WITHDRAWN

WITHDRAWN

CASTE IN INDIA

CASTE IN INDIA

Its Nature, Function, and Origins

J. H. HUTTON, C.I.E., M.A., D.Sc.

*Professor Emeritus of Social Anthropology
in the University of Cambridge*

FOURTH EDITION

OXFORD UNIVERSITY PRESS

Oxford University Press, Ely House, London W.1

GLASGOW   NEW YORK   TORONTO   MELBOURNE   WELLINGTON
CAPE TOWN   SALISBURY   IBADAN   NAIROBI   LUSAKA   ADDIS ABABA
BOMBAY   CALCUTTA   MADRAS   KARACHI   LAHORE   DACCA
KUALA LUMPUR   HONG KONG   TOKYO

Oxford House, Apollo Bunder, Bombay 1 BR

First published (by the Cambridge University Press) 1946
Second edition 1951
Third edition 1961
Fourth edition 1963
Reprinted 1969

Printed in India by Sudhir Balsaver at Usha Printers,
6 Tulloch Road, Apollo Bunder, Bombay 1 BR and
published by John Brown, Oxford University Press,
Apollo Bunder, Bombay 1 BR

CONTENTS

Part III. ORIGINS

Part IV. APPENDICES

Part V

PREFACE

In this edition of *Caste in India* little new matter will be found. One or two minor mistakes have been corrected, an omission or two rectified. A few slight alterations have been made in order to conform to some of the internal changes of administrative boundaries in India, e.g. of the partition of Bombay into Gujarat and Maharashtra; but N.E.F.A. and Nagaland will be found alluded to as if they were still part of Assam. They never had very much in common with the Assam Valley proper, but the same applies to other hill tribes like the Khasi and the Lushei who are still included administratively in the state of Assam. Otherwise there has been no change. That is not intended to imply that the caste system itself has suffered no change, but it is likely that such change as has taken place since the third, or perhaps even since the first edition was published, is hardly yet perceptible in day-to-day social life, at any rate in the villages, in which the great majority of Indians live. It is another matter when it comes to election time, whether for general or local elections, for Professor Srinivas has pointed out that some weakening of the ideas regarding pollution which have permeated the caste system in the past has been accompanied by a greater activity of caste in politics.[1] This need not be regarded as an unfavourable prognostic for India's nationhood; patriotism, like charity, begins at home and the lesser loyalties lead to the greater. Consciousness of their legal rights as citizens has increased among members of low or exterior castes, though this does not imply a consequent increase in status; such an increase has however undoubtedly taken place in some, perhaps in many cases as a result of improvement in economic condition. The present position of caste in India has been admirably reviewed by Professor Srinivas in the volume of essays already referred to, and there are other recent works on caste to which attention ought to be drawn. In the last edition of this book Dr W. H. Newell's article on ' The Brahman and Caste Isogamy in North India ' in the *Journal of the Royal Anthropological Institute*, vol. lxxxv, pp. 101-10, was overlooked, and there have

---

[1] *Caste in Modern India and Other Essays*, pp. 5 sqq. and Essay I *passim*.

appeared since *Aspects of Caste in South India, Ceylon and North-West Pakistan,* edited by Dr E. R. Leach, Dr McKim Marriott's *Caste Ranking and Community Structure in Five Regions of India and Pakistan,* Professor Irawati Karvé's *Changing India: Aspects of Caste Society,* her *Hindu Society: an Interpretation* (see *Man,* 1962, **254**), and Mrs Taya Zinkin's *Caste Today.* The two last items taken together will give an admirable idea of the practical working of caste, in the past and in the present, to anyone unfamiliar with it at first hand; they make an excellent supplement to Professor Srinivas' account of the current political aspects of caste. All of these are of course more up-to-date than I can be, and Professors Karve and Srinivas at any rate have the advantage of seeing the caste system from inside.

My acknowledgements are due again to a number of kindly critics, and to the indefatigable co-operation of the Bombay branch of the Oxford University Press.

NEW RADNOR   J. H. H.
July 1963

PREFACE TO THE THIRD EDITION

MUCH has happened in India since *Caste in India* was first published. The arrival of independence and a purely Indian government has made possible legislation which would have been improper even had it been possible to an alien administration, and the leaders of thought and policy in India seem generally to have come to the decision that the caste system must go. If that be indeed the case it is perhaps partly on the ground that the caste system is a hindrance to industrial development and economic advance, but more particularly under the urge of an altruistic and humanitarian desire for an improvement in the condition of the depressed classes, and a feeling that the caste system is bound up with the untouchability of the exterior castes and is discreditable therefore to a modern society. Legislation then has been undertaken in an attempt to deal with this situation.

In 1931 it was reckoned that the exterior castes numbered over fifty million; in 1951 nearly fifty-two million 'untouchables' were counted; in 1960 the 'scheduled castes' are spoken of [1] as numbering fifty-five million. The Indian Constitution makes special provision for the scheduled castes, and in 1955 the Indian parliament enacted the Untouchability (Offences) Act, which laid down severe penalties for anyone acting on ancient custom to prohibit to excluded castes the use of temples, wells, schools, shops, eating-houses, or theatres, or to treat them as in any way separate or inferior. In the agencies of central and of state governments one post in eight of those filled by competitive examination is reserved for them, and standards and age limits are adjusted to their poorer education; government scholarships are likewise reserved for students from their communities. Caste Hindus are encouraged by the offer of free board and lodging to enter hostels intended to accommodate exterior castes, and all hostels accepting government aid are required to take in a minimum complement of such castes, and seats are reserved for them in the central and state legislatures. There are at the time of writing 76 exterior caste members in

[1] The Delhi correspondent of *The Times*, 22 May 1960.

the Lok Sabha; the Cabinet Minister for Railways is of their community, and the Chief Minister of the state of Andhra Pradesh also. It is not easy to see what more can be done towards abolishing untouchability by legislative action, particularly as it is still practised by many of the exterior castes as between themselves. The experience of Japan, where some similar discriminations against certain castes were abolished in law eighty years ago but still subsist in practice, suggests that such an end can only be attained by very slow degrees and the continued pressure of advancing education and rising standards of living.

Most writers on caste do seem to regard untouchability as inseparably bound up with the caste system, and some as a necessary condition of the survival of Hinduism, but I cannot see it in either of these aspects myself. One writer says: 'It seems that members of a multi-stratified society must feel superior to one group, and assert that superiority if their subservience to another is to remain tolerable. And this apparently human need finds full and inhuman expression in untouchability.'[2] It is possible that this is so, and that the bottom group of all has to take it out in superiority over dumb animals, but the untouchability of certain groups as groups does not apply to the majority of graded castes and cannot therefore be essential to the system. It is a principle which can be observed also in non-Hindu societies which are not graded to anything like the same extent, while societies stratified in some degree at any rate have existed throughout history without it.

However that may be the intelligentsia of India today seem to have made up their minds that the caste system should be got rid of, though it seems clear that in general they fail to comprehend the difficulties, and perhaps the dangers, of such an undertaking—one indeed which would, if carried out at a stroke, wreck the edifice of Hindu society and destroy a growth of some three thousand years or more. In the autumn of 1955 an Indian Conference on Social Work organized a 'Seminar on Casteism and Removal of Untouchability' in order to suggest concrete measures for the removal of untouchability and to 'combat the ubiquitous menace of casteism'. It met under the able chairmanship of Professor M. N. Srinivas, and many and various were

[2] The Delhi correspondent of *The Times* on 2 May 1955.

the views expressed, but it may be doubted whether any but the trained anthropologists and a psychologist or two appreciated the formidable nature of an attempt to jettison the whole structure of their society. The anthropologists included, besides the chairman of course, Dr Smt. Irawati Karvé, and of the psychologists it may be noted in passing that Dr Pandharinath Prabhu agrees with me in regarding the problem of untouchability as quite separable from that of caste. Several speakers pointed out the dangers of too much protection for the untouchable classes, and indeed there had long before been rumours of caste Hindus declaring themselves untouchable to enjoy the untouchables' special facilities. But it appeared that on the whole there had been little effective change of attitude, and it was left to Professor Srinivas to point out, when summing up, that although everyone says that he wishes caste to go ' actions are more or less at complete variance with professed beliefs '.

There have been a number of individual contributions to the study of caste since the second edition of this book was prepared, and some of them of the first importance. Bruce Ryan's *Caste in Modern Ceylon* (1953) is perhaps only relevant for comparative purposes, but no student of caste in India can afford to neglect Dr Karvé's *Kinship Organization in India* (1953); Kapadia's *Hindu Kinship* was published in 1947, Stevenson's *Status Evaluation in the Hindu Caste System* in 1954, and Marriott's *Village India* in 1955. Dr Ghaus Ansari has written in Vienna of caste as it affects Muslims (1954) and Professor Mario Cappieri in Italian of the untouchables (1947). Then there have been valuable studies of specific areas—Professor Srinivas's *Religion and Society among the Coorgs of South India*, a model of its kind, appeared in 1952, Professor L. Dumont's *Hierarchy and Marriage Alliance in South Indian Kinship* in 1957, F. G. Bailey's *Caste and the Economic Frontier* in the same year, and Mayer's admirable *Caste and Kinship in Central India* in 1960. There have likewise been many monographs on individual castes such as Fürer-Haimendorf's *The Raj Gonds of Adilabad* (1948), Dubé's *The Kamar* (1951), and Fr Fuchs' *The Gond and Bhumia of Eastern Mandla* in 1960, and that is to mention merely a small part of all that has been published since I wrote, which is relevant to the study of the caste system.

If I were to take all these into account I should have to go back to India and start again, but, as before, I have done my best to rectify in this edition any mistakes of fact that have been pointed out and come to my notice, and to remedy the fault of one or two omissions. One of my critics chid me gently for saying nothing of the future of caste, but I have no claim to be a seer, and prophecy has no part in my purpose in writing. All that I have attempted here is to achieve a general but factual view of the caste system as a working whole and the principal cohesive factor in the society of Hindustan as I knew it, and to examine briefly the various views put forward as to how it came into being. I write as an ethnographer and perhaps, in a very modest way, as an historian. Not for me the misty visions of Durkheim nor even the more objective horizons of Radcliffe Brown. I am neither a psychologist nor a sociologist, and general theories of human society and religion are little relevant to my theme. In so far as such theories are valid their validity must be of an universal nature; but the caste system as observed in India is an unique phenomenon, and can only have arisen therefore as the result of local historical and particular impacts. Moreover I am far from feeling confident of the possibility of man's ascertaining from inside human society any permanently valid rules of human behaviour therein. In moments of pessimism I see mankind devolving into monstrous communes of fixed pattern comparable to societies of ants, wasps, termites, or dung-beetles. In such an event it would no doubt be possible (for apes or angels) to codify its rules of behaviour and predict its reactions to stimuli. And perhaps it is only a Victorian and non-evidentiary belief that in the very long run the better prevails over the worse, which unseats the nightmare. Meanwhile the chief characteristics of human society, as I see it, are its incredible adaptability to environment, its extreme unpredictability in behaviour, its infinite variety, and its innate folly. Instances a plenty will be found in the pages that follow.

J. H. H.

NEW RADNOR
Midsummer, 1960

PREFACE TO THE SECOND EDITION

In this second edition of *Caste in India* the author has to acknowledge with thanks his indebtedness to the many kind reviewers of the first edition for improvements in this one. He has done his best to take advantage of all criticisms except one or two which he found it impossible to accept, and one which required something beyond his powers: having no Sanskrit he was compelled to continue to rely on translations of the *vedas* and *puranas* instead of consulting the original texts. He has moreover made little attempt to recast his material in the terms of India and Pakistan as they appear after their achievement of independent status, but has thought it wiser to retain the terminology of the India with which he was personally familiar. In the few passages containing words, references, or quotations from Greek literature Roman script has been substituted for the Greek lettering used in the original edition. Otherwise he has added a little, he has altered a little, and he has to thank Mr Martin Rowlands of the School of Geography in Cambridge for two admirable maps, one showing areas, the other places and geographical features. The general aim in these maps has been to insert all places mentioned in the text, and, with the object of keeping the maps as clear as possible in a small space, such places only.

It should perhaps be added that it was largely the appreciative reception of the first edition by Indians that encouraged the author to publish a second, and to get it done in India itself, a country to which his lasting gratitude is due. And in this connexion the author has to acknowledge not only the generosity of the Cambridge University Press in allowing him to transfer the work to another press when the first edition was sold out, but also the courtesy and the efficiency of the printers and publishers in Bombay.

J. H. H.

NEW RADNOR
22 November 1950

FOREWORD TO THE FIRST EDITION

IT is probable that some sort of an apology is needed from anyone who is bold enough to add to the great mass of literature that already exists upon the subject of Indian caste. A recent Indologist in America claims to have compiled a list of over five thousand published works on this subject; so obviously some justification is needed for adding to their number. Nothing like that quantity, however, will be found in the list of works cited in this volume, which does not claim in any sense to deal exhaustively with the subject. Only an encyclopaedia could do that. It does attempt, however, to offer a brief conspectus of the various aspects of caste, since, when trying to give to my classes a general idea of the nature of the problems involved, I was unable to find any single book of moderate size to which I could send students for what I regarded as a satisfactory outline of the subject. Two compact books in English there certainly are, both fairly recent and each admirable after its kind; they have been freely cited in this volume, particularly in chapter VII. But the one deals merely with existing phenomena omitting, generally speaking, questions of origin and of wider significance; the other has its treatment of origin based on theories of race which are no longer valid in the light of present knowledge, while its treatment of existing facts is limited to northern India, though the caste system is probably found at its strongest in the south. In this outline some attempt has been made in brief not only to consider origins, but also the place of caste in the social and economic order of Hindustan.

Besides the two authors referred to above there are a number of others whose works have been quoted freely. All will be found in the bibliography at the end of the volume. Even where facts referred to are within my own observation and experience, I have, wherever I could, given a reference to some printed authority in which the matter can be followed up.

An apology is also perhaps required for certain inconsistencies in the pages that follow. . . . In the text I have [not often used diacritical marks] but in the glossary I have endeavoured to mark all long syllables where a knowledge of the quantity is needed to afford some approach to a correct pronunciation. Again, the termination *-an* in South Indian caste names is sometimes replaced by the honorific *-ar*, or the final *n* may be omitted; and there are almost inevitably inconsistencies in transliteration from Indian alphabets into Roman. But the inconsistency which has proved the most disconcerting to the proof-readers in the University Press has been a tendency to fluctuate between singular and plural forms for the names of castes, and above all my unpredictable and unrepentant practice of using singular and plural verbs indiscriminately where the subject is the name of a caste. As however ' caste ' is a collective noun I hold that I am entitled to use either number in the verb that follows, and I have deliberately declined to be unnecessarily (as it seems to me) consistent in this matter. If the reader is offended thereby, I offer him my apologies—*pro formā*.

I have to acknowledge the kindness of the Government of India in giving me leave to reproduce as appendices to this volume an appendix (II) and a chapter (XI) from my report on the Indian census of 1931; the two together form part IV of this volume. I have to thank Mr J. Brough, of St John's College, Cambridge, now of the British Museum,[1] for his important help in the matter of *prăvără*, and Rajkumar Sahib Prafulla Chandra Bhanj Deo also for some assistance in the same field. Dr Alma Wittlin has helped me in the matter of references, but I have to thank in particular Miss Maureen O'Reilly for reading my proof sheets and still more for the laborious and exacting work of verifying almost all the references and checking my bibliography. I must thank Professor Raymond Firth also for very kindly reading through my proofs, and not the least of my acknowledgements are due to my friend Dr Mary Edwards, but for whose kindly and persistent instigation I should probably never have set my hand to plough this furrow at all.

J. H. H.

CAMBRIDGE
31 October 1945

---

[1] Since 1948 Professor of Sanskrit in the University of London.

PART ONE

THE BACKGROUND

CHAPTER I

INTRODUCTORY

THE subcontinent of India has been likened to a deep net into which various races and peoples of Asia have drifted and been caught. It is of course divided from the rest of Asia by the high barrier of the Himalayas and from the other parts of the outside world by sea. This isolation has not prevented numbers of races from migrating into India, but it has led to the development of society on peculiar lines of its own. Together with Pakistan India [1] contains nearly a fifth of the world's population, some 530 millions of people, and being a natural geographical unit there is inevitably much that this great population has in common. At the same time it is composed of all sorts of different elements of great diversity, of different creeds, different customs, and even different colours. All these varied peoples have been enabled to live together, in conditions of comparative stability and forming what may be described as a multiple society, by the caste system, which must probably be regarded as having developed as a sort of organic response to the requirements of the particular case. Geographical circumstances have imposed a certain unity on the inhabitants of the peninsula, whereas the diverse origins of the people have dictated variety. The view put forward in this volume is that it is caste which has made it possible for both requirements to be satisfied within a single social system, a system, moreover, which has proved historically to be very stable. It has proved capable of absorbing any intrusive society, and no intruders have yet succeeded in revolutionizing it, though it is not so rigid that a caste cannot rise in the social scale. Some castes, it is true, are so low in the scale that

[1] This work having been originally written before their separation, the term 'India' is hereafter used generally in its geographical and historical values to refer to the whole peninsula in which India in its more recent sense and Pakistan are included.

1

they are regarded as outside the ordinary pale of society and suffer disabilities accordingly, but that is perhaps an incidental rather than an essential feature of the caste system.

Each caste is a social unit in itself. The customs by which it lives are generally different in some respects from those of other castes, and are sometimes in marked contrast to those of any other caste at all. Persons of one caste do not marry those of another. The extent to which persons of one caste will eat or drink with those of another is strictly limited by unwritten laws and everybody knows who is affected by them. Even a change of religion does not destroy the caste system, for Muslims, who do not recognize it as valid, are often found to observe it in practice, and there are many Muslim castes as well as Hindu; and when some reforming body breaks away from Hinduism and repudiates caste, it becomes something very like a new caste of its own. Jews and Christians also in India often form castes or bodies analogous to castes.

There are thought to be some 3,000 castes in India, and it would need an encyclopaedia to deal with them all. Some are derived from tribal or racial elements, some are occupational, being of the nature originally perhaps of guilds of artificers or craftsmen, some are territorial, some religious, and so forth. The original bond which united the members of a caste has often been different in different cases, but it is suggested that the society of the country as a whole has been built up by the integration of these different units into an organic community, and one into which a new unit is fitted without difficulty, while any group that breaks away from other units can as easily form itself into a new cell within the structure, and will indeed find it almost impossible to do anything else.

To get some idea of the various peoples which have contributed to this society one must consider what is known of migrations into India. To judge by other areas of south-east Asia it seems likely that the earliest human inhabitants of the Indian peninsula of which any trace survives were Negritos— very dark pygmies with 'peppercorn' hair, marked steatopygia, and generally between 4 and 5 feet high. There are several such tribes still surviving in Malaya and the Philippine Islands, and there are somewhat kindred tribes in New Guinea. They have survived in an almost unmixed form in the Andaman Islands in the Bay of Bengal, though in rapidly dwindling numbers, and traces of their blood are possibly to be seen in some of the forest tribes of southern India, like the Kadars of the Cochin forests, in occasional individuals in remote and hilly areas such as the Rajmahal Hills just south of the Ganges river in Bihar, where such a case has been reported,[2] and in occasional remote Naga villages on the north-east frontier between Assam and Burma. But of these Negritos nothing more than the merest trace remains on the mainland, and one can only conjecture that at some remote date they may have inhabited southern and eastern India. In the extreme north-east of India, in the Naga Hills of Assam again, there are traces of other negroid tribes akin to Papuans and Melanesians, traces which can be seen readily in culture and in art, and which occasionally appear in physical traits.

Whether or not we are to count the Negritos among the races which have contributed to India's population, there is no doubt about the Australoid race which is often alluded to as pre-Dravidian or proto-Australoid. This is a racial element which may be ultimately allied to the so-called ' Brown Race ' of south-east Europe, or which may have developed from a subhuman ancestry in south-east Asia itself. The type is allied to the aborigines of Australia and to primitive races spread over the Indian archipelago and is very widely spread all over India, particularly among the lower castes and humbler classes of society. It is found in the least adulterated form in some of the more primitive of the southern Indian hill and forest tribes, but generally appears mixed with other elements in all grades of society, though it is much less evident among the higher classes than the lower. It is characterized by very wavy, even curly, hair, a broad nose and rather coarse features generally, and by a darkish skin. There can be little doubt but that the ancestors of people of this type formed the bulk of the population of the Indian peninsula at some very early date, and probably before anyone else, except perhaps Negritos, had entered it. How and

---

[2] Guha, *Racial Ethnology of India,* p. 130 and Pl. VIII, fig. 4. It may be pointed out here that on the previous page Dr Guha mentions frizzly hair as occurring not infrequently among the Angami Nagas. This statement needs some correction. Such hair is very rare among Angamis, less rare among Kachha Nagas, and not infrequent among Konyak Nagas, where occasionally it seems to be characteristic of certain clans or villages.

when the subsequent types came to arrive in India is a matter of conjecture almost until we reach historic times. What light we have on the matter is supplied by inferences drawn from languages, culture and physique.

There are some thirty different groups of languages spoken in India, each of which consists of from one to five or more different vernaculars. Half a dozen of these belong to the family known as Austric, which since it is the most widely dispersed is probably one of the oldest families of human speech. The peoples who still use branches of this family of speech in India, or branches of other families which show traces of affinity with Austric tongues, are to be found in hilly and afforested areas where they have been comparatively free from external contacts. Several tribes whose language is now classed with other families seem to have formerly used Austric languages. In physique such tribes have a good deal that suggests that they contain strong pre-Dravidian or proto-Australoid elements, but with considerable admixture of later comers of a more refined type, and an appreciable dash of something that is common to Mongoloid types, for without showing pronounced Mongolian features they suggest that sub-Mongoloid type which is sometimes met with on the fringes of purely Mongolian areas and may represent an ancient marginal and less highly specialized Mongoloid stock. As there are two distinct families of Austric languages in use in India it is possible that there have been two routes of migration from central Asia, one round the west end of the Himalayas, the other somewhere to the eastward of them. The languages used may be spoken of as Kolarian in the former case, Mon-Khmer in the latter, which is confined in India to one area in Assam, while the Nicobar Islanders in the Bay of Bengal also speak a language intermediate between the two branches, but probably derived from the east.

The speakers of Kolarian languages in India are few in number and scattered in distribution, but languages of the Dravidian family are widely spoken over large and contiguous areas. Not only does the whole of India south of the Godāvari river use these languages, but there are more or less isolated survivals like Brahui in the north-west and Malto in the Rajmahal Hills, as well as certain words and sounds used generally in northern India which indicate that Dravidian languages

were once spoken over the whole peninsula.   No certain affinities
have been established outside India, but it seems likely that
these languages entered India from the north-west coming
perhaps from Asia Minor, or at any rate from that direction,
via Mesopotamia. The physical type particularly associated with
these languages is probably closely related to that which is predominant in the Mediterranean, though it is generally found
now in a state of mixture with other types, particularly with a
round-headed type suggestive of Syria, Armenia and the Iranian
plateau. There are many cultural parallels between south
India in particular and the older civilizations of Mesopotamia,
Syria, and Crete, and it is probable that many waves of immigration have taken place, all more or less of the same type of
people. Probably the earliest of these were of a more or less
unmixed long-headed type, the later comers being increasingly
mixed with rounder-headed peoples from the highlands of Asia
Minor and perhaps Iran.

At some later date, probably in the third millennium B.C.,
when there seems to have been much disturbance of races and
peoples in the southern Russian steppe and in Iran, a wave of
round-headed peoples seems to have come in from the north-
west and passed down the west coast as far as Coorg. From
there some no doubt trickled through what is now the Mysore
state into the Tamil-speaking area of southern India, missing
the Malabar coast, which is cut off by the Western Ghats from
the rest of south India, and reaching the Telugu-speaking
Andhra country just south of the Godavari river in even less force
than the Tamilnad. A section of these round-headed immigrants
seems to have crossed India to what is now Bengal, probably
moving south of the Jumna and Ganges rivers for most of the
way. It is possible that these immigrants introduced what is now
known as the outer band of Indo-Aryan languages, and it is
possible that they were also the first to introduce a patrilineal
form of succession; but these are very much matters of conjecture.

The first invasion of India of which we have any sort of record
was that of the ' Āryans '[3] of the Rigveda somewhere about
1500 B.C. These people definitely used an Indo-European

[3] ' Aryan ' is really a linguistic term and ought not to be used as if it
were a racial one; it is only used here for want of a better term, and
because it is familiar.

language, and it is not unlikely that they had, at any rate to some extent, fair hair and blue eyes. Their religion was a form of nature worship, expressed in the hymns to their nature deities which we know as the Rigveda. These people occupied and settled in the Punjab in the north-west of India, later sending colonies farther east and filtering through central India into the south. Over the whole of northern India Aryan languages have generally superseded all others, and though they have never succeeded in doing this in southern India, they have naturally succeeded in modifying some of the languages of that part of the peninsula.

These Indo-Europeans were followed in subsequent centuries by many invasions on a smaller scale. Between 500 B.C. and the beginning of the Christian era northern India was invaded by Persians and Greeks, and after them by the Sakas or Scythians and by the Kushans, who were a nomad tribe from Central Asia. Again in the fifth century A.D. another horde of nomads from central Asia, the Huns, invaded northern India. In the eighth century the Muslim invasions began with an Arab invasion of Sind, and Muslim invasions of one sort or another continued until the establishment of the Mughal Empire in the sixteenth century, by which time the Portuguese had already founded their settlement at Goa. From the other direction the Mongoloid Shans had invaded Assam, and Mongolians no doubt already occupied the higher mountains all along the northern fringe of India.

It is from such diverse elements that the peoples of India are derived, and although the development of the caste system and its stabilization have crystallized the peoples of India into a large number of fairly 'watertight' communities, the barriers between them were less rigid while the system was in its early development than they are now, and even now they are not all immutable. Consequently the differences between caste and caste, in so far as they are racial, are rather differences of degree of mixture than absolute differences of race and type. In some cases it is easier to differentiate between Indian racial types by area than by caste,[4] and of course it is possible that in the course of time different geographical environments may have played some part in establishing physical differences between the inhabitants

[4] *Vide* Guha, op. cit., particularly with reference to his map on p. 129.

of different areas, since environmental differences, e.g. between the Thar Desert and the humid coasts of southern India, are extreme.

It is in the south probably that the most ancient types survive, for, while the climate has favoured the growth of heavy forest most in the south, the shape of India has tended to drive early inhabitants southwards under pressure, no doubt, of migrations and invasions from the north. In this introductory glance at the background of caste, then, it will be convenient to start with the south of India, and the most primitive of the people to be found there, working northwards and then across India from west to east, and thence north-westwards again into the Himalayas which form the northern boundary of the Indian peninsula. It will be understood that in a survey so restricted of an area so vast and a population so varied it is only possible to generalize on broad lines.

Note. In line 2 of page 3 above I have substituted ' possibly ' for the ' probably ' of the first two editions in deference to the criticisms of several Indian reviewers whose knowledge of physical anthropology is likely to be less superficial than mine. At the same time it seems to me on purely general grounds that the Negrito is unlikely to have been absent from the mainland of the Indian peninsula; traces of him have been reported from the Persian Gulf (Giuffrida-Ruggeri, *First Outlines of a Systematic Anthropology of Asia*) and he is visibly present in the Bay of Bengal, the Golden Chersonese, and Indonesia. If he was present in India he is likely to have left some traces in the existing population, for man is an incorrigible miscegenator. Of some such physical strain in the Naga Hills, with its many cultural links with Melanesia, I feel confident from personal observations. Since writing the above a team of five physical anthropologists of the University of Calcutta's Anthropological Department have made a detailed physical survey of the Kadar, and conclude that the features which some anthropologists (including myself) had taken to indicate a Negrito strain are really due to a negro admixture. See *A Physical Survey of the Kadar of Kerala*, by S. S. Sarkar, Gautamsankar Ray, M. R. Chakravartti, A. R. Banerjee, and Papia Bhattacharjee, Memoir No. 6 (1959) of the Anthropological Survey of the Government of India.

CHAPTER II

SOUTHERN INDIA

PERHAPS the most primitive of the south Indian forest tribes is that of the Kadar of Cochin State, a tribe in which the proto-Australoid element is definitely predominant. For an unquestionable Negrito we have to go outside the mainland of India to the Andaman Islands. The Kadar have only got some suggestions of similar physical characteristics, but, like the Andamanese, they live by hunting and the collection of forest produce. They bury their dead, observe no period of taboo after a death has occurred in the family, and erect no memorial. They file or chip the incisor teeth to a point. Like the Andamanese the Kadar are very rapidly dying out, largely, apparently, as the result of their having taken to opium and distilled liquor, which has been given them by alien contractors employing their services.[1]

Another tribe of southern India living in an extremely primitive way by hunting and digging for roots is the Mala-Pantaram tribe of Travancore. Their principal or only weapon and implement is a stick with the point hardened in the fire, and they have no domestic animal except the dog. Being entirely dependent on hunting and food collecting they need about two square miles of forest per head to support themselves. Their form of burial is very simple; the dead are just buried where they die and the group leaves the place and moves elsewhere. They are nomads within a limited area, and their dwellings either rock shelters or flimsy huts of leaves. Unlike most of their neighbours they are not matrilineal, but reckon descent through the father. A very similar tribe is that of the Paliyan of Madura district. They, too, do not cultivate, and live entirely by collecting forest produce and snaring and trapping wild animals and birds; they own no personal property except the clothes they wear, a few of the simplest utensils, a digging stick like that of the Pantaram, and a bill-hook. They depend largely on wild honey and on the sale of the wax from its combs. To get the honey a man is commonly let down over

[1] *Report on the Census of India*, 1931, vol. 1 (India), pt. iii-B, pp. 213 sqq.

the cliff by a rope of twisted creepers and dislodges the bees' nest with his digging stick. Most Paliyar cannot count beyond the numbers of their fingers and toes.[2]

A little less primitive in their mode of life than the Pantaram and Paliyan are Malavetan, Thantapulayan, Urali and other similar tribes, mostly of hybrid origin though predominantly proto-Australoid, who practise a shifting or migratory cultivation in addition to hunting and food collecting. Many retain individual primitive traits of social behaviour of one sort or another. Some of the Malavetan, for instance, chip their incisor teeth to a sharp point like the Kadar;[3] the Thantapulayan women wear (or did till recently) a skirt of leaves or grass; the Urali are particularly given to making tree houses 50 feet or so above the ground, and it is in such houses that their women seclude themselves at adolescence, menstruation and even at childbirth, which takes place in isolation, advice and instructions being shouted from a distance to the woman in travail. The hills and forests of Travancore, Cochin and the other parts of southern India contain a number of tribes of this kind, many of them—the Mala-Arayan for instance—matrilineal, others patrilineal, and some, like the Ulladan, in an intermediate stage in which the property of a man passes half to his sons and half to his sister's sons. All of them, probably, practise cross-cousin marriage, in the form of a union between a man and his mother's brother's daughter. The weapons and implements of the most primitive ones consist of a digging stick and a wooden spear, and nowadays often a mild steel bill-hook purchased in the towns. The less primitive use also the bow and the pellet-bow, and in a few cases, that of the Muthuvan of the Palni Hills for instance, the blow-gun. Some, like the Kannikan, have the institution of the bachelors' hall, a hut where all the unmarried men live, or at any rate sleep, in common, and most of them have a headman of some sort who settles disputes, and performs minor administrative functions, with the help of a council of elders. All are regarded as more or less outside the pale of respectable Hinduism.

[2] Ibid., pp. 195 sq.
[3] L. A. K. Iyer, *Travancore Tribes*, I, p. 159, and illustrations at pp. 145, 149.

The peoples of southern India, other than the primitive jungle tribes of pre-Dravidian race, are roughly divisible into four groups—those of Telingana or the Andhra country, of the Tamilnad, of the Carnatic, and of Kerala. The first of these corresponds roughly with the distribution of the Telugu language, which is spoken along the east coast of India from the Pulicat lake, a little north of Madras itself, in the south to Kalingapatam at the mouth of the Vamsadhara and the Orissa boundary in the north. Inland it stretches back into Hyderabad (formerly the Nizam's Dominions), to Sandur and to the eastern districts of Mysore south of that. The second occupies the whole of the eastern side of India south of Pulicat lake, from the Coromandel coast, that is, to the Western Ghats from Cape Comorin to the Nilgiri Hills. This is the home of the Tamil language. The term 'Carnatic' is liable to some misinterpretation. It has become obsolete possibly on account in part of the confusion to which its use may give rise. Historically it has been used to signify the low country between the Eastern Ghats and the Coromandel coast, while its one-time synonym 'Canara', probably of the same derivation etymologically, has been similarly limited to the lowlands between the Western Ghats and the sea.[4] Here the term Carnatic is taken to cover the Tulu- and Kanarese-speaking countries of Kanara, Mysore, and the adjacent parts of Bellary and Dharwar, together with the little plateau of Coorg where Kodagu is the vernacular—that tract of Dravidian-speaking country, in fact, which lies south of Maharashtra and north of Kerala, and extends eastwards towards the meeting-place of Telingana, or the Andhra country, and the Tamilnad on the east coast. Kerala may be said to extend from Kanara down the Western Ghats and the Malabar coast to Cape Comorin. On this coast, including the states of Cochin and Travancore, the language is Malayalam. To the north of Kerala is the real Karnātaka, where the language is Kanarese, and the great cultivating castes of Okkalīga and Lingayat, a caste of sectarian origin, co-exist in the same sort of rivalry as the Kapu and Kamma castes of Telingana.

All languages mentioned here belong to the Dravidian family. Each linguistic area contains people and castes of all grades of

---

4 *Vide* Yule and Burnell, *Hobson-Jobson*, s.vv. 'Canara' and 'Carnatic'.

society, but while very many of them correspond to some more
or less equivalent body in another area there are differences of
character and custom as well as of language which distinguish
them. The Telugu language has often been compared in
mellifluence to Italian, and the upper-class Telugu approxi-
mates to the south-east European in physical type. This is particularly marked in the case of the Telugu Brahman. The Telugu
caste of Kapu, which uses the familiar title ' Reddi ', is probably
the most numerous single caste in the south of India. It numbers two or three millions, mostly cultivators, farmers and
landowners. Socially they take a place next to Brahmans in
many districts, and claim an origin from northern India and
kinship with the Rathor clan of Rajputs. The caste is split
up into a large number of sections, some of which show traces
in their customs of the former existence of a matrilineal system,
while one section, the Morasu, is noticeable for a custom by
which at the marriage of the first daughter, or alternatively at
the birth of the first grandchild into a family, the bride's mother
or the wife of the grandfather's eldest son must amputate at
least one joint of the third and fourth fingers of her right hand
at a temple of Bhairava. The custom was practised at any
rate up to the end of the last century.[5] Some of the Panta
Reddis of Conjeeveram have totemistic septs which taboo the
totems with which they are associated. Generally speaking, the
inhabitants of the Andhra country appear to be more volatile
and ' temperamental ' than their neighbours, and in particular
are noted for the outbreaks of rioting between the castes of the
Right Hand and of the Left, two ancient factions in which the
low castes of Mala and Madiga are respectively prominent as
protagonists. The Chindu dance performed by Madigas with
bells on their legs at marriages, and festivals generally, has had
to be prohibited in several districts on account of its infuriating
effect on the Malas, and of the resulting riots.[6] The Tamil
seems generally to be of a harder-headed, more practical turn
of mind than the Telugu, similar musical gifts being combined
with a peculiar aptitude for mathematics and physics. The
Tamil community—Brahmans in particular—have produced

[5] Vide Thurston, Castes and Tribes, v, pp. 75 sqq. The same practice
used to be followed by the Okkaliga of Mysore and Kanara. Vide Iyer and
Nanjundayya, The Mysore Tribes and Castes, iv, pp. 225 sqq.
[6] Vide infra, p. 70.

physicists whose names are well known in Europe. Among the
lower classes of the Tamilnad are the criminal tribes known as
Kallar and Maravar, more or less professional cattle thieves
who have a notable bull cult very suggestive of the Mediterranean, whether of ancient Mycenae or of modern Portugal.
Bulls with sharpened horns are driven to fury, and the young
man who wishes to distinguish himself and prove himself a
desirable match for the lady of his choice must jump on the
bull's back and recover a cloth from its horns.[7] Another caste
of the Tamil country with rather unusual customs is that of the
Kottai Vellala who live in a walled fort of some 20 acres extent,
inside which no male of any other caste is allowed to enter
and outside which no woman of the Kottai Vellala caste is
allowed to go.[8] The family dwelling-house passes to the
youngest daughter, and a daughter who marries continues to
live in it until her younger sister marries. The caste is a very
small one, a contrast in this respect to the Kallar. Tamils of
the poorer classes have emigrated in large numbers as labourers
to Ceylon and also to Malaya and elsewhere.

The caste known as Kammalan or Panchala should be mentioned, as it consists of the artisans of five occupational sections—
goldsmiths, braziers, carpenters, stonemasons, and blacksmiths.
They claim descent from Viswakarma, the architect of the
gods, and equality with Brahmans. They intermarry (though
the goldsmiths will not intermarry with the blacksmiths) and
have most elaborate guild organizations. When, as they sometimes do, they bury their dead instead of cremating them, they
use a stone-lined grave, in which apparently they place the
deceased in a sitting position, in contradistinction to the cultivating castes who do not line the grave with stone and generally
bury the body extended. The Chetti, a caste of bankers,
brokers, shopkeepers, moneylenders and traders, have a large
number of subdivisions; being in general wealthy and of much
business acumen their social importance is greater than mere
numbers would warrant. One other Tamil caste must be
mentioned here and that is the more humble one of the Kuruba,
whose traditional occupation is the keeping of sheep and the
weaving of woollen cloth and blankets. They seem strictly to

[7] Thurston, *Castes and Tribes*, III, p. 75.
[8] Thurston, *Castes and Tribes*, IV, pp. 33 sqq.

belong to the Kanarese country, but are found in both Andhra and the Tamilnad and are remarkable for the fact that they still erect cromlech-like rough stone dolmens over the graves of their dead. In choosing a bride they are very particular that the whorls or natural partings in her hair shall be such as are accounted fortunate, a prejudice common enough in India and Arabia in estimating the value of cattle or horses, but perhaps unusual outside south India as applied to human beings.[9]

While the society of Kanara is generally speaking not dissimilar to that of the Andhra and Tamil countries, the physical type of at any rate the higher classes varies from it and shows some affinity to that of Bengal, possibly because both areas constitute the limits more or less of the main infusion of round-headed stock before the invasion of the Rigvedic ' Aryans '. Kerala, on the other hand, has been the stronghold of an ancient type of society which predates any ' Aryan ' invasion and was probably at one time virtually universal in India. The Malabar coast is a long strip of very fertile tropical country cut off on the east by the high mountains and thick forests of the Western Ghats from easy communication with the Telugu- and Tamil-speaking areas, a strip narrowing in the north in the neighbourhood of Goa and in the south at Cape Comorin, so that it is virtually shut off by mountains from land communications. Such external contacts as it has experienced until comparatively recent times have been mostly by sea, and the influences of Arab traders and of immigrants from Malaysia via Ceylon—the route by which came also the coconut, a staple product of Malabar—are readily traceable in certain sections of the population. It is no doubt the landward isolation of the Malabar coast which has been responsible for the long survival there of the matrilineal system. Until the passage of special legislation within the last fifty years, the great majority of the castes of Malabar lived under a system of society in which all real property and the family name were inherited through the women of the family instead of through the men. Any property acquired by a man went not to his own children but to his sister's children, for his own children inherited the family name and property of their mother and her brothers, not of their father.

[9] Thurston, *Castes and Tribes*, III, pp. 133 sqq.; *Ethnographic Notes*, pp. 146 sq.

This system is not without advantages of its own, but succumbed in other parts of India to a patrilineal one which probably came in with Indo-European tongues or earlier. In Malabar it was retained by nearly all castes, the most important being that of the Nayars, a more or less military society in which the men tended to go off on fighting or marauding expeditions leaving their wives to live in their own maternal homes, a state of society familiar also in Malaysia. The Nayars formed the aristocracy of Malabar, and the lower castes were and are mostly organized on a similar social scheme, but the priestly caste of Brahmans, called Nambudri, hold a peculiar position in the country. They seem to have come originally from northern India, and to have entered Malabar at a much later date than the Nayars, and they observe the rule of primogeniture and a patrilineal system of inheritance. The eldest son marries a Nambudri Brahman wife and their children inherit the paternal estate. The younger sons form matrilineal alliances with Nayar women, and their children inherit from their mothers and mothers' brothers on the Nayar pattern. At least that was the rule until recent legislation made it possible for the paternal property to be divided and inherited by younger sons who can now hand on property to their own children. The Nambudri Brahman women marry Nambudri Brahman men only, so that, as all the younger sons of Nambudri families married Nayars, they used to find it difficult to get husbands at all. The family system of the Nayars naturally tended to preserve a much greater social freedom for women than is common elsewhere in India, and female education has gone much further in Malabar than in most other parts. This is not only the case in Nayar society but in many other Malabar communities—among Syrian Christians, for instance, for Malabar contains a large number of Christians, the earliest converts having been converted by Nestorian missionaries of the Syrian church, possibly in the first century A.D. and traditionally by St Thomas the Apostle, but probably not later than the fourth in any case. The Cochin State on the Malabar coast also contains some very ancient Jewish communities which claim to have been in south India at least since the Roman destruction of Jerusalem.[10] They are

[10] Achan, ' A Hebrew Inscription from Chennamangalam ', in *I.A.*, July 1930.

divided into the White Jews of pure Hebraic descent and the Black Jews who include local converts and persons of mixed descent. Linschoten remarks that the White Jews speak good Spanish and says that they came direct from Palestine, and Crooke classifies them with Spanish Jews as Sephardim.[11] The Moplahs (Mappila) of Malabar are generally regarded as partly of Arab extraction, much reinforced by local converts. The more southerly have the reputation of being exceptionally fanatical Muslims, and in frequent rebellions have earned a reputation for complete disregard of personal safety in their religious zeal, which has also shown itself in attempts at wholesale conversion of Hindus to Islam by force.

Among the non-Nayar Hindu castes of Malabar mention must be made of the Tiyar, a caste corresponding to the Shanan of the Tamil country, whose traditional occupation is the extraction of toddy from palm trees, and the Iruvan, who seem to have reached Malabar by sea from the Indian archipelago by way of Ceylon; the Panan caste also is of interest for its picturesque practice of the curing of sickness by dancing in the guise of demons about the body of the sick, a practice used also by the Malayar, as well as by the Parava caste.

The landward isolation of the Malabar coast from the rest of the Indian peninsula has led to the survival there of ancient forms of society. It has also led to the survival of ancient physical types, for the immigration of broad-headed elements, probably coming down the west coast of India from the Iranian plateau somewhere about the third millennium B.C., has hardly penetrated this area at all, and the Nambudri Brahmans from north India were also a long-headed breed, so that the Malabar head is almost universally narrow. The little mountain plateau of Coorg, however, presents a great contrast in this respect. The Kodaga (or ' Koraga ') population here, from which the plateau takes its name, is tall, stalwart, broad-headed and comparatively fair-complexioned, and though Hindu, like that of Malabar, has preserved and developed a distinct culture of its own with greater freedom from the restrictions of caste and a long tradition of martial independence and self-reliance which may be compared in some respects with that of Switzerland among the nations of Europe. On the birth of a Kodaga boy a miniature

[11] *Things Indian*, p. 293.

bow and arrow are put into his hands as a symbol,[12] and athletic
contests of one kind or another form a common feature of
ceremonial or festive gatherings.[13] The uniform brachycephaly
of these mountaineers, in marked contrast to the dolichocephaly
of most of Madras, indicates Coorg as the southern extremity
of a prehistoric penetration down the west coast of India of
an intrusive broad-headed element which has retained on this
plateau its original character with comparatively little admixture
of other racial stocks. It is in marked contrast to the next
most numerous people now living in Coorg, the Yeruvas, who
are dolichocephalic and of markedly Australoid affinities. The
Kodaga population is marked by a straight and narrow nose,
whereas the Yeruva, who is incidentally of much lower stature,
has a broad and flat one.[14]

Associated with no other community in southern India in their
physique or in their society is the rapidly vanishing Toda tribe
of the Nilgiri Hills. This remarkable people subsists by the
keeping of buffalo herds and dairies in extremely primitive
conditions. Though inheritance is through the male, the social
system involves joint families in which one woman has several
husbands. The cow buffalo is never eaten, but a bull buffalo
calf is killed and eaten sacramentally annually and the office of
priest is indistinguishable from that of dairyman. In fact, the
dairy practice involves a ritual which makes it amount to a sort
of religion. In physical type the Toda is a contrast to the
neighbouring tribes of the Nilgiris by his hairiness, and is otherwise more suggestive physically of the Nambudri Brahman
perhaps than of any other type of southern Indian, though poles
apart from him culturally and socially. In general, of course,
the Toda seems to approximate more to northern than to
southern Indian physical type, and it is conceivable that he
represents a very ancient migration of cattle-keepers from Iran
hybridized with some local type, and that his culture embodies
traditions going back to the prehistoric time when dairying was
a new invention. In contrast to the pastoral economy of the
Todas are the intensive agriculture and gardening of the Badaga
tribe, a very much more numerous people, some 50,000 in

12 Richter, *Manual of Coorg*, p. 141.
13 Holland, *Coorgs and Yeruvas*, p. 59.
14 Ibid., p. 81.

number. Though primarily agricultural, they follow all kinds of pursuits from that of lawyer to that of scavenger. By origin they seem to be immigrants from Kanara who have migrated south-eastwards, but they show little or no trace of the broad-headedness characteristic of the Konkan, being, on the contrary, extremely long-headed. Among their ceremonials is that of fire-walking, in which numbers of persons walk across a pit some 15 feet long filled with glowing embers to the sound of music played by Kotas, a caste who supply the musical as also the artisan element in the Nilgiri Hills. The fire-walk is undertaken as an act of worship of the god Jadeswami and with some reference apparently to the fertility of nature.

In the centre of the northern half of southern India is the plateau known as the Deccan (literally the ' South '), most of which, with Berar to the north of it (Berar belongs rather to central or to western than to southern India), constituted the dominions of the Nizam of Hyderabad. The population is mainly Hindu and differs little from that in British India on its borders, the cultivators in the east, for example, being indistinguishable from those of the Andhra country, and those in the north being largely Gonds as in the adjoining districts of the Central Provinces. In the forests of the south we find the primitive tribe of the Chenchus, living by hunting, and, though nowadays helping out their existence by a little agriculture of the most primitive kind, really dependent otherwise on the collection of forest produce. They occur also in the reserved forests of the neighbouring districts of what was British India, a very primitive tribe of proto-Australoid type like those already alluded to farther south.

Although the population of the Nizam's dominions was Hindu, the Nizam was a Muslim ruler and the nobility of the state were of Arab extraction, many of them with pedigrees that went back to the ancient aristocracy of Arabia in the time of the Prophet.

CHAPTER III

WESTERN, CENTRAL, AND EASTERN INDIA

To the west of the Nizam's dominions lay the province of Bombay occupying the west coast from south of the Portuguese colony of Goa to the gulf of Surat in the north. All down this west coast the physical type is more markedly broad-headed than elsewhere in the plains of India, though brachycephaly is also strong in Bengal. Trading and business castes have brought manufacturing towns like Bombay and Ahmedabad to a high level of prosperity, particularly by cotton spinning, and trade connexions overseas go back to a very early date. Among the trading castes, particularly in Gujarat, the northern part of the former Bombay province, Jains are well represented, as well as Hindus, the Agarwalas, originating from the United Provinces, largely Jain by religion, Oswals and Jaiswals from Mewar in Rajputana, Khatris from the Punjab, and Bhatias, and the Muslim Khojas. Bohras, a caste from Baroda State, do, or used to do, a good deal of business with Spain, and in 1931 there were some two hundred of them in business in Bilboa, Malaga and other towns there. Among the seafaring castes the Kharvas of Kachh, Kathiawar, Cambay, etc., seem to be of Rajput extraction. They are hardy sailors, and besides manning the country craft that ply up and down the west coast of India, to Aden and Zanzibar, and as far east as Singapore, they are familiar as lascars in the liners running between Bombay and Europe.

Prominent in 'big business' in Bombay is the Parsi community. The Parsis, who are Zoroastrians by religion, emigrated from Persia about the eighth century A.D. to avoid compulsory conversion to Islam. They have been foremost among Indians to adopt European manners and customs, and as a community are one of much wealth, culture and refinement. They have an unusual way of disposing of their dead, who are not buried as by Muslims, nor burnt as by most Hindus, but exposed on the tops of Towers of Silence where the bodies are eaten by vultures and the fleshless bones disposed of in a well below. As a physical type the Parsis are more distinct from the generality of Indians of Bombay than another community of foreign extraction, the Ben-i-Israel, who seem to have arrived a couple of centuries earlier from Arabia. These Jews are claimed to be representative of the lost ten tribes, as they are said to have no names which can be shown to be later than the Captivity.[1]

Gujarat and Maharashtra are coastal states, and while overseas trade is a natural activity of some of their population other sea-faring activities occupy many more. The numerous and humble caste of Koli, dark in complexion and coarser in feature than the trading classes, often cultivate the soil, but are also much occupied with fishing and with manual labour in the mills. Physically they approximate in type to the jungle tribes and Bhils referred to below. Often employed as labourers, their tribal name has been taken over in English as a synonym for the unskilled labourer of India and elsewhere in the tropics—the 'coolie'. From a tribe the Koli has become a Hindu caste, but retains in his appearance the physique of the earlier inhabitants of India. Above him in the social scale is the widespread cultivating caste of the west coast, the Kunbi, the typical peasant of western India who probably contributed largely to the rank and file of that fighting race the Marathas. The Marathas, first heard of in the thirteenth or fourteenth century, came into prominence as a fighting race in the seventeenth century and nearly became masters of India in the eighteenth. Their leaders rank as Kshatriyas, though racially probably of the same extraction as the shepherds and cultivators who supplied the rank and file of their armies. In fact the word 'Maratha' in its narrower use is applied to a society in which Rajputs or quasi-Rajputs, at the top, with Kunbis, Dhangars (shepherds), and Goalas (cowherds) practise hypergamy, each group taking wives from the one below, causing a superfluity of women at the top and a scarcity at the bottom of the social scale. One sect of Kunbi, known as Kadva Kunbi, claim to have been created by the goddess Parbati, wife of Shiva, from the perspiration at her waist (*ked*); they worship the goddess Umia Mata at Unja in the Kadi district, and marriages take place only once in nine to twelve years 'when the goddess speaks', an occasion determined by divination. Even unborn children are married on such an occasion, the mothers performing a marriage ceremony on an

[1] A useful account of this caste will be found in Enthoven's *Tribes and Castes of Bombay*, I, p. 67.

understanding that it shall be valid if the two infants prove to be of different sex. Girls for whom no husband can be found when the goddess speaks, are married to a bunch of flowers which is thrown into a well or a river, after which the girl can remarry as a widow when occasion offers.[2] Several of the Maratha clans seem to be totemic,[3] and the Marathas in general worship, among others, a god spoken of as Khandoba (*khanda* = a sword), a warrior incarnation of the Supreme Deity who is depicted on horseback with two women, a wife, a Baniya (merchant caste), in front of him and a mistress, a Dhangarin (shepherd caste), behind him.[4] The spring festival was celebrated by a foray. The Marathas are noted for the part played by women in public life, for their simplicity of living and the affection of their leaders for their original village. The Marathan rise against the Mughals affords perhaps the sole instance in earlier Indian history of a movement which was primarily rather national than religious, in spite of the appeal it made to anti-Islamic feeling. The term ' Maratha ' in its wider aspect is used to indicate a number of castes from Brahmans downwards. Of the west of India Brahman castes one may mention the Chitpāvans with their fair complexions and occasionally even grey eyes, while of equal intellectual attainment probably is the important caste of Prabhu, occupationally writers, who have often held important administrative and official posts. Maharashtra, the name of the country of the Marathas, where the Marathi language is spoken, is generally associated with the word Maratha, but it has been suggested that it is really derived from the word Mahār which is the name for a widespread exterior[5] caste of that country. Its social status is degraded on account of the occupations it follows, but it is commonly associated with certain village services, and the fact that the Mahars are commonly regarded as authorities on village boundaries has been cited as evidence that they are the original inhabitants of Maharashtra. This is not impossible, as they represent an older stratum of population than the broad-headed Kunbi or the fair-skinned Brahman and are numerous and ubiquitous.

Though outcaste the Mahars are Hindus, but this is more

---

[2] Desai, *Glossary of Castes, etc.*, pp. 43 sq.; Enthoven, *Tribes and Castes,* II, p. 145. [3] Enthoven, *Tribes and Castes*, III, pp. 10 sqq.
[4] Russell, *Tribes and Castes of the Central Provinces*, IV, p. 204.
[5] For the expression ' exterior caste ' see Appendix A.

doubtful in the case of some of the jungle tribes that still survive in small numbers in the west of India, tribes such as the Chodhra or the Katkari, who pick up a meagre and nomadic living by collecting forest produce, or sometimes settle down as labourers on the land of their employers. One famous tribe of western India, however, is still numerous and vigorous, and that is the Bhil tribe, an important section of which is to be found in the former Bombay province, though it extends widely into Rajputana to the north and into central India eastwards. Bhili, the tribal language, is an Indo-Aryan tongue, but it probably replaces an older Dravidian tongue, and perhaps a Kolarian language before that. The tribesmen, partially Hinduized now in most districts, but in some professing a rather unorthodox form of Muslim faith, still retain their tribal organization and tribal consciousness. Most of them are now peaceful cultivators, but in the past they have been renowned for brigandage and lawlessness. They are a smallish, swarthy race, very expert in the use of the bow. There are a number of different sections of the Bhil tribe each divided into many exogamous and totemistic clans. They have been said to venerate the horse above other animals, but their chief festivals are those in honour of the dead. They are inveterate believers in witchcraft, and their women, who have much freedom and influence, used in former times to accompany their menfolk into battle, using slings with great effect.

Associated like the Bhils with western India, with Rajputana and with central India, as well as with the Deccan, is the caste known as Banjara or Lambadi, a nomad caste of traders and cattle herdsmen with reputed criminal propensities. Their former occupation consisted largely in supplying grain for campaigning armies. They moved about, as many of them still do, using their oxen as pack animals for transporting grain and living in temporary camps. They used to do not a little business in the disposal of loot and in the purchase and sale of children. Their women are noted for good looks, domestic freedom, and a remarkable headdress in which a shawl is raised above the head by a wooden horn resting on the back hair.

Turning eastwards from Bombay to central India there is little marked change in the higher classes of society until the centre of the peninsula is passed. Indeed, the influence of the Marathas carried their language at one time right over to the confines of Orissa, where many of the common people use a dialect called Halbi which is based on Marathi. The Bhils of Bombay also reappear in the Central Provinces, where they occupy the Vindhya and Satpura ranges, but soon give way to other tribes more typical of the central forests and highlands. Before the Marathas, Rajputs from northern India had pushed into the centre and south through the forest passes of the Vindhya Hills and set up local dynasties in small states, often intermarrying, it would seem, with aboriginal rulers, and central India held till 1948 [6] numbers of Rajput or quasi-Rajput states. Of the aboriginal tribes the Baiga are possibly the most ancient survival that still retains a tribal consciousness. They practised until recently, and perhaps still, in places, practise a shifting cultivation of a primitive type, using only the hoe and abjuring the plough; and their marriage system has features that suggest a survival from some long-abandoned system of marriage classes analogous to those of the aboriginal Australians. It is still not excessively uncommon [7] for a Baiga grandparent and grandchild to be married—the difference in age of course may be even less than 30 years in a people where unions are normal at the age of 15 and not unknown at that of 12. Possibly there is a belief in the reincarnation of a dead man in his grandson or of a dead woman in her granddaughter which makes it only proper for a couple to be reunited when the one who has died young is reborn while the widowed partner still lives.[8] At any rate, a belief in reincarnation of this kind has been widely held in many parts of the world.

The Baiga now speak a dialect of Hindi, but the Gond tribe, who constitute the most numerous element among the forest tribes of central India, have a language of their own that belongs to the Dravidian family. Over large areas they have settled down as ordinary villagers cultivating the soil with the plough, though in forest areas they retain their primitive life and customs. Their national weapon is the *tangi*, a type of light axe with a narrow, curved vertical blade, which every Gond man

---

[6] Though the States Reorganization Act was not passed till 1956, most of the smaller States were merged into larger units soon after Independence.
[7] *Vide* Elwin, *The Baiga*, pp. 180 sq. Fuchs reports an analogous custom of the Gond and Bhumia *vide* his *The Gond and Bhumia of Eastern Mandla*, pp. 168-9.   [8] *Vide infra*, pp. 252-3.

carries in the forest and with which they have been known to kill even the tiger in single combat. They are organized in totemistic clans with a ruling clan of Raj-Gonds as socially the most important. This clan has given dynasties to many Gond states and claims Rajput status. The Gonds had at one time a dynasty of considerable importance which had suzerainty over all the Gond country of central India, and the ruins of its palaces are still to be seen. Like the Baiga they are great believers in and practisers of witchcraft, and they have family and tribal gods which vary in number. The legs of their women are elaborately tattooed, but where Gond and Baiga live as neighbours the tattoo is put on (with soot as dye, and thorn prickers) by women of the Baiga tribe, from whom no doubt the Gonds adopted the practice. Human sacrifice used at one time to be practised, but this was far from being limited to any one people, or even any one group of peoples in India.

Although they differ in language the Baiga and Gond are not dissimilar in physical type, and the same applies to Korku, Korwa and other jungle tribes of this area, but the Chamar of the Chattisgarh plateau in the east of it is of a distinctly finer physical make-up than the generality of Gonds, though this might not apply to the Maria Gonds of the Bastar State who hunt the great gaur or ' bison ' of their forests to wear their horns as headgear. The Chamar of Chattisgarh, although belonging to that exterior caste of leather-workers whose touch is polluting to caste Hindus, are here cultivators tilling the land whose women have a great reputation locally for their handsome features. There are other people too on the Chattisgarh plateau of more primitive type similar to those in the adjoining plateau of Chota Nagpur. Chota Nagpur, while not actually part of the Central Provinces, for it falls in the province of Bihar, is racially closely bound to central India, and geographically part of it, and the tribes which people it, having remained in their comparative isolation for longer than their neighbours in the plains, still retain their tribal society. Some of them, the Oraons, for instance, like the Gonds, speak a Dravidian language, but more of them use one of the Kolarian languages which have elsewhere been superseded either by a Dravidian or by an Indo-Aryan tongue, or first by the one and then by the other. Several of them retain the institution of the bachelors' dormitory,[9] where the boys of the village spend three years in educative discipline, the younger boys working under the direction of the elder. Except in language and in some of their minor institutions, they do not differ greatly from their Kolarian-speaking neighbours, who inhabited Chota Nagpur before they did and who retain their distinctive tribal organization, even though their villages are now territorially mixed up with those of the Mundas. The Mundas are the most important of these other tribes, perhaps, but really form one people with the Kharias, Hos, Kols, Bhuiyas and others, all of whom have a similar territorial organization, which is shared by the Oraon, and make a tribal feature of the Spring Hunt for which a number of villages assemble annually. The Munda tribe in particular puts up rude stone monuments for its dead somewhat resembling the so-called 'cromlechs' of Britain. Another tribe very closely akin to this group is the Santal tribe, well known as hunters and labourers, who rebelled in 1855 largely as the result of the exactions of moneylenders and dispossession from land under civil court decrees.[10] This vigorous tribe, originally located in the Santal Parganas of Chota Nagpur, has colonized the empty areas of the Rajmahal Hills and is now widespread in the Central Provinces, Bihar, Bengal and Assam. The pre-Santal occupants of the Rajmahal Hills are the Malers, a tribe using, like the Oraons, a Dravidian language, and apparently like the Brahui of Baluchistan, an outlying remnant of the former Dravidian-speaking population of northern India generally.

On the southern side of the Chota Nagpur plateau and in the east of the Central Provinces the forests and broken hills house other remnants of Kolarian-speaking tribes such as the Juangs whose women, at any rate till recently, used petticoats of leaves, which in hot dry weather shrivel so fast that frequent departures to the forest for a change of garment are said to be necessary. Another nomadic jungle tribe of this area and with similar affinities is the Birhor, who subsist without agriculture and are reputed to represent the Padaeans of Herodotus and to have had the practice, shared with the Massagetae and appar-

[9] Elwin, *The Muria and their Ghotul*, Pt. II ; Roy, *The Oraons*, pp. 211 sqq.
[10] Hunter, *Annals of Rural Bengal*, ch. IV ; Bradley-Birt, *Story of an Indian Upland*, ch. VII ; see also *Modern India and the West* (ed. O'Malley), pp. 421-30.

ently some of the ancient Irish, of displaying their affection for their deceased relatives by eating their bodies in piety.[11] If the Birhors ever did have this custom, they have abandoned it for at least a couple of generations, but similar customs are not unknown in other parts of the world, and there is nothing inherently improbable in the tradition of its having existed among the Birhors.

From the Chota Nagpur and Central Provinces border the hilly country extends towards the east coast and continues to be the home of primitive tribesmen until the coastal plain is reached. Some of them, like the Gadaba and the Bondo, retain their Kolarian language, others like the Bhatra now use either Halbi, a dialect much influenced by Marathi, or Oriya, the language of the Orissa plain, or both. As in the case of the Maria Gonds, there is a noticeable suggestion of the Mongolian about many of these tribesmen. Perhaps, as it shows little trace of the epicanthic fold in the eye, it should be called palaeo- or proto-Mongoloid, and is more typical of the fringes of the Mongolian area than the centre and may be due to an early distribution of the Mongolian type before the more pronounced features were developed. There it is, however, for several trained observers have noticed it, particularly in the tribe known as Sawara which has a distinctive language and culture in the Orissa hills. The language is Kolarian, and the culture has much in common with other Kolarian-speaking tribes, particularly in the setting up of stone monoliths, but differs from that of its neighbours in the use of irrigated terraces for the growing of rice, a feature more suggestive of Assam than of the Orissa or central Indian hill tracts. The funerary cult of the Sawara involves cremation of the body, accompanied by the construction of a temporary house for the soul and the erection of a menhir, in a special grove reserved for that purpose, when the ghost goes to join his ancestors. Periodically a secondary funeral feast is held to commemorate all those who have died since its last celebration.

A people more numerous than the Sawara and one which has attracted much more attention in the past is the Kond or Kondh (commonly written Khond) tribe, nearly allied to the Gonds of central India both in speech and culture—indeed, it is probably

[11] Dalton, *Ethnology of Bengal*, p. 220.

to be regarded as a branch of that people, and the names are perhaps really identical. The Konds are notorious for the trouble they gave by opposing the suppression of infanticide and still more by their obstinate addiction to the use of human sacrifices carried out often in a very cruel manner. Here the life of the dead victim was associated with the harvest, and the harvest consequently liable to fail if no life had been provided to quicken and vivify the seed. The victims were sometimes kidnapped from the adjoining areas, sometimes provided by families in whom the duty was hereditary from among their members. The Kond women tattoo themselves like Gond and Oraon women, and the warriors used to dress like the Maria Gond with a flamboyant headdress of bison horns and feathers.

The inhabitants of the Orissa plains no doubt share, in the cases of many castes, the same racial origins as the tribesmen of the hills. One caste now scattered throughout India, that of the migratory earth-workers known as Odh,[12] has a traditional origin from Orissa, and, it has been suggested, has affinities with Kolarian tribes. The quasi-military Khandait caste of Orissa now claims the rank of Kshatriya, but probably has closer local ties than such a claim would suggest. The same may apply to the numerous cultivating caste of Kalta. Orissa is a famous land of shrines and pilgrimages, the most famous being the temple at Puri where Vishnu is worshipped in his incarnation of Krishna, the Lord of the World (*Jagan-Nath*). This is the temple from which the car of Jagannath is dragged by pilgrims, some of whom have in the past immolated themselves under the wheels. The festival is probably a Hinduized survival of an ancient fertility ceremony, but it is associated with a temporary relaxation of the more rigid restrictions of caste, and it is probably the catholicity of the worship of Krishna under the form of Jagannath which has made it such a popular place of pilgrimage for Hindus. Jagannath is a god of the people, or at any rate has been, and although outcastes were excluded from the temple, even washermen could go into the temple court where they could catch a glimpse of the idol, and rice once offered to the god can no longer be a vehicle of any contamination, so that outside the gate a hundred thousand pilgrims of all castes

---

[12] Enthoven, *Tribes and Castes*, III, pp. 138 sqq.; Thurston, *Castes and Tribes*, V, p. 424.

can eat together and no one be defiled. Sir William Hunter, indeed, recorded [13] that he had seen a Brahman priest accept this food from the hand of a Christian. Pilgrimage to Jagannath secures all sorts of earthly blessings and gives liberation from sin. Indeed, on the entry of the pilgrims by the Lion Gate of Puri a man of the scavenger caste used to strike them with his broom to sweep away all sin and compelled them to promise not to disclose the secrets of the shrine. [14]

Geographically Assam is separated from Orissa by the great province of Bengal, much larger than either, but culturally these two small provinces have had much in common and probably retain remnants of a common culture which once spread over both sides of the Ganges delta, but which has been greatly modified at the centre by later intrusive elements both of race and culture. While Orissa consists of a coastal plain with jungle-clad hills behind it, Assam proper is a riverine plain with hills almost all round it. Like Orissa it contains Hindu shrines of great antiquity and survivals of ancient and probably pre-Hindu fertility cults. But it differs from Orissa in having a much stronger Mongolian element in its population. Traces of this are to be seen not only in the ordinary cultivating castes like Kochh and Kalita but occasionally even in the higher castes whose forebears migrated from the United Provinces, while the Ahoms of the Assam valley represent the Shans from Burma who conquered the country in the thirteenth century A.D. Many of the Brahmans and Kayasthas of the province have names which embody Ahom titles, and the Assamese language, though belonging to the Indo-Aryan family, contains many Shan words in its vocabulary. The hills round the valley contain a great variety of tribes with probably more diversity of custom and language than any comparable area in the world. The valley is drained by the Brahmaputra river, which after debouching southwards from Tibet turns westwards and runs roughly from north-east to south-west. On the north bank the very Mongoloid tribes are linguistically and physically allied to the Tibetans and Bhutanese. The Daflas, Abors and Mishmis all inhabit inaccessible forest-clad mountains subject to an extremely

[13] *Orissa*, I, p. 86.
[14] Ibid., p. 142. It is probable that by now (1946) outcastes are again admitted to the temple of Jagannath.

high rainfall. Accustomed for centuries to descending on the plains for loot and blackmail, it is only in comparatively recent years that they have been reduced to behaviour which is more or less peaceable, and no very detailed accounts of them have been published.[15] The Apa Tani tribe in this area has an elaborate system of terraced irrigation, but the agriculture of the other tribes is much more primitive. On the south bank of the Brahmaputra and occupying the hills running thence south-wards to the Bay of Bengal are the two groups of tribes known to us as the Naga tribes and the Kuki-Chin tribes, together with some intermediate ones which have cultures with something in common with both these groups. Between them they use some forty different languages or more. In some Naga villages two quite different languages are used on opposite sides of the village street, and though one of the two will be understood by everyone the other will remain a private language unknown to half the village. Customs and cultures differ almost as much as languages, although all Nagas are head-hunters by predilec-tion at any rate. Some use a primitive method of shifting culti-vation, clearing the forest, sowing crops for a couple of years and then letting the land go back to jungle till the growth is ready to cut and burn again; others, on the other hand, have a careful and elaborate system of irrigation, leading water round the contours of their steep hills for miles to flood their rice terraces. While some have sacrosanct chiefs so sacred that they must not touch the common soil, others are governed by councils of elders, and others again are extreme democracies. All are more or less ancestor worshippers. Like the hill tribes of Orissa they erect monoliths as memorials for their dead and vehicles for the operation of the life-essence of the dead in the fertiliza-tion of the crops. Indeed, the head-hunting cult itself is based on a belief in a regular cycle of life which is a material essence residing particularly in the head and which can thus be abstracted from one owner and carried off to benefit the village and family of the head-taker. The Kuki-Chin groups of tribes, on the other hand, are almost all organized under the rule of hereditary chieftains and used to be slave-raiders rather than

---

[15] Since the above was written Sachin Roy has made a good start on the Abor with his *Aspects of Padam-Minyong Culture* and Fürer-Haimendorf has published *The Api Tanis and their Neighbours.*

head-hunters. They are very clannish indeed, with great loyalty to fellow-clansmen and to their chiefs. The Mongolian element is stronger in them than in the Nagas, who, in spite of their Tibeto-Burmese languages, have racial and cultural links with the peoples of the Indian Archipelago and the Pacific Ocean. The Nagas and Kukis are patrilineal, but that is not the case with the Khasis and Garos who inhabit the hills to the south of the Brahmaputra running westwards towards Bengal. Both these tribes reckon descent through the mother rather than through the father. Among the Khasis property in land or homestead passes from a mother to her youngest daughter, who also inherits the office of family priestess.[16] Where the head of the state—there were twenty-two small Khasi states—is hereditary, the chieftainship passes to the chief's youngest sister's eldest son, but several of the Khasi states have elected rulers.[17] Although the women own the property, only the men have votes at election time, that is, when a local ruler is being elected, for if it is a matter of electing a member of the Assam Legislative Council, women, under a recent electoral law, have a vote as well. The Garo tribe, like the Khasis, inherit name and property through the mother, but a woman's daughter is expected to marry her father's sister's son as a matter of course, so that while the ownership of land passes from mother to daughter, the management of the estate passes regularly from uncle to nephew in a different family, and it is a rule that when his uncle dies the nephew, his sister's son, that is, must marry his mother-in-law as well as her daughter whom he has already married.[18]

Half-way between the Himalayas and the Bay of Bengal is the state of Manipur. The Maharaja and the principal inhabitants of this upland valley, a place of great natural beauty, are Hindus, but before the state was Hinduized it had a culture of its own, probably Shan or Chinese in origin, and survivals of this are still to be seen in the distinctive costumes and customs of the inhabitants. Among other distinctive

---

[16] Gurdon, *The Khasis*, p. 83.   [17] Ibid., sect. III (pp. 62 sqq.).
[18] Playfair, *The Garos*, p. 68. The Caribs make marrying the wife's mother (as well as her daughter) an alternative to complete avoidance (Briffault, *The Mothers*, I, p. 264, quoting La Borde, and Quand), and Spencer cites an instance of a Tierra del Fuego native marrying his wife's mother during her daughter's life (*Spencer's Last Journey*, p. 72).

features are its national sports of polo, played between whole villages on small ponies on their grazing grounds with unlimited numbers a side (it was from here that Great Britain adopted the game in a modified form), and boat racing, an annual event in which elaborate dragon-boats are rowed, as in China, by crews in special gala dress while the spectators on the banks also take part by helping to push off the boat they support when it runs aground on the muddy bank.[19]

There are many immigrants in the plains of Assam. Some of them are labourers in tea gardens, the bulk of whom are Hindus, as are most of the Assamese proper, while some have been converted to Christianity. They come from all parts of India, but mostly from Chota Nagpur and the neighbouring parts of central India. The majority of the more recent immigrants into Assam, however, were Muslim cultivators from Bengal, sturdy, industrious, but rather turbulent people who tended to oust the Assamese from the south and west of the valley. The Sylhet and Kachar districts of southern Assam, which belong geographically to Bengal, had, long before the emergence of Pakistan, already become in effect Bengali colonies, the Kachari, who once ruled there, having become quite unimportant numerically. They are allied in origin to the Garo, Kochh, and the people of the north bank of the Brahmaputra river, and in the hills still speak their own distinctive language.

Between Orissa to the south-west and Assam to the north-east the population of Bengal seems to contain a brachycephalic element of population comparatively lacking in the other two, which has perhaps come down the Ganges valley, but which is much more prevalent in Bengal than it is in Upper India generally. There is also in Bengal a brachycephalic Mongolian element to be seen in the people of the Chittagong Hills on the Burma border and at the foot of the Himalayas, but the broad-headedness which is typical of the Bengali Brahman and found also in other castes of high standing like Kayastha and Baidya is of a different character and to be associated with that found in western India. It seems to be strongest in the highest caste and to decrease with descent in the social scale. Thus the Chandals or Namasudras who are low in social position are

19 Hodson, *The Meitheis*, p. 52.

longer headed than the Brahman. or Kayastha of Bengal and the Rajbansi and Bauri still more so.[20] On the other hand, the Namasudra is often fair-skinned and apt to be leptorrhine in some contrast to the bulk of the Muslim population of Bengal which is dark-skinned and rather flat-nosed, suggesting a considerable strain of the Australoid type, a type also apparent in many of the lower-class fishing and cultivating castes such as Bagdi, Bauri, or Kaibartta.

It is the cultivated and educated Bengali who has been probably more than any other Indian the interpreter of the Englishman to the Indian. Although no more intellectually acute probably than the educated Madrasi, Parsi, Maratha, or north Indian, the receptivity of the Bengali has made him very quick to appreciate and to reproduce the British point of view, and often to carry it with characteristic subtlety to a logical conclusion to which the English themselves would be unlikely to take it, particularly in the interpretation of legal principles. Bengali literature, too, in an English form is probably more familiar to Englishmen than that of other parts of India, largely as a result of the activities of Tagore, a Pir-Ali Brahman of Bengal, and of Bengali novelists such as Bankim Chandra Chatterji and Romesh Chandra Dutt. The area known as the Bikrampur pargana in the Dacca district is famous for the extremely high proportion of lawyers, clerks, and *literati* generally whom it supplies or used to supply widely to northern and eastern India, but particularly, of course, to Calcutta, which, taken with the contiguous municipality of Howrah, is one of the most populous cities in the British Commonwealth. Calcutta, although naturally predominantly a Bengali city, contains people from all over India and Pakistan to say nothing of foreigners, and had a population of one and a half million as long ago as 1931. The commercial abilities of the Bengali are displayed by such castes as those of Shaha and Teli, but it would be a mistake to think of Bengal as a purely Hindu province. In point of fact the Muslims actually outnumber the Hindus, their stronghold being eastern Bengal,[21] where a very high proportion of the cultivators are Muslims. The bulk of the Muslim population are no doubt of more or less aboriginal extraction

[20] Risley, *Tribes and Castes of Bengal, Anthropometric Data,* I, vii.
[21] Now, of course, East Pakistan.

converted to Islam, but the aristocracy includes a number of ancient families of Arabic or Mughal lineage. It is the Bengali Muslim of eastern Bengal and of Sylhet who supplies a very high proportion of the Indian seamen and lascars serving in British merchantmen. In the extreme east of Bengal the Chittagong Hill Tracts contain more or less Mongolian tribes, some of them Buddhists like the Maghs and Mru, others like the Chakma more or less Hinduized, but all really having more in common with the hill tribes to their north in Assam than with the inhabitants of the plains of Bengal. In the Himalayan and sub-Himalayan areas again many Mongoloid tribes, like the Lapcha, are found, and in the delta areas of eastern Bengal a number of Feringhees, now mostly cultivators, who claim descent from the Portuguese pirates who once occupied Chittagong and thence in the seventeenth century raided Bengal as far west as Dacca and Calcutta.

CHAPTER IV

NORTHERN INDIA

PROCEEDING up the Ganges one passes from Bengal into Bihar, and thence into the province of Awadh (Oudh). These areas form a meeting place of the outer and inner bands of Indo-Aryan languages and are likewise, at any rate in the case of Bihar, the area of change from the broad-headed Bengali type to the long-headed type characteristic of Upper India. Hereabouts was the stronghold of Buddhism before it was overthrown and extinguished by the Brahmanistic reaction, while farther to the west, between the Ganges and the Jumna, was the centre of Hinduism *par excellence*, the sacred land from which Brahmans were distributed to many other parts of the peninsula. There are of course many castes and classes of Brahmans, and they are not all so intellectual and refined as the high-class pandits of Benares. Moreover, it is only a minority of the Brahman castes which exercises priestly functions. Brahmans practise in all the learned professions as lawyers, land agents, clerks, etc., and act not infrequently as cooks, since most Hindus will eat food cooked by a Brahman of good standing. It is probable that more than one racial element has gone into the composition of most Brahman castes, and perhaps they represent the priesthoods of what were once different, even antagonistic, religions, but there is no gainsaying the fact that the Brahmans of Upper India in general have preserved their purity of blood and their intellectual ascendancy for a very long period. Brahmans like the Gayawals of Gaya, who maintain themselves in idleness on the offerings of pilgrims to their holy city, or the Chaubes of Mathura, who are more celebrated for their skill in wrestling than in learning, are generally held in comparative disrepute.[1] Apart from Rajputs, the castes which probably stand next to Brahmans in social position and are in some ways allied to them are the Bābhan and the Bhāt. The Babhan are land-holders particularly associated with Bihar and claim to be Brahmans who have given up the priestly function for a life of agriculture. Their social divisions, however, suggest affinities with Rajputs rather than Brahmans. The Taga caste

[1] Crooke, *Northern India*, pp. 99 sq.

of the Upper Ganges valley and the neighbourhood of Agra have similar traditions and a similar status. The Bhats, who claim a Brahman extraction, as the similar caste of Chāran does a Rajput one, are hereditary genealogists and heralds who used in particular to act as escorts to protect persons and property passing through areas of freebooters in northern India where brigandage was almost a profession. The Bhat secured a safe passage for his convoy by committing suicide if it were plundered, when the firm belief that the plunderers would be for ever haunted by his outraged ghost was enough to deter them from becoming the cause of his death.[2]

The great cultivating caste of Bihar and Awadh is that of the Kurmi, a caste equivalent in status to the Kunbi of the Maratha country; while the Ahirs, graziers, occupy much the same sort of position. Very numerous also in this part of India, though absent elsewhere, is the caste or tribe known as Bhar who have sunk to the class of labourers and small cultivators, but who seem at one time to have been the ruling people of Bihar. Many old forts and reservoirs are attributed to them. The Kalwar who distils spirit from molasses or from the flowers of the *mahwa* tree has a status as low as the Bhar, not because he represents a conquered and dispossessed tribe, but on account of his occupation; and occupation again is also in part at any rate the reason for the low standing of the Pasi who taps the toddy palm for liquor, the Dhobi, who is a washerman, the Khatik who is a butcher, or the Chamār who tans hides and works in leather. Below all these are the scavenging castes, the various grades of Bhangi or sweeper and the numerous caste of Dōm. The Doms, though serfs and outcaste for centuries if not millennia, possibly represent a once respectable tribe. Przyluski[3] would identify them with the Odumbara, a more or less legendary tribe of shepherds in the Punjab. They are hereditary executioners, and their assistance is necessary at funerals to hand the wisp of lighted straw with which the chief mourner ignites the pyre, but they perform any menial work, are often nomadic and are most unorthodox in their willingness to take food from anyone except a Dhobi, and food, at that, of any kind at all, on which account the Dom is very offensive to the

[2] Ibid., pp. 107 sqq.; Malcolm, *Central India,* pp. 131-9.
[3] *Les Udumbara.*

orthodox Hindu, though he acts on occasions as a musician. The Doms in the Himalayan foothills, in Kumaon and Garhwal, have retained a considerably higher status and something of their tribal organization, and are subdivided into various artisan groups practising different crafts. These hill Doms now repudiate any connexion with the scavengers of the plains.[4] Going westwards from Upper India into Rajputana one enters the most romantic area in the peninsula, a land of ruined forts and ancient strongholds, famous for deeds of valour and self-sacrifice, crowning rugged heights above old and picturesque towns. Many are the monuments to long-dead warriors, stones carved with a horseman and his weapons and the heavenly bodies, and still frequent are the stones carved with a single upraised arm indicating the place where a widow burned herself upon her husband's funeral pyre. There are many inhabitants besides Rajputs—the famous Bhil tribe has been already mentioned; the Bhilala are hybrids of Bhil and Rajput ancestry; the Mina are a tribe of marauders, for that is what they used to be, closely akin to the Bhil in character. There are other tribal communities too, Meo, Mer, and Merat for instance, and many castes of cultivators and others often claiming quasi-Rajput status, like the Lodha, and the great Baniya or trading castes— Agarwala, Oswal, Parwar and so forth, who likewise claim to be of Rajput stock like the Charan or bards; but the Rajput clans are the people who matter here.

Both by tradition and in physical characteristics the Rajputs appear to be of mixed origin. Popularly they are regarded as the lineal descendants of the Rajanya warriors who invaded India in the Rigvedic age and who at that time took precedence even over Brahmans. A recent writer has associated some features of their culture with a still earlier race of invaders with a matrilineal culture,[5] while it is pretty clear from many traditions and inscriptions that the Rajput clans were augmented by Saka, Kushan, and Hun invaders at a much later date.[6] It is possible that the traditional division of the Rajputs into

---

[4] Turner, ' Caste in the Kumaon division and Tehri-Garhwal State ', in the *Report on the Census of India*, 1931, vol. I, pt. iii B, pp. 17 sqq.; Crooke, *Tribes and Castes*, II, s.v. Dom

[5] Ehrenfels, *Mother-right in India*, pp. 158 sq.

[6] Crooke, Tod's *Annals and Antiquities of Rajasthan*, pp. xxxi sqq.; Baines, *Ethnography*, p. 31.

descendants of the Sun, of the Moon, and of Fire, reflects such a threefold origin and that, while the descendants of the Sun and of the Moon go back to the Rigvedic age and earlier, the Fire-descended Rajputs were of later origin and became Rajputs in virtue of a ritual of purification by and rebirth from fire after the Hindu reaction against Buddhism had devastated its Rajput supporters. There are generally said to be thirty-six royal clans of Rajputs, but the lists vary and some include the Huns, and also the Jats, which latter are more often regarded as a lower caste and who are perhaps derived from comparatively late immigrants. Indeed, the distinction between the Rajput and the Jat is in some degree more social than racial, and the same applies again to the distinction lower down the scale between the Jat and the Gujar. The principal clans of the Solar line are those of Sesōdiya, Kachwahā and Rathor; of the Lunar line those of Yādava and Tonwar; and of the Fire-descended lines those of Ponwar, Chauhan, Parihar and Solanki. Some inscriptions record the marriage of Rajput princes, among the Sesodiya, for instance, with Hun wives. Many of the dynasties still ruling in Rajputana states in 1946 can be shown to have been established between the seventh and eleventh centuries A.D. The earliest Sesodiya inscription in Rajputana is dated A.D. 646, when that clan migrated eastwards from Gujarat to rule in Udaipur. The Bhatti, a sept of the Yadava or Jadu clan, came in the eighth century to Jaisalmer and still rules there, and about the same time the Chauhan settled in Sambhar, but later migrated southwards to Sirohi, Bundi and Kotah states. The Kachwaha came from Gwalior to Jaipur early in the twelfth century, and the Rathor settled in Jodhpur in the thirteenth. The Princes of Bikaner and of Kishengarh also belonged to this illustrious clan. It has been said of this clan, which is freer than most from taboos on food and drink, that they are soldiers first and Hindus after that. The Rajputs, with their quasi-feudal tribal system, their romantic character and chivalrous valour, and their punctilious regard for personal honour, have been well described by Tod in his *Annals and Antiquities of Rajasthan*, which, although his speculations as to origins and affinities are out of date, has rightly been described as ' the most comprehensive monograph ever compiled by a British officer describing one of the leading peoples of India '. The adventurous disposition of the Rajputs was not confined to the men, for their women often shared the dangers of war and sport and often exercised a healthy influence on public as well as on domestic affairs. It was usual for them to burn themselves on their husband's pyre, and there are many authentic stories of the final sacrifice of their lives in the rite known as *johar* in order to save themselves from dishonour in the hour of defeat. The Bhats, already mentioned, acted as genealogists, bards and preservers of tradition for the Rajputs, while the Baniya classes largely provided the revenue and ministerial administration required by Rajput chiefs.[7]

The population of the Punjab—the land of Five Rivers—which has often proved the best of all recruiting grounds for the Indian army, falls generally into three groups—Hindu, Sikh and Muslim—but the differences between them are rather religious than racial, at any rate if the Pathans and Baluchis of the western Punjab be excluded. For the Punjabi Muhammadan who provided such an important element in the Indian army is commonly of Rajput extraction, as are many of the Sikh rulers, while the Jats who form perhaps the most important element in the population of the Punjab may be either Hindu or Sikh or Muslim, though the last are in the minority, and the typical Punjab Jat is probably a Sikh. The Jat is a typical yeoman, devoted to agriculture and not particularly concerned in satisfying the requirements of orthodoxy, at any rate as a Hindu, so that he takes a lower social level than the Rajput. His industry is unceasing and every member of his family shares the work in the fields. His reputation for stolidity and reticence has caused him to be described as having ' grown grave and impassive like the great white oxen ' which he prizes so highly.[8] The Sikhs of the Punjab started as a sect within the Hindu pale about the end of the fifteenth century. It was the great Guru, Govind Singh, about the end of the seventeenth, who organized them on a military and political basis and who emphasized the social aspect of the first Guru's reforms. Taught by him the Akali Sikhs at any rate discard the sacred thread of the ' twice

[7] Cole, *Rajputana Classes*, ch. iv ; Russell, *Tribes and Castes*, iv, pp. 414 sqq.; Enthoven, *Tribes and Castes*, iii, pp. 290 sqq.; Rose, *Tribes and Castes*, iii, p. 300 ; Ibbetson, *Panjab Castes*, pt. iii ; Crooke, *Tribes and Castes*, iii, p. 27.   [8] Crooke, *Northern India*, p. 93.

born ' (i.e. initiated) Hindu, repudiate caste, eschew the use of alcohol and tobacco, the wearing of hats or caps, and the eating of all meat not killed by decapitation; the Akali Sikhs pay no bride-price, make no pilgrimage to the great Hindu shrines, forbid witchcraft and the taking of omens, the observance of social impurity at births and deaths, and Brahmanical usages in worship. On the other hand, they accept the Hindu ways of attaining communion with the deity. Strict Sikhs not only always wear ' the five K's ', but will not eat food not cooked by a Sikh who is himself wearing them at the time of cooking. These five K's are *kesh* (uncut hair), *kirpan* (a dagger worn in the hair), *kanga* (wooden comb), *kachh* (shorts) and *kara* (iron bracelet). Sikhs are fond of athletics and games; they make very good mechanics, and their fighting qualities are too well known to need comment.[9]

Two important castes in the Punjab who are much more often Hindu than Sikh or Muslim are the Khatri and Arora castes, which stand in a reciprocal relationship very similar to that of Rajputs and Jats. The Khatri at any rate claim to be of Kshatriya origin, but the principal pursuit of both these important and numerous castes is trade.[10] Much of the commerce of Afghanistan and central Asia is in Khatri hands, and they have at all times shown great administrative ability. Some of them are Muslims, when they are known as Khoja. These Punjab Khojas are generally Sunni, but the Khojas of Bombay, derived largely from the Hindu Lohana caste of Sind, are Shiah and followers of the Aga Khan.

As the Rajput is to the Jat so is the Jat to the Gujar,[11] but the Gujar, though physically and in his social system not so very different from the Jat, is a poorer cultivator and by preference a herdsman. The Gujars seem to have become established in the Gujarat district of the Punjab before the seventh century A.D. and to have come in with one of the Hun invasions. They are often associated with the Ahir caste, which is also a caste of graziers rather than cultivators, but is quite distinct from the Gujars. Very low down, almost at the bottom of the social scale in Hindu society, comes the numerous caste (or tribe) of Chuhra, which does the scavenging of the Punjab and

---

[9] Rose, *Tribes and Castes*, I, pp. 676 sqq.
[10] Rose, *Tribes and Castes*, II, pp. 501 sqq., 507.
[11] Ibid., pp. 306 sqq.; Ibbetson, op. cit., pp. 182 sqq.

which is possibly here the parent caste of the Chamar or tanner. The Chuhra has been held to be the remnant of an aboriginal tribe, but in point of fact his physical type differs but little from that of other inhabitants. His outcaste position is due largely to his occupation, and when he turns Sikh he becomes a Mazhbi, and the taint of his origin prevents his ever being admitted to full social equality with the Sikh of Rajput or Jat origin, despite the Sikh repudiation of caste. When he turns Muslim he becomes a Musalli and again retains some taint of his despised origin.[12]

It has already been pointed·out that the Muslims of the Punjab, except for the Pathans and Baluchis of the west, are generally of similar race to the Sikhs and Hindus and are commonly Jat or Rajput in origin. There are, however, others, the Awans for instance who claim to be Arabs by extraction and claim descent from Ali, the Prophet's son-in-law. They are exclusively Muslim and probably the descendants of some of the earlier Muslim invaders of the tenth century or earlier.[13]

The earliest Muslim invaders appeared in the eighth century in Sind, and this small province has since been predominantly Muslim in religion, but the blood of the inhabitants is mixed indeed. Sind seems at one time to have been occupied by Rajput clans, and it is possible that in some cases clans were still Buddhist when forcibly converted to Islam by conquering Arabs from the west. There are, however, clear traces of the Sakas and Huns in Sind, and the clan known as Mahăr probably preserves the name of the Epthalite Mihirs. The Rajputs of the tenth century succeeded in expelling the Arabs, but were converted to Islam by the later Muslim invaders from the north. The Rajput title Jam is still used by Muslim descendants of the old Rajput houses. Of the non-Muslim castes the Bhatias and Lohanas are among the most important. They are very similar in custom, both are trading castes, and the Bhatias at any rate probably of Rajput extraction. The Bhatia are mostly Hindu, but the Lohanas are many of them Sikhs.

Of the Muslims of Sind, many are of Baloch origin, particularly in the west, and they are often organized as the followers

---

12 Rose, *Tribes and Castes*, II, pp. 182 sq.
13 Ibid., pp. 25 sq.; Ibbetson, op. cit., pp. 169 sq.

of some particular *pir* or 'saint' holding office as a religious and hereditary leader.[14] These *pirs* exercise great influence on their adherents and obtain very considerable revenues from the offerings of their clientele over whom they used to enjoy quasi-judicial and executive powers. In some cases, in spite of their saintly title, they have been little better than leaders of banditti. A notorious case in point is that of the Pir Pagaro or 'Pir of the Turban'. This *pir* is a hereditary religious leader descended from a family which entered Sind with the Arabs in A.D. 711, whose followers, known as Hurs, form a sect of quasi-religious criminals. A position not unlike that of a *pir* is also held by the head of the Muslim community known as Meman or Momin who in Sind consist of Lohanas converted from Hinduism to Islam by the descendants of a Muslim saint who died at Baghdad in the twelfth century A.D. They still retain certain non-Islamic customs such as that of not allowing a daughter or widow to inherit property and of consulting astrologers, but are very punctilious about performing the pilgrimage to Mecca.

West of Sind lies the mountainous country of Baluchistan. The dominant race is the Baloch, which is probably derived from Iranian stock that migrated into its present country between the mid-thirteenth and mid-fifteenth centuries A.D., having been originally located somewhere about the shores of the Caspian Sea. The Baloch tribes may be divided roughly into two groups, the northern or Sulaimani Baloch and the southern or Makrani Baloch, separated from each other by the Brahui tribes. Baluchistan is at present an arid and inhospitable country of rock and sand sprinkled with oases and the remnants of bygone earthworks suggesting that it was once a country of woods, springs, and plenty, 'a land of fountains and of depths, drawing water from the rain of heaven', though now steadily turning into desert under the encroaching sand and needing to be irrigated by means of underground waterways. Parts of it contain as few as one inhabitant to 50 square miles. The Rind tribe is said to be of Arab stock, but differs little physically from the other Baloch tribes, all of which have been

[14] Burton, *Sindh*, ch. VIII ; Mead and MacGregor, *Report on the Census of Bombay*, 1911, I, pp. 205 sqq.

modified by admixture with the Brahui. The Baloch are organized in tribes, each with a chief whose post is hereditary in a
particular family; they are nomads by instinct and where it is
possible still prefer the wandering pastoral life, though circumstances nowadays often compel them to settle permanently in
one place as cultivators. Where they are still nomadic, their
villages consist of little enclosures of rough stone masonry 3 or
4 feet high over which a temporary roof of matting is spread
while the hut is occupied. When the time comes the occupants
move off to another grazing ground, taking the roof with them.
Their wealth consists in camels, cattle, sheep and goats, and
their life is extremely primitive, although the making of carpets
is an important industry. By inclination they are bandits and
cattle-lifters, and the title *Rahzan* (='Highwayman') is a title
of honour.

The true Baloch type is brachycephalic [15] and the Baloch
clans are patrilineal, but the Brahui, the other important indigenous people of Baluchistan, were probably long-headed originally and traced their descent and kinship through the mother.
They speak, too, a Dravidian language completely different from
Balochi and allied to those in southern India. It is no doubt
an isolated remnant of what was once the general linguistic stock
of northern India as it is now of southern. The Brahui have
largely absorbed Baloch blood and so much admire the short
Iranian head that they mould their children's skulls to make
them shorter headed; they bind their foreheads with a smooth
tight bandage, give them soft pillows of millet, and in the case
of a girl, the shape of whose head is more important than that
of a boy's, they bore three or four holes in the ears so that if by
chance the infant turns on the side of her head the pain makes
her turn on to her back again, till the back of her head is permanently flattened. Balochis and Pathans, however, also follow
similar practices, and the Brahui even goes so far as to attempt to
mould the head-forms of his domestic animals—lambs and kids—
while horses are bandaged to give them a slender foreleg above
the knee. But the Brahui does not seem to practise female
(as well as male) circumcision as many of the Baloch tribes do.

Of the other tribes in Baluchistan the humble nomad Lori—
travelling tinkers, and workers in gold and silver, minstrels,

[15] Cf. Dames, *The Baloch Race*, p. 11.

musicians, midwives and menials—call for mention. They seem
to correspond in some respects to the Dom of northern India,
but claim descent from the youngest son of the Prophet's uncle
and an origin from Aleppo. They are gipsies and most at home
on the Makran coast, but nomadism is typical of all Baluchistan.
A third of the population live in tents or temporary huts, and
a very great proportion of the population migrate with the
seasons either from one part of Baluchistan to another or from
Baluchistan to the plains of Sind and back again.[16]

On the North-West Frontier proper, as in Baluchistan, we are
almost outside the range of caste. Many of the nomads who
are to be met with in Baluchistan are Pathan *pawindas* or
' caravanners ' from Afghanistan. No satisfactory distinction can
be made between the terms ' Pathan ' and ' Afghan ', but the
term ' Pathan ' is commonly applied to several millions of
mountaineers occupying the mountains in the north-west of
India on both sides of the Afghanistan frontier and speaking
the Pashto language. Their emigration towards India seems to
have begun about the fifteenth century and probably started as
an annual migration leading to permanent settlement. Their
migration into the Kurram valley is recent and two tribes of
Pathans are still nomads. They are now bounded roughly by
Persia on the west, Dardistan on the north, Baluchistan on the
south and the Punjab to the east. The Pathans are not organized politically but tribally in a number of well-known tribal
groups—Ghilzai, Mohmand, Afridi, Wazir, Orakzai, Yusufzai,
Mahsud, and so on. The tribes are subdivided into septs and
families, each group having its leading man—malik—while the
malik of one group, generally the eldest member of the tribe,
acts as chief of the whole tribe. He possesses, however, influence
rather than power, and the real authority, in so far as there
is any, rests with the *jirgah* or council of elders, that is, of all
the maliks of the tribe. Each tribe, generally speaking, has a
more or less corporate existence as a geographical, as well as
genealogical, unit. The blood feud is a well-established custom,
and the internal jealousies and dissensions of Pathan groups
are well illustrated by the fact that the same word in Pashto
serves both for ' cousin ' and for ' enemy ' and a derivative both

[16] Bray, *Report on the Census of Baluchistan*, 1911, pp. 42 sqq.

for 'cousinhood' and for 'enmity'.[17] The Pathan has been described as treacherous, bloodthirsty, cruel, and vindictive in the highest degree, but he has a code of honour of his own to which he adheres strictly enough and which imposes on him three sacred obligations: hospitality to all who may ask for it; protection, even for an enemy who comes as a suppliant; and the duty of revenge by retaliation. On the frontier they live in fortified villages with stone houses in commanding positions which serve as watch-towers or as places of refuge. The Pathan tribes formed a very valuable source of recruits for the Indian army of high-class fighting quality.[18]

Towards Dardistan on the edge of the Pathan country are found what is left, after constant harrying by the Afghans, of the Red and the Black Kafirs. These tribes were, till recently at any rate, head-hunters, speaking a very early form of the Sanskrit language, using carved wooden vessels more suggestive of Scandinavia than of India, and tripods described as Grecian in type. One account describes them as burying their dead erect in the snow, as extracting the heart and liver, burning them on an altar and sometimes eating the ashes out of piety. They erect carved wooden memorial figures of their dead and used to be given much to dancing with great activity, though now most of them have been more or less compulsorily converted to Islam. In view of their language and their physical type with lightish hair and eyes, tall stature and long heads, it seems not unlikely that the Red Kafirs at any rate may represent something like the original stock of the Indo-European invaders of India in the second millennium B.C.[19]

Going eastwards among the Khos of Gilgit, the Dards, Baltis, Brokpas, and Burusho, the physical type is broader headed and darker, and among the Kanets of the Kulu valley, and the Garhwalis, who again form an important element in the Indian army, a shorter dark long-headed type is found akin to that of the Indian plains. In Ladakh and in Lahaul and Spiti the inhabitants become definitely more Mongoloid, and this latter type predominates among the Gurkhas of the independent state of Nepal as it does likewise in Sikkim and Bhutan to the east

[17] Rose, *Tribes and Castes*, III, p. 219 n.
[18] Barton, *India's North-West Frontier*; Rose, op. cit., III, s v. Pathan.
[19] Robertson, *Kafirs of the Hindu-Kush*; Biddulph, *Tribes of the Hindoo Koosh*, pp. 128 sqq.; Guha, *Racial Ethnology of India*, p 136.

of it.   The people of Lahaul and Spiti are cut off for six months of the year from the Punjab province, of which these are out-lying domains, by heavy snow, and the poverty of their country, which will only support a very scattered and sparse population, has assisted in perpetuating, if it has not actually contributed to establishing, a social system which contrasts very markedly with that of both the Muslim and Hindu societies of their neighbours. By religion they are Buddhists and their social system is one of fraternal polyandry, in which a number of brothers share a wife between them, and in this way contrive to rear a family in common on the inhospitable slopes of the rugged country they inhabit.   The Kanets of the Kulu valley to the south, who are Hindus, used apparently to have, and perhaps still have, a somewhat similar practice by which brothers might share one wife or more than one.[20]

Here in the snow-clad mountains which form the northern barrier shutting off the Indian peninsula from the rest of Asia we must leave this brief glance at the peoples who inhabit it. They are, as has been seen, almost unbelievably diverse, and while climate, habitat and ecology vary greatly in what has been described as a subcontinent—it ranges from about the eighth degree north of the equator to the thirty-sixth—the variety of the people who live in it is far greater.   It is this variety which it has been sought to illustrate in the foregoing pages, and this being so a certain obvious lack of proportion has been unavoidable.   As much space has been given to disappearing peoples like the Todas or the Andamanese, numbering two or three hundreds, as to great and important castes of as many millions.   The great majority of castes, of course, have not been mentioned at all,[21] but an attempt has been made to give a very brief account of enough of the physical and cultural types of India to indicate the very great diversity of the people of that country.   The system which has made it possible for so many and so different communities to live and develop together in common political units while retaining their own social systems and customs is the system of caste, and whatever drawbacks that

[20] Rose, *Tribes and Castes*, s.vv. Kanet, Lahula, Lama; Majumdar, ' Cultural Life of the Khasas ', *J.R.A.S.B.*, VI (1940), no. 1.
[21] About one in ten of castes (exclusive of the much more numerous sub-castes) find mention in this volume.

system has and whatever injustices it involves, there can be no doubt but it has enabled the peoples of India to establish a stable society which has withstood and survived all military and political disturbances and the various vicissitudes of some three thousand years. That there is room for reform in its operation no one will question, but it should at the same time be recognized that the caste system has had and no doubt still has a value of its own in the integration and stabilization of Indian society, and it is doubtful whether without it such diverse racial and cultural elements could ever have been combined to the extent to which we find them combined at the present day. Indeed, it is only against this background of almost incredible diversity of racial origin and of social custom that the phenomenon of caste can be appreciated and understood.

PART TWO

CASTE

CHAPTER V

ITS STRUCTURE

LET it be understood at the outset that it is not intended to give here an exhaustive account of individual castes, their ceremonies, and their machinery for regulating their relations with other castes, nor of their own internal conduct, nor of the historical developments of caste as reflected in Brahmanical scriptures, but rather to examine the nature and origins of the caste system, its function in Indian society, and the broader relations of caste to race and religion in India.

A great deal has been written about caste and more or less from this aspect, but most of those who have so written have approached the question from a single viewpoint, theoretical or social, and have tended to regard caste as an institution which, whatever has been contributed from other sources, has in the main a single and a simple origin. And the origin ascribed to the institution has varied with the writer. To the present writer, however, caste appears to be an institution of highly complex origin, an origin so complex indeed that in its very nature it must be limited to a single area; and that, no doubt, is why it is only found in India. For although social institutions that resemble caste in one respect or another are not difficult to find elsewhere, and some of them undoubtedly have some association with caste in their ultimate origin, yet caste in its fullest sense, caste, that is, as we know it in India, is an exclusively Indian phenomenon. No comparable institution to be seen elsewhere has anything like the complexity, elaboration and rigidity of caste in India. Indeed, on reflection, it is apparent that caste as known in India might be expected to prove to be unique. If it were a simple institution, it could hardly fail to be more widely distributed; and accordingly we do find a wider distribution for certain important or striking features of caste. But highly complex as it is, caste could only arise within a limited area in which all the elements contributing to it were associated over a long period of time. It is virtually inconceivable that the association of circumstances necessary to produce so complex an institution as caste is in India could ever be found in more than one area of the earth's surface; and it is probably significant that the geographical limits within which the institution is manifest are such as have offered in the past very considerable obstacles to perennial communications or easy contacts of any kind.

The word 'caste' comes from the Portuguese word *casta*, signifying breed, race or kind; *homem de boa casta* is 'a man of good family'. The first use of this word in the restricted sense of what we now understand by caste seems to date from 1563 when Garcia de Orta wrote that 'no one changes from his father's trade and all those of the same caste (*casta*) of shoemakers are the same'. Yule and Burnell, who quote this passage,[1] follow it by another from a decree of the sacred Council of Goa in 1567 describing the Gentoos (Hindus) as dividing themselves 'into distinct races or castes (*castas*) of greater or less dignity, holding the Christians as of lower degree, and keep them so superstitiously that no one of a higher caste can eat or drink with those of a lower'.

To define a caste is harder than to give the derivation of the term. Risley defines it as 'a collection of families or groups of families bearing a common name; claiming a common descent from a mythical ancestor, human or divine; professing to follow the same hereditary calling; and regarded by those who are competent to give an opinion as forming a single homogeneous community'. He goes on to add that the caste name is generally associated with a specific occupation and that a caste is almost invariably endogamous, but is further divided, as a rule, into a number of smaller circles each of which is endogamous, so that a Brahman is not only restricted to marrying another Brahman, but to marrying a woman of the same subdivision of Brahmans. This definition is open to question on the ground that descent from a mythical ancestor is claimed rather by the *gōtra*, the internal exogamous division of the endogamous caste, than by the caste as a whole; further,

[1] Yule and Burnell, *Hobson-Jobson* (1903), s.v. Caste.

although the endogamous subdivision of a caste is a genuine
and common feature of the institution, it is doubtful if the
unqualified term Brahman can rightly be used as the name of
a caste at all. It is probably too vague to be of value, for
though the Brahman belongs to one of the four original *varna*
or 'colours' into which Rigvedic society was divided, a *varna* is
very far from being the same thing as a caste, the Hindi word
for which is *jāti* or *jāt*. The relationship between *varna* and
jat is dealt with later on.

Ketkar defines caste as ' a social group having two characteristics: (1) membership is confined to those who are born of
members, and includes all persons so born; (2) the members
are forbidden by an inexorable social law to marry outside the
group. Each one of these groups has a special name by which
it is called, several of such small aggregates are grouped together
under a common name, while these large groups are but subdivisions of groups still larger which have independent names.
Thus we see that there are several stages of groups and that
the word " caste " is applied to groups at any stage. The words
" caste " and " subcaste " are not absolute but comparative in
signification. The larger group will be called a caste while the
smaller group will be called a subcaste. A group is a caste or a
subcaste in comparison with smaller or larger. When we talk of
a Maratha Brahmin and Konkan Brahmin, the first one would
be called a caste while the latter would be called a subcaste;
but in a general way both of them might be called castes. . . .
These divisions and subdivisions are introduced on different
principles. In this way two hundred million Hindus are so
much divided and subdivided that there are castes who cannot
marry outside fifteen families.' [2] Here again the definition is
not entirely satisfactory as there are a number of castes for
instance, particularly in southern India, which have been
recruited, and continue to be recruited, from the mixed offspring
of other castes which are not members of the caste itself, as well
as from those who, having a similar origin, are already members
of the caste; such castes are the Ambalavasi caste of Malabar,
the Shagirdpesha of Orissa, the Chasa caste of Orissa, and the
Karan caste of Orissa. It is perhaps noticeable that the first of
the above-mentioned four castes is one of temple servants, while

[2] *History of Caste in India*, p. 15.

the latter three are all occupational, the Shagirdpesha being domestic servants, the Chasa cultivators and the Karan writers, corresponding to the Kayastha farther north. Generally speaking, however, the definition is valid, though there are still parts of India where caste is fluid enough to make it possible for persons to acquire a caste into which they were not born. Again, in eastern Bengal there is a subcaste of the Baidya caste which intermarries on equal terms with the Kayastha and it is said with Sunris also, the children always taking the caste of the father.[3] Further, while all castes and many subcastes are strictly endogamous, many subcastes are not, but intermarry with other subcastes within the same caste. N. K. Dutt refrains[4] from defining caste, but describes its features: members of a caste cannot marry outside it; there are similar but less rigid restrictions on eating and drinking with a member of another caste; there are fixed occupations for many castes; there is some hierarchical gradation of castes, the best recognized position being that of the Brahmans at the top; birth determines a man's caste for life unless he be expelled for violation of its rules; otherwise transition from one caste to another is not possible; the whole system turns on the prestige of the Brahman.

This description of Dutt's is a normally accurate description applicable to India as a whole. If it needs qualification, it is in the matter of the possibility of transition from one caste to another, for besides the case in Orissa of Chasas who become Karans, there are places on the fringes of northern India where the offspring of a high-caste father by a low-caste mother can in the course of a few generations be accepted as belonging to the higher caste,[5] as provided for by the laws of Manu, though the provision has been a dead letter in orthodox Hinduism for hundreds of years. There were also Indian states in which the secular ruler still had power to bestow caste as well as to take it away, for a Loi of the Manipur State could be made into a Manipuri with the status of a Kshatriya and could wear the sacred thread by the authority of the Maharaja. Senart's description is more comprehensive: 'Figurons-nous un groupe corporatif,

---

[3] Risley, *Tribes and Castes*, s.v. Baidya (I, p. 47). Cf. also Bhattacharya, *Hindu Castes and Sects*, p. 161, and Gait, *Report on the Census of Bengal*, 1901, § 611 (p. 379).   [4] *Origin and Growth of Caste in India*, p. 3.
[5] Rose, *Tribes and Castes*, I, pp. 41 sqq.; and cf. Forsyth, *Highlands of Central India*, p. 416.

fermé, et, en théorie du moins, rigoureusement héréditaire, muni d'une certaine organisation traditionnelle et indépendante, d'un chef, d'un conseil, se réunissant à l'occasion en assemblées plus ou moins plénières; uni souvent par la célébration de certaines fêtes; relié par une profession commune, pratiquant des usages communs qui portent plus spécialement sur le mariage, sur la nourriture, sur des cas divers d'impureté; armé enfin, pour en assurer l'empire, d'une juridiction de compétence plus ou moins étendue, mais capable, sous la sanction de certaines pénalités, surtout de l'exclusion soit définitive soit révocable, de faire sentir efficacement l'autorité de la communauté: telle en raccourci nous apparaît la caste.'[6]   The truth is that while a caste is a social unit in a quasi-organic system of society and throughout India is consistent enough to be immediately identifiable, the nature of the unit is variable enough to make a concise definition difficult. If it be enough to define the system, the following formula is suggested—'a caste system is one whereby a society is divided up into a number of self-contained and completely segregated units (castes), the mutual relations between which are ritually determined in a graded scale'.   But it would be hard to claim that to define a caste as one of a number of such units was completely satisfactory.

One of the difficulties in defining caste is caused by a certain fluidity which shows itself most often perhaps in fissiparous tendencies, but sometimes of recent years in a tendency towards the amalgamation of analogous castes with a view to the exercise of social and political influence. Thus in 1931 there was a widespread movement on the part of various cattle-keeping castes—Ahirs, Ahars, Goalas, Gollas, Gopas, Idaiyans, etc.—to combine under a new caste name as Yādava, though how far,

---

[6] Senart, *Les Castes dans l'Inde* (1927), p. 35. This passage may be somewhat freely translated as follows: ' We must conceive of a group, united, closed, and at least in theory hereditary, provided with a measure of organization which is traditional and independent, with a headman, and with a council ; a group that meets when need be in more or less full assembly ; that is often combined in the keeping of certain festivals ; that is bound together by a common occupation, and shares common customs in regard particularly to marriage, to the consumption of food and drink, and to various cases of pollution ; finally, a group which has the power to maintain its authority by means of a jurisdiction which, though rather attenuated, is capable of making the authority of the community effectively felt by the imposition of various penalties, the most important being permanent or temporary expulsion from the group: such in epitome, as it seems to us, is a caste.'

if at all, such a movement would involve reciprocity in the matter of marriage is uncertain. On the other hand, the tendency of many castes to split up and throw off fresh endogamous units has persisted from very early times. Risley [7] draws attention to this and ascribes to the fissiparous nature of caste decadence and sterility in Indian art. The medieval guild, he says, was capable of expansion and development and could give free play to artistic inspiration, whereas ' a caste is an organism of a lower type; it grows by fission; and each step in its growth detracts from its power to advance or to preserve the art which it professes to practise '. Attention has also been drawn to the process of the splitting up of castes into various endogamous sections by W. Kirkpatrick, [8] who regards the various gipsy castes of the south-east Punjab and the western part of the United Provinces as endogamous sections of a single original family. Change of occupation is also a common cause of the splitting up of castes into subcastes. Thus the Khatiks, a caste of butchers, has subcastes of Bekanwala, pork butcher ($<$ ' bacon '); Rajgar, mason; Sombatta, ropemaker; Mewafarosh, fruiterer, etc. Formerly fissions of this kind were often the result of migration or of political or social environmental factors, but latterly they have more often perhaps been the result of attempts by the well-to-do elements in a despised caste to cut adrift from their humbler caste brethren and raise themselves in the social scale by finding a new name and a dubious origin associating them with some higher caste. [9]

This process of separation is generally the sequel to the segregation of part of the caste into a subcaste which for a time has accepted wives from other subcastes while refusing to give daughters to such subcastes, thus establishing first of all the position of a superior subcaste, the claim to superiority generally being based on a change of occupation. The final step is to refuse to take wives from other subcastes and then to adopt a new name and deny all connexion with the caste of origin. Conversely the Kaibarttas of Bengal, perhaps a tribe originally, were long regarded, and regarded themselves, as a single caste divided occupationally into Jaliya Kaibarttas who practised the calling

[7] *People of India*, p. 270. And see Wise, *Notes on the Races, Castes and Trades of Eastern Bengal*, pp. 194 sq.
[8] ' Primitive Exogamy and the Caste System ', *Proc. A.S.B.*, VIII, no. 3, 1912. [9] *Vide infra*, pp. 112 sq.

of fishermen and Haliya (or Chasi) Kaibarttas who lived by
agriculture. But as the latter is a respectably regarded mode
of life while fishing is a despised calling, in the course of time
the practice arose on the part of the Haliya Kaibarttas of exacting high prices for their daughters when married by Jaliya
Kaibarttas while themselves refusing to marry Jaliya women.[10]
Eventually the Haliya Kaibarttas broke away entirely, banning
all intermarriage with the Jaliya Kaibarttas, and succeeded in
getting recognition as a separate caste under the name of
Mahishya.[11] The same caste probably affords another instance
of the tendency of castes to split up, as the Kewat caste appear
to have belonged originally to the same caste as the Kaibarttas,
and the names were synonymous in Orissa after the two were
quite distinct in Bihar and Bengal.[12]

With reference to the respective status of subcastes, it should
be made clear that that status is no less variable than that of
castes in different localities. Thus in the district of Cawnpore
in the United Provinces the caste of Dhanuk has five subcastes:
Laungbarsa, Badhik, Kathariya, Hazari and Taihal. In the
eastern part of the district each of these subcastes has become
an endogamous unit of its own. In the southern part of the
district the three latter are endogamous, but Laungbarsa and
Badhik intermarry to the extent that Badhik men take Laungbarsa wives, but Laungbarsa men do not take Badhik wives.
In north-west Cawnpore only Hazari and Taihal are closed
endogamous units; the other three subcastes practise some form
of intermarriage with one another. In north-east Cawnpore
only the Taihal subcaste is strictly endogamous, the other four
practising again some form of hypergamous or reciprocal intermarriage.[13] This case is typical of the extreme variability of
status found as between subcastes, and of the very variable
pattern of the caste system in general. In one instance hypergamy is practised in alternate generations: a Brahman of the
Asht-bans subcaste of the Bunjāhi section of Saraswat Brahmans
in the Punjab may marry a wife from the Bans-puj subcaste of
that group; but if the son by such a marriage does the same,
he loses status for he must marry an Asht-bans. Hypergamous

10 Risley, *Tribes and Castes*, I, s.v. Kaibartta; Wise, op. cit., p. 299.
11 Gait, op. cit., § 612, p. 380 ; Risley, *People of India*, pp. 117 sq.
12 Risley, *Tribes and Castes*, loc. cit.
13 Blunt, *Caste System of Northern India*, pp. 49, 128.

marriages between the Bans-puj and Asht-bans subcastes are thus limited to alternate generations.[14]

The practice of the higher subcaste in refusing to marry wives of the lower while allowing and even encouraging the man of the lower to marry wives from the upper, as mentioned above in referring to the Kaibartta caste, is contrary to what might be expected in a system in which the principle of hypergamy is so deeply rooted, but it is not unique. Nevertheless, the much more usual pattern is that shown by the Sadgops for instance, in which the superior subcaste takes wives from the inferior but refuses to give daughters to men of the inferior in marriage.[15] In Assam a Rabha man can marry a Kachari girl without any obstacle, but a Kachari man can only marry a Rabha girl after undergoing a special ceremony of purification. The Rabhas generally speaking are probably stricter Hindus than the Kacharis. The practices of hypergamy, that is, of seeking a bridegroom in a higher caste or subcaste than that of the bride, of isogamy, or marrying a spouse from the same caste, and of hypogamy, or seeking a bridegroom in a caste or subcaste lower than that of the bride, will have to be referred to later when dealing with the origins of caste, but it will be convenient here to make the workings of hypergamy clear as it is a widespread feature of the caste system and extends even to matrilineal castes like the Nayars, whose women may never marry husbands of inferior status to themselves. A good illustration of the working of hypergamy may be taken from the practice of the Rarhi Brahmans of Bengal. This caste is divided into subcastes known as Kulin and Srotriya, the latter being again subdivided into Siddha, Sādhya and Kashta Srotriyas. A man of the Kulin subcaste can take a wife from the Kulin, Siddha Srotriya or Sadhya Srotriya subcastes; a man of the Siddha Srotriya from his own or from the Sadhya Srotriya subcaste: a Sadhya Srotriya man or a Kashta Srotriya man can only take a wife from his own subcaste. Conversely, while a Kashta woman can marry only another Kashta Srotriya, a Sadhya can marry Sadhya, Siddha Srotriya, or Kulin, and a Siddha Srotriya woman can marry a man of her own subcaste or a Kulin, while a Kulin woman can marry a Kulin only.[16]

[14] Rose, *Tribes and Castes*, II, p. 126.
[15] Risley, *Tribes and Castes*, II, s.v. Sadgop.   [16] Ibid., I, p. 146.

The Rarhi Brahman pattern of hypergamy is clearly liable to lead to an excess of unmarried girls in the Kulin subcaste, since their choice of bridegrooms in that subcaste is much more limited than is the choice of brides, who may be taken from three subcastes. This superfluity perhaps, together with the duty incumbent on respectable Brahmans of getting their daughters married before puberty, has led to the practice known as ' Kulinism ' by which a man of a Kulin subcaste [17] would often marry a large number of brides, whom he never intended to support, in order to remove from their parents the risk of failure to get their daughters married. Bhattacharya [18] states that the practice might be considered brought to an end by a ruling of the Calcutta High Court that Kulins were bound to maintain their wives, but this opinion was probably unduly optimistic. Many Brahmans would no doubt forgo any claim to have their daughters maintained in order to get them respectably married by the proper time, and O'Malley [19] mentions the case of the Kulin Brahman who as recently as 1911 had married sixty wives, but no doubt the abuses to which Kulinism led at one time are now very much reduced.

Hypergamy among the Rajputs is of a different pattern to that of the Rarhi Brahman. The Rajputs as a whole are divided into a large number of exogamous clans of which some are of higher rank than others, while generally speaking the Rajputs of the west are regarded as of purer blood and better standing than those of eastern India. Thus while theoretically any Rajput can marry any other Rajput who belongs to a clan other than the clans of his parents (and sometimes grandparents), generally speaking a bridegroom of superior status is sought for a girl, while a boy can marry into a clan of lower standing than his own; and while a boy looks eastwards for a bride of lower rank the girl goes westwards for a husband of higher rank than her own. One result of hypergamy is to put a price on bridegrooms instead of on brides, and it is significant that while a high price for bridegrooms is paid where hypergamy

[17] Kulinism is not confined to Brahmans. There are Kulin Kayasthas, for instance, and Kulin Sadgops. The origin of hypergamy is dealt with by Rivers in a paper with that title in *The Journal of the Bihar and Orissa Research Society* for March 1921. [18] *Hindu Castes and Sects*, p. 41.

[19] *Indian Caste Customs*, pp. 9 sq. Cf. Wilson, *Indian Caste*, II, pp. 206 sqq.; Risley, *Tribes and Castes*, I, pp. 440 sq.; Risley, *People of India* (1915), p. 180, cites an interesting parallel to Indian hypergamy from Madagascar.

prevails, hypogamy, on the other hand, is associated with a bride-price. Hypergamous marriages, in which the status of the bridegroom is higher socially than that of the bride, are known as *anulōmă*, i.e. with the grain (lit. 'with the hair'); hypo-gamous marriages, on the other hand, are *prătilōmă*, against the grain, that is, against what is natural or proper, since the status of the bride is in this case higher than that of the bride-groom.

According to Risley,[20] among the Rajputs of Bihar the *gōtra* is tending to supplant the clan as an exogamous unit. Like the clan, the *gōtra* or *gōt*, by derivation a 'cowshed',[21] is an exo-gamous unit of individuals theoretically descended from a single ancestor. A *gotra* is in fact a clan, and, indeed, a Rajput clan is spoken of as a *got*, but in their existing state clan and *gotra* are not by any means conterminous in Rajput society. In castes other than Rajput the *gotra* is the normal exogamous subdivision of the endogamous whole, but, as in the case of the composition of a caste by subcastes, the composition of a caste or subcaste by *gotra* is extremely variable and often anomalous. Blunt, for instance, speaks [22] of castes or endogamous subcastes in which there is only one *gotra*, the Kashyapa, mentioning specifically the Ojha Lohar and the Kalwar. Whatever the case be in the Kalwar caste, the Ojha Lohar are stated by Crooke [23] to have what seems to be a minimum complement of eight Brahmanical *gotras*. For it will often be found that the *gotras* of the Brahman castes appear under the same names in other castes also, however humble, though many castes, of course, have many *gotras* the names of which are not common to the Brahmans and are often peculiar to themselves. Clearly the nomenclature of the *gotra* has often been borrowed from the Brahmanical system and has not by any means always been applied to a similar exogamous unit by the borrower. In the case of a caste with a single *gotra* for instance, marriage must be regulated not by a true *gotra* system but by degrees of prohibited kinship which are observed in the caste marriage system. What might be called the type-form of the *gotra* system is the Brahman one in which

[20] *Tribes and Castes*, s.v. Rajput.
[21] At one time, no doubt, the family cattle shared the family dwelling, as until comparatively recently in parts of Great Britain (Peate, *The Welsh House*, ch. iv).
[22] *Caste System*, p. 44 ; Majumdar, *Pseudo-Rajputs*, p. 169.
[23] *Tribes and Castes*, III, p. 376.

the seven patriarchal sages or *rishis*, traditionally the seven sons of Brahma, founded seven or rather eight *gotras*. The list of *rishis* varies in different sacred books, but their *gotras* are as follows: Kashyapa, Vasishtha, Agastya, Bhrigu, Gautama and Bharadvaja (the two sometimes bracketed as Angirasa), Atri, and Viswamitra.[24] In addition to these there are ten *gotras* founded by Kshatriyas who became Brahmans[25] and innumerable other *gotras* founded by descendants of the original seven (or eight) *gōtrakara rishis*. The Brahmanical *gotras* are to be found in many castes other than Brahman. The usual explanation given is that whereas among Brahmans the *gotra* represents actual descent from the original *rishi*, in other castes the descent is from an individual for whom such a *rishi* acted as family priest. In many cases it may be taken as certain that the name of a Brahmanical *gotra* has merely been adopted by some pre-existing exogamous unit for the sake of appearance; it is conceivable that in a few cases the existence of identical *gotras* in different castes may go back to a time when the constitution of society was less rigid, and individuals of different *varnas* (*vide infra*, pp. 64 sqq.) were enabled sometimes to change their *varna* and status in society. Generally speaking the *gotra* is a strictly exogamous group among Brahmans, though even here castes are found in which the *gotra*, though existing, is not the exogamous unit. For instance, the Sakaldwipi Brahmans of Bihar are divided into *purs* or sections which do not coincide with their *gotras*; here the *pur* is the exogamous unit, and provided marriage takes place outside the *pur* it may be within the *gotra*, and a similar system is reported of the Saraswat Brahmans of the Punjab.[26] Among many of the lower castes and more recent adherents to the Brahmanical religion, the *gotra* may actually represent a pre-Hindu exogamous unit, or it may be a purely arbitrary division which has little practical bearing on exogamy. Sometimes it represents a territorial rather than a kinship unit, and it is to be noted that in many parts of tribal India also village or locality tends to supersede the clan or sept as the exogamous unit. Thus many of the *gotras* of the Golapurab caste of the Agra district are named after villages and some after occupations,[27] while the Bhuinhar or Babhan caste of

[24] Wilson, *Indian Caste*, II, pp. 14 sqq.   [25] Blunt, *Caste System*, p. 43.
[26] Bhattacharya, *Hindu Castes and Sects*, pp. 48 and 56.
[27] Crooke, *Tribes and Castes*, II, p. 423.

Bihar are divided into territorial or functional units as well as into Brahmanical *gotra*, and where exogamy based on the territorial unit (*mul*) conflicts with that based on *gotra*, as it must frequently do, since everyone belongs to both sets, the *mul* prevails over the *gotra*.[28] The Khangars of the Central Provinces have four subdivisions, Rai, Mirdha, Karbal, and Dahāt; the first three intermarry hypergamously, Rai taking wives from Mirdha and Karbal but not giving wives to them, while the fourth is endogamous, being looked down upon for keeping pigs. But, independently apparently of these hypergamous divisions, the tribe as a whole is divided into some thirty or more *gotras* which are really exogamous totemistic clans.[29]

The Dumal, an agricultural caste of Orissa, has three sections (*barga*) based apparently on occupation, three sections (*mitti*) based on territorial origin, and three sections (*gōt*) based on totemic clan. The rule of exogamy takes all three into account, and it is necessary for the bride and bridegroom to have at least one of them different but not necessarily more than one.[30] The Gonds, or some branches of that race, and some allied tribes and castes base their exogamy on clans worshipping different numbers of household gods, a system possibly analogous to the *pravara*[31] system in origin, and the Nattukottai Chetti trading caste of Madura names its nine apparently exogamous divisions after the nine temples in which they respectively worship. Three of these *kōvils* have exogamous subdivisions, and all advocate marriage with the father's sister's daughter.[32] The Satmulia Goalas of Bihar are organized in territorial *mul*, and a man is debarred from marrying not only into his own *mul* but into that of his mother and from five to seven of his grandmothers and great-grandmothers for four generations back, in addition to which some take account of the *muls* of the female ancestors of the bride as well as of the bridegroom.[33] Quite clearly the internal exogamy of Hindu castes is infinitely variable and every sort of system seems to be represented. Indeed, strictly speaking *gotra* itself is not inherited but is acquired by the ' twice-born '

[28] Blunt, *Caste System*, p. 45 ; Risley, *Ethnographic Appendices*, p. 176.
[29] Russell, *Tribes and Castes of the Central Provinces*, III, pp. 440 sq.; Luard, *Ethnographical Survey of the Central India Agency*, III, pp. 9 sqq.
[30] Russell, op. cit., II, p. 530.   [31] *Vide infra*, p. 58.
[32] Thurston, *Castes and Tribes of Southern India*, v, pp. 261, 265.
[33] Risley, *Tribes and Castes*, I, p. 285.

castes only at the initiation ceremony (*upănăyănă*) at which the sacred thread is assumed. In the case of an adopted son whose *gotra* is not that of his adopting father he will be regarded as belonging to two *gotras* for marriage purposes, unless, that is, he is adopted in infancy before he has undergone the *upanayana* ceremony. In the latter case his *gotra* should be that of his adoptive parent.[34]

The *gōtra* then, though normally the exogamous group within the endogamous caste or subcaste, is very far from being a stable institution of consistent pattern, even among Brahman castes themselves, and the only safe generalization that can be made is that the endogamous caste is subdivided into exogamous groups, usually spoken of as *gōtra* or *gōt*, and theoretically derived either from the *gōtrakara rishis* of early vedic times or from the *gotra* of some Brahman priest who has ministered to a non-Brahman caste; these *gotra*, however, are often in reality exogamous units of various kinds, territorial, occupational, totemistic and so forth, masquerading as or actually overriding Brahmanic *gotra*, and very often spoken of by quite a different term—*illam, kul, mul, phaid, pal, pangat, bani, that, nukh, kuri, khel*, and what not. In Gujarat a *kula* is a subdivision of the *gotra* denoting a kindred or group worshipping the same family god; intermediate to the *kula* and the *gotra* is a larger subdivision of the latter known as *nukha*, or sept, which is the *de facto* exogamous unit.[35] One fact remains more or less constant: the endogamous unit contains within it a number of exogamous units. Even that generalization does not hold good for all of them, as within the endogamous units marriage may be regulated merely by a formal schedule of prohibited degrees of kinship.

Before coming to prohibited degrees of kinship, however, there is a restriction on marriage within the caste which is closely associated with the Brahmanical *gotra* which needs some further explanation, and that is restriction on marriage according to *prăvără*. A *pravara* is a passage, or rather perhaps the names contained in such a passage, in the vedic formula used in the worship of his ancestors by a follower of any particular vedic school; and the use of *pravara* involves the recital, at specific

34 Karandikar, *Hindu Exogamy*, p. 76.
35 Thoothi, *Vaisnavas of Gujarat*, pp. 140 sqq.

points in the sacrificial ritual, of the names of certain quasi-deified ancestors who followed that particular school of vedic worship also followed by the descendant reciting the *pravara*, and who are commemorated in the act of worship. These ancestors, known as *rishi* or sages, are believed to have been the original founders of the family in the case of the Brahmans who recite their names. The *gotra* again is subdivided into a number of *gana* (kindreds), each having its own distinctive *pravara*, though all such *gana* will normally have at least one *pravara* name, the chief name of those used, in common. In a case where two Brahman *gotra* have two chief *pravara* names in common, this is explained by a tradition of adoption, but it is possible that the *pravara* names were not always those of actual but sometimes of 'spiritual' fathers, since a distinction is made between *arsa-gotra* and *laukika-gotra*, that is, between 'spiritual' and 'profane' clans, for *arsa-gotra* means *gotra* as determined by the names of the *rishis* (ṛṣi) used in the *pravara*.[36] If this be the case, there might well be found identical *rishi* names in the *pravara* of different *gotra*. It has been suggested, however, that *pravara* has been used to determine the exogamous marriage unit by Brahmans because the term *gotra* has been loosely used with inexact meaning.[37] Be that as it may, any identity of names in the respective *pravaras* of two families operates as an effective bar to intermarriage, whether or no the *gotra* constitutes such a bar by itself. Castes with no *pravara* ancestors of their own use the *pravara* of their hereditary *purohit* or family priest who, being a Brahman, must have *pravara*, but it is the Brahman castes only which attach primary importance to *pravara*. It should further be pointed out here that certain *gotras* are in any case forbidden to intermarry, presumably on account of some relationship of their respective ancestors. Thus intermarriage is barred, for instance, between the Kashyapa and Vasishtha *gotras*. The ban on intermarriage varies in some *gotras*, and the regulations are meticulous. In the Bhrigu and Agastya *gotras*, for instance, the cult of more than one common *rishi* out of three in the *pravara*, or two out of five, is enough to make such *pravara* a valid bar to intermarriage. In the other

[36] Brough, *Early Brahmanical System of Gotra and Pravara.*
[37] Ibid.

gotras apparently a single *rishi* ancestor common to two *pravara* will act as a bar to marriage between them.[38]

While *gotra* and *pravara* regulate exogamous marriage as between agnates whether the kinship be real or hypothetical, there are also rules of consanguinity which govern marriage between affines as well as agnates, and it is on rules of this kind, of course, that castes which have only one *gotra* depend, though castes with multiple *gotra* observe them no less. The most familiar of these rules is the one known as that of *sapindă*.[39] Under the *sapinda* rule, which is generally observed in castes of good status, marriage is prohibited between any two persons who possess a common ancestor within a certain number of degrees on the father's side and a smaller number of degrees on the mother's. The actual number of prohibited degrees varies in different castes and in different parts of India—seven degrees on the father's side or five on the mother's is sometimes given as the rule; six on the father's side and four on the mother's is a frequent standard, but the degrees on the mother's side prohibited under the *sapinda* rule are sometimes as low as three. A simplified form of this rule which is commonly observed is that no marriage shall take place between two families while the memory of a previous intermarriage lasts. Sometimes this is less exactingly stated in the form that a man shall not take a bride from any family to which his family is known to have given one, while conversely again a daughter may not marry into a family from which a son has taken a bride. Various other rules are in use in different castes. The Ahir are reported to prohibit a man from taking a bride from any of the *gotras* of his four grandparents. Some castes forbid marriage with any descendant of a father's or mother's brother or sister, thus barring all marriage with a first cousin of any kind or his or her child, marriage with a brother's or sister's child being likewise forbidden. Other castes again forbid mar-

---

[38] Brough (op. cit.) says that to bar marriage a majority of *rishi* names must be identical, but it is possible that he is thinking in terms of *pravara* containing the names of three *rishis* only.

[39] The original meaning of *săpindă* seems to be one who is under an obligation, shared with the person using the term, to perform funeral ceremonies for a father, grandfather, great-grandfather, and their wives, in common. The term is derived from the Sanskrit word *pinda*, meaning the cake of food offered to the departed at the funeral ceremonies.

riage with all patrilineal kindred and with the kindred of the
mother's brother, though permitting marriage with cousins
derived from a father's or mother's sister, while others again
allow marriage with all but patrilineal cousins, i.e. have no
real *sapinda* rule at all. Some castes forbid a daughter's being
married into her mother's family, a rule which Blunt explains
on the ground of hypergamy, but which may be a survival of
a matrilineal tradition.[40] The generally accepted simple rule
is that no marriage shall take place between a person and a
child or descendant of his or her father's or mother's brothers
or sisters. Many castes, however, have far more elaborate
rules, a good instance of which is to be found among the
Goalas of Bengal. Here the subcaste known as Satmulia forbids marriage within seven groups of relatives as shown in the
following table, while the Naomulia subcaste forbids marriage
within nine groups:

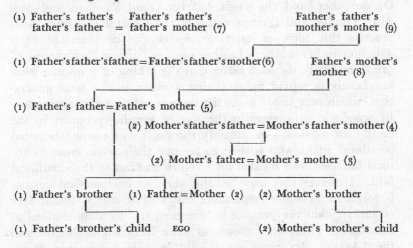

(1) Father's father's   Father's father's   Father's father's
    father's father = father's mother (7)   mother's mother (9)

(1) Father's father's father = Father's father's mother (6)   Father's mother's
                                                                    mother (8)

(1) Father's father = Father's mother (5)

         (2) Mother's father's father = Mother's father's mother (4)

         (2) Mother's father = Mother's mother (3)

(1) Father's brother   (1) Father = Mother (2)   (2) Mother's brother

(1) Father's brother's child   EGO   (2) Mother's brother's child

Here EGO may not marry into any of the lines (1)—(7) if he be
a Satmulia, nor any descendant of (8) or (9) either if he be a
Naomulia.[41] The opposite extreme was to be found at any rate
until recently in one district in northern Bengal where the
Rajbansi caste permitted marriage with a uterine half-sister.[42]
While all Hindu castes forbid marriage between ortho-cousins

---

[40] Brough, op. cit., mentions a verse attributed to Sātātapa which forbids
any marriage into the mother's *gotra*, apparently for either sex.
[41] *Vide* Risley, *Tribes and Castes*, I, p. 287.   [42] Ibid., p. 494.

on the male side, i.e. between the children of two brothers, and
while the great majority at any rate forbid it between ortho-
cousins on the female side also, between the children, that is,
of two sisters, cross-cousin marriage—marriage, that is, between
a man and his mother's brother's or father's sister's daughter—
is widespread and common, particularly in south India, marriage
with the mother's brother's daughter being especially favoured.
In some cases this type of marriage is virtually compulsory.
Among people following the matrilineal system of the Malabar
coast a man often has by custom a prescriptive right to marry
his mother's brother's daughter if he wishes. This custom has
often been interpreted as a conventional compromise to retain
matrilineal inheritance under patrilineal forms, but since it is
followed in the matrilineal castes as well as in many patrilineal
ones it may equally well, if not more likely, be in the nature
of a concession on the part of matriliny to patrilineal influences.
On the other hand, the Baiga, Agariya, Gond, Pardhan, and even
Ahir, Dhulia, and Dhimar castes of the Central Provinces, who
practise this form of marriage, speak of the marriage of a
daughter to her mother's brother's son as ' giving back the milk '
(*dudh lautāna*), the idea being that the taking of a woman from
her family is repaid by returning another in the next generation, which may imply a quasi-economic origin for the custom—
its economic advantages in the way of keeping property in the
family are obvious—or possibly the results of contact between
patrilocal tribes who wished to remove their wives from matrilocal families, who insisted on a return in kind to the matrilocal
fold. However this may be, this very un-Brahmanical custom
is followed in many respectable castes of southern India; Iyer
remarks [43] that the practice is ' creeping in ' to some sections of
Brahmans; Thurston [44] mentions some Deshasth Brahmans and
the ' Ayyar ' Brahmans specifically in this connexion; Steele
records [45] that in the south Maratha country a brother's child
may marry a sister's child provided the *gotra* is different;
inquiries made in the Bombay census of 1911 showed that thirty-
one castes in this area allowed a man to marry his cross-cousin,
paternal or maternal, three to marry his mother's sister's
daughter, and fifteen to marry his mother's brother's daughter,

[43] *Lectures on Ethnography,* p. 130.
[44] *Ethnographic Notes in Southern India,* p. 54.
[45] *Law and Custom of Hindoo Castes within the Dekhun Provinces,* p. 163.

but not his father's sister's. Some castes go still further, for the Kammavan, and probably some others, add a sister's daughter to the category of suitable wives.[46] Marriages of these kinds are so strongly regarded as proper sorts of match that on account of the relationship a boy will often be married to a woman much older than he is. In some of the central Indian tribes and castes the relationship system seems to suggest that at some time in the remote past a marriage class system analogous to that of Australia may have prevailed, for grandparents and grandchildren are found to have a 'joking relationship' impossible between parents and children,[47] as if, as in the four-class system of several Australian tribes, for instance, grandparents and grandchildren fell into respectively marriageable classes. Indeed, in the Baiga tribe marriages actually occur between grandparent and grandchild, specific instances being given by Elwin,[48] who quotes one case of a woman who had two children by her own grandson, so perhaps the list of prohibited degrees in the Book of Common Prayer does not really start with such comic irrelevance as one is inclined to think. In the case of grandparent-grandchild marriage it is possible that the basis of the practice is a belief in reincarnation. If the grandchild is merely the grandparent reborn, what could be more natural than for him or her to be reunited to his or her former spouse? It is possibly significant that these grandparent-grandchild marriages among the Baiga seem to be normally performed with the informal rites used for remarriage generally. The same tribes and castes that have a joking relationship between grandparent and grandchild generally have one between a man and his wife's younger sisters and between a woman and her husband's younger brothers, which is surely a relic of the levirate and sororate, and, indeed, in the Rengma tribe in Assam the relationship between a woman and her husband's younger brother is often (or was till recently) very much more intimate than mere jocularity or even romping. This joking relationship between brothers and sisters-in-law obtains very widely in India, and in Bengal at any rate among castes high up in social status.

Restrictions on marriage then vary very considerably according to caste and locality, and many of the rules observed can hardly

[46] O'Malley, *Indian Caste Customs*, p. 7.
[47] Russell, op. cit., III, p. 72.   [48] *The Baiga*, p. 180.

be said to be exactly relevant to the question of caste. Yet to this extent caste does govern marriage: the caste is almost invariably endogamous and the subcaste very frequently so indeed; the caste either contains within itself exogamous subdivisions, or else observes certain rules restricting the choice of mates; and when those rules, whatever they may be, are broken, the culprit is dealt with by his caste fellows and punished according to the code of his caste. This control is an aspect of caste to be treated later, but it may be stated here that generally speaking, and apart from recognized hypergamous and hypogamous subcaste systems, a person marrying outside the caste is excommunicated. Very often a man or woman marrying into a caste which is definitely recognized as unquestionably inferior in status will be received into the caste of his or her spouse.[49] Very rarely in the case of a man marrying a bride from a lower caste, the original status may be recovered in the course of several generations.[50] This is in accordance with an ancient practice, which had the sanction of the lawgiver Manu, and also of the *Mitākshara*, but which has generally ceased to be observed.[51]

Something must here be said about *varna*, ' colour ', a term which is often confused with caste (*jāti, jāt*) though it is far from having the same meaning. The *varna* seem to have been originally the four classes into which Rigvedic society was divided; that is, the three categories of twice-born, Brahman, Kshatriya and Vaishya, and fourthly the Sudra, below whom were the outcastes. The ' twice-born ' (*dvija*) classes are so-called on account of the initiation ceremony (*upanayana*) at which they are ceremonially reborn and assume the sacred thread, a ceremony not permitted to Sudras. It is probable that in vedic times the lines between these classes were not impassable. According to tradition Kshatriyas could and did become

---

[49] O'Malley (*Caste Customs,* p. 33) cites the practice of the Bauri caste as a common instance of this, but I have known it happen in other castes.

[50] Rose, *Tribes and Castes,* I, p. 42 ; *Laws of Manu* (tr. Bühler), x, 64.

[51] The Code of Manu is dated by Macdonell between 200 B.C. and A.D. 200, but is founded on material of an earlier date. The *Mitākshara* is a juristic work of the eleventh century A.D. based on two *Yājñavalkya-smriti* of *c.* 300 A.D.; its authority is accepted in most of India, but is not necessarily followed in practice, and in this instance may be regarded as generally speaking a dead letter. *Vide* Macdonell, *India's Past,* pp. 58, 163, 165, and Dowson, *Classical Dictionary of Hindu Mythology,* s.vv. Manu-Sanhita and Mitākshara.

Brahmans, Viswamitra, who from a Kshatriya became a Brahman and a *pravara rishi* by his austerity, affording an example. According to the *purana* 'Harivansha',[52] two sons of Nābhāgarishta who were Vaishyas became Brahmans. Even Sudras seem sometimes to have become Brahmans, for the ancestor of the Pokhar Sevaka Brahmans of Rajputana was a Mer who was taught the Yajurveda by a *muni*,[53] and the Vyāsokta Brahmans of Bengal are reputed to be the descendants of a Sudra who was made a Brahman by the *rishi* Vyasa, himself, according to the Buddhist writer of the Vajrashuchi, the son of a fisherman's daughter.[54] The barrier between these classes is still perhaps not entirely impassable, for the important caste of Kayastha, which ranks next to Brahman in Bengal, is now commonly regarded as 'twice-born', and itself claims to be Kshatriya, though it was perhaps more often regarded as clean Sudra a hundred years ago and its status as twice-born is still disputed.[55] They are probably really an occupational caste in origin, and as 'writers' may have been recruited from more than one *varna*.

At the time of the Rigvedic invasion the four *varna* must be held to represent a fourfold division of society into classes— Brahmans who acted as priests, Kshatriyas or Rajanyas who were rulers, nobles and fighters, Vaishyas ($< vish$)[56] the people generally, ordinary householders so to speak, and Sudras, the servile classes drawn from the people of the country. The last term 'does not even occur in the early parts of the collection of the Vedas',[57] while the Brahman was the utterer of prayer and conductor of ceremonial, but apparently had no privilege on that account and attained his greatest dignity as the *purohita* or family priest of kings and princes, of the Rajanya that is, who were the holders of the *raj* or government and possessors of *kshatra*, authority. The highest religious authorities seem to have been the sages or *rishis*, the poetical authors of the vedic hymns, and these *rishis* came from any *varna* and belonged in some cases to indigenous families; both Rajanya and Vaishya

[52] Wilson, *Indian Caste*, I, p. 434.   [53] Ibid., II, p. 172.
[54] Ibid., I, p. 307.
[55] *Vide* Gait, *Report on the Census of Bengal*, 1901, pp. 379 and 381, and cf. Colebrooke, 'Enumeration of Indian Classes' in *Asiatick Researches* (1807), v, pp. 58, 66.
[56] *Vish* is translated 'commonalty' by Keith, *vide* Rapson, *Cambridge History of India*, pp. 91-4.   [57] Wilson, *Indian Caste*, I, p. 204.

had the privilege of conducting certain sacrifices at any rate as
well as Brahmans, whose predominance does not appear until
the later or derivative vedas. Certain colours are associated
with the four *varna*—white with the Brahman, red with the
Kshatriya, yellow with the Vaishya and black with the Sudra;
varna, as has been stated, means colour. It is possible that this
colour distinction is in some way associated with race, as one is
reminded of the ancient Egyptian convention which showed
Egyptians red, Asiatics yellow, Northerners white and negroes
black; Hocart [58] has strenuously attacked this hypothesis and
maintains that the traditional association of the colours of the
four *varna* with points of the compass—white with the north,
red with the east, yellow with the south and black with the
west—has a ritual, not a racial significance, and refers to the
four quarters of an enclosed town allotted respectively as dwelling places to the different *varna*, outcastes having to live, as
they still do, outside the village fence.

However that may be, the *varna* are often claimed not only
to be of the nature of castes but up to a point to be castes—
Brahman and Kshatriya at any rate are terms which seem at
first sight to be still in use as labels associated with particular
castes, while the term Vaishya has come back into use of recent
years, generally with some qualifying adjective and associated
with some particular caste group. As a matter of fact none of
the four terms for *varna* now represents anything but groups of
castes. All Brahmans do not intermarry, but there are many
endogamous Brahman castes. The Rajput does seem to answer
more nearly to the Rajanya or Kshatriya *varna*, but here again
there are very many castes who claim Kshatriya origin and wear
the sacred thread of the twice-born, but do not intermarry; thus
the Khatri,[59] a caste of the Punjab, of the United Provinces
and of Bihar claiming Kshatriya origin, do not ordinarily intermarry with Rajputs and indeed contain a number of endogamous subcastes. The probability seems to be that in vedic times
the *varna* were classes rather than castes, and that post-vedic
scholars, looking for authority for the caste system in the earliest
vedas, have interpreted the nature of the *varna* in terms of the

[58] *Les Castes*, pp. 46 sqq.
[59] For a very full account of the Khatri caste see Crooke, *Tribes and
Castes*, III and Rose, op. cit., II.

caste system as they knew it. At any rate the *varna* of the present day is not a caste, though it may be regarded as a group of castes, and there is a tendency among social reformers to advocate the substitution of four *varna* for three thousand or more endogamous groups of the caste system, a movement which, if successful, would tend to fix a hard and fast line of social cleavage between classes, and which probably underestimates the power and misunderstands the significance of the caste system, its origin, and the important function it still performs in the integration of Indian society.

Like caste *varna* is to some extent fluid. In its earlier history there seem to have been Brahmans by works as well as Brahmans by birth; the whole of the Kshatriya *varna* is claimed by Brahmans to have been extirpated by Parasurama,[60] but if so it has been replaced by manufactured Kshatriyas, and in any case Kshatriya rank is claimed by many whose title is one of function or of creation rather than of inheritance. Numbers of Sudra castes have taken to wearing the insignia of the twice-born, and some of them gain acceptance, after a time, as doing so legitimately.[61] In short, *varna*, like caste, is a somewhat indeterminate expression, and persons belonging to one *varna* in one locality may be otherwise classified in another. It is wider and vaguer than caste, like which it is a variable social unit.

One other aspect of caste must be briefly referred to here. That is, the curious tradition only found in southern India by which certain castes are regarded as castes of the Right Hand and others as castes of the Left Hand. Between these two divisions there is a very strong sentiment of factious rivalry, leading to frequent clashes, often with riot and violence, generally occasioned by some real or supposed encroachment by castes of the Left Hand on privileges claimed as belonging exclusively to the Right. All castes are not concerned in this dual division and its rivalries and animosities. Brahmans, for instance, are spoken of as *Mahajanam* ('of great birth') and are often regarded as belonging to neither division.[62] There are generally said to be eighteen castes of the Right Hand and nine of the Left, but when it comes to stating the names of these

[60] See Dowson, op. cit., pp. 230 sq.
[61] For example see Majumdar, *Pseudo-Rajputs*, pp. 156 sqq.
[62] Schoebel, *L'Histoire des Origines et du Développement des Castes de l'Inde*, p. 94.

nine or eighteen much difficulty is experienced, and accounts
are found to vary. Buchanan [63] gives a list, but the terms
are Kanarese, do not always tally with the Tamil, and are in
some cases apparently purely occupational. A list is given by
Aiyangar,[64] but that of the castes of the Right Hand is clearly
incomplete. Oppert [65] gives a list which shows at least fifty-eight
castes of the Right and at least five of the Left, but it is difficult
to identify all the castes in his lists, which contain other obscur-
ities also.[66] The principal castes of the Left Hand are the following: Beri Chetti, Vaniyan (who yoke two bullocks to their
oil-press), Devanga (weavers), Golla (cowherds), Panchala (five
artisan castes—carpenters, masons, goldsmiths, coppersmiths, and
blacksmiths), Chakkiliyan (leather-workers), Bedar, Palli, and
Pallan (cultivator and soldier castes). In the Chakkiliyan caste
the men belong to the Left Hand, but their women-folk to the
Right Hand. One authority—Dr Macleane, quoted by Oppert [67]
as stating it ' in the Administration Manual, vol. I, p. 69 '—has
stated that the male Palli belonged to the Right and the female
to the Left Hand. The same statement is recorded by Thurston [68]
as having been made by the Census Superintendent of 1871,
but he adds that this has not been confirmed by recent investigations. Indeed both earlier and later authorities return the
Palli as belonging unequivocally to the Left Hand. Buchanan
so mentions them in 1800,[69] and the famous Chingleput judge-
ment of George Coleman in 1809 [70] does the same. Fully Right-
Hand castes include at any rate the following: Balija, Banajiga
and Komati (trading castes), Vaniyan (who yoke one bullock
only), Chaliyan and Seniyan (weaving castes), Janappan (hemp
dressers), Kusavan (potters), Melakkaran (musicians), Shanan
(toddy drawers), Ambattan (barbers), Vannan (washermen),
Idaiyan (shepherds) Vellala, Paraiyan, Mala, Holeya (cultivating
castes), Kurava, Odde, Irula, Vedan and Vettuvan (mostly

---

[63] Francis Buchanan, *Journey through Mysore, Canara and Malabar* (1870),
I, pp. 53 sq. [ch. II].   [64] M. Srinivasa Aiyangar, *Tamil Studies*, p. 95.
[65] Gustav Oppert, *On the Original Inhabitants of Bharatavarsa or India*,
pp. 57 sqq.
[66] Other references to this division into Right and Left will be found in
Thurston, *Castes and Tribes*, e.g. I, p. 35 ; II, pp. 4, 11, 121 ; III, pp. 40, 117
sq.; IV, pp. 295, 330, 332 ; V, pp. 474 sq.; VI, pp. 15, 91 ; in Sonnerat,
Voyages aux Indes, I, pp. 54 sqq.; in Hayavadana Rao, *Indian Caste System*,
pp. 73 sqq.; and in Love, *Vestiges of Old Madras*, I, pp. 118 sqq.
[67] Op. cit., p. 65 n.   [68] *Castes and Tribes*, VI, p. 15.
[69] Loc. cit.   [70] See Oppert, op. cit., p. 62, n. 59.

labourers). In addition to the above there seem to be, as already stated, the women of the Chakkiliyan or Madiga caste, but the Right- or Left-handedness of castes differs apparently to some extent with locality. Thus the Kaikolans,[71] a weaver caste associated with Devanga, belong to the Left Hand, but the *devadasis* (dancing girls) and *nattuvans* (teachers of dancing girls), drawn from the Kaikolan caste, belong to the Right Hand. Conversely, there are sections both of Komatis [72] and Chaliyans [73] which belong to the Left, while the same applies to some of even the Mala in at any rate the Kurnool and Cuddapah districts. There the normal Right-Hand Mala are reported to be spoken of as *Pekinati-vandhlu* or as *Reddi-Bhumi-vandhlu*; the Left-Hand Mala call themselves *Murikinati-vandhlu*, a name said to be applied also to a class of Brahmans. These divisions of the Mala caste are endogamous; the women of the Right Hand do not wear glass bangles nor pierce the left nostril; they remove the bodice at marriage, and they forbid the remarriage of widows. The women of the Left Hand wear the *paita* over the left shoulder except at marriage.[74]

It may be mentioned in passing that one or two authorities seem to have suffered from a tendency to transpose Right and Left. Thus Thurston [75] quotes the Madura District Manual as stating that the Chakkiliyan men belong to the Right Hand and their women to the Left, while Oppert likewise quotes the Madura Manual but in the reverse sense.[76] The latter seems to be the correct version, but Hocart [77] has followed Thurston's, and sees in this division between the sexes an indication of a former dual system of exogamous moieties. Oppert refers to an account which associates the Right and Left Hands with the Saivite and Vaishnavite sects respectively,[78] and himself sees in it a reflection of objections to Brahman authority.[79]

Later immigrants into south India, such as Muslims, Marwaris, and Gujaratis, are, like Brahmans, generally regarded

[71] Thurston, *Castes and Tribes*, III, p. 40.   [72] Ibid., I, p. 35.
[73] Ibid., II, p. 11.
[74] Personal information from the Venerable P. B. Emmet, formerly Archdeacon of Nandyal in the Kurnool District of Madras. *Murikinati* probably = *Murakanādu*, a sect of Brahmans following the White Yajurveda (Wilson, *Indian Caste*, II, p. 52). *Pekinati* possibly = *Vegināḍu* ; see Wilson, loc. cit., p. 54, and Thurston, *Castes and Tribes*, IV, pp. 345 sq.
[75] *Castes and Tribes*, II, p. 4.   [76] Op. cit., p. 66.
[77] *Les Castes*, p. 113.   [78] Op. cit., p. 58.
[79] Ibid., p. 61.

as outside this dual system entirely. The subjects of contention are generally purely social or ceremonial matters, such as the right to use twelve pillars in a marriage booth, to wear certain gold ornaments on both arms, to carry a flag with the emblem of a monkey on it, to ride on a horse or to use a palanquin in wedding processions, or to indulge in certain specific sorts of music or dance.[80] These may seem trivial matters, but the disturbances resulting from such disputes have often been widespread and serious. Certain parallels, in some degree at any rate, are to be found elsewhere in India, though without the dual division into Right and Left. Thus in the Laccadive Islands, where the inhabitants are Muslims, certain clans are not allowed by tradition the use of certain ornaments and symbols, the use of shoes, or the ownership of sailing vessels;[81] again, in central India the use of certain gold ornaments by Chamars has led to riots between them and Rajput neighbours. Srinavasa Aiyangar says [82] that 'similar distinctions may still be found among the Sakti worshippers of Bengal', though he does not regard them as having any connexion with the Madras division. The origin of this peculiar division into Right-Hand and Left-Hand castes will be discussed in another chapter,[83] but it may be noted here that while trading and weaving castes are found in both divisions, the artisan castes belong almost exclusively to the Left and the cultivating castes mostly to the Right. Further, although this division of castes is familiar in the Telugu-, Tamil- and Kanarese-speaking districts of south India, it is not found in the Malayalam-speaking districts, where the *marumakkathayam* system, by which descent is reckoned in the female line, prevails against the *makkathayam* (male line) system of the rest of the peninsula. This fact is possibly not without significance in regard to the origin of the system, though the Abbé Carré in the seventeenth century ascribed it [84] to the use, or disuse, of the left hand in working.

---

[80] *Vide*, for instance, Molony, *Census of Madras*, 1911, I, p. 162.
[81] *Per contra* the Malacheri class which suffers these disabilities has the exclusive right to perform the functions of barber, goldsmith, etc. and of cooking and baling aboard sailing vessels. *Vide The Statesman* (Calcutta) of 6 October 1934 and R. H. Ellis, *Laccadive Islands*, ch. IV.
[82] *Tamil Studies*, p. 96.   [83] See chapter X (*infra*), pp. 149 sq.
[84] *Travels in India and the Near East*, II, p. 595.

CHAPTER VI

ITS STRICTURES

THE marital restrictions of caste have already been treated, as they are vitally involved in the relationship of a caste to society as a whole, but they are very far from being the only restrictions which isolate or, rather, insulate one caste from another. Indeed, it seems possible that caste endogamy is more or less incidental to the taboo on taking food cooked by a person of at any rate a lower, if not of any other, caste, and in the view of the writer this taboo is probably the keystone of the whole system. It is not uncommon in some parts of India for a man of one caste to keep a concubine of a lower caste, or even a non-Hindu, and he is not outcasted by his caste fellows on that ground, though he may be, and often is, on the ground that he has eaten food cooked or served by her or taken water from her hands.[1] This suggests that the taboo on marriage is the necessary and inevitable outcome of the taboo on food and drink, rather than the cause of it. Roscoe, indeed, has pointed out the effect of food taboos in preventing intermarriage between pastoral and agricultural peoples in central Africa.[2]

Now the taboo on food and water as between caste and caste is subject to many gradations and variations. It is often stated that the test of a ' clean caste ', that is to say, a caste of respectable and non-polluting status, lies in whether or not a Brahman can accept drinking water at its hands. Here, of course, as in the case of marital restrictions, there is room for much variation between one locality and another, and any generalization that can be made must be made subject to local variations of custom which may now and then be very striking.[3] Thus in northern India there are a number of Sudra castes from which men of higher caste can take water, whereas in southern and western India the higher caste at any rate will as a rule only take water from men of their own caste or a caste higher than their own.

[1] Russell, op. cit., I, p. 179 ; O'Malley, *Caste Customs*, p. 64 ; and cf. Blunt, *Caste System*, pp. 123 and 124 n.

[2] ' Immigrants and their Influence in the Lake Region of Central Africa ' in *The Frazer Lectures*, 1922-1932, p. 33.

[3] In Bengal a Brahman, or any man of good caste, was forbidden to drink water from the hands of any woman who had no tattoo spot, though this taboo was breaking down in 1889. *Vide* Wise, op. cit., p. 123.

Ganges water, however, can be taken apparently even from untouchables, on account of its sacred character which is beyond pollution. There is a saying also that water is purified by air, alluding to the common practice of pouring out water from one main vessel into the drinking vessel of another. No one in practice drinks out of a vessel belonging to another caste, though theoretically a man can drink from one that has been used only by a higher caste than his own. This would, of course, make it useless to the higher caste owner. In northern India a Brahman will take water poured into his *lota* (drinking vessel) by men of several Sudra castes regarded as clean, e.g. Barhai (a carpenter caste, claiming an origin from the god Viswakarman, the Architect of the Universe), Nai (the barber caste, the services of which are important in much Hindu ritual), Bharbunja (grain-parchers), Halwai (confectioners), Kahar (fishermen, well-sinkers, and growers of water-nuts). The southern Brahman is more particular, and in any case the water distributors at railway stations are always Brahmans, so that anyone can accept water poured out by them. As an instance of the variation shown from place to place the Goala (cowherd) caste will serve. In Bihar Brahmans can take water from them, but not in Bengal, or at any rate in parts of Bengal. In the case of castes lower than Brahman the restrictions on taking water may be somewhat less rigid, at any rate in northern and north-eastern India, but are approximately the same, a caste recognized as clean by Brahmans being similarly recognized as such by other castes.

Restrictions in regard to eating are generally speaking more severe than those which govern drinking, but do not depend, as in that case, on who supplies the food but rather on who cooks it. The cooking is very important, and a stranger's shadow, or even the glance of a man of low caste,[4] falling on the cooking pot may necessitate throwing away the contents. Members of the same exogamous unit can, of course, share each other's food. So, too, as a rule can members of different exogamous groups who can intermarry, for a man must be able to eat food cooked by his own household. Blunt[5] maintains that this commensality is a result of intermarriage, and that until such intermarriage had taken place the two groups could not eat each other's food.

[4] Thurston, *Omens and Superstitions*, p. 109.
[5] *Caste System*, p. 89.

The other way round, however, is perhaps the more likely, if one comes before the other at all, and intermarriage takes place because there is no taboo on interdining. A Kahar employed by a superior caste—Brahman, Rajput, Kayastha, etc.—may eat their leavings so long as he himself is not married;[6] after marriage he may not do so. Some castes will not take food from their own daughters once these daughters are married, even to men of their own caste.[7] The ordinary cooked meal has to be prepared with much ceremony and care, rice boiled in water, or *chăpāti*, that is, bannocks, cakes of unleavened flour or meal mixed with water and baked upon a griddle, form the staple food of most castes, and these must be cooked, as Blunt says, 'with the precautions of a magic ceremony.'. If away from the regular household cooking-place, each man marks off his own cooking-place, makes his own mud oven and cooks apart from his fellows. He may cook for others of his own caste or subcaste also, but so particular are most castes that a number of sarcastic proverbs attach to their scruples—' Thirteen Rajputs, thirteen cooking places', 'Three Tirhut Brahmans and thirteen cooking places', are quoted by O'Malley. A. K. Forbes mentions eastern Brahmans who forbid brothers to use a common cooking-place or even take fire from one another to cook with. He gives details of the elaborate ceremonial of a Brahman meal, and he describes the precautions required of a Nagar Brahman, who must first bathe, dress in clean clothes, which, if cotton, must first have been washed and dried where nothing contaminating could touch them. He must not touch an earthen vessel[8] that has contained water, nor a piece of cotton touched by anyone in a state of ritual impurity unless it has been decontaminated by dipping in *ghi* (liquid butter), nor leather, nor bone, nor paper unless it has Hindu characters on it. He must not touch or be touched by a donkey, pig, dog, or a child old enough to eat solid food. (Such a child being uninitiated would not be bound by caste rules as to food.) Before he begins to eat he must not touch a Brahman who is eating or has eaten. He must not read a printed book while eating, nor a manuscript book unless bound with silk and pasted with pounded tamarind

---

[6] Risley, *Tribes and Castes*, I, p. 374.   [7] Russell, op. cit., I, p 179.
[8] He must himself use metal utensils only, of course. Cf. Stevenson, *Rites of the Twice-Born*, p. 240.

seed paste.[9] No doubt this is a somewhat extreme case, but
it is typical of the sort of restrictions that accompany cooking
and eating, for the eating of grain, cooked with water, is of
the nature of a sacrament. A candidate for admission to the
Mahli caste, for instance, must eat a little of the leavings
of the food of each of the caste-men joining in his initiatory
feast.[10] The women eat separately when the men have finished.
Barbosa records that the king of Malabar ate in privacy, so that
no one saw him, and Nicolo Conti [11] ascribes the reason why
many eat in secret to a fear of the evil eye. Clearly restrictions
of this kind are most inconvenient to travellers, so that it is not
surprising to find special exemptions for other kinds of food.

Food cooked with water as described is known as *kachchā*, and
the restrictions associated with it are much more severe than
those associated with food known as *pakkā*, which is cooked with
ghī—it is said that *ghi*, being a product of the cow, sanctifies the
food cooked with it, just as the sanctity of the Ganges does the
water drawn from her, making it safe against transmitting pollution from one caste to another. Consequently, it is possible for
a Brahman even to buy sweetmeats from a Halwai and eat them
without any need for preliminary bathing or purification. At
the same time parched grain is also reckoned, like food prepared
with *ghi*, as *pakka*, and in view of the passage in the *Satapatha
Brahmana*, quoted by Frazer,[12] which shows that the Brahman
anciently considered rice cakes cooked with water as becoming
identical with human flesh, one may perhaps infer that it is the
combination of grain with water that gives the sacred character
to the *kachcha* food. Perhaps this is on account of a belief
in the identity of the ' soul-stuff ' or life-matter of human beings
with that of cereal plants (a belief which seems to appear again

[9] *Rás Málá* (1856), II, pp. 258 sq., and cf. Blunt, *Caste System,* pp. 97
sqq.; Wise, op. cit., p. 291.   [10] Russell, op. cit., I, p. 168.
[11] Quoted by Crooke, *Things Indian,* p. 227.
[12] *Golden Bough* (1914), VIII (*Spirits of the Corn and the Wild,* II), p. 89.
Mayer (*Caste and Kinship in Central India,* p. 33) adds that salt is ' also a
controlling factor ' in the constitution of *kachcha* food. I do not question
this, at any rate as regards Rajputana, but I am not sure that it obtains
everywhere, for while rice and millet eaters at least usually add salt to the
water they are going to cook in, the ' people of the northern hills use it
with their cooked food as we do ' (Crooke, *Things Indian,* s.v. Salt). The
Portuguese in Goa issued an edict in 1736 by which Indians were prohibited
from using as food ' rice cooked without salt, mixing the salt afterwards
as is done by the Gentios ' i.e. by Hindus. Some of the north-eastern hill
people cook in brine drawn in that form from brine-wells, but the ones
I have observed doing this were not Hindu.

in the ignominy attaching to the occupation of that branch of the Teli caste which extracted the oil from seed as distinct from the comparative respectability of the other branch which merely traded in it) as well as the association of life with water. However that may be, the distinction between *kachcha* and *pakka* food remains very important in that pollution is far more easily transmitted by the former than by the latter, which may be taken by a Brahman from a Halwai, from a Kahar, or from a Bharbunja. *Ghi*, uncooked grain, or vegetables can be bought in the market even from Muslims, but once cooked such food ' becomes Brahmā and so must be treated with sacramental care '.[13]

Another important point to be noticed is that the severity of the food taboo has no relation to the social position of the caste. Blunt [14] has worked out a classification of castes into five groups as follows:

(i) Those who will eat *kachcha* food cooked only by a member of their own endogamous group or by their personal *guru* (spiritual guide), and *pakka* food cooked only by the same or a Halwai or Kahar; to which he should, I think, have added food cooked (*pakka*, of course) by a Bharbunja.

(ii) Those who will eat similar food similarly cooked by the above castes and also by Brahmans.

(iii) Those who will eat similar food similarly cooked by all the above and by Rajputs.

(iv) Those who will eat similar food similarly cooked by all the above castes and by lower castes of rank which they regard as at least equal to their own.

(v) Those who will eat food cooked by almost anyone.

Under these five heads he deals with seventy-six different castes of the United Provinces, but they do not fall into uniform groups, for some which fall into group one as regards *kachcha* food fall into another in regard to *pakka* food about which they are not so strict, whereas there are others who are as strict about *pakka* food as they are about *kachcha*, or even stricter in comparison with other castes. Thus some Brahman castes fall, as one might expect, unequivocally into the first category; other Brahmans in category (i) as regards *kachcha* food fall into number (iv) as regards *pakka* food. The castes of Kachhi, market gardeners and vegetable sellers, Kumhar, potters, and

[13] S. Stevenson, op. cit., p. 246.   [14] *Caste System*, pp. 90 sqq.

some cultivators, such as Kisan and Koiri, fall into the first category on all counts. The Kalwar caste, distillers and liquor-sellers, on the other hand, fall into number (i) for *kachcha* food and (iii) for *pakka;* the Halwai themselves fall likewise into (i) for *kachcha,* but into (iv) for *pakka* food; the Kayastha (writer) caste fall into (ii) for both purposes; the Kahar fall into (iv) for *kachcha* and into (iii) for *pakka* food; and the Agariya, more or less tribal iron-smelters, fall into (iii) for *kachcha* food, but into group (i) for *pakka* food. These instances show clearly enough that each caste almost has a law to itself. Further, as in the case of intermarriage, the taboos of any given caste or sub-caste are liable to vary from one locality to another, and no general rule can be laid down, nor any scale of correspondence between social position and strictness of observance. A Kurmi, for instance, in west Bengal, will not take food cooked by any Brahman except his own *guru,* and his wife will not take the food her husband's *guru* cooks. A Kurmi again will take water from a Santal and smoke from the same *huqqa,* but cannot take the food he cooks, though the Santal can take the Kurmi's.[15] As regards southern India someone has pointed out that while a woman can eat food cooked by her daughter-in-law, whose mother can also eat food cooked by her own daughter, the mother and the mother-in-law cannot eat of each other's cooking.[16]

Besides the restrictions on drinking and eating, similar restrictions are observed on smoking. Where a common pipe is used, it is passed from hand to hand (and thus from mouth to mouth) in turn, a practice at least as intimate as drinking or eating from the same dish. Smoking, in fact, is normally spoken of as 'drinking tobacco'. Sometimes, it is true, a difference is made between smoking in which the mouth-piece is put to the mouth and smoking through the hand or hands folded so as to

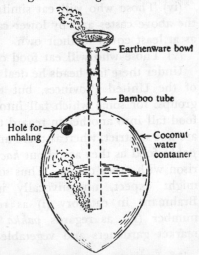

← Earthenware bowl

← Bamboo tube

Hole for → inhaling

← Coconut water container

15 Risley, *Tribes and Castes,* I, p. 536.
16 Molony, *A Book of South India* (1926), p. 109.

make a funnel, the thumb end of which is put to the sucker's mouth while the hand only comes into contact with the pipe [17] or cigarette. Generally speaking, however, smoking comes into the same category as taking water or *kachcha* food, and the usual expression for suspending a man's caste privilege is *huqqa pani band karna*, 'to deny tobacco-pipe and water', which prevents a man from associating with his caste fellows.

Before leaving the subject of food it should be mentioned that there are restrictions on the material of which eating and drinking vessels are made—earthenware, for instance, is tabooed by all higher castes, the reason usually given being that it cannot be made really clean—as well as on the use of certain animals for food. The only castes that will eat beef are untouchables like the Chamar (leather-worker) or some of the scavenging castes like the Dōm. The Dom is reputed to eat tiger's flesh, while the monkey is probably eaten only by primitive tribes, most of whom would taboo tiger flesh. Some castes are at any rate in theory purely vegetarian, but this seems to depend largely upon sect, Vaishnavas being vegetarians, whereas Shaivas and Saktas eat meat. Even where meat is eaten, most respectable castes eschew the domestic fowl and even more the domestic pig. Mutton, goat and game, whether ground or winged, is generally eaten freely, the superior Rajput eating the wild pig as many other castes do. As regards fish, custom varies greatly, more perhaps by locality than by social position. Thus most respectable castes eat fish in Bengal, whereas in the dry and sandy deserts of Rajputana the idea of eating fish causes disgust, and traders coming from there to live in Assam refuse to allow their lorries carrying goods to transport the disgusting creatures. A Marwari *baniya* (trader) has been heard to remark that to carry fish for food was as bad as carrying snakes. Some castes distinguish between fish with scales and those without, and some, the Kewat, for instance, who will not eat fowl or pork, will eat crocodile and tortoise. Certain vegetables are also tabooed in some cases: Agarwalas will not eat turnips or carrots; they and some others bar the onion, and according to Blunt [18] some subcastes bar turmeric and are called *Haldiya*

[17] The ' pipe ' is often just a coconut water-container having an earthenware tobacco bowl, connected with it by a vertical bamboo tube, and a hole in the side of the upper part through which the smoke is inhaled.
[18] *Caste System*, p. 96.

(= Turmeric ones) accordingly, a fact which is rather suggestive of totemism.

Since pollution may be incurred by contact through food or drink it is not surprising that it should be carried by mere bodily contact. Thus contact with a woman during her monthly period, a woman within the tabooed period after childbirth, a man who had lit a funeral pyre and is therefore tainted by death-pollution till purified, or persons in a similar state of ceremonial impurity or taboo, cause pollution and make it incumbent on a Hindu of caste to bathe and wash his clothes before eating or before undertaking any act requiring ceremonial purity. Similar purification is strictly speaking necessary as a result of contact with certain low castes whose traditional occupation, whether actually followed or not, or whose mode of life places them outside the pale of Hindu society. Such castes are those commonly spoken of as outcastes or untouchables. Thus Chamars (they work in cowhide), Dhobis (they wash dirty, particularly menstruously defiled, clothes), Doms (they remove corpses), sweeper castes, and many others who are impure because they eat beef or the flesh of the domestic pig, all pollute a Brahman by contact. Castes lower than a Brahman are generally speaking less easily defiled, but the principle is the same, and contact with castes or outcastes of this category used to entail early steps to remove the pollution. Thus if a Cheruman, or Pulayan, be touched by a Paraiyan, 'he is defiled and must wash his head and pray'.[19]   According to Barbosa a Nayar woman touched by a Pulayan is outcaste for life and thinks only of leaving her home for fear of polluting her family.

As a result of the increase of travelling in public vehicles on the railway or bus routes, pollution of this kind has become so common and its frequent removal so inconvenient that it is no longer treated very seriously by the majority of high-caste Hindus. Indeed, some of the lowest castes in Hindu society are more particular than many high ones; a Kuricchan of Malabar plasters his house with cowdung if it is polluted by the entry of a Brahman.[20]   This is an extreme case, but Blunt has worked out [21] for the United Provinces a table of which castes regard which as untouchable, which is analogous to the lists already

[19] Buchanan, op. cit. (1870), II, p. 151 [ch. XIII].
[20] Aiyangar, op. cit., p. 91.   [21] Caste System, p. 102.

referred to of the varying incidence of taboo on *kachcha* and on *pakka* food. In southern India this principle of untouchability has been carried a good deal further in the observance of what is known as 'distance pollution'. The following of a degrading occupation, or membership of a caste traditionally associated with a degrading occupation, is a cause of pollution by contact, so that Mahabrahmans (i.e. 'Great Brahmans'), though Brahmans, are not accorded the respect due to Brahmans, but are regarded as polluting, because they officiate at the cremation of corpses, no less than the Dom who removes the dead bodies. But while in the north of India prejudice or pride may prevent a Rajput who does not lay hand to a plough from dining with a Rajput who does, mere proximity would not pollute him. In southern India, on the other hand, many castes are regarded as polluting by proximity, and are not allowed to approach within certain distances of Hindu temples; so much is this the case that common expressions of spatial measurement are, or were, *Tiyapad, Chērumapad,* etc., indicating a distance equivalent to that within which a Tiyan or a Cheruman, as the case may be of course, may not approach a man of high caste. At the same time this spatial measurement must be anything but exact, as not only is the polluting distance less for a Nayar, for instance, than for a Brahman, but different standards are mentioned by different authorities. Jonathan Duncan, in his *Remarks on the Coast of Malabar,*[22] says that a Nayar may approach a Nambudri Brahman, but must not touch him; a Tiyan (toddy-drawer) must remain 36 paces off; a Malayan (i.e. Panan, exorcist basket-maker) must remain 'three or four' paces farther; a Pulayan (cultivator and untouchable) must keep 96 paces from a Brahman. A Tiyan must not come within 12 paces of a Nayar; a Malayan (Panan) must keep 3 or 4 paces farther off, and a Pulayan must still keep his 96 from a Nayar as well as a Brahman. A Panan may approach but not touch a Tiyan, but a Pulayan must not even approach a Panan. If he wishes to address a man of higher caste, he must stand afar off and 'cry aloud'. If a Pulayan touch a Brahman, the Brahman must at once bathe, read 'much of the divine books', and change his Brahmanical thread. A Nayar, on the other hand, or any other caste polluted by a Pulayan's touch, need only bathe to purify

[22] *Asiatick Researches,* v (1807), p. 5.

himself. In any case, of course, a Nayar, being a Sudra, has no
sacred thread. Francis Day,[23] writing in 1863, says that an
Ilavan must keep 36 paces from a Brahman and 12 from a Nayar,
while a Kaniyan (astrologer caste) pollutes a Nambudri Brahman
at 24 ft. and a Nayar by touch. Mateer,[24] in 1861, gives 36
paces as the distance within which a Shanan must not approach
a Brahman, and 96 as the distance for a Pulayan; from a Nayar
a Shanan must keep a distance of 12 paces and a Pulayan 66
paces. Wilson,[25] writing some 70 years after Duncan, says that
a Nayar must not come within 3 ft. of a Nambudri Brahman,
an Ilavan or Shanan (equivalent to, or identical with, Tiyan)
within 24 paces, and a Pulayan or other untouchable within 36
paces, while C. A. Innes, in the *Malabar Gazetteer* of 1908, says
that artisans must keep about 24 ft. from a Brahman, while a
Nayadi (a member of a more or less nomad, outcaste and quasi-
aboriginal tribe) must keep 74 ft. away. There may naturally,
of course, have been some changes during the hundred years
covered by these reports. Aiyappan,[26] in 1937, gives a scale of
distance pollution for several castes: a Nayar must keep 7 ft.
from a Nambudri Brahman, an Iravan (Ilavan, Izhuvan, Tiyan)
must keep 32, a Cheruman 64 and a Nayadi from 74 to 124.
The respective distances between these lower castes are calculated
by a simple process of subtraction: the Iravan must keep 25 ft.
from the Nayar and the Cheruman 32 ft. from the Iravan. The
Nayadi when travelling has to avoid not only people of other
castes, but dwellings, tanks, temples, and even certain streams
when people are bathing in them. 'If a Nayadi touches the
water in which men of higher castes are bathing, the water loses
its purificatory qualities so long as the Nayadi is in contact with
it within the sight of the bathers.' At Vilayur there is a *tintal
para* or pollution rock, which marks the limit within which
Nayadis may not approach the village. It is three furlongs from
there to the nearest Hindu house. An Ernadan must not come
within 400 yards of a village or 100 yards of a man of high
caste.[27] If a man is polluted by a Nayadi, he must bathe in

23 *Land of the Permauls*, pp. 322, 323.
24 *Land of Charity*, pp. 32, 46.   25 Op. cit., II, p. 74.
26 *Anthropology of the Nayadis*, pp. 18 sqq.
27 The Ernadan are a small jungle tribe of Malabar which is reported to
have a remarkable custom by which a man marries his eldest daughter as
his second wife (Thurston, *Castes and Tribes*, II, p. 217).

seven streams and seven tanks and let blood from his little finger. Ulladans and Paraiyans are mutually polluted by each other's approach. Innes [28] records that Nayadis had to avoid walking over the long bridge over the Ponnāni river and go miles round, because if they walked over it they would pollute it, or any at least who might make contact with their footprints, while the Ande Koragas of Mangalore District had to carry round their necks a small spittoon since they must not expectorate on the public road for fear of polluting a passer-by who might all unknowing tread where they had spat. Mateer [29] quotes a saying that a Vedan pollutes the road while he is upon it, but a Pulayan pollutes the road by which he has gone. Indeed, in some cases, as already indicated, mere sight might be enough to cause pollution, for apart from the case he mentions of bathers, Aiyappan says: [30] 'Some believe that low caste people should not be seen by them on days when they have to be specially pure.' A correspondent of The Hindu reported (24 December 1932) that in the district of Tinnevelly there were a class of unseeables—a caste of washermen known as Purada Vannan, who washed the clothes of untouchable castes and were therefore doubly polluting. They had to work between midnight and daybreak and were not allowed to come out during the daytime because the very sight of them was polluting.[31] Such 'distance pollution' as that described is still observed in ritual situations, though no longer enforced in ordinary day-to-day secular life.

Since indirect contact and even sight can be polluting, it is clear that the use of the same wells by caste and outcaste would give rise to trouble, though A. K. Forbes [32] mentions wells from which outcastes drew water on one side, and Brahmans 'when they are gone' from the other. A well defiled by the corpse

[28] Gazetteer of the Malabar and Anjengo Districts, p. 102.
[29] Native Life in Travancore, p. 337.   [30] Loc. cit.
[31] Hutton, Report on the Census of India, 1931, vol. I, pt. I, p. 483. O'Malley (Caste Customs, p. 147) quotes James Forbes as saying that a Maratha proclamation issued at Baroch in 1783 forbade the untouchable castes of Halalkhor, Dhed and Chandal to come out of their houses after 9 a.m., and Hobson-Jobson mentions the passage under the heading 'Halalcore' referring to Forbes, Or. Mem. iv. 232. This reference is to the first edition, and the passage has been omitted in the second. It prohibits the castes referred to from coming out of their houses after 9 a.m. 'upon any consideration . . . lest they should taint the air or touch the superior Hindus in the streets'. It should be added that Forbes anticipated that Baskar Rao's durbar would cancel the edict on the receipt of satisfactory bribes to do so.   [32] Rás Máld, II, p. 240.

6

of a dog, etc., had to have water drawn from it five times and
Ganges water or cow's urine poured into it. Where there is
plenty of water, as in Assam and Bengal, it is easy enough to
have different wells, and occasional difficulties can be surmounted by water being drawn from the well by some caste
Hindu and poured out for the untouchable. In the drier parts
of India the difficulty is more serious, and the outcastes have
often had to put up with the most indifferent water supply.
When they have succeeded in asserting their right to use public
wells, the higher castes have usually given up these wells.
Much the same has happened in the case of schools, cremation
grounds, etc., and inevitably restaurants, hairdressers and so
forth catering for caste Hindus have found it necessary to debar
outcaste Hindus from using their services.

In temples there are (or have been) regular scales of distance
beyond which certain castes must remain, and just as caste-
polluting distances vary, so the distance at which temple
pollution is involved varies much in different places. No Iravan
or Tiyan must come within 325 ft. of the curtain wall of the
temple of Guruvayur in Malabar. The sides of the square
enclosed by this wall are each 350 ft. long and the temple is in
the centre of that enclosure. The public road which skirted
the temple at Vaikam was forbidden to be used by untouchables,
and the same applied to that which passed the Sachindram
temple, likewise in Travancore. The former road had to be
realigned to prevent the pollution of the temple. Similarly,
court houses were tabooed to low castes who had to keep from
40 to 100 paces off, and at one court house near a temple
Pulayans used to have to keep 200 paces off and so 'cannot give
their evidence with convenience', as Mateer [33] puts it. Mateer
also records [34] how the temple of Kottayam had to be recon-
secrated because a European passed along the pathway between
the temple and the tank attached to it, and also how in 1873
the Nagerkoil temple had to be purified because it had been
entered by the children of a Brahman who had allowed his virgin
daughter to be remarried after the death of her husband married
in infancy.[35] Generally speaking, Muslims and Christians are

[33] *Native Life*, pp. 343 sqq.   [34] Ibid., p. 333.
[35] Ibid., p. 331.

regarded as inferior to Brahmans and Nayars in Malabar, but as less polluting than the lower castes,[36] but Thurston records how he touched the ladle in a pot in which an Odh woman was cooking her meal and later found that she had been out-casted for subsequently touching the cooking pot.[37] On the other hand Syrian Christians in Cochin and Travancore seem to have ranked as equal if not superior to Nayars.[38] Thurston also records that in Travancore the breath of a courtier may pollute the king, while a low-caste man at a temple must wear a bandage over mouth and nose lest his breath pollute the idol, and a Kudumi woman in her menstrual period must keep 7 ft. away from anyone, cover her mouth and nostrils with her hand, and take care that her shadow falls on no one. So too a potter making a household deity for the Kurubas must cover his mouth with a bandage;[39] and a Brahman may be polluted by a whiff of smoke from a funeral pyre.[40]

This question of indirect pollution has been treated at some length, since it shows so very clearly how intimate is the association between caste and taboo. There are of course a number of other taboos, similar in nature, which are more or less intimately associated with caste. Menstruation of course renders a woman polluting, but the degree of pollution varies with the caste. The case of the Kudumi woman in Travancore has been mentioned, and she must take care to prevent contamination being carried by her breath, or even by her shadow. Childbirth is no less polluting,[41] but whereas the period of pollution for a Brahman in southern India is ten days, it is eleven or twelve for a Kshatriya or an Ambalavasi, fifteen for a Nayar, twenty-eight for a Kuricchan, twenty-eight for a Cheruman in the south but forty-two in the north of Malabar, and four months for a Kadar. On the other hand, the social position of a caste is not necessarily an indication of the length of its birth-taboo, as Nayadi and Paniyan observe ten days only. In some of the more primitive castes the labour has to take place in a separate hut, or in a segregated part of the dwelling-house, as in

[36] Aiyappan, op. cit., p. 18 n.
[37] *Omens and Superstitions of Southern India* (1912), p. 110.
[38] L. K. A. Iyer, *Syrian Christians*, pp. 53 sqq.
[39] *Omens and Superstitions*, p. 26.
[40] Dubois, *People of India* (1879), p. 110 (pt. II, ch. IV).
[41] Innes, op. cit., p. 170.

the case of the Vettuvan who dig a hole in one corner and segregate the expectant mother there alone with some water until the
cry of the child is heard. In the case of birth pollution all the
members of the household are involved for periods which,
generally speaking, increase as the social status of the caste
descends. In Malabar there is an extension of this pollution to
the *tarwād*, that is to say, to all the branches of a joint family
who recognize their descent in the female line from a common
ancestor, and the extension applies to death pollution as well as
to birth pollution.[42] The periods of death pollution are generally spoken of as being varied according to *varna*. The
Brahman must observe mourning for ten days, the Kshatriya
for twelve, the Vaishya for fifteen, and the Sudra for a full
month. This general rule, however, cannot be regarded as
covering all castes, and in southern India at any rate there is
a good deal of variation from it except perhaps for Brahmans.
Thus the pollution period is said to vary in different sections of
the Nayar, while Tiyan, Mukkuvan and Cheruman observe only
fourteen or fifteen days, though some of the latter have a method
of postponing pollution to a convenient season by sealing a
ball of cowdung in a pot and suspending the taboo till the pot
is opened again, when the period to be observed after post-
ponement becomes forty days instead of fourteen.[43] The performance of certain funeral ceremonies also varies according to
caste, Brahmans performing them ' after certain intelligence of
. . . death has been received ', but some other castes, e.g. Prabhu
(a western India writer caste of high standing corresponding to
Kayastha), wait for twenty-five years, and others, e.g. Sonar (goldsmiths), for twenty years, others again for twelve or fifteen
years.[44] During periods of ceremonial pollution, in Malabar at
any rate, a characteristic service known as *māttu* (='change') is
performed for each caste by whatever caste performs for it the
office of washerman. Thus when a Nayar woman is delivered
of a child a woman of the Mannan caste, which washes otherwise
for exterior castes but not for Nayars, brings a change, *māttu*,
of clean clothing (belonging to the washerwoman) and puts it in
the courtyard where she finds her perquisites of grain and a
lamp. A woman of the caste serving the Nayars as barbers and

42 Ibid., p. 103.   43 Ibid., p. 189.
44 Steele, op. cit., p. 228.

midwives (in north Malabar the Marayan caste, which also performs certain functions at Nayar funerals, in the south the Velakkattalavan) takes the clean clothes in and the Mannan woman removes those previously worn by the woman in childbed. On the seventh and fifteenth days the washerwoman is accompanied by a man of her caste who goes through a ceremony before the barber-woman takes the clean clothes indoors. It is essential that this change should be furnished by the appropriate caste in each case.[45] The *māttu* is worn for the purificatory immersion which marks the end of the period of pollution, whether by menstruation or by childbirth, or as a result of death, which causes the pollution of the entire household in which it takes place.

Attention has already been drawn in the first chapter to the variation of marriage rules according to caste; and although the practice of castes in the matter of the age of marriage, and the remarriage of widows, and in particular the taking to wife of the widow of an elder brother, or the practice of cross-cousin marriage, may have varied considerably in the course of years, it is, generally speaking, the caste rather than the individual which determines what custom shall be observed, or at any rate, approved; the behaviour of individual caste men is determined by the decision of the caste as a whole, though the practice approved may vary in different localities.

Another question to which much importance is attached in some parts of India is the right of a given caste to clothe themselves with certain garments, wear certain ornaments, and use certain articles of show or luxury in public. Different materials are prescribed for the sacred thread for different *varna*: that of the Brahman is nowadays usually of cotton, of the Kshatriya hemp, the material used for bowstrings, and of the Vaishya wool.[46] In southern India the wearing of clothes above the waist was formerly a privilege of the twice-born castes, while the Sudra castes themselves until quite recently insisted that it was forbidden to the exterior or untouchable castes.[47] The same prohibition extended to the use of gold or even silver ornaments, of umbrellas, and even of shoes. Farther north cases have occurred of Chamars, for instance, being beaten up for dressing like

[45] Innes, op. cit., p. 170 ; Thurston, *Castes and Tribes*, VII, p. 318.
[46] For a detailed account *vide* Dubois, op. cit., pt. II, ch I and Crooke, *Things Indian*, s.v. Thread, sacred.　　　[47] Mateer, *Land of Charity*, p. 45.

Rajputs or for wearing gold ornaments in a similar way.[48] This restriction on the use of ornaments seems to be of very ancient and widespread observance, as certain clans in the non-Hindu Ao Naga country in Assam, for instance, are not allowed to wear the heavy ivory armlets in use there on both arms, and similar restrictions are in force in the Islamized Laccadive Islands on the extreme opposite fringe of the Indian area.[49] In both cases again failure to observe the prohibition has frequently resulted in violence. Similar prohibitions are found against the use by low castes of horses as mounts for bridegrooms in marriage processions, a common cause of violence or boycott, or of palanquins, the use of which at marriages has often led to disturbances in Madras when used by low castes there and has had the same result in Bengal when used by Namasudras (Chandals). The right to use ornaments, etc., of certain kinds may vary not only as between caste and caste, but also as between castes of the Right Hand and castes of the Left, and Dubois mentions[50] great commotion caused at a festival by a Chakkiliyan's wearing red flowers in his *pagri* which the Paraiyans denied his right to wear.

In keeping with these restrictions as to dress and ornament are the restrictions of language still perhaps obtaining on the Malabar coast, and at one time probably a good deal more widely observed, which compelled members of what may be conveniently called the ' exterior ' castes, as being outside the pale of respectable Hindu society, to use special language when referring to themselves or their possessions; ' when speaking of their bodily members, such as an eye, or an ear, to a superior, they (as must also the Chogans [=Tiyan, Izhavan or Iluvan], and those inferior to them) prefix it by the epithet *old*, such as " old eye ", " old ear ". They are obliged to call their children " calves ", their silver " copper ", and their paddy " chaff ". They commence speaking by saying, " your slave has received permission to observe ". Nairs they must call " Kings ", and Brahmans they must not approach ', etc.[51] The Pulayan ' dare not say " I ", but " *adiyan* ", " your slave "; he dare not call his rice " *choru* " but " *karikadi* "—dirty gruel. He asks leave not to take food,

[48] Hutton, *Census of India*, pp. 485, 486.
[49] See the Calcutta *Statesman* of 6 Oct. 1934 and R. H. Ellis, loc. cit.
[50] Op. cit., pt. I, ch. I (pp. 11 sq.).
[51] Day, *Land of the Permauls*, p. 327.

but "to drink water". His house is called "*mādam*",[52] a hut, and his children he speaks of as "monkeys", or "calves"; and when speaking he must place the hand over the mouth, lest the breath should go forth and pollute the person whom he is addressing.'[53] Conversely, a Brahman may use different expressions when returning the greetings of persons of different *varna*.

Mateer says that if a Pulayan tried to build himself a superior type of house, 'infuriated Sudras' would soon pull it down. From Day we learn that the higher castes also are not without restrictions, obviously as a result of the possibility of breach of taboo, in the matter of building materials: 'In building for those of the higher castes, great care is necessary, as a piece of wood, clothing or drapery will convey pollution, from the lower to the higher castes: as will also coir matting should it contain even one thread of cotton upon it although it is of itself unpollutable, a piece of new cloth may be thrown to a high caste person, who can look at it and toss it back without having been defiled, but should it be old it causes pollution. Floors must be made of chunam [lime plaster], stone, or earth, which are non-conductors, and not of planks: and for the same reason no carpets or mats can be spread. The chequered black and white chunam floors, are therefore usually seen, in the houses of the higher castes.'[54]

It is hardly necessary to labour the differences between caste and caste in matters of custom. Specific taboos are associated with particular occupations, like the taboo on the *pān* cultivations of the Barui (*pān*-growing) caste, which the owner may not enter without bathing and purification and which the Brahman may not set foot in at all;[55] or like the impurity which attaches to the potter's oven; or the taboo which the Let subcaste of Bagdi place on bamboo fishtraps, which they will not use although they fish with nets;[56] or the Sarak caste place on the use of the word meaning ' to cut '.[57] Such differences extend to every kind of ceremonial activity, and many instances have already been given of the sort of variation found. To say

[52] Or, according to Logan, *Malabar*, I, p. 85, ' dung heaps '.
[53] Mateer, *Land of Charity*, p. 45.   [54] Day, op. cit., p. 405 (sic).
[55] Risley, *Tribes and Castes*, I, pp. 72, 73.
[56] Gait, *Report on the Census of Bengal, etc.*, p. 421.
[57] Ibid., pp. 428, 430. The Saraks of Orissa are Buddhist, and those of Bengal still extremely sensitive about the taking of animal life, whence, no doubt, the taboo on a word associated with slaughtering.

nothing more of differences in etiquette and ritual, customs such as those of inheritance, for instance, vary very greatly by caste. In Malabar, at any rate, the matrilineal system of inheritance still survives, according to which a man's property is inherited by his sister's children, and there are traces of it elsewhere in India. Among purely patrilineal castes observing primogeniture the rules of precedence between brothers vary. Some castes hold the senior son to be the first son of the first wife married; others the first son born, irrespective of the wife; others again regard as senior the son first seen by his father. Similarly in the case of twins, while some castes count the elder of the two to be the one first seen by his father, many more count the first to be born the elder son, but many more still, apparently, count the later born to be the elder son.[58]

One restriction on Hindus in general may perhaps be mentioned here, as it applies, or used to apply, with much greater force to higher than to lower castes, and that is the prohibition against going overseas. The causes of the prohibition can only be guessed at, but it has possibly arisen from the feeling that the act of crossing the sea and living in a strange land makes the observance of caste rules so difficult that they are certain to be broken and therefore the mere act of such travel has itself become taboo.[59] However that may be, it entails among strict Hindus the purification ceremony which involves drinking the *panchgavya*—that is, the five products of the cow—milk, clarified butter, curds, urine, and dung all mixed together, than which no remedy is more efficacious for purifying the body from defilement. Cow's urine is likewise a potent cleanser of external defilement, and Dubois[60] noted having seen it used for that purpose. Nowadays, of course, it is common enough for many strict Hindus to cross the sea, and it is probable that the *panchgavya* is reduced to a purely ceremonial minimum for those who have to consume it on return to India.

Restrictions on occupations have already been mentioned in connexion with taboo infections,[61] and are to be generally asso-

[58] Steele, op. cit., pp. 228, 376.
[59] Perhaps it is associated with setting foot on and sojourning on foreign soil which infects the traveller with the taint of the land and its inhabitants so that he also becomes equivalent to a stranger and equally dangerous and taboo.
[60] *People of India*, pt. 1, ch. IV (p. 28) and *vide infra* p. 108.
[61] *Vide supra*, pp. 78 sq.

ciated rather with the Hindu creed in general than with the caste system specifically. Since certain occupations are unclean, e.g. scavenging or flaying cattle, the persons following these occupations become untouchable, and anyone adopting them, unless in company with his caste, must necessarily be outcasted to preserve the whole caste from pollution. Often there is a distinction between the occupation of different subcastes of the same caste. Thus there are two divisions of the Teli caste in Bengal—sometimes distinguished as Tili and Teli—one of which only deals in oil while the other presses it. There seems to be no doubt that both spring from an original caste which pressed oil seeds (*til*) and sold the oil. The pressing of oil seeds, however, is stigmatized as a degrading occupation in the Code of Manu because it destroys life by crushing the seed. This seems to have led to the division of the caste into two, one of which is treated as untouchable, the other not, and the Telis who only sell oil will outcaste a member who should venture to press it. Similarly, those Rajputs of the Kangra valley who refrain from ploughing hold themselves distinct and superior to those who plough,[62] while Blunt [63] records that the bad reputation for chicanery acquired by the *patwaris* (keepers of village land-revenue records and maps) nearly led to the formation of a separate and inferior subcaste of Kayastha by the refusal of Kayasthas in general to have connubial and commensal relations with *patwari* families of that caste. Clearly, therefore, caste may lay occupational restrictions on its members, although mere occupation other than that traditionally associated with caste will not of itself be an offence. The traditional occupation of Brahmans is the teaching and interpretation of the scriptures, but very many Brahmans are employed as cooks, since anyone can take food from them, but they are not therefore put out of caste.

Sometimes occupational restrictions imposed by caste may have a purely economic purpose: O'Malley mentions a case of the Kasera (brass-founder) caste expelling a man who tried to steal a march on his fellow-castemen by working on a day which the caste had decided to keep as a holiday; the Sonars (goldsmiths) of a district in the Central Provinces have a feast at which the castemen take oath that they will not reveal the amount of alloy

---

[62] Ibbetson, *Panjab Castes*, p. 156.   [63] *Caste System*, p. 222.

decided to be mixed with gold by the Sonars on pain of being outcasted.[64] Most professional castes also have regular clienteles, persons for whom individuals perform regular services and from whom they receive fixed dues. Poaching on the 'practice' of a fellow-casteman would be a proper subject for the caste *panchayat* to adjudicate upon. As regards actual change of occupation Blunt[65] sums up the existing position by saying that a change of function will no longer result in a change of caste unless it involves a change of status, and that when such a change of status does occur it will take one of three forms— segregation into a new caste, or affiliation of the new group to another already existing caste, or the creation of a new endo-gamous subcaste within the original caste. (The last is easily the most frequent result.) He instances the creation of the Singhariya caste as a new caste formed by Kahars (domestic servants) who had taken to the growing of water-nuts, of the Gual Nats, wandering singers and dancers who took to trade and now call themselves Badi Banjaras (the Banjara is a wander-ing carrier and trade caste), and of the occupational subcastes of Kahar known as Dhimar (fishermen), Mahar (women's servants), and Kamkar (drawers of water). Progress, according to Blunt, 'has weakened and is slowly killing the functional caste, at all events on its purely occupational side. The road lies open to trade unionism.'[66] As far as the purely occupational side of caste is concerned Blunt's verdict may be accepted, but caste has never been a purely occupational institution, and in so far as it has been occupational it has long performed many of the functions of trade unionism, as Blunt's chapter on caste in rela-tion to occupation shows clearly enough.

Wilson sums up comprehensively the extent to which caste rules govern every member of any caste. Caste, he says,[67] 'gives its directions for recognition, acceptance, consecration, and sacramental dedication, and vice versa, of a human being on his appearance in the world. It has for infancy, pupilage, and manhood, its ordained methods of sucking, sipping, drink-ing, eating, and voiding; of washing, rinsing, anointing, and smearing; of clothing, dressing, and ornamenting; of sitting,

[64] O'Malley, *Caste Customs*, pp. 134, 135.
[65] *Caste System*, p. 236.   [66] *Caste System*, p. 246.
[67] *Indian Caste*, I, p. 13.

rising, and reclining; of moving, visiting, and travelling; of speaking, reading, listening, and reciting; and of meditating, singing, working, playing, and fighting. It has its laws for social and religious rights, privileges, and occupations; for instructing, training, and educating; for obligation, duty, and practice; for divine recognition, duty, and ceremony; for errors, sins, and transgressions; for intercommunion, avoidance, and excommunication; for defilement, ablution, and purification; for fines, chastisements, imprisonments, mutilations, banishments and capital executions. It unfolds the ways of committing what it calls sin, accumulating sin, and of putting away sin; and of acquiring merit, dispensing merit, and losing merit. It treats of inheritance, conveyance, possession, and dispossession; and of bargains, gain, loss, and ruin. It deals with death, burial, and burning; and with commemoration, assistance, and injury after death. It interferes, in short, with all the relations and events of life, and with what precedes and follows . . . life.'

CHAPTER VII

I T S   S A N C.T I O N S

A CASTE has been described as a social unit, and it is in accordance with its character as such that it is, generally speaking, the
guardian of its own rules, that it disciplines its members, expels
them from the community, or readmits them after penalties imposed and satisfaction exacted. It is true that religious authority, normally in the form of the Brahman, plays a part in the
proceedings, but that is only to declare if necessary what pattern
of behaviour has scriptural approval, or what expiations may
be prescribed by religious authority or tradition. Ketkar points
out that an appeal against expulsion from caste to Brahmans is
useless. All that they can do is to specify and administer a
suitable penance; they cannot readmit the culprit to caste.[1]
The fact that their ministrations are necessary for all *rites de
passage* such as birth, marriage, etc., and that they can, if they
choose, refuse to perform the necessary ritual, naturally gives
them a position of very powerful influence, but it does not make
them the final authority in matters of caste.

Nor did the Brahman fail to make the most of his privileged
position as interpreter and arbiter of holy writ, at any rate
according to the Code of Manu. A Brahman need observe
mourning for 10 days only, but a Kshatriya for 12, a Vaishya
for 15 and a Sudra for a month. A Brahman is initiated, and
in the process born again, in his eighth year, a Kshatriya in his
eleventh, a Vaishya in his twelfth, and a Sudra never. A Sudra
may use only the southern gate of a town for carrying forth his
dead, and his killing by a Brahman is equivalent merely to the
killing of a cat, a mongoose, a blue jay, a frog, a dog, a lizard,
an owl, or a crow. To serve a Brahman learned in the vedas
is the highest duty of a Sudra, and if he be pure and serve
humbly he may in another incarnation attain the highest class.[2]
The Brahman is by right the chief of this whole creation;
whatever exists in the universe is the wealth of the Brahman,
who is entitled to it all by his primogeniture; in virtue
of which he is entitled to treasure trove and his property never

---

[1] Ketkar, *Essay on Hinduism.*
[2] *Laws of Manu* (tr. Bühler), IX, pp. 334, 335.

escheats to the king. He is the deity on earth by divine status and the intelligent one by his innate comprehension. He may without hesitation take the property of a Sudra for the purpose of sacrifice, for a Sudra has no business with sacrifices.[3] If a Sudra mention the name and class of the twice-born with contumely an iron nail ten fingers long shall be thrust red hot into his mouth.[4] 'If he arrogantly teaches Brahmanas their duty, the king shall cause hot oil to be poured into his mouth and into his ears.'[5] But no reciprocal punishments are prescribed for cantankerous Brahmans—though they follow mean occupations Brahmans are to be honoured in every way 'for each of them is a very great deity'.[6] Such are the injunctions of the Code of Manu; the Padma Purāna says that immoral Brahmans are to be worshipped, but not Sudras, though subduing their passions, for 'the cow that eats things not to be eaten is better than the sow of good intent'. Vedic rites and prayers are required of the twice-born castes, but they are prohibited to Sudras who may learn only the Puranas and the Tantras. The Code of Manu says that a king shall never execute a Brahman 'though convicted of all possible crimes', but may banish him 'with all his property secure and his body unhurt. No greater crime is known on earth than slaying a Brahman; and the king, therefore, must not even form in his mind an idea of killing a priest.'[7] 'A Brahman, be he ignorant or learned, is a great divinity.'[8] With all this, secular power was hardly necessary.

It is probably significant of the true origins of the caste system that the ultimate controlling authority is secular, and further that the secular authority visualized as responsible in the ancient Hindu authorities is the king. Vasishtha, quoted by A. M. T. Jackson in his 'Note on the History of the Caste System',[9] says (XIX, 7-8): 'Let the King, paying attention to all the laws of countries, castes and families, make the four *varna* fulfil their particular duties. Let him punish those who stray.' Manu prescribes the action of a conquering prince in regard to a conquered realm as follows: 'When he has gained the victory let him duly worship the gods, and honour righteous Brāhmanas, let him grant exemptions, and let him cause promises of safety

---

[3] Ibid., XI, p. 13.
[4] Ibid., VIII, p. 271.
[5] Ibid.
[6] Ibid., IX, p. 319.

[7] Wilson, *Indian Caste*, I, p. 22.
[8] *Laws of Manu* (tr. Bühler), IX, p. 317.
[9] *J.A S.B.*, vol. III, no. 7, July 1907, p. 510.

to be proclaimed. But, having fully ascertained the wishes of all the (conquered), let him place there a relation of the (vanquished ruler on the throne) and let him impose his conditions. Let him make authoritative the lawful (customs) of the (inhabitants), just as they are stated (to be), and let him honour the (new king) and his chief servants with precious gifts.' [10] Clearly here no change in customs is envisaged as a result of conquest, and the new king is charged with governing according to the former customs.

If the secular ruler was the ultimate authority during the early period of Indian history, he certainly continued to be so in the middle ages. Ballal Sen, King of Bengal in the twelfth century, prescribed the order of precedence of different castes of Brahmans in his dominions, and raised the status of some castes, degrading others. O'Malley points out that the fourteenth-century prince Hara Singh Deva of North Bihar 'settled the respective ranks of three sections of the Maithil subcaste of Brahmans and made marriage rules for them; and it should be noted that he was not a Brahman but a Kshattriya.' [11] Hara Singh was later a ruler in Nepal, and there the castes are still under State control; law courts take cognizance of cases involving expulsion from caste, serious cases, that is, such as cattle-killing or the breach of commensal rules, and also determine the caste of the offspring of mixed unions. The hereditary Prime Minister, who was de facto ruler, was the final court of appeal in such caste cases. Minor caste matters are dealt with by caste councils. At the other end of the peninsula the Maharaja of Cochin, a Kshatriya, acted as the final authority in caste matters for Nambudri Brahmans and had the power to raise persons from one caste to another, while final expulsion from a caste required his sanction. [12] In Rajputana the position was similar, for although in most cases the caste councils disposed of caste matters, cases that could not be settled by them were referred to the State courts or to the ruler himself, and Ibbetson reports the creation of a new caste from a section of the Minas by the Maharaja of Alwar, who laid down at the same time rules to govern hypergamy between the new and old castes. [13] In Indore the ruler appointed

---

[10] *Laws of Manu* (tr. Bühler), VII, pp. 201-3.
[11] *Indian Caste Customs*, p. 57.
[12] Menon, *Report on the Census of Cochin*, 1911, p. 69 ; Molony, *Census of Madras*, 1911, p. 180.   [13] *Panjab Castes*, p. 16.

a council of *sastris*, that is, of persons learned in Hindu law, to advise upon or decide on caste questions, subject to the powers of the Maharaja to override their decisions. The Maratha rulers exercised the same powers, both Gwalior and Baroda having councils of *sastris* like Indore, though O'Malley says that the Gaekwar no longer exercised his personal authority in castes other than Maratha castes.[14] It is probable that the powers of the secular ruler in caste questions have been allowed to lapse in many states, and Ibbetson[15] attributes this to the Mughal conquest which he regards as having deprived the Hindus of their natural leaders, the Rajputs, and so strengthened caste rather than otherwise, by leaving matters in the hands of the Brahmans and of caste councils acting under their influence. In the marginal areas and in remoter fastnesses of hills and forests the older order held good, and the Rajput princes in the Kangra Hills classified Brahmans, promoted from one caste to another, and readmitted expelled persons to caste partially at any rate for money payments.[16] The Rajas of the Simla Hill States, of Bastar and Jashpur in the Central Provinces, of the Orissa Feudatory States, all exercised the final power in caste matters, including expulsion from and restoration to caste, and wielded discipline over Brahman offenders as well as over those of lower caste. The Maharaja of Manipur in Assam likewise had power to admit to, to expel from and to restore to caste, and at some time in the nineteen-thirties created a minor local sensation by expelling from caste his own Maharani who had in some way offended him. As in the Kangra Hills, so in Manipur, fines and penalties arising from caste cases constituted a by no means negligible contribution to the privy purse. O'Malley describes the wretched plight of some high-caste subjects of one of the Orissa Feudatory States who refused to accept the decision of their ruler in a caste case, and were themselves outcasted by him in consequence. No priest, barber or washerman could render them any service, with the result that ' they had long beards matted with dirt, their hair hung in long strands and was filthy in the extreme,

---

[14] O'Malley, *Caste Customs*, p. 70.

[15] Op. cit., p. 15, and cf. p. 101. Buchanan says of the Smartal Brahmans of Kolar that they leave the punishment of transgression against caste rules to the transgressors' ' own hereditary chiefs ; at whose desire, however, they reprimand and impose fines on obstinate offenders ', op. cit., 1, p. 213 (ch. v, 8 July 1800).   [16] Ibbetson, op. cit., pp. 16, 101.

and their clothes were beyond description for uncleanliness '.[17] Somewhat similar cases are often to be seen in the completely non-Hindu villages of the Naga Hills where some recalcitrant individual has refused to conform to village opinion and has been in consequence officially ostracized by his fellow-villagers. Beards do not grow much in that region, but such a person's hair, which can only be cut with someone else's help (for scissors are not, and hair is cut by tapping it between a sharp *dao* blade and a little wooden hammer), gets into an indescribable state. Clothes are not much worn, but the effect of ostracism is seen in his house, which decays and falls to pieces since no one will help to rethatch it. His fields fall unweeded and unharvested for want of co-operative labour, and unless he be restored to community life he soon relapses into dire poverty and ex-cessive discomfort. As will be seen when discussing the origins of caste, the parallel here is perhaps not entirely without significance.

The principle that caste is ultimately a matter for the secular or political authority is to be seen carried so far that landlords at any rate in eastern India are apt to interfere in purely caste mat-ters, either because their intervention is sought, or in other cases because it increases their control over their tenants and because, perhaps, the fines can thus be pocketed in whole or in part.[18] So clearly has the principle that the secular power is the final arbiter of caste been accepted in the past, that the Mughal rulers of Bengal and their British successors have in turn found them-selves in the position of judges of such matters. Nor have they always adopted the attitude of the nonchalant Gallio. In Bengal the Mughal governors retained the right to sanction readmission to caste, and O'Malley [19] quotes from S. C. Bose's *The Hindus as they Are* (Calcutta, 1883, p. 167) a case in which a Nawab of Bengal refused to restore a Brahman family that had been put out of caste. He goes on to quote Verelst (*View of the English Government in Bengal* [1772], p. 238) on the instructions drafted in 1769 for British officers in charge of the revenue administra-tion there: ' When any man has naturally forfeited his cast (*sic*), you are to observe that he cannot be restored to it without

---

[17] *Caste Customs*, pp. 65, 66.
[18] O'Malley, *Caste Customs*, p. 72, and cf. Blunt, *Caste System*, p. 127.
[19] *Caste Customs*, p. 59 n.

the sanction of Government; which was a political supremacy
reserved to themselves by the Mahomedans.' Although the
power was waived by Government, which probably misunder-
stood the historic reasons leading to its exercise by the Mughals,
a court known as the Caste Cutcherry was maintained in Calcutta
to settle caste questions, and the British Governor was nominally
head of it, though he deputed the chair to his Hindu Banyan or
commercial agent, who presided over it ' by virtue of the imme-
morial usage of the settlement ', a fact of which Burke made
effective and, of course, misleading use in his indictment of
Warren Hastings.[20] Since then the British Government has
declined to give decisions on caste questions except in so far as
it has been compelled to do so through judgements of the civil
courts when deciding cases of Hindu law. Nevertheless, the
Census Commissioner used to be grievously importuned at every
decade to decide on the claims of castes to be recognized for
something better than their neighbours would allow them to be.
So far from accepting the position of arbiter was the British
Government, that in 1921 the Chief Commissioner of Assam said
that every man's caste was to be returned as what he said it was.
In such circumstances accuracy cannot even be claimed for the
resultant figures, and the return of caste disappeared entirely
from the census schedules in 1941.

The fact that a secular authority is normally the final arbiter
of caste disputes and offences does not entirely rule out religious
jurisdiction. As might be expected in dealing with so varied a
phenomenon, exceptions occur to the general rule. The councils
of *sastris* already mentioned as functioning in Indore and
Gwalior, for instance, are advisory only, but the corresponding
body in Kashmir, known as the *Dharma Săbhā*—' Religious
Convention ', perhaps—appears to have delivered judgements and
to have deprived men of caste in that principality, except possibly
in the case of the Rajputs of whom the Maharaja himself was the
head.[21] In Mysore and in Kanara important religious leaders,
especially among Brahmans and Lingayats, seem to dispose of
questions of caste, the caste councils having little more than ' the
position of inquiring and reporting agencies under them '.[22] So
too in the Assam valley, in the extreme north-east of India, the

[20] O'Malley, op. cit., pp. 60 sqq., *Modern India* etc., p. 369.
[21] Harikishan Kaul, *Report on the Census of the Punjab*, 1911, I, p. 428.
[22] O'Malley, *Caste Customs*, p. 71.

7

Gosains, who are the heads of *satras* or religious colleges or monasteries and who are held in great respect, are referred to when the caste councils find difficulty in dealing with a case. Sometimes the control of caste observance has fallen into the hands of the *guru* or spiritual adviser, who is usually but not always a Brahman. Blunt reports this of the Malalodhi subcaste of Lodha, and Buchanan in 1807 reported from Kerala that the *gurus* ' take cognizance of all omissions of ceremonies and actions that are contrary to the rules of cast (*sic*). Small delinquencies they punish by pouring cowdung and water on the head of the guilty person, by fine, and by whipping. For great offences they excommunicate the culprit; which is done by shaving his head. . . . The excommunication may be removed by the *guru*; in which case he purifies the repentant sinner by a copious draught of cow's urine.' [23] In some castes in northern India there is a regular official, no doubt normally if not always a Brahman in this case, who is called *dhărmādhikāri* (' religious preceptor '), whose duty it is to fix the punishment and who, in Garhwal at any rate, purifies the outcaste for readmission to caste.[24]

The vast majority of caste matters, however, are nowadays disposed of by the caste councils which exercise the final powers of expulsion and restoration to caste as well as imposing fines and other penalties for less serious breaches of custom.

Now it is clear, of course, that with a widely spread caste the ideal of a council for the whole caste is impossible of attainment. The whole caste may, it is true, nowadays, have a *sabha*, an association, that is, with branches all over India and even a central headquarters. But such an organization, if it exist, must be a recent development subsequent to the introduction of a cheap postal system and rapid communications of various kinds, and it has not replaced the old system of caste control for the purpose of the imposition of sanctions, though it may represent the caste for purposes of social or political agitation. The caste council can only act for a limited area, an area small enough for the members of the council to assemble and for members of the caste within the area to have some knowledge of each other as a general rule. In practice the members of the caste in such an area will usually form a nearly related group and are spoken of

---

[23] Buchanan, op. cit., I, pp. 101 sq. (ch. III, 8 June 1800).
[24] Blunt, *Caste System*, p. 127.

collectively; in northern India, as a *biradari* or as *bhaiband*, that is, as a brotherhood, an association of kinsmen. They may, indeed, actually constitute an exogamous unit within the embracing endogamous caste, but none the less act for the caste as a whole in enforcing sanctions on the caste members within their sphere of action. In any case they will not consist of a group so large as to embrace more than one endogamous unit, since an endogamous subcaste will normally have rules varying from those of other such subcastes and each must administer its own rules.[25] Local conditions, such as ease of communication, numbers of the caste residing, and their concentration or dispersal, must determine the area within which the caste council functions. In conditions of this kind there is obviously room for every kind of variety in the nature, constitution and working of the caste council, and since the variation will be no less than that already encountered in the structure of caste and in the restrictions enforced by it, it is both impossible to give here a complete account of all of them, and unnecessary to do so for the purpose of understanding caste. The general lines on which the system works can be indicated by a few examples.

The caste council is commonly spoken of as a *pănchāyăt*, literally, that is, a body of five men, but in practice it is usually very much larger. It may be a permanent institution with a continuous existence, or it may be an intermittent one only called into being when circumstances demand it and dissolved again after its work is done. Similarly, the officials who perform its executive functions, as well as sharing its judicial ones, may be appointed *ad hoc* for the particular purpose in hand, or for a much longer period, or they may be hereditary, or some may be elected while others are hereditary. It has frequently been observed that the lower the caste in the social scale, the stronger its combination and the more efficient its organization. This has been pointed out by Sir William Sleeman,[26] O'Malley[27] and Blunt,[28] and probably by many others, since in northern India at any rate the fact is patent. The *panchayat* of the Baghel Rajputs in Banda has not met for three generations.[29] Indeed,

---

[25] Ibid., pp. 10, 105, 128 ; O'Malley, *Caste Customs*, p. 38.
[26] *Rambles and Recollections of an Indian Official*, I, p. 61 (ch. VIII). Cf. Molony, *Report on the Census of Madras*, 1911, p. 180.
[27] *Caste Customs*, pp. 52 sq. [28] *Caste System*, pp. 104, 106, 125.
[29] Ibid., pp. 125, 127.

the high castes rarely have any organization strictly comparable to that of the lower ones. They may well have a *sabha*, a loose association which may be India-wide, but a *panchayat* and officials, permanent or impermanent, are rarely to be found. The rules of the caste are maintained, in so far as they are maintained, by public opinion and by the feeling of the caste members themselves. Informal ostracism is generally the sanction applied, and it is clear that in such cases some members of a caste will apply the sanction while others will refrain from doing so. Thus as O'Malley points out,[30] Mr Gandhi after his first visit to England was formally excommunicated by the leaders of his caste in Bombay and Porbandar, and was still excluded by them from religious privileges in 1924, whereas the members of his caste at his home in Rajkot had duly received him back into communion on his return home. Persons of influence can sometimes thus afford to act in a manner contrary to the rules and prevailing sentiment of their castes, and can carry it off and often persuade many sympathizers to their point of view, and, indeed, behaviour of this kind has often occasioned the formation of subcastes in the past, such as that of the Pir-Ali Brahmans in Bengal to which the Tagore family belongs.[31] It is possible that this generalization does not apply with the same force to Kerala as it does to the rest of India, since the Nayar caste organizations are very strong, and more extended spatially, than those of the lower castes, which often refer their internal disputes to Nayars.

On the other hand, the caste councils of the lower castes in the south as well as in the north are sometimes extremely well organized. Among the Iluvans of Tinnevelly, for instance, in south India, the caste in each village has its own council and elects two members to a council which controls a union of villages. Each group of from five to seven union councils elects five members of the divisional council which regulates the affairs of the caste throughout the *nādu*, that is, the division or tract of country. The Panikkan, likewise in the Madras Presidency, have a similar though not identical system.[32] A somewhat similar system is sometimes found in northern India, where the Gujar of the United Provinces, for instance, have a small hereditary caste

[30] *Caste Customs*, p. 53, quoting Gray and Parekh's *Mahatma Gandhi*. [31] Wilson, op. cit., II, p. 215. Cf. Molony, *Census of Madras*, 1911, pp. 173 sqq.   [32] O'Malley, *Caste Customs*, p. 40.

panchayat in each village, and a combined *panchayat* of several villages under a headman, who is likewise hereditary, for the trial of grave offences. Generally speaking, however, the caste councils of northern India seem to operate for smaller areas than in the south, and indirect representation as among the Iluvan and Panikkan is not reported. Blunt [33] gives details of the *panchayat* system for twenty-nine castes, in all of which the system differs, and even then the practices of individual castes are apt to vary within themselves according to subcaste or locality. Each *panchayat* has a headman commonly known as *sarpanch*—' head of the five ', the members as a rule being known severally as *panch*, though many other terms are in use for both these offices. The headman is sometimes hereditary, sometimes elected, and the same applies to the members, who may also include vice-chairmen and executive officers who may likewise be hereditary or elected. Election may be for life or for each meeting. Often two systems are combined, the headman being hereditary and the members elected or vice versa. In the case of the Lal-Begis, a scavenger caste in Benares, the organization is modelled on that of a military cantonment. The diversity of constitution prevailing may be illustrated by the variations within a single caste. Thus in the Khatik caste in Aligarh there is an hereditary headman called *chaudhuri* with five *panches* chosen for the occasion, though there is a tendency to choose them on hereditary lines, and the Sonkhar subcaste in Gorakhpur has a headman and six or seven *panches* who are all hereditary. The Poldar subcaste has a headman (*chaudhuri*) and a vice-president (*padhan*) who are both hereditary, but the Saqba subcaste has a headman only who is elected for a single year at the Dasehra festival. In Bulandshahr every village has an officer known as *muqaddam*, who disposes of minor cases, and an hereditary *chaudhuri* with two vice-presidents (*diwan*) to every hundred or so villages.[34] A similar diversity holds good generally as between different castes, and is common between different subcastes of a single caste. Among the Koltas of Orissa, where the headman is hereditary, women have been known to succeed to the office.[35] This is, of course, most unusual, but the Tawaïf of the United Provinces, who are dancing girls, have a head-

[33] *Caste System*, pp. 107 sqq. [34] Blunt, *Caste System*, pp. 109 sq.
[35] O'Malley, *Caste Customs*, p. 41.

woman (*chaudhuraïn*) elected for life, and a *panchayat* of women elected for the occasion. The *chaudhuraïn* must have been born within the jurisdiction of the *panchayat*. The headman of a caste council often has privileges or insignia which possibly suggest that the position is derived in some cases from that of the chief of a tribe. In one section of the Vellalans of Tinnevelly he has a seat on a daïs, while everyone else stands, and is addressed by the title *Irunkol* meaning ' Please sit down '. In other castes the headman may ride on horseback, use an umbrella, wear a gold ring, etc.,[36] and the Bhoksa of the United Provinces address the president of their council as *takht*, ' throne ', while *badshah*, ' king ', and *mehtar*, ' prince ', are among the appellations used by other castes for their headmen.[37] In some castes in south India ' the headman is like a chief with practically absolute power ', according to O'Malley,[38] and he mentions the Maravan caste as an instance.

The jurisdiction of caste *panchayats* is conceived as extending to any matter in which the men of the caste consider that the interests or reputation of the caste require action to be taken against a member of the caste. Clearly there is vast room here for the diversity of practice which has been seen to be characteristic of the caste system as a whole. Here again, too, it is obvious that the castes which have a permanent and continuous system of controlling bodies are likely to exercise a much more rigid control than those which have not, and control will be least among the higher and generally speaking better educated classes whose distribution is wide, who are less tied to a particular locality by individual family ties, and who have learned to ' appreciate the liberty which they enjoy by not being in tutelage to ' any particular caste authority. In fact a proposal to revive caste *panchayats* for the socially advanced Prabhus in Bombay met with a critical opposition, which declared the caste *panchayats* to be ' the greatest of all evils ' as being opposed to individual growth and liberty.[39] The more territorially concentrated a caste is the greater will be its consciousness of itself as a coherent entity and the more stringent is its control likely to be over the individual members of which it is composed.

[36] Ibid., p. 42.   [37] Blunt, *Caste System*, pp. 107 sq.
[38] *Caste Customs*, p. 43.
[39] Mead and MacGregor, *Census of Bombay*, 1911, p. 201.

Generally speaking, then, the offences of which a caste *panchayat* will take cognizance are of the following kinds. Offences against the commensal taboos, which prevent members of the caste from eating, drinking, or smoking with members of another caste or at least of other castes regarded by the prohibiting caste as lower in social status than themselves, are undoubtedly the most important, for the transgression of one member of the caste if unknown and unpunished may affect the whole caste with pollution through his commensality with the rest. Offences involving sex or breaches of the marriage rules of the caste really fall into two different categories: inter-marriage contrary to the caste custom is obviously liable to affect the commensal taboo no less than eating food cooked by a stranger, since for practical purposes that is what is involved; on the other hand, marriage with a widow of the same caste where the caste forbids the remarriage of widows is liable to affect the good reputation of the caste or subcaste among its Hindu neighbours, though clearly no commensal taboo is broken. Any offence in which sex is involved may come under one of these two heads, and the nature and extent of such offences will vary greatly with caste, and locality, and the conditions of life in general. Some castes, for instance, forbid the remarriage of any widow, while others allow remarriage of widows to widowers only, and others again observe no restrictions. Often a subcaste which wishes to raise itself in social status will place a ban on the remarriage of widows, while other subcastes of the same caste continue to allow it. Grave offences against widely accepted precepts of Hinduism, such as insulting a Brahman or killing a cow (i.e., generally, causing its death by neglect or ill-treatment), of which the courts established under British rule will take no cognizance [40] or treat only as minor offences, are likewise subject to caste discipline, though the nature of the reason is not always easy to determine, as besides the feeling of injury to the reputation of the caste the feeling of collective responsibility and the contagious nature of taboo may also come into play. This seems almost certainly the case where the caste *panchayat* takes action, as it does in some castes, on account of the killing of a dog or cat or ass. The same doubt attaches to the sins of being

---

[40] But since the achievement of independence, the government of what were the Central Provinces has made the killing of a cow a cognizable offence.

deservedly or undeservedly beaten with a shoe or put in gaol,[41] for it is possible in their case that it is rather the fear of pollution through contact with cowhide or through eating with someone who has been the guest of the Inspector-General of Prisons that is operative, than any sense of disrepute attaching to the stigma of chastisement or of conviction in a criminal court. It may be likewise such a fear of pollution by contagion that causes a man to be put out of caste, as by the Sansiya, a criminal caste or tribe of Rajputana, for happening to be touched by the petticoat of his mother-in-law or daughter-in-law, or for being struck by his wife's petticoat ' in the course of connubial strife '.[42] Something of the same doubt attaches to offences against etiquette or against caste custom in the matter of feasts and entertainments, while in the latter case again there may be an overlap with offences against the economic interests of the caste such as might be involved in a breach of caste trading conventions, or customs respecting handicrafts exercised, or the collection of wild produce. Where the caste *panchayat* takes the liberty of retrying cases among its members already disposed of by the courts, no doubt it is regarded as in the interests of the caste as a whole that a decision which it finds unsatisfactory should be modified in its effects by the action of the caste, even though the actual decision of the courts of law must be endured. Blunt suggests that such retrials among criminal castes may be concerned really with the clumsiness which has led to the offender's detection.[43] Caste *panchayats* will generally be very much more likely to know the true facts of offences their castemen have committed than the ordinary law courts are, and they undoubtedly resent matters closely touching their community being taken to the ordinary courts, and when the interests of a fellow-casteman are in question the caste may combine to stifle evidence which might lead to a conviction in a court of law. O'Malley [44]

[41] *Vide* Elwin, *The Baiga*, pp. 199, 200, *Maria Murder and Suicide*, pp. 195 sqq. Molony (*South India*, p. 111) mentions a case of a man fined Rs. 200—a very large sum in his case—for being struck with a slipper. He mentions also that a caste council took cognizance of a man who committed the social offence of ' stinking '.

[42] J. Hutton, *Thugs and Dacoits*, pp. 152 sq. Similarly in the Naga Hills of Assam, though no question of outcasting would arise, it is a terrible misfortune for a man to be struck with a woman's petticoat that has been worn, and in one case an infuriated wife petticoated her husband's gun, after which it would never shoot straight again and he had to get a new one.

[43] *Caste System*, p. 116.   [44] *Caste Customs*, pp. 51 sq.

gives two instances of evidence of murder being suppressed in this way. Such instances could probably be multiplied indefinitely by diving into the records of police stations throughout India.

The procedure observed in cases tried by caste *panchayats* is no doubt extremely simple, informal, and untrammelled by the law of evidence [45]—more so probably than even a perusal of O'Malley's account [46] would suggest. At the same time Blunt records a number of cases in which some special procedure is laid down. The Lal-Begi *panchayat* already referred to have a quite elaborate arrangement [47] for determining by indirect consultation the general opinion of the members present. In the Nai (barber) *panchayat* of Bulandshahr an inquiry is called for in a specific formula, uttered when the offender is present, in the words 'Look for hair and flies (in your food) before you eat '.[48] Among the Muslim Chamargaurs of Banda an outcasted man desiring reinstatement has food prepared on a day fixed by himself and summons his own caste brethren, the Hindu Chamargaurs of the place, and some Brahmans; if they consider that he can be reinstated they eat the food, but 'a single dissentient among the Muhammadans, and three or four among the Hindus, would be enough to make his restoration impossible '.[49] The Chandel and Kachwaha Rajputs of Cawnpore require the person ostracized to approach a leading clansman, who calls together the brotherhood, appoints assessors and holds an inquiry; he will not act, however, on any person's motion except that of the ostracized person, and the decision pronounced must be either a confirmation of the ostracism suffered or a complete acquittal.[50] This latter procedure is probably typical on the whole of cases where there is no permanent caste *panchayat*, and it is necessary for some individual, who is anxious to have one, to go to the expense of providing entertainment and setting machinery in motion to get the members of the caste together.

Evidence before a caste *panchayat* is frequently given on oath, and Hindu oaths by Ganges water, or the sacred *tulsi* (sweet basil) plant, or by holding a cow's tail, etc., are commonly used.

[45] See Blunt, *Caste System*, p. 113.
[46] *Caste Customs*, p. 45.
[47] Blunt, *Caste System*, p. 114.
[48] Ibid., loc. cit.
[49] Ibid., p. 126.
[50] Ibid., loc. cit.

Blunt mentions ' a white stone tied round with black woollen
thread' used by the Bhotiyas of Kumaon; no man, he says,
dare tell a lie with his right hand on this stone.[51]   Ordeals of
a more exacting kind are also in use, and accused persons, or
the parties to a dispute, may be required to plunge an arm into
boiling cowdung and extract a coin or pebble, or to hold in the
hand a piece of red-hot iron. An interesting account of the
administration of an ordeal of this kind with dramatic and satisfactory results—the innocent man's arm came unscathed from
the boiling water, while the guilty man's was scalded at the
brink—will be found recorded by an observer of complete reliabi-
lity in the *Journal of the Royal Asiatic Society of Bengal*, vol. II
(no. 1), of 1936.[52]   A less drastic form of ordeal is mentioned
by O'Malley [53] as used by a Brahman subcaste of Sambalpur in
which the accused takes oath that if he is guilty he shall become
blind or his children shall die within a specified time.   The oath
is recorded on a palm leaf which is kept in the temple for the
period named and the accused is temporarily outcasted.   If at
the end of the period he and his family have suffered no evil,
he appears before the *panchayat* with the leaf and applies for
readmission to the caste.   Very close analogies with this form
of ordeal are to be found in use among the Ao Nagas of Assam
who, far from being Brahmans, are in no way Hindus, but as
they have no writing, their oaths are not written down and
deposited in a Hindu temple.[54]

The most familiar punishment imposed by caste *panchayats*
is that which deprives a casteman of the right to receive water,
or the tobacco pipe, from the hands of his fellow-castemen and
forbids them likewise to receive it from him; *huqqa pani band*—
' pipe water stopped '—is the equivalent of the Roman *inter-
dictio aquae et ignis*.   The prohibition on water automatically
prohibits *kachcha* food,[55] and the culprit is for practical purposes
excommunicated from communion with his fellow-castemen.
He cannot have the services of the Brahmans who conduct
ceremonies for his caste, nor of the barbers who shave for it
nor the washermen who wash for it, and if he die under the

[51] Ibid., p. 114.
[52] Dr Norman Loftus Bor of the Indian Forest Service in an article on
' The Daflas and their Oaths '.   [53] *Caste Customs*, p. 46.
[54] Mills, *The Ao Nagas*, pp. 195 sqq.   [55] *Vide supra*, pp. 74 sqq.

ban his corpse must lack the funeral rites which alone ensure a continued existence after death and subsequent reincarnation. An excommunication of this sort may be a temporary penalty for a stated period, for an indefinite time subject to the performance of some required expiation for the fault punished, or for life, in which case the culprit is virtually compelled to seek acceptance in some other caste or to remain in communion with other unfortunates in the same plight as his own. Other forms of punishment made use of are the exaction of fines or feasts to the caste or to Brahmans. The fines may be utilized to buy sweetmeats for the assembled castemen or for putting into the fund which many castes maintain for communal purposes. Other penalties inflicted may be corporal punishment, or the performance of a pilgrimage, or the collection of a fine by begging. Many penalties imposed are intended to humiliate the culprit excessively and often to fit the crime as far as possible somewhat in the manner advocated by the English philosopher Jeremy Bentham at the end of the eighteenth century. Thus corporal punishment may be given with a shoe, for the sake of humiliating the offender. The person responsible for the death of a cow often has to make a pilgrimage with a cow's tail tied to his staff or to beg for his living for a period in the same manner, or accompanied by a cow the tail of which he holds; or he may have to low like an ox at the same time or even to wear the dead animal's hide, horns and hoofs, or have a rope round his neck and straw in his mouth. Shaving the culprit on one side of his head and face and leaving the other adorned with hair is another method of humiliating, or the victim is paraded on a donkey with one side of his face blacked and the other whitened; or he may be compelled to wear a string of old shoes round his neck, while an unchaste woman may have to walk round the village with a basket of mud on her head or with a grindstone hung round her neck. O'Malley [56] mentions as a punishment making a man stand on one leg in the sun with a pitcher of water balanced on his head; also a punishment used by the Nats of Bihar of making the culprit sit in cold water for as long even as twenty-four hours. This penalty suggests an element of purification, though the same can hardly be said of one mentioned by Blunt,[57] who speaks of

[56] *Caste Customs*, pp. 80, 81.   [57] *Caste System*, p. 123.

a Thathera (brazier) of Azamgarh who was immersed for three days up to the neck in a cesspit before going on a pilgrimage to Puri and Benares and feasting the *biradari*. But bathing in the Ganges or even swallowing some of its sand (or mud) very often forms part of a penalty imposed, as does drinking water into which a Brahman has dipped his toe. The element of purification is clearly present, and in another punishment described by O'Malley [58] the proceedings probably involve a more elaborate symbolism than mere washing, for a Ravulo husband, who has ill-treated his wife, has to enter a fish-trap shaped like a hencoop and his wife sits on it; both parties then go to that part of the house in which corpses are washed, and are there washed as if they had become corpses; the wife then acts as if widowed, breaking a cooking-pot and her bangles, after which she returns to her father's house and is free to marry again. This looks rather as though a permanent divorce were effected by a symbolic birth of the husband from his wife who thereby becomes his mother whom he cannot marry, a severance which is illogically but emphatically reinforced by the death of both parties and a widowhood as well. One may compare with this symbolic birth, if so it be, the symbolism by which a Chamar who has abducted a married woman has to suck her breasts as a sign that he henceforth regards her as his mother, and would therefore be guilty of incest if he continued his liaison with her, before he restores her to her husband. [59] Blunt [60] records some two dozen varied punishments, specific cases, inflicted by the *panchayats* of various castes.

Perhaps the most familiar form of expiation is that of ingesting what is known as *panchgavya*, the five products of the cow, a mixture of milk, curds, ghee, cowdung, and cow's urine. O'Malley calls it ' a sovereign purge for impurity ', and mentions a modern substitute spoken of as *panchamrata* (five nectars) which substitutes honey and sugar for the last two ingredients, a degenerate concession to civilized squeamishness. Fees to administering Brahmans are involved in either case. Sometimes purification is very elaborate. Among the Urali of Trichinopoly, if a man

[58] *Caste Customs*, p. 82.   [59] O'Malley, loc. cit.
[60] *Caste System*, pp. 117 sqq. An account of the formal expulsion from caste, and of formal readmission, as practised by Gonds and Bhumias in eastern Mandla will be found in Fuchs, op. cit., pp. 214 sqq.

has seduced a girl of the caste they have to be married, and they and their relatives purified by bathing in 108 different pools of water, by walking over the buried head of a sheep with the blood of which they are smeared, by further bathing, by the drinking of cow's urine, by bathing again, and finally by feasting the *panchayat*.[61] The sheep here is possibly associated with the scapegoat idea, which, like the idea of sin-eating, appears in some caste ceremonials for purification. Among the Uppiliyans of Trichinopoly a man called 'the man of two lights' has to eat a meal in the polluted house with his hands tied behind his back, and in the Central Provinces several castes pay an *agua*— one who goes ahead—to eat the first mouthful at a penitential feast, by doing which he takes on the sins of others.[62]

Purification and expiation is followed by the readmission to ordinary communion of the erring casteman, but life expulsion may be the penalty for heinous offences, and it may likewise follow errors or misfortunes for which the unhappy victim is in no way to blame. If a Nambudri woman commit adultery she is outcasted and a funeral ceremony is performed for her as if she were dead,[63] as, indeed, she is to her caste, but if a husband take back an erring wife or a father receive home an erring daughter, they, too, are liable to be outcasted. The Dombo of Vizagapatam district outcaste a man who has been eaten by a tiger,[64] and although this may not affect him in his existence just ended, it will presumably do so hereafter, and the practice throws some light on one of the points of view involved in the observance of caste, as does also the fact that in some castes persons who die unmarried are buried instead of burned.[65] Many Assamese girls forcibly abducted by Burmese soldiery in the invasion of 1822 were turned away from their homes when the Burmese withdrew.[66] No less unfortunate are, or were, the miserable wretches who were taken to the banks of the Ganges to die in odour of sanctity and were ill-advised enough to recover. To die half-immersed in the Ganges with Ganges mud

[61] O'Malley, *Caste Customs*, p. 77.   [62] Ibid.
[63] Thurston, *Castes and Tribes of Southern India*, v, p. 223 ; performing the funeral ceremony is the accepted form of excommunication in Kerala, and is not restricted to Nambudris.
[64] Molony, *Census of Madras*, 1911, I, p. 181.
[65] Blunt, *Census of the U.P.*, 1911, p. 122.
[66] Benudhar Rajkhowa, *Short Accounts of Assam*, p. 92.

in one's mouth secures, according to the Agni Purāna, aeons of
bliss hereafter, but if the virtue of the water and mud be such
that the moribund escape death, then mother Ganges has
rejected her votary. He is dead and his property has passed
to his next of kin. He must live an outcaste, and his own
family may not consort with him and must know him no more.[67]

---

[67] According to O'Malley (*Caste Customs,* p. 87) such persons are no
longer outcasted but are none the less regarded as disgraceful.
   One may compare the Greek practice mentioned by Plutarch (*Roman
Questions,* v), but here the ostracism was remedied by a ceremony of rebirth.
In the Naga Hills of Assam it is, or was, an actionable offence to spread an
untrue report of a person's death.

CHAPTER VIII

ITS FUNCTIONS

THE previous three chapters have been concerned with the manner in which caste operates, and the functions of caste in regard both to the individual casteman and to the caste as a whole will already be evident from what has been said. It will therefore be necessary here to do little more than recapitulate and generalize on certain aspects of the foregoing. Something more is perhaps necessary when it comes to considering the society as a whole, and it will be convenient to treat of the functions which the institution of caste performs first, very briefly, from the individual's point of view, then from that of the caste as a body, and finally, at somewhat greater length, from the point of view of society and the State.

From the point of view of the individual member of a caste the system provides him from birth with a fixed social milieu from which neither wealth nor poverty, success nor disaster can remove him, unless of course he so violate the standards of behaviour laid down by his caste that it spews him forth—temporarily or permanently. He is provided in this way with a permanent body of associations which controls almost all his behaviour and contacts. His caste canalizes his choice in marriage, acts as his trade union, his friendly or benefit society, his slate club and his orphanage; it takes the place for him of health insurance, and if need be provides for his funeral. It frequently determines his occupation, often positively, for in many castes the occupational tradition is very strong indeed, commonly negatively, since there are many pursuits, at any rate in the case of all but the lowest castes, which he cannot follow, or can follow only at the cost of excommunication from the society to which he belongs. It must often happen that membership of a caste will take the place of attachment to a political party, since in such cases as disputes between castes of the Right Hand and of the Left his views on the merits of a dispute and the side he is to support are predetermined for him by his caste membership.

Thus the practice of his caste dictates to each member customs to be observed in the matter of diet, the observance of ceremonial in Assam can, in fact, be generally measured by the number of persons belonging to that community who are in Government service.' Caste then may in some cases serve communities (but never individuals) as a ladder for rising in the social scale.

It is no doubt one of the functions of a social system to hand on from generation to generation that pattern of skill, knowledge and behaviour which we speak of as a culture, the benefits and advances achieved in man's struggle to control environment, using that word in its widest sense, of course. The caste system is peculiarly fitted to hand on culture patterns and particular items of culture, though from its isolating tendency it is probably ill-adapted to growth and change. Craft secrets are well safeguarded and perpetuated by occupational castes, and the caste generally functions as a guild or a trade union. The caste acting as an occupational guild can effectively influence the action of individuals or of corporate bodies outside its own membership. In an eastern municipality dependent for its sanitation on the manual labour of one of the scavenging castes a strike of sweepers and dustmen may have the most devastating effect on the comfort and health of an urban population. Commerce has been held up by strikes of buffalo-drivers in Calcutta dissatisfied with regulations. There is nothing to prevent united action by a big caste from having very considerable influence on the election of political representatives, though interference of this kind with elections would probably be anything but beneficial to the political life of the community.

In the religious sphere the caste system so operates that the caste can change or modify its social and religious observances in accordance with changing ethical standards or the trend of public opinion. It is familiar enough to find castes that are wishful to rise in the estimation of the general public insisting on their members giving up the keeping, and eating, of pigs or chickens. The Kacharis of the remote and isolated Dhansiri valley who in 1910 all kept and ate chickens had by 1920 almost entirely eliminated the barndoor fowl from their economy as the result of uplift propaganda received probably from Kacharis living in the Hinduized atmosphere of the plains of Cachar. Similar movements among the Gonds of the Central Provinces are called ' purification ', and the villages which have eliminated fowls and pigs from their domestic economy are known as '*shivraj*'.[3] Another of the first steps usually taken by a low caste wishing to rise in public esteem is to place a ban on the remarriage of widows in order to bring their practice in that respect into line with the orthodox Hindu teaching on the subject and with the prevailing behaviour of the higher castes. There seems, of course, to be no reason why caste should not be activated in the opposite direction to liberalize the Hindu tradition, but in point of fact it generally seems to have functioned hitherto in the direction of increasing restraint, and, in view of the element of taboo in its origin, this is perhaps only what could be expected.

The third aspect of the functions of caste, and the most important, is that which has regard to the State, to the society as a whole. The functions which caste performs for the individual may be and are performed for individuals by other institutions in other societies. The functions performed by caste for the caste group as a body will be found performed in some more or less analogous way in other systems by such social groupings as exist in them. But caste is an unique institution found only in India, and the functions which it has performed and still performs for Indian society as a whole are not found elsewhere. Furnivall[4] has described British India as the outstanding instance of a country where what he calls 'a plural society' has proved stable. Furnivall attributes this to castes having given a religious basis to inequality, but it is undoubtedly due largely also to the fact that the caste system has afforded a place in society into which any community, be it racial, social, occupational or religious, can be fitted as a co-operating part of the social whole, while retaining its own distinctive character and its separate individual life. Even Sherring, whose indictment of the caste system is as savage as it well could be, admits that 'caste promotes cleanliness and order, and is, in a certain sense, a bond of union among all classes of the Hindu community'.[5]

Many instances could be given throughout historic times of the way in which this function has been performed by caste. The Huns, it is true, are no longer recognizable under that name, they seem to have been absorbed into Hindu society under

[3] Information given personally by Dr Verrier Elwin.
[4] *Netherlands India*, p. 464.
[5] *Hindu Tribes and Castes*, III, p. 274.

the guise of Rajput clans, but the Gujar caste has retained its ancient tribal name, and that is the rule rather than the exception. Many are the tribes who have now become castes. The Meitheis of Manipur are still to some extent in the process, or were until recently, for while part of the tribe have been Hindus for some seven hundred years or so, perhaps, their ruler, who is one of them, can still take non-Hindu tribesmen into caste as Kshatriyas, giving them the right to the sacred thread. Indeed it is (in 1960) less than two hundred and fifty years since the Maharaja abolished ancestor-worship and dismissed the indigenous priests from the temples of the local deities and superseded them by Brahmans.[6] Many such instances can be given of tribes or peoples which have apparently within comparatively recent times become castes—Koli in western India, Chuhra in the Punjab, Dom in the United Provinces and elsewhere, Turi, Musahar, Agariya in Bihar, Rajbansi and probably Kaibartta in Bengal, Kochh and Rabha in Assam, Badaga and Paliyan in Madras, and so forth. Instances could also be given of many tribes and peoples who, while not yet strictly speaking castes within the pale of Hindu society, are, like the Gond and the Bhil, rapidly assuming such a position. Both these tribes are in a fair way to become integrated members of Hindu society, even though they may retain part at any rate of their own customary law. Customary law in India, as Bouglé has rightly pointed out,[7] attaches not to area as in the West, but rather to groups, i.e. to caste.

It is not so easy to give instances of occupational groups taken into Hindu society from outside as a ready-made caste. Instances could be more easily given of occupational groups which have migrated from one part of India to another and formed a new caste group in the new area which has become completely separated from its original caste. This appears to have happened more than once in the case of Brahmans as well as of labouring castes like weavers or oil-pressers. New castes have also been formed by the segregation of subcastes or of occupational groups within castes, and these have been accepted as independent castes just as tribes and peoples have been. A recent case typical of the segregation of a new occupational caste within the community is perhaps to be found in the

---

[6] Hodson in *Folk-Lore*, XXIII, p. 182.   [7] Op. cit., p. 184.

secretion of a caste of motor-car drivers. Enthoven writes: [8] 'Modern India, having created a caste of chauffeurs from the menials who tend motor-cars, is almost ripe for a Rolls Royce caste rejecting food or marriage with the Fords.' He should rather have called it a Rolls-Royce subcaste, for at least it would start in that way and, if true to pattern, reject first the giving of daughters to Fords while not hesitating to take wives from among them, secondly, the eating of food with them, and finally, all connexion of any kind, discovering a long-forgotten descent, not shared by Fords, from some Brahman or Kshatriya ancestor who drove the fiery chariot of Surya in the misty dawn of mythology. Whether Enthoven be right or not in stating that a caste of chauffeurs actually exists, he is most certainly right in emphasizing 'the quite disproportionate importance attached in India to trifling differences arising from one reason or another in the conduct of small groups of individuals'. 'Workmen who wear pagris', says Bouglé,[9] 'will have nothing to do with workmen in belts; the caste which mends shoes refrains from making a pair of them', and he goes on to quote Rhys Davids [10] to the effect that it takes three distinct craftsmen to make a bow and arrows, though here we are not so far from our own middle ages when the bowyer's and the fletcher's were separate crafts. Such an attitude of behaviour is probably the inevitable consequence of a system in which each of many component elements has been integrated on a principle of preserving as essentials any features peculiar to itself and tending to distinguish it from other groups. For this is, in effect, what the caste system has done and still does.

In a similar way religious groups, groups in many cases formed in defiance of and in protest against the caste system, have found themselves relegated, whether they wish it or no, precisely into the position of castes in that system which they have aspired to reform. Indeed, unless they were to succeed in destroying the system, as the followers of the Buddha nearly did, it is difficult to see what other outcome such a movement could have unless it broke away from Hinduism altogether. The Sikhs are a case in point. The comparatively unimportant division of them known as the Sahejdari Sikhs still claim to be within the Hindu

[8] Reviewing Dutt's *Origin and Growth of Caste in India*, vol. I, in the *J.R.A.S.* January 1932. [9] Op. cit., p. 215.
[10] *J.R.A.S.*, October 1901, p. 863.

pale, but the more vigorous and independent Sikhs of the
Keshadhari persuasion have repudiated the claim to be called
Hindus, though still sometimes intermarrying with Hindu
families. A typical instance of the religious sect turned caste is
that of the Lingayats, a caste which started as the followers of
Bāsava, a teacher of the twelfth century who preached the
repudiation of caste. They wear as the symbol of their faith a
small silver box containing a stone phallus (*linga*), ' the loss of
which is equivalent to spiritual death '.[11] A similar sectarian
caste is possibly to be found in the Kabirpanthis, followers of
Kabir, who addressed himself to both Hindus and Muslims, and
was particularly popular among weavers; but the somewhat
similar sect of Satnami, largely recruited from Chamars, is careful not to override the demands of caste.[12]

While incorporations of occupational and sectarian groups
have been, as they are now, more or less automatic and inevitable, given the creation of the group in the first instance,
the incorporation of tribal, national, or political groups appears,
on the other hand, to have taken place as a result of deliberate
policy, and to have been used as an administrative device from
the earliest historical times. Jackson [13] quotes Vasishtha to the
effect that the king should pay attention to all the laws of
countries, castes and families and make the four *varna* fulfil
their respective duties; he quotes Apastamba ' who says that if
those who have broken caste rules fail to perform the penance
prescribed by their spiritual guide, he shall take them before the
king ' who shall ' reduce them (to reason) by forcible means ',
short of corporal punishment and servitude if Brahmans, but
with punishments which may amount to death in the case of
other castes. He also quotes Manu (VII, 201-3, Bühler's
translation) as follows: ' When he has gained victory let him
duly worship the gods, and honour righteous Brahmanas, let him
grant exemptions, and let him cause promises of safety to be
proclaimed. But, having fully ascertained the wishes of all the
(conquered), let him place there a relation of the (vanquished
ruler on the throne) and let him impose his conditions. Let him
make authoritative the lawful (customs) of the (inhabitants),

[11] Enthoven, *Tribes and Castes*, II, p. 344.
[12] Crooke, *Tribes and Castes*, IV, pp. 299 sqq.
[13] ' Note on the History of the Caste System ', *J.A.S.B.*, vol. III, no. 7,
July 1907.

just as they are stated (to be).' Jackson goes on to point out that a large proportion of subcastes bear geographical names, and while some take a name from the kingdom others, particularly the trading and artisan castes, take it from the capital city, and that many traces are to be found of sets of subcastes bearing specific geographical names, which is what we should expect if each of the old tribal kingdoms had its own sections of priests, traders, artisans, etc. He gives among other instances those of *Gujar* subcastes among the castes of Darzi, Sonar, Sutar, Charan, Dhed and Baniya; *Kachela* (or its synonym *Parajiā*) among the Lohar, Sonar, Charan and Brahman castes (Kachela means an inhabitant of Kachh); *Modh* among Brahmans, Baniyas and Ghanchis (from the town of Modhera); *Sūrati* among Ghanchis, Lohars, Mochis and Dheds (after the town of Surat or its district), and a number of other instances all from the former Bombay province. They could, of course, with little difficulty be added to by parallel instances from all over India. Clearly geographical, political and administrative considerations have not been unimportant in the development and operation of the caste system, though the essential concepts of pollution, commensality, and endogamy are ritual rather than economic in nature.

It will be understood then that one important function of caste, perhaps the most important of all its functions, and the one which above all others makes caste in India an unique institution, is, or has been, to integrate Indian society, to weld into one community the various competing if not incompatible groups composing it. Some of these groups have been occupational or religious. Others, and this is more important, have been national, political, and tribal societies that must otherwise have either been absorbed and transformed or remained as unadjusted and possibly subversive elements. Generally speaking conquered peoples and their conquerors blend into one society in which one or other element may in the long run predominate. The Castilians who conquered Spain absorbed the Moors that remained there; Anglo-Saxons, British, and Danes coalesced, and absorbed their Norman conquerors. On the other hand the negroes of the United States remain so far an unadjusted population, while European and Bantu in South Africa remain no less segregated in a different way. The caste system has effectively dealt with problems such as these which other societies have failed to solve. It has involved no doubt disadvantages peculiar to itself which are indicated in the proper place, but this aspect of caste as an integrator of peoples is perhaps not without some bearing on problems facing the world today, where the question arises of incorporating the various nations of the world into some sort of integrated whole which is presumably the only alternative to yet more internecine conflict. ' India ', writes Gilbert,[14] ' has developed a system of castes which, as a scheme of social adjustment, compares rather favourably with the European system of warring territorial nationalities.'

A second very important function of caste has been to act as a political stabilizer. It was this function, apparently, of the caste system which so moved the admiration of the Abbé Dubois,[15] who considered the caste system of the Hindus ' the happiest effort of their legislation '. He regarded the caste system as being responsible for the preservation of India from complete barbarism, and as the sure basis of orderly government, as a defence against despotism, and a means for preserving the arts, and as a sure means of preserving the Hindu pattern of culture under the regime of alien conquerors. At a more recent date S. C. Hill [16] has taken a similar view. He points out that whereas ' in Europe we are accustomed to think of the Political and Social systems of a country as one and the same thing ', the Hindu regards them as distinct, and separable in fact. ' His intimate life . . . the life which to the Hindu really matters, is altogether independent of the political conditions which happen to prevail.' He calls the caste system ' the only Social System ever proposed upon a basis stronger than Force '; it puts into successful practice the only instance of a scheme of social life which is ' entirely independent of any form of political government. . . . The system is permanently stable because of the complete absence of any motive on the part of the ruled for seeking any alteration.'

The admiration of Dubois was not without some justification, and he has not been the only writer to draw attention to the value of the caste system as a stabilizer of society. Indian society

---

[14] *Peoples of India,* p. 82.   [15] *People of India,* pt. i, ch. ii.
[16] ' Origin of the Caste System in India ', §§ x, xii, xiii, xiv (*I.A.,* March-Oct. 1930).

has survived a vast number of invasions, famines, revolutions and social upheavals of all kinds, including conquests by invaders of alien religions essentially antagonistic to Hinduism, and there can be no doubt but this is largely due to the caste system on which that society has constructed itself, a system which has often survived even conversion to Islam or Christianity. Muslim castes are a familiar phenomenon; Momin or Jolaha, for instance, a caste of Muslim weavers; Lalkhani, a caste of Muslim Rajputs; Gaddi, a caste of Muslim graziers; Mirāsi, a caste of Muslim minstrels closely akin to the Hindu caste of Dhārhi, and so forth. Indeed, one Muslim caste, the Turkiya Banjara, have definite *gotras*, three of which have Muslim names—Bahlim, Khilji and Shaikh.[17] As for Christians, it is not very many years since the Madras High Court had to adjudicate on the rights of a Christian congregation which sued its priest for breaking down the wall which divided the aisle of the respectable from the aisle in which sat Christians of the untouchable castes, while Bouglé[18] mentions a church in the Tamilnad with separate naves giving on to a common chancel to accommodate hostile castes. Indeed, Iyer, writing of the Syrian Christians of the Malabar Coast, says: ' The average Indian Christian is a staunch observer of castes. It is a moot point whether he is not stricter in his observance of castes than the average Hindu. There are a large number of Christians in the Southern Districts of the Madras Presidency who even boast of their being firmer, and truer adherents of the caste system than the Hindus.'[19] The reason of the social stability conferred by the caste system is no doubt its provision for the unlimited extension of the society by the inclusion as integral parts of the structure of any number of extraneous, particularizing, or segregative entities.

Again, the caste system does provide for the various functions necessary to social life, functions ranging from education to scavenging, from government to domestic service of the most menial kind; and it makes this provision under the sanction of a religious dogma, the belief in *kărmă*, which renders the superficially inequitable distribution of functions acceptable as being part of the divine order of the universe and a transient episode in the prolonged existence of the individual soul, which

[17] Blunt, *Caste System*, p. 45.   [18] Op. cit., p. 26 n.
[19] L. K. A. Iyer, *Anthropology of the Syrian Christians*, p. 218.

by acquiring merit in one existence may rise in the scale in the next, or which may be suffering from a degradation in caste merely by reason of its transgressions in a previous life. As an important element in this stabilizing effect, caste, as Bouglé has pointed out,[20] puts a damper, so to speak, on the rise of the *parvenu*. The Shanan of southern India, in spite of the wealth they have acquired, have no right to build two-storied houses, to wear gold ornaments, or to sport an umbrella.[21] The very nature of the system discountenances and discourages attempts to surmount existing barriers of rank or occupation or to break down those barriers by intermarriage or by freedom of social intercourse generally. The truth is that caste has developed as a quasi-organic structure in which the caste stands to the society as a whole in a relation almost analogous to that of the individual cell to the greater organism of which it forms part. The many undoubted advantages which follow from a development of this kind are more or less inevitably attended by certain disadvantages to which it will be necessary to draw attention.

This view of the caste system as an organism as it were, a composite unit of many individual cells each functioning independently, must not be taken as precluding a certain fluidity in the system, a power of mutability in caste itself within certain definite limits. Hindu society may be classified very roughly into four grades—that of Brahmans, that of other ' twice-born ' castes deriving in theory at any rate from the Kshatriyas and Vaishyas of the vedic age, that of Sudras, and that of the exterior castes. No one not born a Brahman can any longer hope to become one, though that seems to have been possible in the early stages of Hinduism. Castes in the third category can and do succeed in establishing themselves in the second; castes in the fourth can and do get accepted in the third. That is about as far as the mutability of castes goes. Worldly prosperity and a high level of education enable a caste to rise first in its own estimation, later, and much more tardily, in the general estimation of other castes, so that in the course of time it is able to establish recognition, grudging at first no doubt, but ultimately more or less general perhaps, in a group higher than that to which it belonged by origin. Indeed, Blunt [22] insists that the

[20] Op. cit., p. 212 : ' L'Inde ne veut pas connaître la figure du " parvenu ".'   [21] Bhattacharya, op. cit., p. 259.
[22] *Caste System*, p. 208.

caste system is so mutable that no account of it remains accurate for long: 'its evolution is still proceeding: new castes and subcastes come into existence, old customs fall into abeyance.' This, no doubt, is true enough, but it is not the system that is changing so much as caste details within it. Caste, no doubt, keeps changing, and customs come and go; the pattern alters, but the principles that govern it, the frames that hold the pattern so to speak, are exceptionally constant for a human institution. It has been already suggested that there are certain disadvantages probably inseparable from the advantages of the caste system, and it is necessary to draw attention to these in any attempt to describe the functions which caste performs. Pramatha Nath Bose, in his *History of Hindu Civilisation during British Rule*,[23] has stated that the caste system has acted essentially to impose that attitude of mind needed to raise men from savagery but to stop them half-way on the road to progress. In so far as this is true, and in a great measure it would seem to be true, it is probably the result of the passing on of crafts and skills by means of an hereditary environment in which the son learns as it were unconsciously from the father in the process of his upbringing. It is no doubt this method of transmitting a craft which makes an innovation in method appear sometimes as if it were a sin against the craftsman's ancestors. Sonnerat found it useless to try to get Hindu carpenters to use improved methods of sawing wood,[24] and a similar difficulty is still experienced in the hills of Assam, where the local inhabitant prefers the adze to the saw; and it is noticeable how prevalent in eastern India is the employment of Sikhs as carpenters. The Sikhs, be it noted, belong to an offshoot of Hinduism which has repudiated caste. The fisherman in the play of *Sakuntala* who is reproached with cruelty to fish replies that he cannot be blamed, since it is wrong to give up the calling of one's ancestors however degraded that calling may be.[25] 'Caste makes no compromises,' says Sherring. 'The most ignorant Hindu is able to compel the obedience of the most intelligent.'[26]

It is a possible further disadvantage of the caste system economically that it probably discourages organization from above

---

[23] Quoted by Bouglé, op. cit., p. 140.   [24] *Voyage aux Indes*, I, p. 104.
[25] Quoted by Bouglé, op. cit., p. 21.   [26] Op. cit., III, p. 276.

by the *entrepreneur*, no less than it forestalls ambition on the part of the workman. Durkheim has suggested that the function of the division of labour is to give the individual more freedom by substituting an organic for a rigidly mechanical economy, but the organic structure created by the caste system would seem to have provided for the division of labour on a plan ingeniously calculated to avoid giving just that freedom; for occupation is determined by status instead of contract, and transition from status to contract, which Sir Henry Maine regarded as an essential feature of political progress,[27] is nullified and frustrated. A system of this kind must operate to stifle progress in economic life, giving it an almost paralysing stability. The great strides made in industrial progress in India in the twentieth century have been made in spite of the caste system, not as a result of it. It is likely also that a further political consequence of the caste system has been to simplify the intrusions of foreign invaders by opposing to them a society irreparably split up and unable to combine, a society that has for centuries lacked a national life, so much so, perhaps, as to justify Bouglé's apophthegm that for Hindus patriotism consists in attachment to the caste system and they achieve the paradox of being unable to unite except in the very culture pattern that divides them.[28]

This aspect of the caste system has a specific religious sanction. It has been held to have been established by divine ordinance or at least with divine approval, and the Bhagavad Gita, which probably more nearly than any other sacred scripture fulfils for Hindus the function performed for Islam by the Qur'an or for Christians by the Bible, contains some well-known lines which inculcate the supreme merit of performing one's caste duties. ' One's own duty [i.e. *dhărmă* or caste rules], though defective, is better than another's duty well performed.' [29]   Custom, says the Code of Manu, is transcendent law. Perfection, we are told in the Mārkandēya Purana, can only be attained by the man who does not deviate from the duties of caste.[30]   In the observance of these duties therefore consists what is known as *dharma*, that is, religious observance, moral obligation, righteousness; the word is not easy to translate precisely, but God himself is spoken

[27] *Ancient Law* (1880), p. 170.   [28] Op. cit., p. 194.
[29] Quoted by Hill, loc. cit., March 1930.
[30] Wilson, *Indian Caste*, I, p. 437.

of as Dharmeswar, the Righteous One. At any rate it is clear that the social habits of caste are inextricably tied up with religion, and their sanction is reinforced by the doctrine of *karma* already alluded to. Under this doctrine a man's condition in this life is the result of his conduct in his last incarnation; his high or low caste is therefore the reward or punishment of his past behaviour, and if unsatisfactory can be remedied by acquiring merit in his present life which will raise his status in the next. The Laws of Manu contain the following passage: '(A Sūdra who is) pure', etc., 'and free from pride, and always seeks a refuge with Brāhmanas, attains (in his next life) a higher caste.'[31] No doctrine is more likely to conduce to contentment in this life. 'The ties of caste', writes Sherring, 'are stronger than those of religion. A man may be a bad Hindu so far as the practice of his religious duties goes; but caste rules must be minutely observed, or he will have to reap the consequences of neglect. With many Hindus the highest form of religious observance is the complete fulfilment of the claims of caste; and most of them conceive of sin as a breach of caste discipline rather than of moral law.'[32]

The doctrine of *karma* must clearly help to palliate the apparent inequity of the caste system, but it seems likely that it has been grafted on to it in the course of its development, and is not inherent in its origins. In any case it is quite clear that the caste system has been effectively utilized by the Brahman priesthood to maintain the existing form of Hindu society with the Brahmans as a privileged class, and that caste has been taken advantage of generally by the higher castes to keep the inferior and exterior castes in their respective stations, if not to reduce them to the lowest status possible. It is true that theoretically greater responsibilities rest on the higher castes, but the Brahman reception or rejection of water or food is the measure of the status of any given caste in a given place. And in point of fact a tribe which does not recognize Brahmans or Hinduism at all is generally in a better position socially with regard to the Brahman than the exterior castes whose occupation is degrading according to Hindu law and therefore polluting to Brahmans.[33] Dubois, an admirer of the caste system, has

[31] *The Laws of Manu* (tr. Bühler), IX, p. 335.
[32] Op. cit., III, p. 276.   [33] Webb, *These Ten Years*, p. 201.

described their arrogance [34] and finds it not unnatural after all
in a caste brought up with the idea that they have a right to
everything and owe nothing to anyone. It is not difficult to
give instances of the pollutability of Brahmans. In a story in
the Jātakas two Brahman girls playing at the gate of a city
happen to see two Chandals. They run away at once to wash
and decontaminate their eyes. The reason why it is the general
custom in India for Indian gentlemen to call on Europeans at
as early an hour in the day as possible is commonly believed to
be to enable them to decontaminate themselves so as to take
their morning meal in a state of ceremonial purity.[35] It is not
surprising then that there were castes which had to carry warning
bells like a medieval leper, and that they were treated as one
might expect when they were completely without power themselves and inspired nothing but disgust in persons of higher caste,
a disgust so great that contact with them by sight or by the
passage of a breath of air necessitated ceremonial purification.
The theory that greater responsibilities and obligations rest on
the higher castes is no doubt put into practice in the form of
a more scrupulous cleanliness, a stricter observation of rules of
diet, a truer regard for ceremonial observances; but generally
speaking the responsibilities accepted are rather ceremonial than
moral, and although the Hindu sacred books lay down a rule
of strict asceticism for Brahmans, for instance, and of public
service in the form of religious instruction to be given by them
to other castes, the rule is not taken too seriously by the generality of the Brahman castes. At the same time it should perhaps
be made clear that although there are many different Brahman
castes Brahmans do form a cohesive group with much solidarity,
and, to some extent in spite of caste, constitute a sort of intellectual aristocracy.

The caste system is also open, as a result of the particular form
which its religious sanction takes, to the criticism that it may
act as a screen and justification for persistently anti-social conduct. The fisherman in the Jātaka story justified his sin against

---

[34] Op. cit., p. 36 (pt. I, ch. VI); and see Wilson, *Indian Caste*, I, pp. 390,
411, 426 ; Ketkar, *History of Caste*, pp. 138 sqq.; Dutt, op. cit., pp. 148
sqq., etc.
[35] Dr J. Gonda, in a review of the first edition of this book in *Erasmus*,
refers to a text of Kautilya (*Arthasāstra*, ch. XIX) according to which kings
should receive intelligence, etc. before the daily bath and breakfast.

the fish and against the teaching of the Buddha by an appeal to the practice of his caste. In another case the identical argument is pleaded by a butcher for practising his hereditary trade.[36] Precisely the same justification has been used by many criminal castes to justify their behaviour towards their fellow men. The Thugs undoubtedly made a religion of Thuggee and strangled their victims to the honour of their goddess Bhawāni as well as to the enrichment of their pockets. They worshipped also the sacred pickaxe with which they buried the bodies of their victims and from the position of which they read omens before an enterprise; when hidden in a well this pickaxe rose in the morning of its own accord and came of itself into its custodian's hand; its sound made in digging a grave could be heard by none but a Thug; it was more sacred than Ganges water or the Qur'an, and a Thug who took a false oath on it died within six days. 'They considered . . . that their victims were killed by God, with them as his agents, their appointed job being to kill travellers—to quote the words of a Thug, " just as a tiger feeds upon deer ".' The caste had a life of at least more than five hundred years, as the earliest historical mention of Thuggee is in Zia-ud-Din Barni's history of Firoz Shah, written in 1356, and refers to the capture, and release, of a thousand Thugs at Delhi about A.D. 1290.[37] Other criminal castes, like Korava, regard their criminal practices as justified by if not enjoined on them by their membership of the caste to which they belong and by their common share in its ancestors and traditions.[38] Again, Dubois [39] says of the Kallan caste that they exercise their profession of robber, ' without disguise, as their birthright . . . and conceive their calling no way discreditable to themselves or their tribe, as having legitimately descended to them by way of inheritance. So far from shrinking at the appellation, if one of them be asked who he is, he will coolly answer that he is a robber.'

The above considerations suggest that there may be good reason for Furnivall's criticism of ' plural societies '.[40] In examining their economy he says that a plural society in its political aspect ' resembles a confederation of allied provinces, united by

[36] Hopkins, *Ruling Caste in Ancient India*, p. 120.
[37] J. L. Sleeman, *Thug or a Million Murders*, pp. 8, 19, 23, 27 and *passim*.
[38] Hatch, *Land Pirates of India*, ch. VI.
[39] Op. cit., p. 3 (pt. I, ch. I).   [40] Op. cit., pp. 447 sqq.

treaty or within the limits of a formal constitution, merely for certain ends common to the constituent units and, in matters outside the terms of union, each living its own life. But it differs ', he says, ' from a confederation in that the constituent elements are not segregated each within its own territorial limits ', so that ' The elements are so intermingled that secession is identical with anarchy '. This is not an unfair description of the caste system, and Furnivall goes on to argue that such a society lacks a common will in economic life, and there is in consequence an absence of any common social demand; social wants are sectional, and ' there is no social demand common to all the several elements '. This, he maintains, ' raises the economic criterion to a new place in the scale of social values ', since the only place where the various sections of the community meet on common ground is the market-place, where the highest common factor of their wants is the economic one; the elements of such a society come to regard the production of material goods as the prime end of social life; the social needs of the country as a whole are not apprehended, social demand itself becomes sectionalized, ' and within each section of the community the social demand becomes disorganized and ineffective, so that in each section the members are debarred from leading the full life of a citizen in a homogeneous community; finally the reaction against these abnormal conditions . . . sets one community against the other ', enhancing the need for the society ' to be held together by some force exerted from outside '. Such a force is clearly to be found in the law, ' but in a society which has no common bond but law, Right is superseded by Legality, and the only Duty is not to be found out '. Furnivall clearly regards the rule of law in a plural society as responsible for ' the litigation which is a curse of British India ' and ' the aristocracy of native lawyers and money-lenders which is typical of British India outside the Native States '.[41] One would say at first thought that the caste system had the common bond of religion as well as of law, but we have already seen that the first injunction of religion is to obey caste rules, which suggests that Hinduism fails to act as an overriding bond for the plural societies represented by castes. At any rate those who have known India will see much force in what Furnivall has said.

[41] Ibid., p. 466.

There are also drawbacks to the caste system in India which arise not so much because of the nature of the system as incidentally to its development. One of these is the hardship which is entailed on generations of women in all those castes that aim at raising their position in the social scale. Any caste or subcaste that wishes to rise in the estimation of its fellows, or to claim an origin from some twice-born *varna* to which it is not generally conceded to belong, finds it essential to conform as nearly as may be to the traditional standard of Brahman castes in the matter of insisting on the marriage of girls before they reach the age of puberty, and in forbidding their remarriage even if widowed in infancy. This is a very high price to pay for a shadowy descent from some doubtfully historical *rishi* or for the unsubstantial glories of Rajput blood and state. It is perhaps, however, in its treatment of outcastes, that is, of castes outside the pale of respectable society, the 'exterior' castes as they have been called, that the working of the caste system is most open to criticism. The position of these exterior castes has already been indicated. It may be attributed to failure, wilful or otherwise, on the part of the exterior caste to observe the stricter prohibitions of Hindu society, the prohibition, for instance, against the killing of cattle, which keeps outside the pale tanners, cobblers, and all those who deal in the products of their dead bodies; the prohibition, albeit less stringent, against crushing the oil-seed, which makes the oil-presser an exterior caste; or the ban on alcoholic liquor which makes the toddy-drawer an outcaste. It may be attributed also to the pursuit of some even necessary profession which involves contact with some sort of pollution. One might have expected the washerman's to be a cleanly pursuit, but the fact that it brings him into contact with menstrually [42] polluted clothes is enough to make him an outcaste no less than the scavenger who removes night-soil or dead bodies. And in all cases the nature of taboo is such, of course, that the contagion of the polluted occupation contaminates all members of the caste whatever their individual occupation may be, and to an infinite number of generations.

[42] This taboo is, of course, world-wide. There can be little doubt but the reason why the adjectives 'bloody' and 'bleeding' are, or till recently were, regarded as indecent in English is because they have been used as swear-words with that particular association implied.

9

The number of these exterior castes in India was found at the
census of 1931 to be more than 50 millions, or 21% on a Hindu
population of 239 odd millions. Their position was gone into
in some detail in an appendix to the *Report on the Census of
India*, 1931. Extracts from that appendix have been included
in an appendix to this volume as being germane to the whole
question of caste as treated here. It is quite clear that the
unfortunate position of the exterior castes could be remedied
without destroying the caste system. Their position is the result
of prejudices and taboos which have been operative during
millennia, and cannot be got rid of in a night. That is a
process which can only be accomplished in the course of time,
and with the help of education in its broadest sense. To destroy
the caste system, even if it could be done, might be disastrous
to the society which is constructed on its framework. Religious
beliefs make it tolerable and even reasonable to the members
of that society. No doubt modifications in those beliefs, which
probably will take place in the course of time, which probably
are indeed already taking place, will bring about in their train
a modification of the caste system. At any rate they will make
modification easier, and will automatically improve the position
of the exterior castes. Meanwhile there seems to be no reason
why a great improvement in the position of those castes should
not be made within the system as it exists today, and without
any necessity for destroying a social order which performs a
number of useful functions both for the individual and for the
society. Caste is probably what Professor Bartlett [43] would call
one of the ' hard points ' of Hindu culture, and any attempt to
modify it by a direct attack on it is likely to provoke resistance
and discord, and reformers will need to aim at some ' soft point ',
some other feature of the culture, that is, through which the
' hard point ' can ultimately be circumvented and isolated. The
mere fact that caste is one of the ' chief differentiating cultural
features ' between Western cultures and Hinduism, is, if Professor
Bartlett is to be followed, a reason for scrupulously avoiding any
direct attack on it.

[43] *Anthropology in Reconstruction*, p. 5.

There is yet another function which the caste system probably performs, and that is a genetic one. India is a country in which the male sex generally outnumbers the female. The ratio in 1931 was 1,000 males to 941 females, or, if Hindus alone be considered, to 953, and this inequality is likely to be felt most acutely among Hindus on account of their ban against the remarriage of widows. Now a good deal of fairly recent work on sex ratios has pointed to the conclusion that an excess of males is indicative of a declining population, but this is certainly not the case in India. It is possible that the caste system itself contributes to the preponderance of masculinity. Westermarck [44] takes the view that a mixture of race leads to an increase in the ratio of females to males. He cites a number of observations from various parts of the world to support this view: he quotes Dr Nagel's experiments in the self-fertilization of plants, as producing an excess of male flowers, and several cases of inbreeding herds of cattle in which bull calves greatly exceed heifers, as well as two independent experiments in horse-breeding indicating that fillies predominate among foals in proportion as sire and dam differ in colour. George Pitt-Rivers [45] quotes Heape to the effect that experiments upon dogs indicate that inbreeding produces a high percentage of males. Westermarck, again, quotes the Talmud as stating that mixed marriages produce only girls, [46] and mentions a number of statistics pointing to an excess of female births as the result of mixed marriages. The causal connexion between inbreeding and an excess of male births is not proved, but there is a good deal of evidence to support the theory that pure-blooded societies produce an excess of males, and Miss King's experiments with rats afforded evidence that the normal sex ratio could be changed by breeding from litters which contain an excess of males. [47] Sedgwick, in his *Report on the Census of Bombay, 1921,* [48] pointed out that the Indian caste system with its endogamous caste and its exogamous *gotras* ' is a perfect method of preserving what is called in genetics the " pure line ". The endogamy prevents external hybridization, while the (internal) exogamy prevents the

[44] *History of Human Marriage* (1901), pp. 476-82.
[45] *The Clash of Culture,* p. 111, referring to *Proc. Camb. Phil. Soc.,* xiv, pp. 21 et seq.
[46] *Op. cit.,* p. 479.
[47] Pitt-Rivers, loc. cit.
[48] p. 103.

possibility of a fresh pure line arising within the old one by the isolation of any character not common to the whole line. With the preservation of the pure line the perpetuation of all characters common to it necessarily follows.' Whether this statement of the position be strictly accurate or not it may at least be conceded that if once a caste, whether as the result of inbreeding or of some quite different factor, have acquired the natural condition of having an excess of males, this condition is likely to be perpetuated as long as inbreeding is maintained. Caste, therefore, would appear to be of definite assistance to the Hindu in his superlative anxiety for male offspring. 'There is no heaven for the sonless man.'

PART THREE
ORIGINS

CHAPTER IX

ANALOGOUS INSTITUTIONS
ELSEWHERE

IT has already been said that caste is an exclusively Indian phenomenon, but there are in various parts of the world analogous institutions which resemble caste in one or other of its aspects, and before proceeding to examine the question of how caste originated it will be useful to glance at these institutions, since they are likely to throw light on the origins of caste proper, which are not one but many. It is no doubt the manifold origin of caste in India that is the cause of its being unique, since it is unlikely that a complex combination of factors could be exactly repeated in some other part of the world. It is not to be understood, therefore, that there is any complete analogy to caste in any non-Indian society, but there are a number of social phenomena which offer a parallel to one or other element in the caste system. How mixed in origin caste is is aptly illustrated by Molony,[1] who remarks that the caste table for the Madras census in 1911 suggested 'a division of the inhabitants of England into families of Norman descent, clerks in Holy Orders, noblemen, positivists, ironmongers, vegetarians, communists and Scotchmen'. The difference is that whereas these categories overlap in the English social system, corresponding categories in the caste system would be mutually segregate. Risley has elaborated the idea in his chapter on social types.[2]

An allusion has been made in the last chapter to Furnivall's treatment of 'plural societies'.[3] There he treats caste as one system by which the problems inherent in a plural society are resolved, alternative resolutions being Law, Nationalism, and Federalism, and he suggests that three colonizing peoples—the

[1] *A Book of South India*, p. 106.   [2] *People of India*, ch. II.
[3] *Netherlands India*, ch. XIII.

Portuguese, British, and Dutch—have respectively adopted these three solutions of what is primarily an economic problem. For a plural society is one in which different elements perform different functions. Thus in Siam, he says, the Siamese, Chinese, and Europeans ' have distinct economic functions, and live apart as separate social orders '. Similarly, in South Africa and in the United States there are white and coloured populations exhibiting a not dissimilar phenomenon, and in the French provinces of Canada, English and French Canadians who grow up ' separated by race, language and religion' in two distinct societies. ' Even where there is no difference of creed or colour, a community may still have a plural character, as in western Canada, where people of different racial origin tend to live in distinct settlements and, for example, a northern European cannot find work on the railway, because this is reserved for " Dagoes " or " Wops ".' And in lands where a strong Jewish element is regarded as alien, ' there is to that extent a plural society'. Clearly there is a social phenomenon in this which has much in common with the caste system, particularly in its economic aspect. At the same time it is clearly not caste in the Indian sense, a truth well illustrated by Furnivall's citing Burma as a country of plural society where different functions are discharged by Europeans, Indians, Chinese and Burmese,[4] but one in which there is no caste.[5] Yet Burma from quite a different, and a non-economic, aspect offers us yet another remarkable parallel to caste, as will be seen later.

Another institution in some ways analogous to caste in its economic and also more particularly in its occupational aspect is to be seen, as pointed out by Risley,[6] in the ordinances of the Theodosian Code of the Western Roman Empire in the early part of the fifth century A.D. The intention of these ordinances seems to have been partly fiscal, partly an administrative attempt to ensure the performance of the various functions needed for the social life of the community. The method by which it was sought to do this was to make it compulsory for a man to follow his father's calling, and in certain cases at any rate to compel a man to follow the calling of the family into which he married. Thus owing to a scarcity of bakers not only

[4] Op. cit., p. 467.　　　　　　　　[5] Ibid., p. 465.
[6] *People of India* (1915), pp. 270 sq.

was a baker's son compelled to be a baker, but if a man married a baker's daughter he himself had to become a baker. All public functions were made hereditary; even the *curiales*, the quasi-priestly persons responsible for the secular and religious functions associated with what might be described as municipal wards—aldermen we may perhaps call them, but they were responsible for the collection of taxes—were ordered back to their native cities and compelled to resume their original functions, which they were forbidden to evade by taking government service. They were even denied the right of asylum in the Church. The wine merchant, oilman, butcher and pork-butcher, the transport contractor and the corn merchant, the waterman, the stoker in the public baths, even the senator were all made hereditary and bound to their callings from one generation to another. The troops known as *burgarii* who garrisoned the frontier posts were likewise bound to their military profession by heredity. ' It was ', says Dill,[7] ' the principle of rural serfdom applied to social functions. . . . A man was bound to his calling not only by his father's but by his mother's condition. Men were not permitted to marry out of their guild. . . . Not even the power of the Church could avail to break the chain of servitude.' The latter point illustrates very clearly one aspect in which the society sought to be created or perpetuated by the Theodosian Code, and by similar legislation of the period, differs from caste; that is, in the matter of religious sanction. The society analogous to caste of which the last century of the Western Roman Empire affords an example lacked completely the religious sanction which caste receives from Hinduism. It lacked also the basis in taboo and magic, and other essentials such as the gradual development over a period of centuries or rather millennia. At the same time it affords a definite analogy to the occupational aspect of caste.

A third analogy to caste, also pointed out by Risley, who lays much more stress on this one than on the occupational one, is the racial analogy. He argues[8] that whenever the conquest of one people by another has taken place it has been followed by interbreeding, and by an initial stage of hypergamy; that where the two peoples concerned ' are of the same race, or at any rate of the same colour ', the initial stage of hypergamy passes away

[7] *Roman Society*, bk. III, ch I.   [8] *People of India* (1915), p. 273.

and a stage of complete amalgamation follows. On the other hand, where marked distinctions of race and colour intervene 'the tendency is towards the formation of a class of half-breeds, the result of irregular unions between men of the higher race and women of the lower, who marry only among themselves and are to all intents and purposes a caste'. As instance he mentions the southern States of the U.S.A., 'where negroes intermarry with negroes, and the various mixed races, mulattoes, quadroons and octoroons, each have a sharply restricted *jus connubii* of their own and are absolutely cut off from legal unions with white races'. He goes on to give as further instances the half-breeds of Canada, Mexico, and South America, and the Eurasians of India, and, a better instance, perhaps, the Burghers of Ceylon who are of mixed Dutch and native extraction. By way of a precise Indian parallel he refers to the Khas of Nepal and the Dogras of the Kangra valley, similarly formed by alliances between Rajput or Brahman immigrants and women of the country. He fails to mention the cases of the North American Indians and of the Maoris, which perhaps tell against his argument; but the analogy in any case fails in certain important particulars. It is true that the negro in the southern States has been in many respects kept segregated as a distinct community, prohibited or at least prevented from using the same public amenities as white men. It may be the case that there are different grades of colour each with its own *jus connubii*, and it is certain enough that there is a strong prejudice on the part of the whites against mixed marriages, but the question of taboo and pollution by touch hardly arises.[9] A negro servant to a white man is no strange anomaly, but a Brahman with a Chandal cook is unthinkable, and hardly less so a Rajput with a Dhobi for valet. Conquest and the colour bar may contribute to caste; they may be important factors in the complex; and they help to account for its existence in India; but they are not by themselves the cause of caste, and conditions such as those under which negroes and whites live together in the United States do not form a true parallel to caste in India, and it is doubtful even if any system really analogous to hypergamy has ever existed between whites, octoroons, quadroons, mulattoes and negroes.

[9] But see below, p. 174, n. 4.

What Risley calls ' a singularly complete parallel to the Indian usage of hypergamy' is cited by him [10] quoting van Gennep's *Tabou et Totemisme à Madagascar.* The patrician caste, he says, is divided into six classes endogamous in theory, but in practice allowing a man to marry a woman of a lower class while a woman is ' prohibited by strict taboo' from marrying a man of a lower class. If this is correct of any of the Madagascar tribes, it does not apparently hold good of all of them, as Linton, in his monograph on the Tanala,[11] makes clear that in that tribe, although there are distinct classes of patrician origin, of slaves descended from prisoners of war, and of an intermediate ' commoner' group, and although the patricians disapprove of their women marrying commoners or slaves, there can be no strict taboo on so doing, since such marriages did take place and cases of commoners marrying slaves were comparatively common. In any case these classes seem to be social grades rather than castes, and the prohibition on intermarriage was not one of taboo so much as one of mere social prejudice, while there was no commensal taboo as in India. It is probable that the Madagascar classes therefore can hardly be regarded as castes in the Indian sense, even if the prejudice against social relations between different classes was even greater than similar class prejudices have been and indeed are in most European countries. This view is confirmed by the information given us by Ellis [12] and Piolet.[13] Further, it must be borne in mind that such parallels as Madagascar may have to offer to Indian social structure may themselves be derived from India, since it is quite clear that much of Malagasy culture has an Indonesian origin. Indeed, the account given by the Abbé Rochon of the origin of the Malagasy castes is closely analogous to the traditional origin of the four *varna* in Hindu mythology.[14]

An Indian origin, of course, goes without saying in the case of Ceylon, where caste appears in the ritual of the Buddhist Temple of the Tooth. Hocart insists that royal courts cannot be distinguished from temples, since the king represents the gods, and therefore all the different participants in ritual who are required to shave the king, wash his clothes, etc., are found

[10] *People of India* (1915), p. 180.   [11] *The Tanala,* pp. 137 sq., 143.
[12] *History of Madagascar,* 1, p. 164.   [13] *Madagascar et les Hova,* p. 97.
[14] *Madagascar; or Robert Drury's Journal etc., and a Further description
. . by the Abbé Alexis Rochon* (ed. by Oliver, 1890), p. 368.

at royal courts and at the courts of his vassals and subjects, who imitate his behaviour, down to the mere cultivator of land.[15] This is a point to which allusion is made below in discussing the origins of caste more directly. It is enough here to point out the parallel between the ritual aspect of caste, which requires certain purificatory services from certain sections of the people in Ceylon, in the Buddhist temples, that is, and in India, where, as we have seen, the services of barbers, washermen, etc., are essential for certain ceremonial.

A somewhat similar parallel is to be found in Fiji, where there are chieftains each associated with his own clan and each at the same time an official at the court of the High Chief. Each clan has a specific function to perform in regard to the society of the whole group. The clansmen of the Chief of the Land, for instance, function as a sort of police; those of the Lord of the Village Green preside over public feasts and allot the portions of food; the herald clan may also be the one which dresses the High Chief's head in life, watches over his corpse and buries him when dead; sometimes there is a crier clan which proclaims the Chief's wishes; sometimes even ' chieftains of the dogs ', with clansmen who are the High Chief's dogs, follow him about, and bite the disrespectful. These castes have nothing to do with specialization of crafts, but are graded according to their function. There are what appear to be specialized manual workers forming castes in some tribes, but they appear to be of foreign extraction and are associated with the service of chiefs only. They do not work for pay, are technically superfluous, and are required only for the ritual or quasi-ritual service of the High Chief or of the god of some temple. A great chief may thus have a clan of King's Carpenters who make his official canoes. These sacred canoes are built with a succession of ceremonies unnecessary to the building of ordinary canoes, but requiring the services of builders who know the rites. Similarly, the King's Fishermen undertake the ritual fishing for turtle required for a special feast, and their chief is in charge of the ritual which ensures that turtle and fish shall be plentiful.[16]

Offices and functions of this kind, hereditary in certain families

---

[15] Hocart, *Les Castes*, p. 117. Since the publication of the second edition of *Caste in India*, a detailed account and penetrating analysis of caste in Ceylon has been made by Bruce Ryan in his *Caste and Modern Ceylon*.
[16] Hocart, *Kings and Councillors*, pp. 105 sqq.; *Les Castes*, pp. 140 sqq.

or clans, are or have been of course a fairly familiar feature in many countries. Meek records functional groups of this kind in Africa—the Ba-Nando clan of the Jukun of Nigeria who perform the burial rites of the kings of Wukari,[17] the Ba-tôvî, who are the royal grooms.[18] The hereditary offices held about the royal person in medieval courts in Europe were not very dissimilar, for the office of Royal Butler, Constable of the Royal Household, Master of the Buckhounds, King's Champion and so forth became hereditary in certain families. Obviously this hereditary functionalism does not constitute caste. But we do find cases in Africa in which taboos associated with occupation have operated to prevent not merely intermarriage but any sexual relationship at all between pastoral and cultivating groups.[19]

It is a not infrequent error, too, among Europeans, to suppose that differences of caste are analogous to social differences in Europe. Molony puts the matter in a nutshell when he points out that in England the marriage of the daughter of the house to the cook would be a *mésalliance* on her part, whereas it might very well be in India that in the case of a ruling family of lower caste employing a Brahman cook the discredit of such a union, which 'could scarcely be styled a marriage', would fall on the cook.[20] In any case the essentials of the caste system are as absent from the hereditary functions of the Earl Marshal, or from the families of Butler or Dymoke, as they are from the functional village which affords a somewhat similar analogy to certain aspects of caste. The functional village is not unknown in India. References occur in the Jatakas to functional villages of potters, smiths, wheelwrights, etc., and such communities may be found even surviving today. Thus the Maharaja of Manipur has a village which has the specific duty of providing him with boats,[21] like the King's Carpenters in Fiji. But although the Maharaja and his Meithei compatriots are Hindus, the boat-making village is a Loi village, that is to say, it is a village of one section of his people who have not been received into a Hindu caste. An almost closer parallel to caste is to be found in the medieval practice of segregating tanners on account of their

---

[17] *A Sudanese Kingdom*, pp. 50, 170.   [18] Ibid., pp. 149, 338.
[19] Roscoe, *Immigrants and their Influence in the Lake Region of Central Africa*, p. 34.   [20] *A Book of South India*, p. 107.
[21] Hodson, *The Meitheis*, p. 33.

malodorous occupation. Medieval guilds, too, with their craft secrets and their hereditary nature—for it was much harder for a stranger to enter them than for a son of a member [22]—offer an obvious parallel to the functional caste, even though it is very clearly incomplete. Another incomplete medieval parallel is to be found in the case of some German executioners: the son was compelled to succeed to his father's office, the holder of which was so shunned that he had difficulty in getting priests to give him the sacrament, or a fellow-citizen to let him marry his daughter; the latter difficulty was met by granting him the right to claim as a wife a female sent for execution.

The existence of a caste system in ancient Egypt has been recorded by a number of writers, and it has been suggested that here was to be found the nearest analogy to the caste system of India. Herodotus tells us that there were seven classes or rather ' clans ' (*genea*) of the population in Egypt—priests, fighting men, herdsmen, swineherds, tradesmen, interpreters, navigators.[23] The fighting men were divided into two categories territorially, were not allowed to learn or practise any craft or trade, but must devote themselves entirely to military pursuits from generation to generation, the son succeeding to the father. In regard to the swineherds we are told that the pig was an impure (*miaros*) animal, mere contact with which made it necessary to bathe; the swineherds, although native-born Egyptians, could not enter any temple, and they married among themselves, as no one else would be willing either to give a daughter to one of them in marriage, or to receive a swineherd's daughter as a wife.[24] The priests were also hereditary,[25] and we learn among other things that they bathed themselves in cold water four times every twenty-four hours; shaved themselves completely except when in mourning; drank universally from brass vessels [26] which they scoured daily; and regarded beans as unclean (*ou katharon*) food.[27] When one reads further of the great reverence of the Egyptians for the cow, one inevitably recalls Brahmanism, in spite of the fact that male cattle could

---

[22] Lacroix, *Mœurs etc. au Moyen Age*, p. 313.   [23] Herodotus, II, 164.
[24] Ibid., 47.   [25] Ibid., 37.
[26] Cf. Stevenson, *Rites of the Twice-Born*, p. 240. Brahmans must use brass, or at any rate metal, dishes.
[27] For this taboo on beans *vide* Jevons's edition of *Plutarch's Romane Questions*, pp. lxxxvi sqq.

be sacrificed (as indeed in vedic ritual). The parallel with caste is further emphasized by the statement that no Egyptian man or woman will kiss a Greek on the 'mouth, or use the knife, spit, or cauldron of a Greek or taste the flesh of a clean (*katharos*) ox if cut with a Greek knife.[28] Strabo,[29] it is true, mentions only three classes of Egyptians, but Diodorus records five—priests, soldiers, shepherds,[30] husbandmen, and artificers—and states that these divisions are hereditary and compulsory.[31] Plato (*Timaeus*, 24 A, B) mentions six classes—priests, craftsmen (who are sub-divided—'each keeps to its own craft without infringing on another'), shepherds, hunters, farmers, and soldiers.[32] It all sounds as though a caste system not unlike that of India may have existed in ancient Egypt. Revillout has gone into this question carefully in his *Cours de Droit égyptien*. He instances[33] the cases of a family of architects to the crown, so to speak, who for several hundred years and under all the later dynasties continued to exercise their hereditary calling, and of a family of mummy-wardens in Thebes who followed the same calling from 680 B.C. down to the Roman occupation. But he comes to the definite finding that whatever the nature of these so-called Egyptian 'castes' there is nothing to show that there was any caste system which really resembled that of India, nor anything in the customary laws of Egypt which interfered with social intercourse between these groups or prevented their inter-marriage (no doubt with the possible exception of the case of the pig-keepers), instances of which are known to have taken place.[34] Indeed, in so far as there seem to have been groups analogous to caste in Egypt, they seem to have been rather of the nature of administrative organizations[35] like those of the later Roman Empire, than of quasi-organic development like

[28] Herodotus, II, 41.   [29] XVII, 787.

[30] Shepherds seem also to have been tabooed like the swineherds whom Diodorus does not mention, for when Joseph's family came down into Egypt he told them to tell Pharaoh that they were herdsmen of cattle 'for every shepherd is an abomination unto the Egyptians' (Genesis xlvi, 34).

[31] Book I, ch. VI.   [32] Cornford, *Plato's Cosmology*, p. 17.

[33] p. 136.

[34] 'S'il existait des castes en Egypte, évidemment elles n'étaient pas imitées de celles de l'Inde, et nous trouverions plutôt leurs analogues dans les classes établies, d'après d'anciennes traditions locales par les lois [romains] du Bas-Empire. Or, dans ces lois rien n'interdit les rapports sociaux et même le mariage avec des personnes appartenant à une autre caste.' Revillout, *Cours de Droit égyptien*, p. 135.

[35] Revillout, op. cit., p. 141.

castes in India, a view supported incidentally by Diodorus's statement already quoted. At the same time there is a passage in
the book of Genesis which states that when Joseph's brethren
came down into Egypt and were entertained by him incognito,
food was served separately for Joseph, for his brothers, and ' for
the Egyptians, which did eat with him, by themselves: because
the Egyptians might not eat bread with the Hebrews; for that
is an abomination unto the Egyptians '.[36] This is again distinctly suggestive of caste.

Some other analogies are to be found in modern Africa.[37]
Thus among the Somali of the East Horn there are certain outcaste classes. One of these, as perhaps might be expected since
the craft is so often treated as taboo, is that of the blacksmiths—
Tomal; another is the class known as Yebir, who are credited
with supernatural powers, and feared accordingly, and are able
on the strength of that to levy tribute from Somali families
on occasions of birth and marriage. The third are tanners and
hunters known as Midgan, who are regarded as so unclean that
marriage with them is tabooed, and the Somali who breaks this
taboo is degraded to the class of Tomal. Similarly among the
Masai there is a despised tribe of hunters known as Wandorobo,
and a completely tabooed class of blacksmiths on which Wandorobo as well as Masai look down. Although a Masai proper
may act as a blacksmith without suffering serious loss of status,
the hereditary blacksmiths live apart and a blacksmith may
be killed with impunity by a Masai (but not a Masai by a
blacksmith) and no Masai would stop at a blacksmith's encamp-
ment, nor marry a blacksmith's daughter; his products are
impure and must be purified with grease before use, and even
the very name of ' blacksmith ' must not be uttered at night lest
lions attack the camp.

In the Ruanda and Urundi regions adjoining Lake Kivu and
the eastern Congo a somewhat similar condition has been
observed even more suggestive of caste. Three racially and economically distinct groups occupy co-extensive areas—the pastoral
Tussi (or Tutsi), the Hutu, who are cultivators, and the Twa,
a hybrid pygmy tribe, who are hunters. With the latter neither
Hutu nor Tussi will intermarry or contract a blood brotherhood,
though a Tussi is not absolutely barred from such relations with

---

[36] Book of Genesis, xliii, 32.   [37] See Lowie, *Origin of the State*, ch. II.

a Hutu. The Twa themselves, though despising the agricultural Hutu (and likewise that section of their fellow tribesmen which has given up hunting for the settled life of professional potters), acknowledge the superiority of certain Hutu chiefs and pay tribute to the Tussi king through them. The Tussi look down on the Hutu for eating mutton and goat-flesh, and both Tussi and Hutu despise the Twa for eating poultry and eggs. The Twa act as executioners and as the police force, carry the king in his travels, and chant in royal processions, thus recalling the Doms of India who are commonly minstrels as well as executioners, in spite of being general scavengers of the lowest social scale, and who are also nearly allied to a number of hunting or trapping castes. These instances, however, though analogous to caste in some directions do not constitute a caste system, and in Ruanda there is a secret religious society into which all three classes mentioned are admitted.[38] At the same time they may be of much significance in regard to the origin of caste in India.

On the other side of Africa an analogy to caste is afforded by the *osu* in Ibo society. The *osu* are the descendants of free-born ancestors who were bought by a family or by an individual at the instance of a diviner and offered as slaves to some deity who could not be satisfied by any smaller offering such as that of a fowl or a goat. *Osu* became a class apart and sexual relations of any sort between them and the free Ibo are tabooed. There are other restrictions on their intercourse with the free Ibo; their houses are segregated; and to call anyone an *osu* is a gross insult. The free Ibo regard the *osu* with repugnance, and the explanation given is that they would in the old days have been in fact sacrificed to the deity to whom they are now offered as slaves, and are therefore ritually dead.[39] One is reminded not only of the pagoda slaves in Burma, a very close parallel mentioned later in this chapter,[40] but also of the outcastes rejected by the Ganges.[41]

To return to Asia, an analogy to caste, which is perhaps the most significant of any of them, is to be seen in that country which marches most closely with India, that is, in Burma. And this analogy is important, for no one who knows both India and Burma would for an instant go so far as to hold that the

---

[38] Lowie, loc. cit., p. 32.   [39] Green, *Ibo Village Affairs*, pp. 23, 24, 50.
[40] *Vide infra*, pp. 144 sqq.   [41] *Vide supra*, pp. 109-10.

caste system of India obtained there at all. Yet the Burmese analogue is possibly as near to the essence of caste as any parallel elsewhere, and it does, perhaps, throw an important light on one of the origins, perhaps the most important and primary origin, of that unique institution. It may be noted in this connexion that Burma was on the whole even less affected than India by external contacts and likely therefore to conserve customs and beliefs in a more primitive form than India. Further, while Burma received Buddhism from India when it was there predominant, this Buddhism remained as a permanent part of its culture and there was no development of Brahmanism as in India.

In Burma under the old rule of the Burmese monarchy, seven distinct classes of outcaste were recognized. The most important of these was probably that of Pagoda Slaves. It is regarded as very meritorious in Burma to build or repair a pagoda or even to gild or regild a few square feet of its roof. But no such merit attaches to the service performed by the slaves who keep the pagoda in order. A pagoda slave is such for life, and his children and descendants are pagoda slaves *in perpetuum*: they cannot be liberated even by a king. If a person who is not a pagoda slave marry or be married to a pagoda slave, even unwittingly, such a person and all her or his children, even by a former marriage, also become automatically pagoda slaves in perpetuity. Pagoda slaves cannot be employed in any other capacity than that of pagoda servant. It will be observed that in the last two respects the disabilities suffered are even more severe than those of outcastes in India, though the element of untouchability is not stressed in at all the same degree. The pagoda slaves were largely drawn from prisoners of war, and from prisoners convicted of some offence, but also from quite inoffensive Burmese villagers, who had been nominated for the service by some royal official and were too poor to buy themselves off. The other six outcaste classes consisted of, secondly, Professional Beggars, that is, of vagabonds compelled to live such a life and prohibited from any regular occupation, drawn in the main from the same sources as the first class and to be distinguished from free beggars, who beg by choice and not by compulsion; thirdly, Executioners, Jailors and Police, three functions normally combined, under the rule of the Burmese kings, in the same persons, who though feared, no doubt, when alive, and treated accordingly with circumspection, were treated as offal when dead; fourthly, Lepers, and others suffering from incurable diseases, who were compelled to live with other outcastes outside the ordinary village community; fifthly, Deformed and Mutilated Persons, the horror of the maimed in Burma being very strong, so that death is commonly preferred to the amputation of a limb. The sixth class of outcastes consists of Coffin-makers and other persons occupied with grave-digging, graveyards and the disposal of corpses; the Burmese word for such people is *sandala*, which is clearly the same word as the Hindi *chandal*. The seventh class consisted of Government Slaves, who were cultivators of the royal lands and drawn from the same sources as pagoda slaves.

Persons of these outcaste classes in Burma cannot enter a monastery nor become a *hpungyi* (Buddhist monk). Indeed, they may not enter a monastery even to study, though such an entry forms a normal part of the upbringing of a Burmese child. The effect of marrying persons of these classes has already been stated as regards the pagoda slaves, and is the same in the case of the second class and of the last two classes. How far it would affect the other three classes it is a little difficult to say, as the third class at any rate presumably disappeared as such with the British occupation. Up to that time at least these seven classes constituted an outcaste population distinct from the people with whom social relations were possible.[42] They did not constitute castes, so that there were, so to speak, only incaste and outcaste in Burma, and no 'caste system', but the analogy to one aspect of the caste system in any case is clear enough. The untouchability in Burma is obviously based on taboo. This element can be seen to be present in most if not all of the seven groups above mentioned. In the case of the grave-diggers it is probably the fear of death infection, a fear which is associated with the disposal of the dead among so many of the neighbouring hill tribes. A similar taboo probably operates in regard to lepers and deformed persons, for among the Chin and Kuki tribes on the western frontier of Burma, tribes nearly allied to the Burmese in language and probably of the same racial stock, persons dying

[42] Shway Yoe [Sir J. G. Scott], *The Burman; His Life and Notions*, ii, ch. xvi.

of leprosy or from any similar deforming disease are buried with a different orientation from other persons and regarded as having died a ' bad death ', which apparently makes it impossible, or at least undesirable, that they should rejoin their families in the future life.[43] In the case of the Thado Kuki, to have the lobe of the ear split is enough to prevent a woman so mutilated from joining her kindred in the after life. The taboo on executioners is no doubt associated with the Buddhist prohibition on the taking of life as well as on dislike and contempt for persons following such a calling, while that on pagoda slaves might naturally follow from the fact that they are persons set aside as belonging entirely to the deity. It is typical of taboo that the emotions it evokes are ambivalent, and there is no clear line of distinction between the sacred and the accursed. What is holy may be either, but it is certain that it is dangerous. The contagion by which their state infects any who might associate with them with the same disability is also typical of primitive doctrines of taboo. The untouchable condition of pagoda slaves presumably springs from the fact that they are dedicated throughout eternity to the pagoda or to the deity and have no separate life of their own, being as it were part of the deity or of his shrine. A similar untouchability might extend by analogy to vagabonds and to the cultivators of royal lands, who were drawn like the pagoda slaves mainly from prisoners of war and from convicted criminals. In theory all the misfortunes suffered by these classes are the result of the working of *karma*;[44] the unfortunates who composed them are (or were) in a sense subhuman, they form a link between man and the animals, housing souls suffering in the highest grade of punishment for faults in former lives. Even such taxes as were levied on them constituted vile and contaminated funds, which were used to provide food and accommodation for European foreigners as a subtle insult to the unconscious recipients. This doctrine of taboo on which, it is urged, untouchability in Burma is based, probably precedes in that country the influence of Buddhist culture and is rather a survival, like the cults of the *nats*, from a pre-Buddhistic era, from a period of more primitive beliefs which India no doubt shared before it

[43] See Parry, *The Lakhers*, pp. 406-8 and 413, and Shaw, *Notes on the Thadou Kukis*, p. 56, n. 1.   [44] *Vide supra*, pp. 121 sq.

became Hindu at all. There seems to be common ground here for an origin of caste which, while developing in India into an organic structure of society, has in Burma become stabilized in an undeveloped form or even degenerated so as to affect only a limited part of society, and leaving the main body of the people untouched. For the Burmese as a whole are as free from the working of the caste system as the other peoples among whom analogous institutions have been pointed out.

Analogous to the *sandala* of Burma are the *eta* of Japan. Although no doubt primitive taboos have contributed to their status of untouchability, it is perhaps in this case to be associated primarily with the introduction of Buddhism, and its prohibition on the taking of life, together with influences derived directly from the caste system of India. The *eta* form a community of outcastes, said to be about a million in number, who live on the fringe of Japanese society. So strong is the prejudice against them that the very word *eta*, if it must be uttered, is only whispered. The name seems to have appeared first about A.D. 700 and to be associated with the introduction of Buddhism. Outcaste professions included executioners, butchers, leather-workers, saddlers, cobblers, actors, jugglers, grave-diggers, mid-wives, umbrella- and lantern-makers, ' because they handled oiled paper ', and, as in India in Buddhist times, when they were despised occupations, basket-makers and potters. They were considered subhuman; numbered with the termination *-biki* used for quadrupeds; lived in separate quarters in the village; had to wear distinctive dress; could only marry among themselves; had no social intercourse with other classes, and could only go abroad between sunset and sunrise. ' In the small fishing village of Mihoroseki . . . nothing distinguished the *eta* houses in appearance or marked the boundary of the outcast community. Yet the children on either side never crossed an imaginary line which marked the frontier of untouchability halfway up the street.' [45] In 1871 the then Japanese Government abolished all feudal discrimination, but the effect on the *eta* was in some ways to enhance their depression, for they lost their caste autonomy and such privileges as they had, and in particular the monopoly of their special occupations. In cities

[45] The Tokyo correspondent of *The Times* writing in that paper on 9 September 1958.

and towns it is no doubt possible for a stranger of *eta* origin to conceal it, but, where it is known, he is discriminated against at school, in employment, in trade, and in marriage; *eta* tenant farmers failed to obtain the benefit due to them under the post-war land reforms, and the gulf between them and the ordinary population has yet to be bridged. Their position is not without analogies to that of the exterior castes of Hinduism, but probably both here and in Burma what there is of caste is closer to the Ceylon than to the Indian pattern. This is what might naturally be expected, for Japan was once no less Buddhist than Burma and Ceylon.

Indeed it is possible that light on the origin of the caste system is really to be sought for in societies such as those of Burma, Ceylon, and Japan, where traces of the Buddhistic régime have survived unHinduized. Buddhism and Jainism have much in common, and Professor Tucci has argued that the Jain religion embodies a revival of very ancient rituals and forms 'probably even pre-Aryan'. The Buddhist movement of the sixth century B.C. was a revolt against Brahmanism and probably in part at any rate an attempt to revert to an earlier order. If that be so, it might well be that Buddhist societies incorporated, and have retained, some form of caste earlier in pattern than its systemization by Hindu priests and law-givers. One recalls the fact that the first historical *Tīrthănkăra*, Mahā-vīra, is regarded by Jains as the twenty-third in succession, and that Parswa, who preceded him, is described as the son of a King Aswasena, of Benares, though no Aswasena is known to Brahmanical literature except a king of the 'Nāgas'. We should perhaps therefore be justified on these grounds alone in seeking the ultimate origins of the caste system in pre-Rigvedic India.

Many other analogues no doubt exist in various parts of the world. Those that have been mentioned in this chapter merely afford a few instances of phenomena elsewhere that bear some resemblance to caste. It is on the face of it unlikely that a combination of many of them would occur more than once, and it is not therefore surprising that we find a caste system in India alone.

CHAPTER X

THE TRADITIONAL ORIGIN AND ITS IMPLICATIONS

ACCORDING to Hindu tradition the caste system owes its origin to the four *varna*,[1] which are respectively derived from the Brahman who sprang from the mouth of the deity, the Kshatriya who was created from his arms, the Vaishya who was formed from his thighs, and the Sudra who was born from his feet.[2] To the Brahmans were assigned divinity and the six duties of studying, teaching, sacrificing, assisting others to sacrifice, giving alms and receiving gifts to the end that the vedas might be protected; to the Kshatriya were assigned strength and the duties of studying, sacrificing, giving alms, using weapons, protecting treasure and life, to the end that good government should be assured; to the Vaishya were allotted the power of work and the duties of studying, sacrificing, giving alms, cultivating, trading and tending cattle, to the end that labour should be productive; and to the Sudra was given the duty of serving the three higher *varna*.[3] From mixed unions between the different *varna*, or between the *varna* and the offspring of mixed unions and so forth,[4] come the various castes of which 2378 were actually counted at the Indian census of 1901, some numbering millions, others only a very few individuals. To say that there are some 3000 different castes in India is probably to run little risk of exaggeration. The general nature of hypergamy and the meaning of the terms *anuloma* and *pratiloma* have already been explained.[5] Marriages between members of different *varna* are postulated in this traditional account, and these marriages were either *anuloma* or *pratiloma*. Such unions, and the subsequent ones between the mixed offspring of such unions, are held to account for the various castes, and the Code of Manu and the treatises of Vasistha, Baudhyana, Gautama and others give us lists of the castes so formed. Wilson[6] has worked out a list of 134 castes, including the four *varna*, in order of precedence

[1] *Vide supra*, pp. 64 sqq.
[2] Bühler, *Laws of Manu* (I, 31, 87), pp. 14, 24 ; *Sacred Laws*, pt. II, p. 25 (Vasistha IV, 2), etc., and *vide* Wilson, *Indian Caste*, I, p. 17.
[3] Bühler, *Sacred Laws*, pt. II, p. 199 ; Jolly, *Institutes of Vishnu*, p. 12.
[4] Manu, x, 6 sqq. (Bühler, *Laws of Manu*, pp. 403 sqq.).
[5] *Vide supra*, p. 55.   [6] *Indian Caste*, I, pp. 65 sqq.

as mentioned in the ancient law books. In general principle the *pratiloma* castes rank below the *anuloma*, and at the bottom of the scale are the Chandala, begotten of a Sudra male on a Brahman female, and other mixed castes of Chandal parentage. The lists given by the lawgivers of the origins and functions of the various mixed castes do not always agree among themselves and suggest very strongly a formalist interpretation of a state of society the origins of which were already obscure when these treatises were composed. Senart [7] has made out a very strong case for the view that the Code of Manu is an interpretation in terms of *varna*, that is, in terms of an Indo-European social system analogous to that of ancient Rome, of an existing social order which the terms could not, at any rate at the time of application, be made to fit satisfactorily. In any case one of the questions raised by Manu's scheme of precedence is the reason why a caste of mixed origins should, if *pratiloma*, be so much less respectable than an *anuloma* caste of inferior derivation. The offspring of a Sudra man and a Sudra woman might, on the face of it, be expected to rank lower than that of a Sudra man and a Brahman woman. If we fall back on the principle of hypergamy as an explanation, we are really no better off, as some explanation is equally required for the excessive application of such a principle, if not for its actual existence. It is possible that the explanation is to be found in the results of the impact of patrilineal invaders on an indigenous matrilineal population. In such a case a condition of society would arise in which the offspring of a woman of the patrilineal immigrants by a man of the indigenous matrilineal peoples held an anomalous and ambiguous position. In the case of a patrilineal father and a matrilineal mother the child would have status and kinship with both his father's and his mother's families and would inherit from both, or, whether the marriage were patrilocal or matrilocal, at least from one of them. But the issue of an immigrant patrilineal woman by an indigenous matrilineal male would have no place with either. He could claim no kinship through his mother with her exogamous patrilineal clan, nor through his father with his exogamous matrilineal family. With no claims on kinship or inheritance his status would inevitably tend to be degraded, and the exact causes of this would

[7] *Les Castes dans l'Inde,* ch. II.

very soon be forgotten when both societies adopted the patrilineal system, but would call for expression in definite formulae at whatever date an attempt was made to record in the form of a code the state of society as seen by the early lawgiver. There are one or two passages in the Sutras which distinctly suggest such an interpretation. Thus Gautama (IV, 25, 26) tells us that ' those born in the inverse order (from fathers of a lower and mothers of a higher caste) stand outside (the pale of) the sacred law ',[8] as well as those born in a regular order (*anuloma*) from a Sudra woman, and the Institutes of Vishnu (XV, 37, 38) tell us that children begotten by a husband of inferior caste on a woman of a higher caste have no right to inherit, and ' their sons do not even receive a share of the wealth of their paternal grandfathers '.[9] In passing, it is perhaps significant that the Suta, who is the *pratiloma* offspring of a Brahman woman by a Kshatriya man, takes a fairly high place in Manu's list, far removed from the degraded position of a Chandal who is by a Sudra out of a Brahmani. This would reflect, perhaps, the fact that as between *varna* which were both patrilineal the question of complete lack of status and inheritance would not arise, and there seem to have been Brahman families both of invading and of indigenous stock. It must also be pointed out here that statements as to what constitutes a Chandal are not always consistent, for there appear to have been Chandals by works as well as by birth.

Besides the suggestion made above there are a number of other survivals which suggest that a matrilineal system was once much more widely distributed in India than it is now. Sir Denis Bray's account of the Brahui shows that the traces of a former matrilineal system are clear enough, and the story recorded by Lieut. Carloss of his visit to the cave dwellings of Gondrani in 1838 (*J.A.S.B.*, March 1839), when he was shown the palace of Badi-ul-Jamal,[10] the princess married by the stranger, ' a son of the King of Egypt ', who became king of the matrilineal and matrilocal kingdom, is exceedingly suggestive of Mediterranean affinities, while the Shrine of Bibi Nāni near Hinglaj, also in Las Bela, is a place of pilgrimage ' celebrated from the Euphrates to the Ganges ' and the resort alike of Muslim and Hindu pilgrims.[11] Sir Thomas Holdich says of it, ' the object of their

---

[8] Bühler, *Sacred Laws*, pt. I, p. 197.
[9] Jolly, op. cit., pp. 64, 65.
[10] Minchin, *Las Béla Gazetteer*, p. 40.
[11] Ibid., pp. 35 sq.

veneration is probably the same goddess who was known to the
Chaldeans under the same old-world name (Nana) a thousand
years before the time of Abraham. Nothing testifies so strongly
to the unchangeable nature of the geographical link formed by
Makrán between East and West than (sic) does this remarkable
ziarat hidden away in the deep folds of the Malán mountains.' [12]
Some of the features of south Indian culture suggest not merely
Asia Minor (e.g. the fire-walking ceremonies such as are common
in southern India and formed a feature of the worship of
Artemis in Cappadocia), but Crete. Here there was a cult of
snakes,[13] which, indeed, were vehicles of the soul throughout
Greece, and worship of the mother goddess; here again the
vogue of slender waists for males is very suggestive of medieval
Indian sculpture. The popular sport among the Kallan and
Maravan [14] of jumping on to enraged bulls with sharpened horns
to pluck off a cloth put there for the purpose and prove themselves men in the eyes of their womenfolk is also most remi-
niscent not only of the bull-baiting of Provence, where a rosette
must be snatched from the points of the horns of an infuriated
bull, but likewise of the bull-jumping scenes on Cretan vases,
though in southern India the practice does not extend to
somersaults nor to the fairer sex. Terracotta figurines of the
mother goddess have been excavated in Crete not dissimilar, it
seems, to those from Mohenjodaro, and to others excavated in
1926-7 at Buxar in Bihar from a site 52 feet below the present
surface and 13 feet below the Maurya stratum,[15] which rather

[12] Holdich, India, p. 45. Nana or Nanai was the mother of Attis and
identified with Ishtar, Astarte, Artemis, Anaïtis, or Aphrodite. Alone of
her pilgrims devotees and unmarried girls pay no tax to the State. Naina
Devi of the Kulu valley, where her image is a black stone 3 feet high, and
of places in Sirmur and Bilaspur States, and probably elsewhere in the
lower Himalayas, is likely to be the same goddess.
[13] The cult of snakes is also strong in the lower Himalayas and is found
there in the significant company of Naina Devi, megalithic monuments, and
marriage customs not unsuggestive of Babylon, and of fertility rites which
are spoken of by Rose in Punjab Castes and Tribes as ' Paphian ' but
which are not described. Devi in the hills is often spoken of as Devi Mai
or Devi Mata—the Mother Goddess.
[14] In the case of the Kallan it is to be noticed that they include a boome-
rang among their wedding gifts, practise circumcision, and bury their dead
and perform their Karuppan worship with the face to the north, probably
indicating migration into India by land. The rite of circumcision is paid
for by the boy's father's sister, mother of his potential wife.
[15] Banerji-Sastri, ' Mother-Goddess cult in Magadha ' in The Searchlight
(anniversary number, 1929).

suggest the extension of the Indus valley culture to the Ganges valley. The cult of the bull is common to the early cultures of Crete, of Egypt, of the Near East, of the Indus valley and of Hindu India, and it may here be pointed out that Przyluski [16] suggests a non-Indo-European origin for the name of the god Vishnu and a Dravidian origin for the god himself.

The culture of the early civilization of northern India may perhaps be most conveniently described as pre-Rigvedic Hinduism. Even if this culture disappeared entirely from the Indus valley, it may well have survived across the Jumna with sufficient vigour to react to the Rigvedic Aryans whose religious beliefs it ultimately submerged in its own philosophy. Slater [17] has aptly pointed out that Krishna himself was of Naga descent, and the traditional blue colour in which Hindu art depicts him possibly represents the brunette colouring of the indigenes as distinguished on the one hand from the blond Aryans and on the other from the dusky aboriginals. Slater again points out that Sakra, the chief priest of the Asuras, is stated by the Mahabharata to have become ' the spiritual guide of both the Daityas and the Devas ', thus recording the success of the pre-Rigvedic priestly class in imposing their spiritual authority on the Aryans also, and this same Sakra, or another one, according to the Vishnu Purana, said *mantras* for the success of the Asuras and restored to life the Danavas slain by Indra. His father was the *rishi* Bhrigu whose sons were Brahmans and priests of the Daityas. Clearly there were Brahmans before the Rigvedic Aryans, and we must look for the origin of that caste partly no doubt in the priests of the presumably Dravidian-speaking civilization who may well have shared the mathematical and astronomical knowledge of contemporary Babylonia.

It seems generally to happen that people with a matrilineal system substitute a patrilineal one where the two systems come into contact, and it is likely that the change from a matrilineal to a patrilineal system started to take place in upper India as a result of immigration, while it is not unlikely that the same process tended to substitute the worship of male for female deities. The practice of Hinduizing the female village deities of southern India by providing them with orthodox male

[16] *Archiv Orientální*, IV, 2 August 1932, *vide Indian Antiquary*, January 1933.　　　　[17] *Dravidian Element in Indian Culture*, pp. 55 sqq.

husbands from the official Hindu pantheon is still perhaps going
on. In Madura the fish-eyed goddess Minakshi is annually so
married with great pomp and *éclat*, but in the villages the
goddess is still the real deity, and protectress of the people, rather
than the recognized Hindu gods.   So also in Bengal the *Dharma-
puja-paddhati* records that Adyā the mother of the gods was
married to Shiva with ' traditional ceremonies not enjoined in
the Shastras but somehow or other accepted as inviolable by
them and known as stri-āchāra (lit. female custom)' performed
by women before the Brahmans officiated,[18] and the same author
maintains elsewhere that goddesses have been accorded (in folk-
custom presumably) a higher position than the gods.   According
to the Mahabharata a matrilineal system survived in medieval
India in the kingdom of Mahishmati about the Narbadā river,
where the women had liberty to choose a plurality of husbands,
and among the Arattas, somewhere apparently in the Punjab,
' whose heirs are their sisters' children, not their own '.   With
the exception of the Nambudris, who follow the Rigveda,
Brahmans in southern India, many of whom at any rate follow
the Samaveda, Yajurveda or Atharvaveda, are accustomed to
marry the daughter of their mother's brother.   This is opposed
to the letter and spirit of the Brahmanic code and is clearly
suggestive of a survival of a matrilineal system; orthodoxy would
appear to enjoin the patrilineal prohibition of such marriages.
The Pandyan dynasty seems to have been originally matrilineal,
as Tamil poems are said to allude to its founder as a woman,
and the tradition recorded by Megasthenes [19] is that it was
founded by a daughter of Heracles, while Pliny describes the
people as ' *gens Pandae, sola Indorum regnata foeminis* '.[20] The
worship of goddesses in whose honour annual fairs are held is
more important in the Himalayas of the Punjab and United
Provinces than that of the orthodox gods, and such goddesses,
though now regarded as incarnations of Devi, are frequently
associated with the worship of snakes, while it seems likely that
the Nanagotri Brahmans of Tehri-Garhwal represent families
which originally traced their descent through the female line
(*nana* = mother's brother).

[18] Sarkar, *Folk Element in Hindu Culture*, p. 231.
[19] McCrindle, *Ancient India as described by Megasthenes and Arrian*,
pp. 37, 206, and Pintian's note on Pliny, VII, ii, in the edition of 1669,
vol. I, pp. 402, 403.   [20] *Nat. Hist.*, VI, xx.

This pre-Rigvedic culture seems to have still been vigorous enough east of the river Jumna to react to the stimulus of the Rigvedic Aryans, when these invaders, near cousins probably of the Kassites who about the same time overthrew the rulers of Babylon and established themselves as lords of Mitanni, occupied the Punjab about the middle of the second millennium B.C. Their previous traditions as gleaned from the Avesta are conveniently summarized by Peake and Fleure.[21] Driven from their northern home on account of its becoming ice-bound and uninhabitable they moved south to Sughda (Sogdiana) and Mura (Merv, Bokhara). Locusts and hostile tribes drove them to Bakhdi (Balkh) whence they moved to Nisaya. There they divided, one part going to Haroyu (Herat) and the other probably to Kabul and thence to the Punjab at a date not later than 1400 B.C. and probably a century or so earlier. Their occupation of the country between the Indus and the Jumna, where the Rigveda seems to have been composed, but not written, must have taken the form of migratory movement and was probably effected without much difficulty. The description of their enemies as ' noseless ' suggests conflict with tribes of proto-Australoid affinities, and there seems every probability that tribes such as the Bhils and the Chodhras would have continued to occupy hill and forest areas in spite of previous migrations into northern India from the west and north. If the pre-Rigvedic civilization in the Indus valley had really declined, this may have enabled such tribes to reoccupy parts of the open country. The mention, however, e.g. in the 104th hymn of the first book of the Rigveda, of the cities, castles and great wealth of an enemy whose womenfolk bathed themselves in milk suggests that the ancient civilization was far from being extinct, and it is not impossible but that many aborigines were employed as servants and as auxiliary troops or as allies against the invader, a practice which was common enough in medieval India. Alternatively, the description of the Dasyus as ' noseless ' may itself have been a tradition taken over from previous invaders and ' telescoped ' in the matter of time and association. The development of a written literature clearly took place at the second stage of their invasion, described by Rapson [22] as a colonizing

[21] *Merchant Venturers in Bronze*, p. 130.
[22] *Cambridge History of India*, I, p. 47.

stage in contrast to that of mass migration. It is just at such a stage that amalgamation with the pre-existing inhabitants is most likely, and the influence of the latter can clearly be traced in the change in vedic religion which appears even in the tenth book of the Rigveda, and in the Yajurveda, as well as in the Atharvaveda, for this last consists, principally at any rate, of magic, while the pantheistic philosophy later developed in the Upanishads is already apparent in the tenth book of the Rigveda. Pargiter [23] points out that though the name of the compiler of the Rigveda was well known to the later epic and puranic tradition, the very mention of Vyasa is ignored or suppressed in vedic literature. It is possible to infer from this that the immediate post-Rigvedic Brahmans may have been the inheritors of the pre-Rigvedic tradition which was adverse to the Rigveda and supported the indigenous deities by preference. It is possible that the contest between Vasistha and Viswamitra, as a result of which the Kshatriya became a Brahman, may symbolize the amalgamation of the two cultures, and Viswamitra's formal renunciation of Kshatriya ways the final ascendancy of the pre-Aryan religion. In any case it is highly probable that the post-Rigvedic literature, in which the tenth book of the Rigveda must be included, would contain importations from pre-Rigvedic indigenous tradition, while the cerebral dental consonants apparently acquired by the Indo-Aryan from the indigenous languages [24] ' play an increasingly important part in the development of Indo-Aryan in its subsequent phases' just as the use of rice and the areca nut, equally of pre-Aryan origin, has affected the subsequent developments on the cultural side. The development of the art of writing may have gone on simultaneously and have been, as suggested by Macdonell,[25] no doubt first used for purely secular purposes and not at first regarded as proper for application to religious hymns and formulae. This would fit in with a derivation from the signs on the Mohenjodaro seals which seem to have been primarily used for commerce, as cotton fabric bearing a seal impressed with an Indus valley stamp has been recovered from a prehistoric site

[23] *Ancient Indian Historical Tradition*, p. 9.
[24] Rapson, *Cambridge History of India*, I, p. 49.
[25] *India's Past*, pp. 50 sqq.

in Iraq.[26] It seems unlikely in the extreme that the language, religion and culture of the invaders could have been influenced by the pre-existing civilization without an admixture of race taking place, and the fact that later tradition and literature definitely describe some of the *rishis* and their descendants as non-Aryan indicates that this admixture extended to the priesthood,[27] as it probably did to all other classes. Thus the legends of the origin of the Baidyas of Bengal, a caste not only of acknowledged respectability and the repository of traditional medical knowledge, but also one which provided a ruling dynasty in the eleventh century A.D., have been justly interpreted as indicating a matrilineal origin,[28] while another version definitely describes their descent as *pratiloma* in spite of its being ascribed to the Twin Brethren of vedic mythology. It is tempting to see in the two strains the origin of the two great Rajput houses of the Sun and of the Moon, the latter typical of Mesopotamian cults while the former is more suggestive of the Rigveda.[29] The Agnikula branch was probably added at a later date to include the conquering families of Hun or Saka origin. On the other hand, the Brahman in the Rigveda seems to have been second in social importance to the Rajanya, and it seems not impossible that traditions of the conflict between the Brahmans and the Kshatriyas and the extermination of the latter by Parasurama represent a revolt led by a priestly class of mixed origin, which would naturally have the support of the people in general, against the Rigvedic aristocracy.

A further reflection of this amalgamation of two cultures, one patrilineal, the other matrilineal, is possibly to be seen in the employment by Hindus of the daughter's or sister's son or husband in certain rites as an alternative to the employment of

[26] Sayce, *Antiquity*, June 1927, p. 205 n., and see also Marshall, *Mohenjo-daro and the Indus Civilization*, vol. II, pp. 380, 425 sq. Both quote Scheil, *Revue d'Assyriologie*, xxii (1925).

[27] Some of the *rishis* actually appear to have had a sort of totemistic origin ascribed to them: ' Achela Muni was born of an elephant, and Kesha Pingala of an owl, and Agastya Muni from the *agasti* flower, and Kausika Muni from the *kusha* grass, and Kapila from a monkey, etc.' (quoted by Wilson, *Indian Caste*, I, p. 297, from the *Vajra Shuchi*, a Buddhist *sutra*). [28] See Risley, *Ethnographic Appendices*, p. 185.

[29] Ehrenfels [*Mother-Right in India*, chh. B 3 (5), 7 (1), and 9 (2) 3] has ingeniously argued a continuity of culture between the moon-descended Rajputs, the Nayars, and the matrilineal peoples of the Indus civilization.

a Brahman.[30] It is hardly necessary to point out that such circumstances, under which patrilineal invaders took wives from matrilineal indigenes, would also operate very strongly towards the erection of a purdah system. The woman under the matrilineal system has a freedom not dissimilar to that of the man under the patrilineal. The woman taken from a matrilineal society and having ties of language, kinship, acquaintance and custom with that society, but expected to live according to strange and probably repugnant domestic and marital rules, could only be effectively restrained to that end by cutting off her freedom of movement in and association with the society to which she belonged. It may appear at first sight that the case of a Nambudri Brahman cohabiting with a Nayar wife is a contrary instance, since she does not observe purdah at all, but the fact that in this case the children follow the matrilineal system supports the argument that purdah was necessary to the combination of a patrilineal system with the practice of taking wives from a matrilineal society. In the case of the younger son of a Nambudri Brahman his Nayar wife continues to live, and brings up her children, in her own house, in which her husband is only a visitor. She rarely if ever visits his home, and even then is much restricted in the parts of the building to which she can penetrate. Only sometimes in royal households has the Nambudri husband quarters of his own. That purdah should exist so strongly in the case of the Nambudri wives of the elder sons may be explained by the necessity for maintaining a barrier against the encroachment of a matrilineal environment and by the possibility if not probability that the Nambudri already practised purdah when they first arrived in Malabar. That the purdah system was alien to the Rigvedic Aryans when they invaded India the Rigveda itself is a witness, while there is nothing whatever to associate it with the Dravidian-speaking stock, which seems to have followed the matrilineal system in which purdah has no natural place at all. It is perhaps significant in this connexion that purdah is generally weaker in the south of India than in the north, and in Madras at any rate gets weaker from north to south, where, conversely, caste gets stronger. It is conceivable that the same

---

[30] Rose, *Punjab Tribes and Castes,* I, p. 392 ; Turner, *Census of the U.P.,* p. 561. Some Brahmans also recognize the sister's son as the family priest. Wise, op. cit., p. 127.

circumstances gave rise to the practice of the pre-puberty
marriage of girls as to that of purdah, and infant marriage again
is least prevalent in the extreme south.

Various views have been held as to the origin of the custom of
child marriage. It seems never to have extended to the Malabar
coast and is not nearly so prevalent in the extreme south, along
the east coast, or in the north-west as in the west, in Bengal and
in the Deccan. Clearly it is very ancient, and the suggestion that
attributes it to the Muslim invasions is not even momentarily
entertainable. Megasthenes presumably refers to the practice
when he records that the girls of the Pandaian kingdom bear
children at the age of seven, adding that they are old at 40.[31]
Risley regards the custom as due primarily to hypergamy which,
by limiting the choice of bridegrooms, impels parents to marry
off their girls at the earliest age possible. Whether hypergamy
has or has not contributed to the establishment of the custom,
it might equally well have been due, as it almost certainly is
in one tribe in Assam, the Lhota Nagas, to a paucity of women
and the necessity of making sure of a wife before someone else
snapped her up, and not to a paucity of bridegrooms in a country
where males exceed females. Gait regards infant marriage as
the result of the impact of 'Aryan' and 'Dravidian' and a device
to guard against pre-marital communism, and this again has
possibly been a contributing factor. More weight, however, than
was given by him seems due to the late Sir J. Campbell's opinion
quoted on p. 271 of his (Gait's) 1911 *Census Report*. Campbell's
opinion was that early marriage was due to a belief in the danger
of dying with unfulfilled wishes combined with the great wish of
a Hindu to marry and have children. As stated this is probably
the wrong way round. The wish to marry and have children
is the cause of the fear of dying unmarried. The penalty for
failure to marry is extinction in a future existence. This belief

[31] McCrindle, *Ancient India as described by Megasthenes and Arrian*,
Frag. LI (p. 115); Pliny, *Nat. Hist.*, VII, ii. What is presumably the earliest
recorded age of pregnancy anywhere is one at 6 years which was observed at
the Victoria Zenana Hospital in Delhi in June 1932, when a girl who
had only been born on 8 October, 1925, gave birth to a child. The case
was investigated and established by Dr Kean, the woman physician in
charge of the case. Since first printing this note, however, a case has been
reported from Lima, Peru, of a girl's having given birth at the age of
five years and eight months. At the time of the report's appearing in an
English newspaper both mother, aged 16, and child aged 10, were said to
be attending the same school (*Cambridge Daily News*, 16 May 1949).

appears in the tradition of primitive tribes from Assam to Fiji, of which it has been said that ' no unwedded spirit has ever yet reached the Elysium of Fiji '.[32] Duarte Barbosa records of the Nayars that ' the woman who dies a virgin does not go to paradise ', and this idea is still so lively in some parts and castes of India that the corpse of a person dying unmarried is married before cremation.[33] In China this feeling is so strong that the very souls of the unmarried dead are married and given in marriage *post mortem*, and that the idea is not absent in Europe may be inferred from the belief once current in England that maids who died unwed ' lead apes in hell '. It would be rash to say that a superstition of this kind was the cause of early marriage, but it seems more than probable that the underlying idea which imputes blame to failure to marry and propagate is the same as that which enjoins fertilization at the earliest opportunity.

On the Malabar coast, owing to the prevalence of the *marumakkathayam* system,[34] the position of women generally has been better than in any other part of civilized India. The Nambudri Brahmans, however, follow the *makkathayam* system, and the great majority of Nambudri women must have been condemned by ancient custom to remain unmarried, as the eldest son only in a Nambudri family married a wife of his own caste. The others marry Nayar women with whom they live in the form of union known as *sambandham*, easily dissoluble by either party. Recent legislation has now enabled the younger brothers of a Nambudri family to contract marriages within their own caste, and has given legal recognition and binding effect to *sambandham* marriages (as was done in Cochin State by the Nayar Regulation of 1920), whether hypergamous or endogamous, while securing to the wife the right of divorce and, with her children, the right of maintenance by the husband, together with the right to inherit a moiety of undisposed self-acquired property left by the husband. By the customary law all responsibility for the maintenance of the children lay with the woman's family, and any property acquired by the husband reverted to his family at his death. Obviously modern conditions called for some relaxation of this customary law, for the *marumakkathayam*

---

[32] Williams, *Fiji and the Fijians*, I, p. 244.
[33] Thurston, *Ethnographic Notes*, pp. 105 sqq.; Rivers, *The Todas*, pp. 392, 701. [34] *Vide* p. 70, *supra*.

system, perhaps the best in the world when taken by itself, has possibly in the past been exploited by the Nambudris to their own profit. But it would be as great an error to replace the *marumakkathayam* system by the ordinary *makkathayam* one as to suppose that the former is either primitive, barbarous or in any way less respectable than the latter, although it is less widely distributed. On the contrary, it seems likely that the *marumak-kathayam* was the ancient and civilized system, which was replaced in most countries of southern Europe and southern Asia by the *makkathayam* under the stress of conquest by a ruder people from the steppes of southern Russia.

Another possible survival of matrilineal or at least of matri-local customs is to be found in the practice, widely spread in India, under which a man, known as a *ghar-jawai*—that is, as a ' house-son-in-law '—or some such equivalent term, goes to live in the house of his prospective father-in-law. It is commonest perhaps when the girl's father is well-to-do and has no sons, in which case the son-in-law is expected to take up residence there permanently, but it also occurs in cases where the girl's family is very poor and requires the help of an able-bodied man, and likewise where the bridegroom is very poor and unable to pay a marriage price in cash. In such cases the normal period for which he must work to obtain his wife seems to be three years, during which time connubial intercourse is theoretically at any rate not allowed to him, and though the prospective son-in-law is maintained by his father-in-law-to-be he has no claim to inherit in case of his death. This practice is known in the United Provinces as *bina* marriage and is particularly associated with castes derived from tribes, castes such as Chero and Kharwar, which are probably Kolarian in origin, but also Gonds. Blunt [35] mentions the following other castes as using *bina* marriage: Bind, Ghasiya, Majhwar, and Parahiya. Turner [36] adds the names of some of the Kanjar and Nat castes and mentions one division of Nats among whom a bridegroom married in this way must stay and serve as long as his wife's parents are alive, failing which he becomes liable for a money payment, which is fixed by the tribal panchayat to meet the case. As Turner points out,[37] the practice, in the case of a poor son-in-law who goes to live

[35] *Census of the U.P.*, 1911, p. 220. [36] Ibid., 1931, pp. 311 sqq.
[37] Loc. cit.

11

permanently in the house of a rich father-in-law and is virtually paid to become a *ghar-jawai*, is widespread and found in all castes from Brahman downwards; he names a score of such castes in the United Provinces in which either this practice has been reported, or the analogous one of *ghar baithna*, where a man goes to live in the house of a widow with no male collaterals, or both. Marriage by exchange, either direct or (the more popular form) three-cornered, is practised in the same areas, and in one or two castes of Nats and Kanjars the custom of adopting a daughter survives, though under strict Hindu law only a son can be adopted.[38]

A probable survival of the matrilineal culture of south-west Europe, south-west Asia and the Indian peninsula is to be found in the practice in India of dedicating girls to the service of the god in Hindu temples. Girls so dedicated are known as *devadasis* and commonly live as prostitutes, but it has also to be borne in mind that a life of immorality is not necessarily the consequence of such dedication. In several castes in Madras, particularly in Bellary and the neighbourhood, it is the practice, if a male heir be wanting, to dedicate a daughter in the temple. Thenceforward she becomes by established custom the heir to her parents' property and can perform their funeral rites as if she were a son. She takes to herself a mate of her own selection of any equal or higher caste, but continues to live in her father's house, and her children take his name and belong to his family and not to their father's. If she has a son, he inherits the property and continues the family, while if she has a daughter only the daughter will in her turn become a *basavi* and renew the attempt. No social stigma attaches to her, but perhaps rather the contrary, for her presence at weddings is auspicious, probably because she cannot become a widow.

[38] Though not apparently relevant as traceable to matrilineal institutions, an unusual item of marriage ritual reported by Turner in the same context may perhaps be mentioned here in passing. He writes of ' the curious custom observed by Goriyas of the Gorakhpur district (who appear to be the outcome of fusion between a sub-caste of Mallahs and a sub-caste of Kahars). Before the rite of *sendhurdan* (marking the parting of the bride's hair with red lead) is performed the bridegroom leaves the wedding party in assumed umbrage and goes and sits on a roof erected specially for the purpose. The bride then goes to him and entreats him to marry her saying " My lord, come and marry me. You need do no work as I will work and earn money for you." The bridegroom and bride then descend from the roof and the marriage proceeds. The origin of this peculiar rite is unknown. . . .'

Clearly no immorality is inherent in this custom, which is merely a method of temporarily reverting to the *marumakkathayam* system when the family lacks a male heir and the *makkathayam* system proves irksome or inadequate. It amounts in fact to a method of adoption, but, being quite other than the orthodox Hindu form of adoption which prevails in northern India, suggests an origin in the very different form of society which still survives on the Malabar coast, and was no doubt at one time more widely prevalent.

The western Asiatic affinities of the *devadasi* custom of the Tamilnad, for it is perhaps only there that the custom is still general, are clear enough. Besides the familiar account given by Herodotus of the offering made by women of their chastity in the temple of Mylitta at Babylon, a reference to which custom is made also in the 43rd verse of the Epistle of Jeremy in the Book of the apocryphal Prophet Baruch, Lucian mentions the same custom at Byblos in Phoenicia; there the goddess of a temple, connected at a very early date with Egypt, was a fish from the waist downwards and had by her temple a pool of sacred fish with a stone *chattri* in its midst, and a woman had the alternative of shaving her head and offering her hair [39] instead of her chastity. Lucian, as a matter of fact, puts it the other way: 'the women who do not chuse to be shaved are obliged in lieu of it to expose their persons, and submit to the embraces of strangers in the public market-place for hire, during the space of one whole day; the money arising from it is consecrated to the service of the goddess and expended on a sacrifice to her.'[40] Hair was offered by Argive maidens to Athene before marriage, and those of Megara offered clippings of their hair at the tomb of Iphinoe; in Delos both youths and maidens offered their hair before marriage at a tomb of corn-maidens in the sanctuary of Artemis; hair was polled and offered to the goddess of health at Titane near Corinth whose image was 'swathed in strips of Babylonish raiment', and it is still shorn and offered to the Virgin at Tenos as a thanksgiving for recovery from sickness; at Troezen every maiden before marriage dedicated a lock of her hair, in this case to a male deity, in the temple of Hippolytus. In all these cases, with the possible

[39] Cf. pp. 232 sqq., *infra*.
[40] *On the Syrian Goddess*, in *The Works of Lucian*, tr. Francklin, vol. IV, p. 354.

exception of that of the goddess of health, the association seems
to be between hair and fertility of the soil and of the body,
and it is probably the same association in India that makes
the Abbé Dubois remark on the commonness of the offering
of hair in temples by men and women in fulfilment of a vow.[41]
This practice obtains now even at the *darga* of the Mirgan Sahib
at Nagore in Tanjore district, where there is a tank, such as
those commonly found at Hindu temples, to which Hindu
women come to bathe who have vowed their hair to the Muslim
Saint. The element of a vow seems also to have entered into
the practice of sacred prostitution at Comana in Pontus, where
Strabo records that people assembled on account of vows made
to sacrifice to the goddess, describing the place as ' full of women
trafficking in their persons, the most of them sacred ',[42] that is,
to the moon goddess. Similar customs were observed at the
Phoenician colony of Sicca on the north African coast; at Helio-
polis in Syria likewise women prostituted themselves from religious motives; and in Armenia, at the temple of Anaïtis, Strabo
tells us [43] that ' they dedicate male and female slaves, a fact in
no way remarkable, but further the most illustrious of the people
dedicate their virgin daughters, who according to custom prostitute themselves for a long period in the service of the goddess
and are afterwards given in marriage '. Similarly, it appears that
in some Indian temples it is usual for a *devadasi* to serve for
a period in the temple and thereafter be kept as a concubine
outside. Consecrated hetaerae were associated with the worship
of Aphrodite at Corinth, and an inscription from Tralles in
Lydia is referred to by Frazer [44] which shows that the custom
obtained in Asia Minor as late as the second century A.D. ' It
records ', he says, ' of a certain woman, Aurelia Aemilia by name,
not only that she herself served the god in the capacity of a
harlot at his express command, but that her mother and female
ancestors had done the same before her.' Strabo records a practice of dedicating girls in the temple of Ammon in Egypt not
dissimilar to that in Armenia, except that in the case of Ammon
the deity was male and the dedicated girls, when given to a
human husband after serving their term as the wives of the

41 *People of India*, III, iii.
42 *Kai alloi de kat' euchēn aei tines epidēmousi, thusias te epitelountes
tē theō . . . plēthos gunaikōn ergazomenōn apo tou sōmatos, hōn hai
pleious eisin hierai* (Strabo, XII, 559).   43 XI, 532.
44 *Golden Bough*, V, p. 38.

god, were mourned as dead. This practice of marriage to the god appears again, but at an earlier date, in Mesopotamia. Marduk and the Sun-god Shamash both had female votaries who were married to them and who had human children, and the word used for these dedicated women was the same as the Hebrew word for a temple harlot. It is hardly necessary to point out that the *devadasi* is likewise married to the god, but may have children by men. Dedications of virility were also made in the temple of the Syrian goddess whose priests were eunuchs who had dedicated themselves by castration, and it is possible that an Indian survival of the same cult is to be seen in the dedication of natural eunuchs or otherwise deformed males to the goddess Huligamma, and in the cult of the goddess Chatushringi, whose temple on a hill near Poona is served by men (said to be natural eunuchs) who dress in women's clothes and spend their lives begging and worshipping the goddess, at whose temple they collect in large numbers to celebrate the Dasehra. In the Deccan besides the girls dedicated to the god Khandoba as *murli*, boys (*vāghyā*) are also dedicated and are brought up as temple servants and mendicants. This god, Khandoba, is worshipped at the Dasehra in association with Ekavira, who is definitely a fertility goddess worshipped during the Dasehra in Maratha households in little ' Gardens of Adonis '. In any case the general parallel between the practice in southern India and that in Syria and Asia Minor is too close to be fortuitous, and offers another link between Dravidian India and the eastern Mediterranean. It is true that the Asian deity was more often a goddess and that in India a god is served, but there is much evidence to suggest that in India, as in Greece and Italy [45] and as also in Asia Minor, the mother goddess and a matrilineal system preceded a change to a patrilineal system introduced by invaders. It is, of course, impossible to dissociate the custom by which all worshippers propitiate the deity once in their lives by an offering of their chastity from that of dedicating some individuals to do it for a period of their lives. Indeed, the custom alluded to above of dedicating a daughter as a *basavi* for the sake of reviving the otherwise inoperative

[45] *Vide* Frazer, *Golden Bough*, II (*The Magic Art and the Evolution of Kings*, II), ch. XVIII. The institution of kingship under a matrilineal system seems to have accompanied the worship of the mother goddess.

marumakkathayam inheritance rather suggests that the practice of dedication in one form or another, real or symbolic, may have at one time been the universal concomitant of the matrilineal system in India as in Asia Minor or in Cyprus. It is possible that the *talikettu* ceremony on the Malabar coast points in the same direction; the Brahman explanation of it as a purificatory sacrament,[46] read with Hamilton's account of the Zamorin's nuptials,[47] is not antagonistic. At any rate the custom of dedication prevailed as far west as Cyprus, where there was a custom (Herodotus mentions it) similar to that of Babylon, and on the African coast to Sicca Veneris and probably to Carthage herself. The Cyprian shrines were connected in form in respect of their horn and pillar cult with Crete and Mycenae, while the cones which were the emblem of the goddess at Byblos and other places in Asia Minor have been found in the most ancient sanctuary of Cyprus and as far west as Malta. There can be little doubt but that the custom of consecrated prostitution originates in a commerce regarded (on some principle of sympathetic magic, perhaps) as essentially necessary to ensure that life should be propagated and that the earth should fructify. According to Bernier[48] the virgin married to Vishnu at Puri consulted the god as to the abundance of the coming harvest, an association which is most significant. Marco Polo, in giving an account of the custom of prostitution to strangers in the province of Kamul, tells us how it was indignantly prohibited by the Emperor of China. The order was obeyed for three years and then rescinded, as it was found that the land became barren in consequence and the earth no longer brought forth her fruit in due season.[49]

The division of society into two groups, castes of the Right Hand and castes of the Left Hand, has already been mentioned in an earlier chapter.[50] It is natural to suppose that it reflects some acute division of society which, though it apparently convulsed the other Dravidian-speaking provinces of southern India, failed to affect the Malabar coast, since such a division is absent in the Malayalam-speaking area, though lively enough in the

46 Iyer, *Cochin Tribes and Castes*, II, p. 29.
47 *New Account of the East Indies*, p. 310.
48 *Voyages de François Bernier*, II, p. 105.
49 Bk. I, ch. XLI (Yule, I, p. 210).
50 *Vide supra*, pp. 11, 67 sqq.

Telugu, Kanarese and Tamil countries. In the three latter the *makkathayam* principle of inheritance through the male is the prevailing order, in spite of occasional survivals such as the *basavi* system referred to above. In the former, however, the *marumakkathayam* system still prevails and has prevailed almost without exception [51] until a recent date. The inference that the factions of the Right and Left Hand arose as a result of the introduction of the *makkathayam* principle, which some castes were unwilling to accept, is inescapable. The fact that the women of one or two castes belong to one faction while the men belong to another does nothing to weaken this inference, since there is nothing more likely than that the women of a caste might be opposed to a change of this kind while the men were wishful to adopt it,[52] and it is to be observed that in the only case in which the women are certainly reported to differ from their menfolk the women belong to the Right Hand and their menfolk to the Left. Moreover, in the case of the Madiga caste the women are often made *basavi* or are dedicated as *devadasis*, for whom the matrilineal system is important, while in the Kaikolan caste (a Left-Hand caste) also, in which the same practice obtains, the women sometimes belong to the Right Hand.[53] Further, it is to be noted that while the cultivating classes support the Right Hand, which we may take perhaps to represent the form of society which conformed to ancient practice, the artisan castes all support the Left-Hand faction. These claim that their privileges were bestowed on them by a goddess—Kali.[54] Brahmans and other castes from northern India are generally regarded as not concerned in the rivalry of the two factions. Further, there is a strong tradition in southern India that where burial is

[51] One exception in Malabar is the Chaliyan caste of cotton weavers, and while some of them are of the Right Hand others are of the Left, the latter being regarded as superior, though numerically much weaker. Some of the caste follow the *marumakkathayam* rule, others (it may be the Left Hand, but we are not told) the *makkathayam*. In any case the caste appears to be an immigrant one, and this is confirmed by the fact that some of them are patrilineal. See Thurston, *Castes and Tribes*, II, pp. 11 sq.

[52] Among the Jats men claim the right to marry a deceased brother's widow, while women vehemently deny it. Wise, op. cit., p. 125.

[53] According to Rose (' Caste ') *devadasis* of the Right restrict their favours to the caste to which they belong, whereas those of the Left Hand are much more promiscuous, a distinction which seems to support the theory advanced here that the *devadasis* of the Right Hand are merely adhering to an original matrilineal system.

[54] Buchanan, *Journey through Mysore, Canara and Malabar*, ch. II (1870, vol. I, p. 54).

resorted to for disposing of the dead, either on account of poverty or for climatic or other reasons, burning of course being the preferred method of disposal for Hindus, cultivators normally use a simple grave, whereas the Panchala, that is, the five artisan castes, line and cover their graves with stone slabs, a contrast in practice which is suggestive of two different cultures, a metal-using culture having perhaps been immigrant into an area of primitive cultivators still in the stone age.

Be that as it may, there is one obvious inference to be drawn, if the hypothesis of the origin of the Right- and Left-Hand factions here advanced be accepted; and it is an inference, more-over, which is not without support from other considerations; that is, that some sort of a caste system, or something closely analogous, existed in southern India along with a matrilineal culture antecedent to the infiltration of Rigvedic Hinduism from the north. This would support the view advanced by Oldham [55] that caste as we know it is the result of the imposition of 'the varna tradition' upon conditions found in India at the Rigveda period. He suggests that 'the influence of a Brahmanic hierarchy' was 'exerted with the object of embracing within their fold the indigenous tribes and social groups' already occu-pying the country 'and of establishing at the same time an organization that would conform broadly with the tradition of the sacred hymns'. This conclusion accords in some degree with that of Senart referred to above,[56] but it would be rash to regard the caste system, as it has since developed, as a deliberate construction so much as the result of the reactions of indigenous institutions of taboo, pollution, purification and so forth to what was perhaps a conscious political or hierarchical policy adopted by the Rigvedic invaders and their successors towards the com-munities they found in the land.

The complete and emphatic change over from the matrilineal to the patrilineal system, which seems to have taken place throughout almost the whole of India except the Malabar coast, is perhaps to be attributed to the sudden spread of some new and convincingly satisfactory, even if illusory, idea. Such an idea—an idea of an exclusive importance to be attached to paternity in breeding—may have arisen from the observation of

[55] In a review of Ghurye's 'Caste and Race in India' in Man, XXXII, 268 (1932, 316).   [56] p. 150 supra.

some notable or characteristic feature derived from the bull in any herd in which a number of cows are served by a single bull. Sir Arthur Olver, late Principal of the Royal (Dick) Veterinary College in Edinburgh, and at one time a Colonel in the Indian Army Veterinary Service, writes to me of 'the far greater influence of a sire in a herd as a whole than of any particular female. Siring as he may from fifty to a hundred or even more calves in a season, the bull is bound to have a more profound effect on the herd'. Among matrilineal peoples accustomed to attach little importance to paternity, an observation of that kind might well spread with a conviction devastating to existing theories of descent, and cause a swing over to an extreme opposite view, such as that now generally held in Brahmanic doctrine which regards woman as merely the soil, a soil in which the paternal seed germinates and grows, it is true, but which contributes little or nothing to the new creation except nourishment. It is possibly significant in this connexion that a pastoral society has generally been found to be associated with pronounced male domination.

CHAPTER XI

OTHER THEORIES; FACTORS IN THE EMERGENCE OF CASTE

THE earlier European observers of the caste system were content to regard it as an artificial creation, as a device of a clever priesthood for the permanent division and subjection of the masses, or even as the creation of a single lawgiver. Thus the Abbé Dubois, among others, speaks of it as the ingenious device of Brahmans and clearly regards it as made by, and for, them. But it is impossible to accept such a view. So deeply rooted and pervasive a social institution as the caste system could hardly have been imposed by an administrative measure. It is organic rather than artificial, and the same criticism applies to the occupational theory of caste advocated by Nesfield in his *Brief View of the Caste System*. Nesfield regards occupation as the exclusive basis of caste distinction and emphasizes the fact that artisans working in metals rank higher than basket-makers, for instance, and other primitive callings which do not involve the use of metals. Caste he regarded as a natural product of society in the creation of which religion played no part at all. This theory will hardly stand critical examination. It is true that basket-making is an occupation of one of the lowest castes; at the same time the blacksmith's caste is very far from being more highly esteemed, though it must presumably be later in point of time, than that of the coppersmith or the goldsmith. Moreover, this scheme does not explain at all the varying positions of agriculturists who are of low castes in certain parts of southern India but generally of respectable if not of high caste in northern India. It should, however, be mentioned in this connexion that it does appear to be a custom in southern India, or in parts of southern India, to provide a craftsman, that is, a man of the carpenter's or blacksmith's or goldsmith's profession, with a grave made of stone slabs in a cist form in place of the simple unlined grave which is given to a cultivator, and this does suggest either a difference in status or in custom between the aborigines and immigrants who brought in tools and crafts, or in the alternative some difference in eschatology between the cultivator and the craftsman. Moreover, if the origins of the caste system were, as

Nesfield maintains, totally independent of religion, they have undoubtedly received a religious sanction since.

Nesfield's view is, however, in some measure supported by Dahlmann in his *Das Altindische Volkstum*. Dahlmann regards Indian society as organized originally into three natural groups— the priesthood, the nobility, and the bourgeoisie—which are, in his opinion, found in every civilized community, representing the divisions of the people respectively concerned with the religious, the political, and the economic branches of the national life, and which correspond to the three twice-born *varna*; these groups he conceives as split up into a number of smaller groups and communities, some based on relationship, others on community of occupation. Caste sprang not from the four *varna* but from the infinite number of corporations and of groups of relatives into which these four *varna* were divided. There was, he considers, a steady progress of development from classes to corporations and from corporations to castes. Agriculture was originally the prime factor in the economic life of India; a rival developed in the form of trade and industry, and the principle of division of labour became so important that it became regarded as the duty of the ruler to base his economic policy on the division of labour and distinction of occupations. On the basis of the old division by classes, corporations gradually arose and guilds of traders and hand-workers came into existence. Community of interest among persons following the same craft gave rise to a corporate organization, and technical skill was passed on from father to son. Families of craftsmen thus arose bound together by a community of interest which gave rise to a corporate organization and formed a guild. It is this guild which is really the basis of the caste system. Here again this view fails to account for a great deal in the caste system. The German guild is cited by Dahlmann as a close parallel, but it involved no ban on commensality between one profession and another and no prohibition of intermarriage, nor is it conceivable that a distinction based solely on function could develop into the vivid and lasting prejudices that accompany caste distinctions in India.

Blunt [1] follows Dahlmann and accepts also Risley's theory, holding that the origin of caste must be sought for in the peculiar

---

[1] *Census of the U.P.*, pp. 323 sqq.

circumstances of a complex system of society—' a society of classes with a cross-division of guilds '. The classes were largely a matter of colour, and the ultimate result was a society divided into groups of all shades of colour, all degrees, that is, of mixed blood. Meanwhile guilds were growing up which contained recruits of all classes and which developed strong self-governing organizations; within each such guild would be found little groups each with the same class prejudice against corrupting their blood by intermarriage. Each guild would thus become an endogamous caste with endogamous subcastes. In confirmation of this theory Blunt finds first that the functional caste is made up of subcastes which are themselves endogamous, whereas the non-functional castes are endogamous as a whole, but are not so generally made up of endogamous subcastes; secondly, that the functional castes have much more powerful governing bodies (*panchayats*) than the non-functional; and thirdly, that while the non-functional castes claim descent ultimately from a common ancestor, the functional ones do not. The instances given by Blunt of functional castes include Brahman, Kayastha, Sonar and Lohar, of non-functional Rajput, Khatri, Jat and Bhar. These, he says, are made up of exogamous sections instead of endogamous. The facts are, however, by no means so simple as Blunt here suggests, for exogamous *gotras* are to be found in functional as well as non-functional castes, while the latter, though they may claim a common origin, do not as a rule claim a common ancestor, whereas certain functional castes do claim a common ancestor in Viswakarma.

Chanda also traces caste to race and function. ' Colour or race difference, real and fancied, together with hereditary function, gave birth to the caste system. But as newer groups formed or attached themselves to the Arya nations, the absurdity of regarding them all as distinct colours or *varnas* was recognized, and the theory of *varnasankara* or mixed caste was started to explain their origins.' [2]

Senart, in his well-known work *Les Castes dans l'Inde*, seeks to account for caste in an entirely different way. He does not maintain that the caste system springs only from primitive ' Aryan ' elements but regards them as most important in the creation of the caste system, as he stresses the importance of commensality

[2] Chanda, *Indo-Aryan Races*, p. 36.

and derives the exclusive commensality of caste from the family worship and family meal of the primitive *gens* or clan, although he compares it, not very satisfactorily, with the Roman *tribus* and the Greek *phylē*. He regards the ' Aryan ' invasion as having resulted in a mixed race with two orders of scruples about purity, one order based on purity of descent and the other on purity of occupation. These scruples led to the formation of new groups among which the priestly class alone maintained a solid feeling of *esprit de corps*, using its moral power to establish the caste system. This it proceeded to interpret in terms of the traditional division into four classes, accounting for the multiplicity of existing groups by a theory of mixture and by ascribing the lower social level of certain castes to their extraction from irregular unions. This theory also is open to serious criticism. Dahlmann has attacked it as postulating a completely non-existent simplicity of society at the time of the Rigveda, when, he says, the majority of Indians had no longer the rude customs of a pastoral people but a wide and, in some respects, a highly developed civilization in which custom and ritual were well developed. In any case Senart's explanation of the exclusive commensality of caste as derived from the family meal and sacraments shared with the family ancestral spirits cannot be regarded as satisfactory. A caste in India hardly ever claims a common ancestor. It is the *gotra* which, like the *gens*, does so, and it is the *gotra* which, like the *gens*, is an exogamous unit. The caste is not a clan and is not analogous to a clan, and, whatever the origins of this particular feature may be, identical *gotras* are actually found in different castes, so that caste is not analogous to a *tribus* or a *phylē* any more than it is to the *gens*. Senart, however, has clearly seen that neither race nor occupation or function is by itself enough to cause a caste system to come into being, or to account for its restrictions on commensality and marriage.

Sir Herbert Risley, in his book *The People of India*, on the other hand, has relied mainly on theories of race and hypergamy to explain the caste system, which he clearly regards as primarily due to colour differences and to a system of hypergamy resulting therefrom. In order to base caste on hypergamy Risley finds it necessary to presuppose a hypothetical point at which the result of intermarriage between fair invaders and dark aborigines

provides enough women for the society in question to close
its ranks and become a caste, although there still exist outside
it more women of the same community from which it has been
drawing its wives and with which it has been in more or less
intimate relation. The position of negroes in the southern states
of the U.S.A. has been cited as offering a parallel case, and the
view is supported by Westermarck;[3] it finds a certain measure
of confirmation perhaps in the laws passed in the Union of
South Africa against the intermarriage of white and coloured
races; but it fails to offer any satisfactory explanation of the
taboo on commensality. It is no doubt true that separate railway carriages, separate restaurants, even separate townships, are
provided for negroes, but no pollution takes place [4] as a result
of employing negro servants, and there is no hard and fast line
which is really analogous to a caste division between, say, quadroons and octoroons, nor have the social factors which might
have tended to produce similar results in India ever succeeded
in making Muslims, Anglo-Indians or Eurasians into a caste in
the Hindu sense, and where Muslims do form a real caste it
is always one which has been converted to Islam from pre-Islamic
inhabitants while retaining its original caste organization.[5] A

[3] *History of Human Marriage* (1901), pp. 365-7.
[4] At the same time it is necessary in this connexion to draw attention to
a passage quoted by Dr Little in ' The Psychological Background of White-
Coloured Contacts in Britain ' in *The Sociological Review*, XXXV, 3, n. 4
from *Deep South*:
' The belief in the organic inferiority of the negro reaches its strongest
expression in the common assertion that the negroes are '' unclean '' . . . .
There remains a strong feeling that the colour of the negroes is abhorrent
and that contact with them may be contaminating. There is generally a
strong feeling against eating or drinking from dishes used by negroes, and
most of the whites provide separate dishes for the use of their servants.
The idea of uncleanliness is also extended to any clothing worn by negroes,
as was dramatically shown when a negro customer returned a coat which
she had bought from a white clothing merchant. The clerk was unwilling
to accept the coat, and when the assistant manager accepted it, the clerk
said to another clerk: '' This is perfectly terrible; I think it is awful. We
can't put that coat back in stock.'' She hung it up very gingerly and did
not touch it any more than necessary.' (*Deep South : A Social Anthropological Study of Caste and Class*, Allison Davis and B. B. and M. R. Gardner,
p. 16.)
The attitude to negroes indicated here is most suggestive of the caste
system.
[5] But according to Professor Vesey-FitzGerald exclusive Muslim communities having a caste organization exist outside India, the 'Ibadis of the
M'zab in Algeria, for instance, while Ismai'li sects in India tend to organize
themselves in secret societies with esoteric rituals and a dreadful penalty of
excommunication (review of *Caste in India* in the *Bulletin of the School of
Oriental and African Studies*, XII, p. 246).

system of hypergamy is no doubt explicable as a result of the impact of colour prejudice on a caste system, but it is difficult to see how it can give rise to caste. In general its action presupposes just such facilities for intermarriage and commensality as the caste system tends to suppress.

Several other writers on caste explicitly follow Risley or are content to take his theory for granted. Professor N. K. Dutt,[6] while criticizing him, adopts his racial theory of origin in effect, though he attaches much more value than Risley to the account of caste in the Code of Manu. Mr Hayavadana Rao[7] and Dr Ghurye[8] likewise regard caste as having arisen largely as a result of racial differences. Ghurye emphasizes in particular the factor of priestly manipulation by Brahmans attempting to maintain the purity of race of Aryan invaders. One cannot but believe, however, that for priestly interference of this kind to be effective in setting up so far-reaching and complicated a system as that of caste, it is necessary to assume the pre-existence of certain of the essential factors in that system which would predispose the population generally to accept an extension of them. Colour prejudice and racial exclusiveness have been common enough in the history of the world, but they have nowhere else led to such an institution as caste, and it would be rash to suppose that they could have done so in India of themselves. On the other hand, race and colour prejudice have no doubt made an important contribution to the development of the caste system, and it may be that they have played such a part in the crystallizing of that institution as to justify the statement that it could not have come down to posterity in its present form without having been subjected to the reagent of racial prejudice and discrimination. Indeed, Risley's test of the nasal index as indicative of the position of a caste in the social scale has been regarded by both Ghurye[9] and S. C. Roy[10] as holding good in a broad sense for northern India. If indeed it does so, there are a number of striking exceptions to the general rule.

Ibbetson[11] has, like Ghurye, laid great emphasis on the exploitation of their position by the Brahman caste which he supposes

[6] *Origin and Growth of Caste in India*, ch. I.
[7] *Indian Caste System*, p. 66.
[8] *Caste and Race in India*, ch. VII.   [9] Op. cit., pp. 108 sqq.
[10] ' Caste, Race and Religion ', in *Man in India*, XIV, no. 2, p. 79.
[11] *Panjab Castes*, pt. I.

to have 'degraded all occupations except their own and that of their patrons of the ruling class'. He explains caste as arising from a combination of tribal origins, functional guilds and 'a Levitical religion', and has laid the greater stress on the tribe. It is, of course, clear enough that certain tribes are responsible for the formation of certain castes, and no less clear that certain castes are, or have been in the past, restricted to certain occupations, but Ibbetson's explanation of the origin of caste is really only a summary of certain of its obvious features. These features —tribes, guilds, and religious monopolies—have no doubt contributed to the growth and extension of the caste system, and done much to consolidate and perpetuate it, but they cannot be regarded as causes. They are features which are not unique but common to many societies in many countries, whereas caste is found in India and nowhere else. Given caste, a tribe, a guild, or a priestly order may very easily become a caste, but failing the essentials of the caste system there is nothing in them, with the possible exception of the priestly order, which will produce a caste.

Quite a different origin for caste is argued by Hocart,[12] who apparently regards the whole system as originating in ritual. He regards the four *varna* as a division of the people devised primarily for ritualistic purposes; they represent the four points of the compass, as do the colours white, red, yellow and black. The ritual appears to be a duplication of some ancient fertility rite in which two divisions of the people were involved, representing the sky and the earth, and to be focused on the king as representing the deity, or as being himself the deity incarnate, and the functions of various castes are derived from the offices performed by them in the daily ritual of the royal court. Hocart's conclusions are, however, based on his observation of the existing ritual of the Buddhist Temple of the Tooth at Kandy and not on direct acquaintance with caste in India. The functions of the washerman and barber necessary to purificatory ceremonies have struck him, and he seems to regard the corresponding castes as having been created by local imitation of royal courts on a small scale by petty rulers and landed proprietors, each of whom must have, like the divine or royal model, a barber and a washer-

[12] *Les Castes*, passim. Bruce Ryan, in a note on p. 180 of his *Caste in Modern Ceylon*, remarks: 'Hocart's attempt to interpret caste in purely ritual terms must be utterly discarded.'

man and other ritual functionaries, so that there grew up classes of people each performing separate ritual functions, which classes developed into closed castes. This view, however, offers no explanation of the taboos on commensality and intermarriage which are essential to the caste system, unless it is conceived that any performance of ritual functions is vitiated if the performer is in any way contaminated by association with persons who do not or cannot perform them. In such a case ideas of taboo, *mana*, and magic must be postulated which might themselves be enough to account for the formation of caste without bringing in at all the idea of ritual. In any case, it is perhaps less unconvincing to suppose that the performance of the ritual was first associated with particular groups because that was their customary work than that association with the ritual led to the formation of the caste. At the same time it must be admitted that Hocart's theory does supply a unifying factor in the caste system in that all over India castes are to be found with, up to a point, similar ritual as well as social and economic functions from Brahman down to washerman.

A theory of the origin of caste which combines both functional and racial origins has been put forward by Slater in his *Dravidian Elements in Indian Culture*. He emphasizes the fact that caste is actually stronger in southern than in northern India, and suggests that caste arose in India before the Aryan invasion as a result of occupations becoming hereditary and marriages being arranged by parents within the society of the common craft because sexual maturity is early and trade secrets were thus preserved. As a result of magic and religious ceremonies also, exclusive occupational groups were built up, marriage outside which became prejudicial and contrary to practice. The Aryan invasion had the effect of strengthening a tendency to associate difference of caste with a difference of colour and of strengthening also a tendency for castes to be placed in a scale of social precedence. Slater also maintains the existence in the pre-Aryan society of India of an order of priest magicians which he associated, rather unnecessarily perhaps, with Egypt and a heliolithic cult. Dutt,[13] to whose views reference has been made above, takes a somewhat similar view of the impact of an Aryan culture upon pre-Aryan occupational classes

[13] Op. cit., pp. 28 sqq., 106.

already endogamous on account of occupational prejudice and the preservation of trade secrets. Ghurye [14] takes a rather similar line, and suggests that the southern Indian peoples, before their contact with Indo-Aryan culture, probably shared the ideas of primitive peoples about the power of food to transmit qualities, while ideas of untouchability arose from ideas of ceremonial purity first applied to aboriginals in connexion with sacrificial ritual and the theoretical impurity of certain occupations.

Ghurye's account of caste was published in 1932, but before that Bonnerjea, in an article in *The Indian Antiquary*,[15] had explained caste as due to primitive belief in magic, with which he credits both Aryan and pre-Aryan, while accepting Risley's view apparently of the operation of hypergamy and the invading Aryan who married into indigenous peoples until a group had enough women to close its ranks and become endogamous. It is the Aryan invader whom he regards as primarily responsible for the institution of caste. The continuance of caste, once established, he regarded as resting on the occupational basis, the occupation being primarily that of being a magician, and therefore no doubt specially skilled in the craft or occupation pursued. No doubt the common practice by craftsmen of the worship of the tools of their craft could be cited in support of such a view. The tools, like the craftsmen, would be associated with the particular *mana* involved in the craft, and it would be necessary or desirable to keep *en rapport* with them. Even before that, Rice in 1929 published an article in the *Asiatic Review* [16] which he later elaborated in his *Hindu Customs*, ascribing the origin of caste to totemism and the taboos which commonly accompany it. He emphasizes in this connexion the holiness of the kitchen and the principle that food is a ready conveyor of injurious qualities in totemistic and primitive belief.

Gilbert [17] has pointed out that early Tamil literature refers to different peoples as inhabiting the different geographical divisions of the coast, the cultivated lowlands, the pastoral, mountain and desert areas. The Peravadar lived on the coast by fishing, the Vellalar and Velir cultivated irrigated land and

---

[14] Op. cit., p. 145.
[15] ' Possible Origin of the Caste System in India ', April 1931.
[16] ' The Origin of Caste ', *A.R.*, vol. xxv. It is understood that Dr B. S. Guha advanced a theory somewhat similar to that of Rice and Bonnerjea in a thesis for Harvard University in 1924, but that thesis has not been consulted.   [17] *Peoples of India*, p. 29.

the Karalar drier land thus producing rice, millet, and pulse in the lowlands, the Idayar and Ayar herded in the uplands, the Kuravas occupied the mountains and the Maravar the desert. He suggests that this ecological differentiation of early groups offers a possible basis for caste differences, and later points out [18] that the surface distribution of different mineral resources has helped to determine caste distribution, as the Pudukottai bangle-makers must live near the river beds where bangle earth is available, Uppiliyars (salt workers) must live near salt deposits, Upparas where saltpetre is available and so forth, while the distribution of rivers and sea coasts 'characterizes the location of fishing and boating castes' and plant areas the distribution of toddy drawers and betel growers.

We may at this point go back to the theories of an earlier writer, Oldenberg, as published in his article 'Zur Geschichte des indischen Kastenwesens'.[19] Here he criticizes Senart's views and points out (in a footnote) that endogamy is more likely to have originated with the aboriginal inhabitants of India than with the Aryan invaders. He also rejects the view that restrictions on commensality originated with the Aryan invaders. The orthodox account of castes of mixed origin he regards as a fiction for the admission to the caste system of indigenous tribes or of despised sections of the Aryans, and also of functional groups which had sprung up outside the three recognized Aryan classes but which rendered necessary services. In this way he regards the Rigvedic threefold division of the people into classes as having been modified till it developed into a number of castes marked off from each other by endogamy and with other restrictions, partly derived from restrictions on the original Rigvedic classes and partly adopted from the aborigines. The transition from class to caste was reached when a man remained a member of his original group irrespective of his profession. Such a stage marks the beginning of caste even though the fullness of caste in its modern sense may not have been reached. Oldenberg quotes Fick's *Die sociale Gliederung im nordöstlichen Indien zu Buddhas Zeit* (Kiel, 1897) for evidence from Pali literature for the evolution of caste, or rather for the social organization of north India in the early Buddhist period. He finds the term

[18] Op. cit., p. 56.
[19] In *Zeitschrift der Deutschen Morgenländischen Gesellschaft*, LI, pt. 2 (1897).

jati applied to Brahmans, Kshatriyas, Chandalas, Nishadas, etc., that is, to the *varna* and to tribal groups, whereas tradesmen and artisans are termed *kamma* and *sippa*, and they appear to be organized in *sreni* or associations of persons following the same occupations which made their own laws or rules and exercised jurisdiction over their members. The occupations would tend to become hereditary and their guilds, under a system of restrictions due to fear of pollution, would become more and more detached until they hardened into regular castes, while racial or tribal groups would follow a similar course. Oldenberg, then, regards caste as derived from class, guild and tribe segregated into permanently separate groups by heredity and by restrictions on marriage and commensality and a fear of pollution, which were derived partly from the Aryan invader and partly from the aboriginal inhabitants.

This fear of pollution has also been stressed by Ketkar, who points out that ' the chief principle on which the entire system depends is that of purity and pollution ',[20] a view which has not escaped Ghurye [21] and which has been endorsed by Sarat Chandra Roy.[22] Both these authors, however, regard this insistence on ceremonial purity as inherently associated with the Rigvedic Aryans, whereas it is not improbable that it was taken over in part at any rate from a more ancient civilization, a view which would probably receive the support of Professor Murphy, who suggests that the very ample provision for washing and bathing revealed in the ruins of towns of the Indus civilization indicates that the ancient inhabitants of India laid special stress on ablutions and purification long before the advent of the Rigvedic invaders, and that they laid an emphasis on the necessity for ceremonial purity which has been inherited from them by the later Hinduism.[23]

It will be convenient here to refer again to the paper published by A. M. T. Jackson [24] on the history of the caste system in which he refers to Colebrooke's work and emphasizes the importance to the development of the caste system of the internal government of castes. He lays stress on the fact that under

20 *History of Caste,* p. 121, and cf. pp. 28 sq. and 116 sqq.
21 Op. cit., p. 144.
22 ' Caste, Race and Religion ' in *Man in India,* vol. XIV, no. 2, p. 85.
23 *Lamps of Anthropology,* pp. 120, 127.
24 ' Note on the History of the Caste System ', *J.A.S.B.,* vol. III, no. 7 (July 1907).

Hindu rule the authority of the king was frequently called in to compel castes to keep to their proper functions. The effect of the exercise of royal jurisdiction would be to establish gradually a body of caste custom, and in the case of a caste spread widely throughout several kingdoms several bodies of different customs would be created, giving rise inevitably to subcastes or to different castes. The political condition of ancient India was particularly favourable to just this kind of fission; Megasthenes, for instance, reports a hundred and eighteen different kingdoms. As a matter of fact a very large number of subcastes (e.g. of Brahmans) do bear geographical names, and the same geographical name often appears as the name of subcastes of different main castes, a number of instances of which are given by Jackson from Bombay. Thus both the Ghanchi and Muchi castes have subcastes called Ahmadabadi; both Ghanchi and Kansaras have a subcaste called Chāmpāneri (Chāmpāner was the seat of a Hindu dynasty early in the fifteenth century, but has long been uninhabited); Brahmans, Charans, Sonis and Lohars have a subcaste called Kachela or its synonym Parajiā, and 'the name Kachella occurs in inscriptions as early as the eighth century' for the people of Kachh. Jackson gives many other instances of place-names for subcastes, and suggests that while the instances he gives are all from Bombay province the number could be multiplied indefinitely by research in the rest of India. It may here be pointed out [25] that recurrent famines are likely to have had a fissiparous influence on castes not dissimilar to that exercised by political disarticulation.

Linton has drawn attention [26] to the probability that India, or at any rate part of India, formed at some time in its past part of the Austronesian region in which there has been since palaeolithic times 'a fundamental pattern of organization on the basis of small endogamous groups. This pattern', he says, 'assumes various forms, but it is linked with a predominant importance of kinship as the basis for organizing the reciprocal behaviors of the group's members'. In such a system, he suggests, it would be an easy matter for caste to develop in response to frequent invasions and to the emergence of an

[25] *Vide infra*, p. 186.
[26] In a review of *Caste in India* (first edition) in *J.A.O.S.*, vol. 68, no. 2, April-June 1948.

urban culture, as it would provide 'a flexible mechanism for
encapsulating foreign elements' and for developing guild systems
to their logical conclusions.

The theories of the origin of caste so far referred to mostly
contain some important contribution to the subject. At the
same time it is clear that they often lay stress on the phenomena
rather than the causes of the caste system, and in particular
scarcely one of them lays enough emphasis on the importance
of the primitive conceptions of taboo, *mana* and soul-stuff in
contributing to its formation. This cannot justly perhaps be
said of Sarat Chandra Roy, who does indeed accept the hypothesis that a belief in *mana* and 'soul-substance' has contributed
to the development of caste, which he regards as 'the outcome of
the interaction between the Indo-Aryan *varna* system on the one
hand, and the tribal system of the pre-Dravidian and the occupational class system of the Dravidian, on the other'. These
he regards as having been cemented into the caste system by the
Indo-Aryan concept of *karma* and 'a certain "taboo-holiness"
that came to be attached to the Brahman for his accredited
possession of a special spiritual energy (*brahma-sakti*) born of
the predominance of the *sattva guna* [fundamental quality of
revealing light] sustained and stabilized through well-disciplined
continuance'.[27] The emphasis laid on the contribution of the
karma concept is important, but generally speaking Roy seems
to attach too much weight to the philosophic aspects of
Hinduism and attempts to interpret the institution of caste
in terms of ethical principles and an idealism which probably
had little to do with its primary origin. It is readily admitted
that nearly any unpromising material even of the grossest kind
may be found sublimated to form the principle of a noble
philosophy, but the institutions of human society are generally
the result of conflicting principles in which self-seeking and
economic considerations play almost as great a part as superstition, while sublimation comes in at a later stage when the
results are appreciated as being far from ideal.

[27] 'Caste, Race and Religion', in *Man in India*, vol. XVII, no. 4, p. 254.

CHAPTER XII

CONCLUSIONS

SEEING that light is required on the origin of caste it would seem not unreasonable, as in the case of religion, to examine first those cultures that survive in India least altered from antiquity in case they can illumine origins elsewhere obscured by changes and developments due to growing civilization and to external contacts. Caste, as it now is, is an institution which has grown and developed through many centuries, but since it is so firmly rooted in India, and since it is found nowhere else, it would appear almost certain, on the face of it, that its first beginnings are to be sought in India and not outside, and we have fortunately in the more inaccessible corners of this vast country still a few tribes whose primitive conditions of life have changed so little in a thousand years as to be witnesses of value. Pliny the Elder, writing in the first century A.D., mentions [1] a great valley in the Himalayas called Abarimon inhabited by wild men; the Assamese still speak of the hillmen who remain hostile and have not come under the influence of the plainsmen in that precise term, *ābari manu*, untamed folk; and Ptolemy,[2] writing in the second century, locates ' the Nanga-logae, that is the realm of the naked ', precisely where the *Naga lōg* are found today, some tribes of them still unclothed, still, in 1948, untouched by contact with the people of the plains, tribes who had never seen a white man nor a horse nor knew what is gunpowder, and whose language is still unspoken by anyone outside their own community save some of their immediate neighbours. Hinduism, Buddhism and Islam have never penetrated here, and caste as it exists in the plains is unknown and undreamed of, but nevertheless institutions are found which seem to throw a definite light on caste and religion as they have developed in another environment.[3] Thus in the unadministered area to the east of the Naga

---

[1] *Nat. Hist.*, VII, ii. It has been justly pointed out (Sachin Roy, *Aspects of Padam-Minyong Culture*, p. 1) that when Pliny wrote the Assamese language, as such, had not yet been formulated. Whether such a derivation could have been possible from the eastern Prākrit vernacular from which Assamese evolved, I am not philologist enough to have the least idea.

[2] *Geography*, VII, ii, 177.

[3] Cf. Hodson, *Naga Tribes of Manipur*, pp. 82 sq., and ' Genna in Assam ', *J.R.A.I.*, 1906, p. 92.

Hills, where each village is an independent political unit, there is very often to be seen a distribution by villages of certain occupations. Thus some villages make pots but do not weave cloth; others weave, and others again are occupied principally with blacksmiths' work, the one village bartering its products with its neighbours, when not prevented by mutual hostilities, in spite of differences of language, customs and sometimes perhaps of race between one village and another. Here we have clearly an aspect of occupation distinctly suggestive of the caste system; and, indeed, the remnants of such a condition seem to have survived in northern India until the Buddhistic age, as the Jatakas indicate that certain trades were localized in separate villages, some containing potters, others smiths and so forth. But this is not the only feature suggestive of caste. It frequently happens that upheavals in village politics end in battle, vendetta and sudden death, and that as a consequence part of a village community, usually an exogamous clan or sept, is compelled to migrate to some other village. It might be anticipated that a group of weaving families would be welcomed in a pot-making village which only obtained cloth by barter, and vice versa, and up to a point this is indeed the case; numbers are strength, and such immigrants are generally welcomed and allowed to settle and cultivate—but not to ply their ancestral craft when that differs from the occupation of their hosts. That is taboo, and should the strangers insist on it they must again go elsewhere to some village in which it is permitted. Instances of this have occurred within the writer's personal knowledge (compare also Hodson, *Naga Tribes of Manipur*, p. 47), and the underlying feeling seems to be that the practice of the tabooed craft will affect the crops and the fruits of the earth generally, perhaps because it is an offence to the ancestral spirits who are usually regarded as the source of fructification, or it may be that the particular form of *mana* or *aren* which enables the manufacture of the article made by the strangers is liable to neutralize the corresponding magic on which the traditional village industry depends. Here, however, there is, generally speaking, no taboo on commensality or on inter-marriage, and for the sources of these aspects of caste we must look elsewhere.

For a possible source of the commensal taboo, however, we need not look far from that of the occupational one. The same

Naga communities which we have been considering afford abundant instances of taboos on certain foods, of a vivid belief in *mana* or, as the Ao Nagas call it, *aren*, and of the magical effects of food on the consumer. Certain foods are peculiar to certain exogamous clans, or at any rate are in many cases associated with clan ceremonial, and it may be offered as one hypothesis that the presence of strange craftsmen practising their craft is condoned or rather rendered less dangerous by the prohibition of intimate relations with them, reducing thus the inconvenient strictness of one taboo by erecting another which at the start may be less irksome. That this is in accordance with the spirit of the primitive society under consideration is demonstrated by the readiness with which in some tribes the proximity of Christian converts is tolerated, even though they cultivate on tabooed days, provided they live outside the village fence and therefore form a more or less separate community, though here again commensality is not barred, except indeed in so far as the Christians refuse to eat such flesh as they are taught to regard as ' meats offered to idols '. Another hypothesis, and there is no reason to suppose the suggested explanations to be mutually exclusive, is the theory that the food of strangers is itself dangerous. Senart's citation of the taboo on strangers at the family meal would doubtless lead back to this, and Rice's view of the taboo on commensality as derived from a belief in totemism agrees in effect with the hypothesis here put forward, since both depend for their force on the belief in *mana* and in the resulting taboo on food or other contacts, which may be infected with the dangerous soul-matter of strangers; this soul-matter is particularly perilous if such strangers have new and, what is the same thing, mysterious arts and therefore magical powers. Thus when the writer was touring in previously unvisited Naga territory in 1923-4 he found villages which not only objected to accepting presents or purchase-money of any kind from the strangers, or to parting with any possession to them for fear of the influence to which they might thus become subject by proxy as it were, but which actually destroyed mats or other property lent to build shelters when the visitors who had used them had gone, and threw away their tainted coins in the jungle. The differentiation between cooked and uncooked food as a vehicle of pollution so familiar to any observer of caste in India is likely to be traceable to this view of the infection, by the act of cooking, of the food cooked with the *mana* of the cooker. Thus a Brahman can buy *ghi*, grain, or vegetables in the market, even from Muslims, but ' once such food has been cooked, it becomes Brahmā, and so must be treated with " sacramental care " '.[4] Similarly, among the Maori, to quote Eldon Best, ' the most soul-destroying thing according to native ideas ' is *tamaoa*, deprivation of *tapu* by means of cooked food. In the case of the Maori, however, it is the low-caste man who dare not eat of the chief's dish, whereas in India it is the high-caste Brahman who must not eat any food cooked by a man of a lower caste. A taboo on intermarriage could easily be traced to a similar source if not to the same one (among the Mafulu of New Guinea no girl who is not a near relative of a bachelor may even see him eat), since there is little use to a man in a wife who cannot cook for him. In Orissa there is a whole caste known as Chattarkhai which consists of descendants of Hindus who were outcasted for having taken food at relief kitchens in 1866. The caste consists of two endogamous sub-castes, one of which is of Brahman derivation, the other being derived from other castes.[5] Famines must have been an important factor in the splitting up of castes.

Ideas about soul-stuff or life-matter and of the necessity of protecting it by the observance of taboos are common over the whole area of south-east Asia and Australasia from India to New Zealand, though how far they represent undeveloped primitive ideas and how far they are the remnants of some more developed philosophy it is difficult to say. They have been described by Mills for the Ao Nagas, by Marshall for the Karen of Burma, by Warneck for the Batak of Sumatra, by Kruijt for the Toradja of Celebes, by Keysser for the Kai of New Guinea. Traces of these beliefs are very widely spread, and the present writer has given a brief account of them elsewhere.[6] Generally speaking this life-matter is finite and concrete, if invisible, but liable to be attracted and drawn away by any more powerful manifestation of the same principle or to be otherwise harmed if not protected. Its transferability has made it the underlying

---

[4] Stevenson, *Rites of the Twice-Born*, p. 246.
[5] O'Malley, *Caste Customs*, p. 30.
[6] In the Frazer Lecture for 1938, at Oxford, on *A Primitive Philosophy of Life*.

motive in ceremonial and perhaps other cannibalism, in head-hunting, and in human sacrifice, none of which is unknown in India. Life-matter may be inherent in apparently inanimate objects. Warneck says of the Batak: 'Soul is awarded to the *house*, the *hearth*, the *boat*, the *hatchet*, the *iron* and many other instruments not because they are fetiches, but because their usefulness is proof of their soul-power.' [7] One is again reminded of the Indian craftsman worshipping the tools of his craft.

These beliefs in life-matter, or soul-stuff, are closely associated with beliefs in *mana* and with the practice of magic. According to the Kai of New Guinea mere words have their own soul-stuff, which we may perhaps here call *mana*, just like a person's name, and a mere form of words may have its own efficacy—like a *mantram*. Wherever the belief in *mana* prevails a corresponding belief in the value of taboo as a protective measure is also to be found. It is possible that ideas of *mana* and taboo have been distributed to Indonesia and the Pacific from the Indian peninsula. Hocart has pointed out the analogy between the barber, *ambattan* in Tamil, whose business it is to shave heads, and the *mbota*, a clan in Fiji, who alone can touch the chief's head. [8] The Malayo-Polynesian word *tabu* itself seems to contain the basic meanings of segregation and refuge, [9] but it is abundantly clear that the ideas of *mana*, magic, and taboo have from a very ancient period been shared by India with Indonesia and the Pacific. Food taboos have already been mentioned, and they are particularly striking in connexion with caste. According to Handy [10] the 'eating tapu' in Polynesia requires 'men and women and persons of different degrees of sacredness' to eat separately, since 'a loss of *mana* would be incurred by the more sacred person as a result of the shared food's acting as a conductor'. This is precisely the outlook required for a taboo on commensality between caste and caste. Roy [11] has criticized this argument on the ground that the Brahman is at the head of all castes, yet his food can be taken by anyone, whereas the Polynesian chief's food cannot be taken by a man of lower position who would be destroyed by infection

[7] Quoted by S. C. Roy, ' Caste, Race and Religion ', in *Man in India*, XIV, no. 2, p. 117.
[8] ' India and the Pacific ', *C.J.S.*, vol. I, pt. IV, p. 176.
[9] I. H. N. Evans, ' Kempunan ', in *Man*, xx, 38 (May 1920).
[10] *Polynesian Religion*, p. 49.
[11] ' Caste, Race and Religion ', in *Man in India*, XIV, no. 2, p. 111.

with the chief's more powerful *mana*. This criticism is perhaps
inoperative when one regards the two systems as extreme developments in different environments from a common and primitive
basis. It is not suggested that the caste system has developed
from ideas of soul-stuff, *mana*, magic and taboo alone; only that
without these ideas it could not have developed.[12] If these ideas
alone were enough, one might expect to see a caste system in
every island from the Nicobars to Easter, instead of only in
India. At the same time Roy himself supplies evidence of a
precisely similar outlook to that of the Maori within the system
of Indian caste. If a Brahman enter the quarters of the Holeyas,
' they turn out in a body to slipper him, in former times it is
said to death ',[13] while a party of Brahmans who passed through
a Paraiyan hamlet had to run to escape cowpats and broomsticks
because contact with them meant ruin to Paraiyans.[14] The
taboo on a Brahman's entering a Barui's *pānbari* has been
mentioned earlier.[15] Again, ' when a Brahman has been in a
Kuricchan's house, the moment he leaves it, the place where he
was seated is besmeared with cowdung to remove the
pollution '.[16] Roy himself again tells us that the pre-Aryan
inhabitants of India had developed the art of magic to such an
extent that the Aryan immigrants into northern India called it
Asura Vidya, ' the science of the Asuras '.[17] Here, surely, is the
basis on which through a number of factors, too complex to have
occurred together elsewhere, the caste system of India has come
into being and developed into a unique social system found
nowhere else in the world. It is probably significant that one
observer reports that in Gujarat, at any rate, caste taboos are
stricter as one goes down in the social scale. High-caste Hindus
are less particular about their water than castes of lower social
position, and ' restrictions on intercourse increase as one goes

[12] Handy (*Polynesian Religion*, p. 318) sees a common element in *mana*
and the Vedic *brahma* and says: ' Similarly, I believe the tapu system as a
body of rules to prevent improper contact of the superior divine with the
inferior common or corrupt, to be an example of divergent evolution from
the same system out of which came also the Indian caste, with its untouch-
ableness, eating rules, purifications.'
[13] ' Caste, Race and Religion ', in *Man in India*, xiv, no. 2, p. 136,
quoting Capt. J. S. F. Mackenzie in *The Indian Antiquary*, ii, p. 65 (1873).
[14] Ibid., p. 137.
[15] p. 87 *supra*.
[16] S. C. Roy, ' Caste, Race and Religion ', in *Man in India*, xvii, no. 4,
p. 242 n., quoting Thurston (*Castes and Tribes*, iv, p. 126).
[17] Ibid., p. 232.

from the top to the bottom of the caste system. The Brahman, Vania, Rajput and Kanbi castes must marry their girls within their caste or subcaste, but they may eat together within the large circle of their whole caste. . . . But the artisan and depressed classes are more strict both with regard to food and marriage.'[18] Reasons have been given for supposing that castes of some sort preceded the impact of the Rigvedic invaders, but it is not suggested that these invaders did not play an important part in developing the system as it exists today. On the contrary, it is urged emphatically that the Indian caste system is the natural result of the interaction of a number of geographical, social, political, religious, and economic factors not elsewhere found in conjunction. No doubt ideas of magic, *mana*, taboo and soul-substance were not wanting among the Indo-Europeans themselves. Parsi priests have to undergo elaborate ceremonies of purification, and while in a state of purity must eat no food cooked and drink no water drawn by anyone but a man or woman of the priestly class.[19] 'With Parsis eating and drinking are religious rites.'[20] The *mana* principle appears in the Buddhist religion as *iddhi*[21] and in Islamic beliefs as *kudrat*.[22] In Hinduism it is familiar as *sakti*. It seems likely, however, that it was largely the social and political impact of the Rigvedic invaders with their definitely graded social classes that was responsible for introducing the principle of social precedence into a society already divided into groups isolated by taboos.

The general Hindu feeling about the caste system is that it has been 'established by divine ordinance' or at least with divine approval. Reference has already been made to the well-known lines in the Bhagavad Gita which inculcate the supreme merit of performing caste duties, which take precedence of all other obligations, including even those of friendship and kindred. Perfection, it is said, is only attained by the man who

[18] Desai, *Hindu Families in Gujarat* (Baroda, 1932), quoted by Roy in 'Caste, Race and Religion' (*Man in India*, XIV, no. 2, p. 147). According to Dalton (*Ethnography of Bengal*, p. 160 n.) some Kharias are excessively particular about the rules of pollution in regard to cooking vessels: 'He may not allow even his wife to cook for him, and if a stranger enters a house in which he keeps his earthen drinking and cooking vessels, and water pots, every vessel is polluted and the whole are destroyed or thrown away.'
[19] Roy, 'Caste, Race and Religion', *Man in India*, XIV, no. 2, p. 177.
[20] Modi, *Anthropological Papers*, pt. II, pp. 63, 64, quoted by Roy, loc. cit.
[21] Roy, loc. cit., p. 155.   [22] Abbott, *Keys of Power*, p. 3.

does not deviate from the duties of caste. Observance of caste, therefore, is equivalent to *dharma*, that is, to religious observance, righteousness, moral obligation. *Dharma* is not easy to translate accurately, but the term *Dharmeswar*—the Righteous One?—is used for God. In any case it is clearly the result of this teaching that social habits, caste customs, are inextricably tied up with religion. The Brahmanic codes have insisted that every community should obey its own rules. That insistence took place first at a stage in social evolution at which law consisted, largely at any rate, of a code of taboos. Hence the development of the caste system and the unusual success with which the growth of a 'plural' society [23] was attended in India. Inevitably communities incorporated into such a society would overlap; a person belonging to one group by tribal descent might belong to another by occupation. Hence, perhaps, castes of mixed origin like the Prabhu, Karan, or Kayastha, not to say Brahman. Hence also the apparently irrelevant association of caste with religion, coupled with a great variety of sanctions.

By way of conclusion an attempt may be made to recapitulate a number of the more obvious factors which have been indicated as probably contributing to the emergence and development of the caste system.

The geographical isolation of the Indian peninsula as a whole and of individual areas within it.

Primitive ideas about the power of food to transmit qualities.

Similar ideas of totemism, taboo, *mana*, and soul-stuff, or life-matter.

Ideas of pollution, ablution, purification, and ceremonial purity with associations of ritual sacrifice.

Ideas of the exclusive family, ancestor worship, and the sacramental meal.

Beliefs in reincarnation, and in the doctrine of *karma*.

Belief in magic associated with crafts and functions.

Hereditary occupations, and trade and craft secrets.

Guilds and associations of that character and various factors in the development of economic life.

Clash of antagonistic cultures, particularly between cultures with matrilineal and patrilineal modes of descent.

Clash of races, colour prejudice, and conquest.

[23] *Vide supra*, pp. 115, 127 sq.

The development of classes with exclusive religious and social privileges.

Individual isolation of tribes and polities, and their inclusion without absorption in larger administrative units.

Deliberate economic and administrative policies.

Exploitation by a highly intelligent but by no means entirely altruistic hierarchy which had evolved a religious philosophy too subtle for the mass of the people.

Even in this inclusive list, however, it is difficult to feel at all sure that all the more important factors contributing to the emergence of that unique social phenomenon, the caste system, have been included. Probably enough emphasis has not been laid in previous theories of the origin of caste on the geographical aspects of the situation. The fact is, many roads of migration have led into India—and have ended there. This has resulted in the accumulation of a large number of societies of very different levels of culture and very varying customs in an area in which they have neither been mutually inaccessible nor without some measure of individual isolation. The mere inescapable necessity of finding a *modus vivendi* on the part of a number of different cultures has probably played a not unimportant part among the various factors that have combined to cause the caste system to develop. At the same time it is pretty clear that in previous attempts to account for caste insufficient importance has been attached, not only to geographical and migrational considerations and to the clash of matrilineal and patrilineal societies, but more particularly to that complex of beliefs in *mana*, taboo and magic which surrounds the primitive philosophy of soul-stuff or life-matter which is so widely spread and so deeply seated in the mainland of south-east Asia and in the islands of Indonesia and the Pacific. To illustrate the strength of those ideas in India up to the present time an appendix on their relationship to Hinduism has been added to the account of caste given in the foregoing chapters, though the higher esoteric philosophy of Hinduism is treated as entirely outside the scope of this volume.

PART FOUR
APPENDICES

APPENDIX A

THE POSITION OF THE EXTERIOR CASTES

THE substance of this Appendix has been taken with some abridgement, but with little other change, from Appendix I to my *Report on the Census of India*, 1931. No attempt has been made here to deal with events that have taken place since 1931, but the position of these castes had probably altered very little between that year and the outbreak of war with Japan in 1941. Since that war came to an end, change has probably been more rapid, but from what it is possible to learn from correspondents in India and from articles in Indian periodicals, the rate of change is a great deal slower than many Indians appreciate, and in the more remote areas, where communications are slow and difficult, it has probably been of a negligible quality in spite of new laws and of genuine attempts to help the exterior castes, particularly on the part of the Central Government. At the same time it has been a very remarkable and striking circumstance that the new Constitution for India should have been piloted through the assembly by a person who belonged himself to one of the exterior castes, and a circumstance that cannot be without real and weighty significance for the future.

The term ' exterior ' for the Hindu castes hitherto known as ' depressed ' was originally suggested by the Census Superintendent for Assam and was adopted in the report [1] as the most satisfactory alternative to the unfortunate and depressing label ' Depressed Classes '. It has been criticized as being the same term as ' outcaste ', only of five instead of two syllables, and it must be admitted that ' exterior ' is but old ' out ' writ large. At the same time it is here submitted that outcaste, with an *e*, has not unnaturally attracted to its connotation the implications of the quite differently derived outcast, with no *e*. Outcaste correctly interpreted seems to mean no more than one who is outside the caste system and is therefore not admitted to Hindu society, but since in practice the exterior castes also contained those who had been cast out from the Hindu social body

[1] i.e. *Report on the Census of India*, 1931.

for some breach of caste rules, 'outcaste' and 'outcast' were in some cases synonymous, and the derogatory implications of obliquity attaching to the latter term have unjustly coloured the former, a taint which is not conveyed by the substitution of the word 'exterior', which may connote exclusion but not extrusion. The term *a-varna*, 'without *varna*' or outside the four *varnas* (*vide* pp. 64 sqq.), is sometimes used and aptly expresses the same idea.

The instructions of the Government of India for the taking of the 1931 census concluded with the following enjoinder:

'The Government of India also desire that attention should be paid to the collection of information conducive to a better knowledge of the backward and depressed classes and of the problem involved in their present and future welfare.'

In that connexion the following instructions were issued to the various Superintendents of Census Operations [1931] in India:

'For this purpose it will be necessary to have a list of castes to be included in depressed classes and all provinces are asked to frame a list applicable to the province. There are very great difficulties in framing a list of this kind and there are insuperable difficulties in framing a list of depressed classes which will be applicable to India as a whole.'

A subsequent instruction ran as follows:

'I have explained depressed castes as castes, contact with whom entails purification on the part of high-caste Hindus. It is not intended that the term should have any reference to occupation as such but to those castes which by reason of their traditional position in Hindu society are denied access to temples, for instance, or have to use separate wells or are not allowed to sit inside a school house but have to remain outside, or which suffer similar social disabilities. These disabilities vary in different parts of India, being much more severe in the south of India than elsewhere. At the same time the castes which belong to this class are generally known and can in most parts of India be listed for a definite area, though perhaps the lists for India as a whole will not coincide.'

The question of the preparation of lists for each province was discussed at a meeting of the Superintendents of Census Operations in January 1931 before the census took place. It was agreed that each province should make a list of castes who suffered disability on account of their low social position and on account of being debarred from temples, schools or wells. No specific definition of depressed castes was framed and no more precise instructions were issued to the Superintendents of Census Operations, because it was realized that conditions varied so much from province to province and from district to

13

district even, within some provinces, that it would be unwise to tie down the Superintendent of Census Operations with too meticulous instructions. The general method of proceeding prescribed was that of local inquiry into what castes were held to be depressed, and why, and the framing of a list accordingly. It was decided that Muslims and Christians should be excluded from the term 'depressed class' and that, generally speaking, hill and forest tribes, who had not become Hindu but whose religion was returned as Tribal, should also be excluded, and in the numbers of the exterior castes given below these principles have been followed. A note on the depressed and backward classes in Assam submitted to the Franchise Committee by the Superintendent of Census Operations for that province affords a very clear example of the way in which these principles were intended to be applied and have been applied by Superintendents of Census Operations, and an extract from it is given towards the end of this appendix.

Both for social and for political reasons it is obviously necessary to know the number of these classes not only in India as a whole but also in different provinces. The matter is of importance not only with reference to their representation in the body politic, but also with reference to any social work that is to be done towards raising them from their present backward position to one more nearly comparable with that of more advanced social groups.

The Census Commissioner in 1921 (*Census of India*, 1921, vol. I, part I, para. 193) gave what he describes as *minimum* numbers of the depressed classes in various provinces, making a total of 52,680,000. This figure, he states, must be taken as a low estimate, since it does not include all those who should have been included, and he says: 'We may confidently place the numbers of these depressed classes, all of whom are considered impure, at something between 55 and 60 millions in India proper.' Of the $52\frac{1}{2}$ million for which the Census Commissioner gave actual figures, less than $43\frac{1}{2}$ million were to be found in British India. This figure agrees fairly well with the 42 million odd given as the figure of depressed classes by the Franchise Committee of 1919. It is also not greatly at variance with the $44\frac{1}{2}$ million estimated by the Nair Central Committee of 1929 as the figure of depressed classes in British India, but it varies very considerably from the Hartog Committee's figure of approximately 30 million. Clearly it is time that some more definite figures were obtained than the estimates hitherto employed. There are, however, a considerable number of difficulties in arriving at a determined figure.

The definition to be used in arriving at the figure of depressed classes is a very difficult matter. The following possible tests are to be considered:

(1) Whether the caste or class in question can be served by clean Brahmans or not.

(2) Whether the caste or class in question can be served by the barbers, water-carriers, tailors, etc., who serve the caste Hindus.

(3) Whether the caste in question pollutes a high-caste Hindu by contact or by proximity.

(4) Whether the caste or class in question is one from whose hands a caste Hindu can take water.

(5) Whether the caste or class in question is debarred from using public conveniences, such as roads, ferries, wells or schools.

(6) Whether the caste or class in question is debarred from the use of Hindu temples.

(7) Whether in ordinary social intercourse a well-educated member of the caste or class in question will be treated as an equal by high-caste men of the same educational qualifications.

(8) Whether the caste or class in question is merely depressed on account of its own ignorance, illiteracy, or poverty, and but for that, would be subject to no social disability.

(9) Whether it is depressed on account of the occupation followed, and whether but for that occupation it would be subject to no social disability.

Now it is obvious that several of these tests themselves involve an unknown factor—What is a clean Brahman? What is the line between a high-caste and a low-caste Hindu, since both adjectives may and ordinarily would have a merely comparative sense? What constitutes pollution or what constitutes the right to use a temple, since here again there are grades from those who must remain entirely outside and not approach a temple at all to those who are admitted to the inner sanctuary? In deciding what is an exterior caste, none of these tests can be taken alone. From the point of view of the State the important test is the right to use public conveniences—roads, wells and schools— and if this be taken as the primary test, religious disabilities and the social difficulties indirectly involved by them may be regarded as contributory only. Some importance must be attached to them, since obviously if the general public regards the persons of certain groups as so distasteful that concerted action is resorted to in order to keep them away, persons of those groups do suffer under a serious disability. It is not enough to say that a road is a public road, and that if *A* considers himself polluted by the presence of *B* at a distance of 30 yards and no compulsion rests on *B* to remove himself from the road to let *A* pass, the disability is *A*'s and not *B*'s, since *A* must leave the road or be polluted. That is all very well if *B* and his friends are in such a position as to be able to impose on *A* the position of being the one to leave the road. If, however, it is possible for *A* and his friends, by boycotting *B* and his friends for certain purposes, to bring pressure on *B* to disregard his legal rights and to conform to *A*'s religious prejudices and leave the road whenever *A* is seen at a distance, clearly *B* has in practice no freedom of action in the matter of the road, whether his religious scruples are involved or not. This question of the use of roads has been taken as an illustration, but in point of fact the restriction of the use of roads is one which seems to be generally disappearing and has possibly disappeared to such an extent that the question may be ignored as far as British India is concerned. The use of wells, however, is another matter, and the disability of the exterior castes varies from not being allowed to approach the village well at all to the position, common in Bengal, in which persons of certain castes may not draw water themselves but must await someone of a clean caste, who draws water for them at the well. The question of schools is another very real problem for the exterior castes, since in many parts of India if they sat inside the school they would be made to suffer in some other way by the higher castes using the school; and whereas the acquisition of reading and writing, at least, may be taken for granted in the case of the children of any Brahman, and of other castes as well, it is an exception in the case of the exterior castes, the presence of whose children is disliked in the school by their social superiors and whose children, if they read at all, must sit outside in the sun and dust. It is often argued that untouchability is merely dependent on the occupation, so that an untouchable person or caste abandoning an unclean occupation becomes touchable. This may be true in a literal sense, but it is not true morally, since members of exterior castes who may have abandoned their traditional calling for two or three generations are still liable to be treated as outside the pale of decent society, and their presence is apt to be regarded as an offence by members of interior castes, while they would not be ordinarily admitted to social functions on a footing of equality.

For purposes therefore of deciding what persons are to be included in the numbers of the exterior castes, it has been necessary for each province to deal with the problem in its own way and to produce its own list. It is not possible to say generally that such and such a caste is exterior to Hindu society and to apply that dictum to the whole of India. It may be possible to do so in the case of certain castes, such as those of Dom and Bhangi, but it certainly is not the case that a caste which is depressed in one part of India is depressed everywhere. Consequently, each provincial superintendent has had to draw up his own list, taking into account the various factors enumerated above, and to reckon as depressed only those castes or classes who definitely suffer from serious social and political handicap on account of their degraded position in the Hindu social scheme. So much is this the position that, in the Central Provinces for instance, the castes to be treated as depressed for purposes of census figures have varied from district to district, and no list is possible at all which is applicable to the whole of the province for all the castes concerned. Many castes and tribes who would be included by some, at any rate, of the tests mentioned above have been excluded from the list on the ground that they suffer no tangible disability as a result of their inferiority in the Hindu system. Many primitive tribes, for instance, are in an ambiguous position by reason of their not really being Hindus at all. Such tribes, when they come within the Hindu system, often become automatically depressed, largely on account of the fact that they have no prejudices against occupations and food which are taboo to interior Hindus. On the other hand, the socially superior individuals of these identical tribes are very frequently able to get themselves incorporated into the Hindu system as Rajputs or Kshatriyas, though their fellow-tribesmen may remain exterior. In some cases, however, a complete tribe has succeeded in establishing its claim to a more or less equivocal twice-born status. In these circumstances, therefore, non-Hinduized hill and forest tribes have been excluded from the total of the exterior castes, as, until they reach the stage of incorporation in regular Hindu society, they do not really suffer by their potential position in that scheme. Similarly, criminal tribes have not been included unless their condition be such that, even if they ceased to be criminal by habit or profession and lived as peaceable and law-abiding citizens, they would still be depressed on account of their social position as distinct from their occupational stigma. Again, there are numbers of castes which, though they are regarded by interior Hindus as ceremonially polluting and as such that from their hands water cannot be taken, have in many cases such strong caste organizations and include so many individuals of substance and education that they have built up for themselves a strong position which obviates the need of any special measures for their social, political or religious protection. It is these considerations which have caused the Census Superintendent of Cochin State to exclude the Iruvan from the number of those depressed, while the Shaha, Teli and Mahishya of Bengal and Assam would themselves protest at any such inclusion.

The note on the Depressed and Backward Classes in Assam by the Census Superintendent for that province, which forms an appendix to the Assam Census Report [1931], affords an excellent example of the facts and considerations taken into account in determining what constitutes a depressed caste. In the case of Assam, the numbers of the exterior castes are so high in comparison with the total number of interior Hindus, or rather the number of interior Hindus is so comparatively small in a province in which the number of backward classes and hill tribes is high, that the disabilities attaching to depression are slight compared with those in most provinces, but the factors to be taken into account are the same everywhere. The non-Hindus and the hill and forest tribes included by the Assam Census Superintendent as backward classes have been excluded from the figures given in the table opposite, which amount for all India to just a little over 50 millions.

These then being the numbers of the depressed classes in India, some estimate is necessary of their position at the present time [1933], and it has already been pointed out that their disabilities can be roughly divided into two categories. First, that under which they are barred from public utilities, such as the use of roads and tanks, and secondly, their religious disabilities which debar them from the use of temples, burning grounds, *mats* and some other institutions. In addition to the above, but arising out of the second of these, there are the disabilities involved in relations with private individuals, such as the services of barbers and the admission to tea-shops, hotels, or theatres owned by private individuals. A resolution of the Anti-Untouchability Conference of 1929 in Madras regretted 'to note that in Restaurants, Coffee Hotels, Hair-Dressing Saloons, Water Pandals, etc., notices are hung prominently excluding the untouchables', and the Census Superintendent for the Central Provinces writes: 'The fact that a sweeper may sit beside a high-class Hindu in a railway carriage or a motor-lorry without any question of his right to do so has not yet made it any more easy in the interior for a touring officer to persuade cartmen of some castes to carry his sweeper from camp to camp. In fact, in certain districts it is always essential to employ at least one cartman of humble caste for this purpose.'

Theoretically perhaps the admission to Hindu temples would be enough, once it is conceded, to remove all the other disabilities, for the temple is not merely a religious institution but is also in many ways a social one, for the term must be taken to include such buildings as *namghars* in Assam, which, as temples do in some parts of India, serve as a village hall or a town hall for the public generally. A temple also contains a school, so that the absence of the right of entering the temple may debar an individual from the possibility of attending the school. In some Hindu temples, such as the Parbati Temple in Poona, the Kalarama Temple at Nasik, the Hajo Temple in Assam, it has been in the past the practice to admit non-Hindus, such

Province or State	Total population	Total Hindu	Total exterior castes	Percentage of exterior castes on Hindu population	Total population	Percentage of exterior castes who are literate
India	350,529,557	239,195,140	50,195,770	21	14	1.9
Provinces	271,431,549	177,727,988	39,064,009	22	14	1.6
1. Ajmer Merwara	560,292	434,509	76,816	18	14	2.2
2. Andamans and Nicobars	29,463	7,618	512	7	2	?
3. Assam	8,622,251	4,931,760	1,829,009	37	21	3.1
4. Baluchistan (Districts & Administered Territories)	463,508	41,432	5,702	14	1	6.9
5. Bengal	50,114,002	21,570,407	6,899,809	32	14	5.0
6. Bihar and Orissa	37,677,576	31,011,474	5,744,393	19	15	0.6
7. Bombay	21,854,866	16,621,221	1,750,424	11	8	2.8
8. Burma	14,647,497	570,953	No return of caste	—	—	—
9. Central Provinces & Berar	15,507,723	13,338,223	2,818,346	21	18	1.5
10. Coorg	163,327	146,007	24,803	17	15	1.5
11. Delhi	636,246	399,863	72,883	18	11	1.4
12. Madras	46,740,107	41,277,370	7,234,104	18	15	1.5
13. North-West Frontier Province	2,425,076	142,977	5,468	4	—	3.6
14. Punjab	23,580,852	6,328,588	1,279,459	20	5	0.8
15. United Provinces of Agra and Oudh	48,408,763	40,905,586	11,322,281	28	23	0.5
States and Agencies	*79,098,088*	*61,407,152*	*11,131,761*	*18*	*14*	*3.1*
16. Assam States	625,606	272,890	1,421	—	—	12.9
17. Baluchistan States	405,109	12,249	20	—	—	?
18. Baroda State	2,443,007	2,152,071	203,043	9	8	10.3
19. Bengal States	973,336	641,662	30,822	5	3	?
20. Bihar and Orissa States	4,652,007	4,194,878	631,864	15	14	1.0
21. Bombay States	4,468,396	3,921,088	348,574	9	8	2.8
22. Central India Agency	6,632,790	5,852,204	797,902	17	12	0.3
23. Central Provinces States	2,483,214	1,788,401	252,732	14	10	0.5
24. Gwalior State	3,523,070	3,271,576	678,119	21	19	?
25. Hyderabad State	14,436,148	12,176,727	2,473,230	20	17	0.6
26. Jammu & Kashmir State	3,646,243	736,222	170,928	23	5	0.5
27. Madras States Agency	6,754,484	4,323,150	1,960,370	45	29	13.8
Cochin State	*1,205,016*	*780,484*	*125,339*	*16*	*10*	*4.8*
Travancore State	*5,095,973*	*3,134,888*	*1,769,735*	*56*	*35*	*14.9*
Other Madras States	*453,495*	*407,778*	*65,296*	*16*	*14*	*3.5*
28. Mysore State	6,557,302	6,015,880	1,000,326	17	15	1.4
29. North-West Frontier Province (Agencies and Tribal Areas)	46,451	13,651	542	4	1	
30. Punjab States	437,787	383,883	94,347	25	22	0.3
31. Punjab States Agency	4,472,218	1,887,249	392,999	21	9	
32. Rajputana Agency	11,225,712	9,578,805	1,565,409	16	14	0.4
33. Sikkim State	109,808	47,074	2,029	4	2	?
34. United Provinces States	1,206,070	950,724	208,864	22	17	0.2
35. Western India States Agency	3,999,250	3,245,768	318,220	10	8	1.9

as Christians and Muslims, to a point to which the untouchable Hindus were never admitted at all.   It is, however, not quite certain how far under present conditions the actual right of admission to a temple would, if conceded, remove the social disabilities of the depressed castes, since it might have the effect of merely driving the higher castes to shun the temples to which the untouchables were admitted.[2]   In any case the right varies much in different places.   An Iruva or a Tiya in Malabar must stay 325 feet from the curtain wall of the temple of Guruvayur, for instance, and this wall encloses a space 350 feet square with the temple in the centre.   Yet the Iruva have not been treated, in Cochin State at any rate, as a depressed caste at all, since, though deprived there likewise of temple entry, they are otherwise well-to-do and not ill-educated.

As regards the civil rather than the religious disabilities to which the depressed classes are at present subjected, the first one mentioned above is the right to use the public roads; up to how recently the use of public roads has been debarred in certain cases may be gathered from the fact that the untouchables of Travancore made an organized attempt in 1924 to obtain the use of roads which skirted the temple at Vaikom. These roads were public roads, maintained by the State for the use of everybody, but, on account of their proximity to the temple building, the untouchables were not allowed to use certain sections which skirted the temple too closely.   Ultimately, as a result of *satyagraha*, the temple compound was enlarged and the ban on the roads was removed, the roads having been realigned so that their users were no longer within the polluting distance of the temple.   In 1926, and again in 1930, a similar case occurred in Travancore in connexion with Sachindram Temple, which is one of the richest in the State. Here again the depressed classes wanted the right to use a road maintained by public funds and belonging to the State.   In the matter of the use of roads generally, however, the depressed castes are no longer in the position in which some of them were when the *Mangalore District Gazetteer* was written, when the Ande Koraga had to carry a spittoon round their necks as being so highly polluting that they could not be allowed to expectorate on the public road.   It has recently been reported however that a caste has been found in the Tamilnad, the very sight of which is polluting, so that its unfortunate members are compelled to follow nocturnal habits, leaving their dens after dark and scuttling home at the false dawn like the badger, hyena, or aard-vark.   *The Hindu* of 24 December 1932 writes of them as follows : ' In this [Tinnevelly] district there is a class of unseeables called Purada Vannans.   They are not allowed to

---

[2] This in fact is reported to have been the result in Malabar, where most well-to-do households have a private shrine.

come out during day-time because their sight is considered to be pollution.' Sóme of these people, who wash the clothes of other exterior castes, working between midnight and daybreak, were with difficulty persuaded to leave their houses to interview Mr A. V. Thakkar, who described them as coming only after repeated persuasion and then with 'their whole bodies shaking and trembling'.[3]

The case of wells has already been alluded to, and is a far more widespread and real grievance than any which may still survive in regard to the use of roads. Generally speaking, if the exterior castes have succeeded in asserting their right to use public wells, the higher castes have given them up. Here again the difficulty about the use of wells will be found to be most prevalent in the drier parts of India where water is scarce. In Assam this difficulty is not worth mentioning, and in Bengal, where it exists, it is usually got over by water being drawn for the exterior castes by some interior-caste Hindu. This arrangement is obviously open to certain drawbacks, but it is not so serious as the custom in many parts of upper India and southern India which prohibits the exterior castes from having water at all from the well which is used by interior Hindus. The same applies to the use of *dhărămshālās* and of public burning ghats and burial grounds, in regard to all of which the position of the exterior castes is much the same as it is in regard to the use of wells.

With regard to schools, the Director of Public Instruction for Bombay, reporting for the year 1928-9, remarks that admission to schools was not refused to the children of the depressed classes in the schools under the control of any local body except the District Local Board at Ratnagiri, the District Local Board of the Nasik District (some schools only), and in the Ahmedabad and Surat districts. In the latter districts the students generally used to sit in temples, *dharamshalas* or private houses and the pupils of the depressed classes were objected to, but the objection was withdrawn on warning being given that in this way the schools would lose any grants that they enjoyed from the Government. How far this withdrawal of objection was effective is doubtful, since at any rate in one case the depressed classes at Surat had to withdraw their children from the school as a result of the indirect pressure exerted on them by higher castes. Similarly, in some cases the depressed caste pupils find it better to sit outside the schools, as, if they sit inside, they are boycotted and compelled to leave the school. Thus at Kaira in April 1931 some Dheds took their seats with other Hindu boys in the municipal school. Kaira had been one of the centres of Mr Gandhi's activities and no objection was raised on that day, but when the parents of the interior-caste

[3] Cf. *supra*, p. 81, n. 31.

boys heard of it they threatened a boycott of the school and of the teacher if the Dhed boys were allowed to sit with theirs, or even to occupy the same classroom, with the result that the next day the Dheds were refused admission to the school premises. On the other hand, in Sind and in the central and southern divisions of Bombay it was reported that there were no primary schools managed by the local authorities which refused admission to the children of the depressed castes. Similarly, in Assam no inconvenience appears to have been experienced by the exterior castes in the matter of school attendance. On the other hand, in many parts of India the inconvenience is greater than it is in Bombay. Very few of the exterior castes attend schools nominally accessible to them in Negapatam, Kumbakonam, Tinnevelly, Cocanada, Bezwada and Narsapur and other towns in southern India, though in Madras, Madura, Sivaganga and some other towns a number of children of the exterior castes attend schools which are not especially reserved for them and which are not boycotted by the higher castes. In most parts of southern India it is necessary to have special schools for the exterior castes, since it is not yet possible to induce the higher castes to study in their company. In July 1931, when it was decided to admit exterior castes into all the aided schools, a number of schools had to close, and from some other schools the higher caste children were withdrawn. Similarly, in Baroda State the abolition of separate schools in November 1931 is reported to have caused great resentment among the caste Hindus, who in some cases withdrew their children from schools and in others destroyed the crops of the exterior castes or poured kerosene oil into the wells used by them. In Bengal the Rural Primary Education Bill, passed in 1930, appears to have been opposed by members representing the caste Hindus, and it is alleged that this opposition was aimed at depriving the non-caste Hindus, and also the poorer Muslims, of the benefits of literacy. In Cochin State, on the other hand, much has been done to open all educational institutions to the exterior castes, though this has involved in some cases the removal of the school to another site, while cases have occurred of some ill-treatment of the castes now admitted to the schools. Generally speaking, however, during the last decade [1921-31] the exterior castes at school in Cochin increased in number from some 1,500 to some 14,000 and out of 700 recognized schools only three were still reserved to the higher castes in 1931, and a Protector of the backward and depressed classes had recently been appointed. Cochin, however, is probably in many ways exceptional.

In regard to the matter of the right to enter Hindu temples, the exterior castes were advised by Mr Gandhi not to attempt to gain entry, as God resided in their breasts. A temple, however, as has been pointed out, is more than a purely religious institution, and the right of temple entry is by some regarded as the key position with regard to the removal of untouchability. The claim to enter temples is not opposed only by high-caste Hindus; even *Justice*, the organ of the anti-Brahman Party, writes as follows:

'For many centuries these peoples, most of whom until recently were Animists, were content to worship at their own shrines, and to try to force themselves into Hindu temples is not . . . to make themselves popular. Nor can we think that any grave wrong is done by their continued exclusion . . . they would be better occupied in improving their own condition than in a violent attempt to assert rights which no one had heard of till a few years ago.'

There is, on the other hand, a definite movement among many more advanced Hindus to remove the ban on temple entry,[4] a movement which has since the census (of 1931) been given much impetus by Mr Gandhi's fast and the negotiations following it for the admission of untouchables to Hindu temples generally, and it may be mentioned as an instance of this that eight temples of a Telugu community in Bombay were reported to have been opened to untouchables in February 1930. On the other hand, recent cases of attempts to obtain entry by exterior castes had led to violence. Some 2,000 untouchables collected outside the Kala Ram temple at Nasik on 3 March 1930, and a meeting which attempted to bring about a settlement was stoned by the orthodox. Ultimately some 150,000 Mahars and Chamars were reported to have collected at Nasik and the temple had to be closed for about a month to keep them from entering it. The admission of caste Hindus by a private passage ended in violence in which the orthodox were the aggressors, and which was extended to Mahar villages in the neighbourhood, where the exterior castes were violently attacked by caste Hindus, their wells polluted and in some cases their houses burned. A similar attempt to force an entrance a year later had similar results, and in December 1931 the same sort of situation arose on an attempt of the exterior castes to bathe in the Ramakund, the sacred pool at Nasik, and again in April over the dragging of the *rath*. Similarly at Singanallur in south India the question of entry to a temple led to a free fight in 1930, and at some other places also. In Nagpur a temple was voluntarily opened to untouchables, and in the Dacca Division in Bengal a *satyagraha* of 9 months' duration ended in the temple doors being forced open by a band of high-

[4] A Congress 'Independence Day' pledge runs: 'We know that the distinction between Caste Hindus and Harijans [i.e. the exterior castes] must be abolished', and a Brahman political leader has actually declared: 'We want intermarriage to make the people biologically one'.

caste women who sympathized with the *satyagrahis*. This was in May, but it was reported in October that the temple was deserted by high-caste Hindus. One wonders therefore how far the higher castes are likely to make use of a pan-Hindu temple recently endowed at Ratnagiri with a view to providing a common place of worship for all castes.

The prohibition against exterior castes entering the Hindu temples naturally raises the question whether they can really be called Hindu at all. Generally speaking, the answer must be that they are definitely Hindus; they worship the same deities and, though they are refused entry to the temples, boxes are placed outside, at the limits to which they can approach, to receive their offerings. The degree of Hinduism does, however, vary considerably; thus the Mahar and Chamar in general are very decidedly Hindu, whereas the Chuhra of the Punjab is very doubtfully so, taking a Hindu tone when living by a Hindu village, a Muslim tone in a Muslim village, and that of a Sikh in a Sikh village. Possibly the Chuhra should really be described as tribal by religion, and the possibly connected Chodhra of the Bombay Presidency are definitely regarded as a forest tribe rather than a caste. In any case, in the Punjab the question has been partly solved at this census by the Chuhra returning himself as an *Ad-Dharmi*, that is to say, a follower of the original religion. For him it means the customs immemorially observed by his caste or tribe, but of course the term might mean very different things to different peoples. In the Punjab its use as distinct from Hindu (in other provinces the exterior castes have frequently returned themselves as *Adi-Hindu, Adi-Dravida*, etc., with a similar implication to that of *Ad-Dharmi*) is probably a political expedient in order to obtain more effective representation on the provincial legislative body, and, in spite of the occasional use of the word ' Hindu ' with reference to caste Hindus and excluding the exterior castes, it must be held that these castes generally are Hindu by religion even if they are not Hindu socially, hence the expression ' exterior caste ' is suitably applied to castes who follow the Hindu religion, but are not admitted to Hindu society.

This social bar tends to foster conversion to the Sikh faith, to Islam, or to Christianity, though even after conversion the social stigma does not vanish at once. This is hardly to be expected. The Mazhbi Sikhs are looked down upon by the Sikhs who are not Mazhbi.[5] The southern Indian Christians distinguish between the castes of their converts in their seating

[5] A reviewer of the first edition of this book, writing in the *Journal of the Royal Asiatic Society,* drew attention to experience of caste in the armed services in the war of 1939-45. He stated that while Hindus of varying castes were willing to feed with each other and with adherents of other religions, they were not prepared to do so with men recruited from

accommodation in churches, and the dislike of the exterior castes does not immediately disappear when they turn Muslim. At the same time, once they are converted it does not take them very long before they can rise in the social scale, and in the case of Indian Christians in southern India a period of about three generations often, perhaps usually, sees them accepted as the equals of previous converts of most castes.

There are other points in which the exterior castes suffer socially. Thus exception is taken to their wearing the ornaments usually worn by higher castes, and in some cases they are not allowed to wear gold ornaments at all. Cases are on record in which Chamars, for instance, have been beaten for dressing like Rajputs, and the mounting of an exterior caste bridegroom upon a horse for his bridal procession has led to a boycott of the caste in question by the higher caste neighbours. In December 1930 the Kallar in Ramnad propounded eight prohibitions, the disregard of which led to the use of violence by the Kallar against the exterior castes, whose huts were fired, whose granaries and property were destroyed, and whose livestock was looted. These eight prohibitions were as follows:

'(i) that the Adi-Dravidas shall not wear ornament of gold and silver;

'(ii) that the males should not be allowed to wear their clothes below their knees or above the hips;

'(iii) that their males should not wear coats or shirts or baniyans;

'(iv) no Adi-Dravida shall be allowed to have his hair cropped;

'(v) that the Adi-Dravidas should not use other than earthenware vessels in their homes;

'(vi) their women shall not be allowed to cover the upper portion of their bodies by clothes or ravukvais or thavanies;

'(vii) their women shall not be allowed to use flowers or saffron paste; and

'(viii) the men shall not use umbrellas for protection against sun and rain nor should they wear sandals.'

In June 1931, the eight prohibitions not having been satisfactorily observed by the exterior castes in question, the Kallar met together and framed eleven prohibitions, which went still further than the original eight, and an attempt to enforce these led to more violence. These eleven prohibitions were:

the exterior castes. He went on to say that while such persons were often enlisted in ordinary units formerly, ' even the exigencies of the recent war have permitted only of their being taken into special formations '. And from this he infers that untouchability seems likely to endure ' as the vital criterion '. It had however long been the practice to enrol Mazhbi Sikhs, who are Chuhra by extraction, in separate pioneer units.

' 1. The Adi-Dravidas and Devendrakula Velalars should not wear clothes below their knees.

' 2. The men and women of the above said depressed classes should not wear gold jewels.

' 3. Their women should carry water only in mud pots and not in copper or brass vessels. They should use straw only to carry the water pots and no cloths should be used for that purpose.

' 4. Their children should not read and get themselves literate or educated.

' 5. The children should be asked only to tend the cattle of the Mirasdars.

' 6. Their men and women should work as slaves of the Mirasdars in their respective Pannais.

' 7. They should not cultivate the land either on *waram* or lease from the Mirasdars.

' 8. They must sell away their own lands to Mirasdars of the village at very cheap rates, and if they don't do so, no water will be allowed to them to irrigate their lands. Even if something is grown by the help of rain-water, the crops should be robbed away, when they are ripe for harvest.

' 9. They must work as coolies from 7 a.m. to 6 p.m. under the Mirasdars and their wages shall be for men Re. 0-4-0 per day and for women Re. 0-2-0 per day.

' 10. The above said communities should not use Indian Music (Melam, etc.), in their marriages and other celebrations.

' 11. They must stop their habit of going on a horse in procession before tying the Thali thread in Marriage, and they must use their house doors as a palanquin for the marriage processions and no vehicle should be used by them, for any purpose.'

Similarly, in Bengal the use by a Namasudra bridegroom of a palanquin in a marriage procession led to a disturbance, and other instances could probably be quoted from other parts of India.

It is not suggested that the eight or eleven injunctions of the Kallar would be taken very seriously by anyone but themselves, but they are quoted here to indicate the attitude often adopted towards the exterior castes.

Economically the exterior castes in eastern India are generally speaking self-supporting and by no means desperately poor. In western India their position often is that of scavenger or village menial, for whose service there is a certain amount of necessity which is recompensed by a traditional provision of certain village lands or by other methods of payment in kind. The trouble frequently is that the number of these menials has become superfluous and they none the less expect to be fed by the village for unwanted services, and if they do not get so fed they steal the grain, no doubt regarding it as theirs by right. In southern India again the exterior castes are generally derived from various classes of cultivating serfs who until recently were tied to the soil. In northern India their economic position varies a good deal, since leather-workers for instance in industrial towns find a ready livelihood, whereas the exterior castes in the agricultural areas, where they can only obtain the worst land and the worst wells, are very often extremely poverty-stricken.

The origin of the position of the exterior castes is partly racial, partly religious, and partly a matter of social custom. There can be little doubt but the idea of untouchability originates in taboo. Reminiscences of such a taboo are still to be seen in Burma, where grave-digging is a profession involving a social stigma of a kind which will not permit of association with persons of other professions. A comparison of this custom with the position of those who dig graves for the hill tribes in the surrounding areas leaves little doubt but that the repulsion originates in the fear of some sort of death infection, and the underlying idea is not that the person himself is polluted by unclean work but that his mere association with death may infect others, with whom the grave-digger comes into contact, with the probability of dying. The treatment of washermen all over India as a depressed caste is almost certainly traceable to a similar taboo, the objection perhaps arising from an association with the menstrual clothes of women and consequently an infection which, in the first instance, is magical, though it later comes to be regarded merely as a matter of personal cleanliness. The untouchability which has originated in taboo has undoubtedly been accentuated by differences of race and the racial antipathies which seem common to every branch of the human family and have reinforced the magical taboo. An instance of this sort of thing may again be found in Burma, which, as there is no caste there in the Indian sense, is useful as providing indications of the process of caste formation. Here pagoda slaves, the status of whom is hereditary, are looked down upon by other classes. In general, pagoda slaves have been recruited from non-Burmese races. Large numbers of Arakanese, Talaings, Manipuris and Siamese have been settled in various parts of Burma by various conquering monarchs as slaves of different pagodas. This racial element is probably to be traced again in the prohibition of the wearing of ornaments by certain castes. Thus in the Ao tribe in the Naga Hills of Assam one of the subtribal groups, which is apparently of different origin to the rest of the tribe, is not allowed to wear ivory on both arms. Similar restrictions are found in the Laccadive Islands. The same element probably appears in the practice of hypergamy, and one of the first steps which any section of an exterior caste takes in order to raise its social standing is to deny to other sections the right to marry its daughters though continuing for the time being to take wives from among them. Thus have the Haliya Kaibartta severed themselves from the Jaliya Kaibartta and established themselves as a separate caste, no longer depressed, and even so a section of the Namasudra is now attempting to segregate itself. Indeed, as between different sections of the exterior castes prejudice is just as strong as between the interior castes and the exterior castes generally. The Mahar in Bombay have objected to sharing their counsels and conferences with Chamars, and Mahar and Chamar have unanimously spurned the Bhangi. Similarly, in Madras Pallans have objected to being classed with Chakli whom they regard as no less inferior to them than the Paraiyan, though all alike are untouchables to a good-caste Hindu. Religion, of course, with its apparatus of holy vessels, sacred animals and sacrosanct priests, has also contributed to the creation of the idea of untouchability; and society in general by its natural dislike of certain unclean occupations and by its very proper antipathy to criminal professions has done much to depress and stereotype the position of the exterior castes.

In 1916, and again in 1920, the Government of India called for a report as to the moral and material conditions of the depressed classes and for proposals for their amelioration from all local governments. The records of the consequent reports will be found under *Proceedings of the Government of India in the Home Department*, nos. 130-1 of July 1916, 329-41 of August 1920.

During the decade 1921-31 a good deal was done, particularly in Madras, to benefit the exterior castes in various ways. Not only did the Madras Government appoint a Commissioner of Labour entrusted with the task of encouraging the education of the depressed classes and of looking after their economic interests, but many private societies were also at work. Besides a number of Christian Missions, the Depressed Classes Union, the Poor School Society, the Social Service League, the Andhra Deena Seva Sangam, and the Depressed Classes Mission of Mangalore are some of the institutions working for this object. The Arcot Mission started an agricultural school, and Local Boards were also spending money towards the same end. In addition to this much was done by the Self-Respect movement and the Depressed Classes Conference. The actual steps taken by the Government of Madras included, besides the appointment of a Commissioner of Labour, the insistence on the right of admission of exterior caste pupils into all publicly managed schools, the refusal of grants-in-aid to privately managed schools which did not admit exterior caste pupils, the removal of publicly managed schools from places inaccessible to exterior castes, the opening of special schools and hostels for the exterior

castes, the remission of their fees, and the provision of scholarships and of special facilities for the training of exterior caste
teachers. On the economic side the Government of Madras
took steps towards the provision of house sites for the relief
of congestion and for purposes of freeing the exterior castes
from oppression by their landlords, the organization and running of co-operative societies, the provision of drinking water by
constructing new wells and repairing old, the provision of burial
grounds and sanitary requirements for the exterior castes, the
assignment of land for cultivation both by reservation for and
free assignment to exterior castes of lands not classed as valuable, that is, lands not affected by irrigation projects, and by
reservation for exterior castes of lands classed as valuable and
assignment to them on payment of market value in easy instal-
ments. As a result of these measures some progress was
made. In 1920 there were 150,000 pupils of exterior castes in
schools; in 1930 there were 230,000. Over 100,000 of these were
in Christian Mission schools and many of the remainder in
schools maintained by the societies mentioned above. Most of
these schools are only primary schools, there being only about
2,700 pupils in educational institutions above the primary stage,
of whom about fifty only were in colleges. Out of 230,000 reading in schools in 1930 about 7,500 were girls. Of the 230,000
only 16,000, however, were reading in ordinary schools not
reserved for exterior castes, while over 70,000 pupils who did
not belong to the exterior castes were reading in schools specially
maintained for those castes. As compared with the rest of the
population, while about 6 per cent of the population of Madras
was going to school when the census (1931) took place, only
about 4 per cent of the exterior castes were at school, and of
that total less than 1 per cent was beyond the primary stage.
Economically very considerable sums had been spent by the
Madras Government during the past ten years in financing and
organizing co-operative societies for the acquisition of land for
house sites and for the granting of agricultural loans and for
purposes of flood relief, rural credit and collective bargaining.
In 1920 there were over 14,600 members of exterior castes in
about 100 co-operative societies; as a result of the work done
during the decade there were in 1931 about 2,000 such societies
consisting mainly of exterior castes, and during recent years new
societies have been registered at the rate of over 100 a year.
Over 55,000 house sites have been provided and some 300,000
acres of land have been assigned to exterior caste cultivators.
But at the time of the 1931 census there were still six districts
in Madras untouched by the activities of the Commissioner of
Labour. In Bombay, apart from the work done by private
institutions among which the Servants of India Society is very

14

prominent, little has yet been done. In November 1928 a Committee was appointed by the Government of Bombay to inquire into the condition of the depressed castes and aboriginal tribes in the Presidency. As a result of the recommendations of that Committee an officer was appointed in 1931, charged with the duty of watching over the progress of, and of upholding the rights of, the backward classes. In addition to that, a Resolution of the Government of Bombay directed the recruitment of members of the depressed classes in the police. It is perhaps significant that the Committee found it necessary to include in their recommendations an addition to the Government Servants' Conduct Rules framed with a view to enforcing polite treatment of the depressed classes by the officials of Government. Many of the Indian States have also recognized the necessity for special measures for the uplift of exterior castes, in particular, Baroda, Cochin and Travancore; while in Gwalior and Jaipur action has been taken more particularly in regard to the criminal tribes, of which there are considerable numbers in those States. In Jaipur areas of land have been allotted to the criminal tribes and special schools have been opened for the education of their children, and the same has been done in Gwalior.

The occasion of the 1931 census, coming as it did at a time when political reforms appeared imminent, complicated the already plentiful difficulties in the way of getting an exact return of numbers of exterior castes. A number of conflicting forces were at work, as, apart from the natural desire of individuals of exterior castes to raise their own social status by making themselves out to be something other than they were recognized to be by their neighbours, a definite movement was set afoot by the Hindu Mahasabha for the return of all Hindus as Hindu simply, with no qualifications of caste or sect. In 1928 the Hindu Mahasabha itself passed a resolution declaring that the so-called untouchables had equal rights with other Hindus to study in schools, and to use wells and roads and temples, and the same resolution called on priests, barbers, and washermen to afford their services to untouchables. At the 1931 census, however, political considerations probably outweighed all else, and many efforts were made to induce untouchables to record themselves as ' Hindus ' and nothing else. The exterior castes themselves were, however, generally alive to the fact that their interests required their numbers to be definitely known; at the same time they were not unconscious of the fact that it might be advantageous to them to represent as many castes as possible as being depressed in order to swell their numbers and importance. Consequently, while in the Punjab the All-India Shradhanand Depressed Classes Mission was calling on the exterior castes to return themselves as Arya Hindus instead of, for instance, Achuts or Dalits, the exterior castes' own leaders were calling on their followers to return themselves as *Ad-Dharmi* [6] by religion and not Hindu at all. In other provinces the associations of the exterior castes were representing as 'depressed' castes which very doubtfully fall into that category and many of which have been excluded on scrutiny. Generally speaking, however, it is believed that the figures for the exterior classes obtained at the 1931 census have been accurate on the whole, and the methods adopted in different provinces to determine what constitutes an exterior caste have already been referred to, while extracts from some of the Provincial Reports will be found below.

ASSAM.

The treatment of the subject by the Census Superintendent of Assam has already been mentioned as typical of the method adopted in all provinces at this census. He writes as follows:

'"*Hindu Exterior Castes.*" This, as I have confessed, is an expression to which I plead guilty. I am by no means proud of it and it is open to many criticisms. I have, however, asked many Indian gentlemen to give me a better one but they have not succeeded. The expression, as it stands, connotes castes which are Hindu castes but which are outside something and that is really what I mean to imply.

'What are they outside? The answer is that they are outside the social pale of Hindu Society; that they are "below the salt"; that they are on the other side of a barrier which prevents them from moving upwards.

'But before going further I must define what I mean by "Hindu Exterior Castes".

'By this expression I mean castes recognized definitely as Hindu castes whose water is not acceptable and who, *in addition*, are so deficient as castes in education, wealth and influence or, for some reason connected with their traditional occupations, are so looked down upon, that there seems little hope of their being allowed by Hindu Society to acquire any further social privileges within—at any rate—the next decade.

'By the use of the word "exterior caste" I certainly do not intend to imply that such a caste can never raise itself to a higher level. On the contrary, I intend to imply that this can happen, as it actually has happened in the past, and that an exterior caste may in the course of time possibly become what I may call an "interior" one.

'It is impossible to lay down any simple test to distinguish members of the Hindu exterior castes in Assam from others. The main test to distinguish "clean" castes from "unclean" castes is whether the water of the caste is accepted by members of the upper castes. A caste whose water is acceptable is known

[6] i.e. ' of the original (aboriginal?) religion '.

in the Surma Valley as "*jal-chal*", and a caste whose water is not accepted may be conveniently defined as "*jal-achal*". In Assam the words "*pani chale*" and "*pani na chale*" are in vogue. But we cannot apply this simple test alone in order to find out which castes are exterior and which are not. It is true that all exterior castes are *jal-achal*, but it is not true that all *jal-achal* castes are exterior. For example, in the Sylhet district the Shahas are technically a *jal-achal* caste, but they are a very wealthy and influential community who are treated with considerable respect in society, and by a peculiar social convention are permitted to purchase their brides from the higher castes.

'The Shahas are, in fact, a good example of a caste which though technically unclean have by their own efforts raised themselves to a position in which the upper classes simply cannot afford to ignore them.

'I have not therefore classed the Shahas as an "Exterior Caste". One of my friendly critics, Babu K. C. Dutta, Extra-Assistant Commissioner, has taken up this point:

"You do not class", he writes, "the Shahas as an exterior caste simply because of their education and the wealth and influence they command. Yet they are not *jal-chal*, they are not allowed entrance into the *Thakurghar* of the cleaner castes, and the disability is not likely to be relaxed in the next decade. I do not concede for a moment that the disabilities that bar the Shahas are any more pronounced in the case of the less influential and uncultured castes. These exterior castes are suffering from want of education, wealth, culture, in fact, all that contributes to social influence. As soon as they have achieved these, their position will be akin to that of the Shahas—neither clean nor depressed."

'The Shahas are, of course, exterior to the extent that they fall on the other side of the great line which divides Hindu Society—the *jal-chal* line—but though this line is still of great importance, other things must be taken into consideration.

'If, for example, the Patnis and Namasudras could shake off the tradition which associates them with occupations regarded as low (most of them are now cultivators, but tradition associates them with fishing and boat-plying) and could acquire, as a caste, a reputation for wealth and culture, they would, I admit, be in much the same position as the Shahas are today.

'This process will, however, take many generations, and in the meantime they are, in my op...ion, clearly suffering from greater disabilities than the Shahas, the disabilities being the very absence of those factors which have made the Shahas a respected caste.

'Thus, while the *jal-chal* line is a useful line of division between the upper and the lower castes, it is not of much use as a test for determining the " Exterior Castes ". Nor does the test of temple entry afford us much assistance.

' Generally speaking, in the Surma Valley all castes which are "*jal-achal*" are not allowed into the actual *Thakurghar* of temples in which the higher castes worship and are not allowed to assist in the ceremonies by bringing tulsi and flowers with which to decorate the idol. *Jal-achal* castes are, however, allowed "darshan" and are permitted to come into the compound of the temple. In the Assam Valley where the "*Namghar*" generally takes the place of the temple the same principle holds good, but a distinction is made between different classes of *jal-achal* castes. Nadiyals and Banias,[7] for example, are not allowed at all into the *Namghars* of higher castes, whereas Katonis and Suts are allowed in some districts to enter the part not regarded as particularly holy, i.e. they are not allowed to enter the *Monikhut*.

' The whole matter being, therefore, so indeterminate, how, it may be asked, can I possibly venture to say, with any degree of certainty, what castes are exterior? The only possible method was to find out by local inquiry in each district the general social position of all castes which might be thought to come under the definition of " exterior castes ". This is the method I adopted. . . .

' Caste in the Assam Valley is not, as elsewhere, chiefly a functional division; it is really a racial division and functional castes are very few.

' Probably for that reason Hinduism in that valley is tolerant towards the tribal communities which have not yet been completely absorbed into its organism. It must, in fact, be extremely difficult for an Assamese Hindu to despise at heart a man whose Hinduism is open to considerable doubt, but who considers that he is just as good a man as any Koch or Kalita. In fact, people like the Deoris consider that they are much better and don't care who knows it. Nobody can be depressed who hits you with a big stick if you attempt to show your contempt for him.

'As a result the only castes in the Assam Valley which can be called exterior are castes which are either traditionally associated with some degrading occupation (such as selling fish) or whose traditional origin is associated with a bar sinister. About some castes in this valley there is, however, no possible doubt. Let us deal with these first.

' There is, I consider, no doubt that in the Assam Valley the caste which at this census has adopted the name of Bania and

---

[7] i.e. ' Brittial-Bania '. The term ' Brittial-Bania ' was itself a recently adopted term, a substitute probably for Dom or Hari. The use of the term ' Bania ' (Baniya) is a mere usurpation from the name of the trading castes of Rajputana and elsewhere in northern and western India.

which at previous censuses was styled Brittial-Bania is an exterior caste. Some of the leading men of this community have in fact informed me that their position in society is hopeless and have asked to be classed as a depressed caste.

'That this caste is an exterior caste is also the unanimous opinion of all responsible officers whom I have consulted.

'Nor is there any doubt about the large class which has now adopted the caste name of Kaibartta—and which was previously known as Nadiyal; nor about the Charals of Lower Assam who now call themselves Namasudras with their offshoot the Hiras. The general opinion about all these castes is unanimous.

'Thus the Census Officer, Dhubri, reports:

"Namasudras or Nadiyals or Jaluas or Charals or Kaibarttas or Doms are considered untouchable by caste Hindus who neither admit them into their places of worship nor take water touched by them."

and the Census Officer, Jorhat:

"Among the indigenous Assamese castes the following are depressed:
"(1) Kaibarttas or Nadiyals or Doms.
"(2) Brittial-Banias.
"(3) Hiras or Charals (found in Lower Assam only)."

'From Darrang comes further evidence:

"That Doms, Nadiyals, Namasudras, Charals, Hiras and Brittial-Banias are depressed is admitted by the members of the community themselves who were consulted", writes the Census Officer.

'In fact, in every district of the Assam Valley the opinion is unanimous that the Brittial-Banias and the Kaibarttas (which name may be taken to include Charals, Nadiyals, Hiras and all the other names which from time to time have been applied to various branches of this family) are the most exterior castes in the whole of the Assam Valley.

'These castes are socially "outside the pale", and though the Brittial-Banias have worked hard to improve their position and have a considerable number of educated men amongst them they appear to be as far off as ever from any sort of social recognition.

'Ancient custom and practice have ordained that members of these castes are to be treated as practically untouchable. It is true that the former necessity of taking a bath if touched by a member of one of these castes has fallen into disuse, but a Brahman officer of about 30 years of age has informed me that when he was a small boy he had to take a bath if, by accident, he was touched by one of the hated Doms.

'Above these castes came others whose position seemed to me for a long time to be extremely doubtful. They are the Naths or Jugis (known in Upper Assam as Katonis) and the Suts who are also commonly called Borias.

'A careful study of the position of these castes has, however, convinced me that I would be wrong to class them as exterior. ... The truth about the Naths and the Suts appears to be that they are exterior castes who have made considerable efforts to raise themselves socially and that their efforts are beginning to bear fruit. There is a bar against them, but they are beginning to break through it: they are really "superior exterior castes" who are moving upwards. There is, in fact, hope for them. As one Assamese officer has briefly expressed it:

"All Assamese low castes have a chance of rising in the social scale except the Doms and Haris whose case is hopeless."

'The Suts and Naths do not themselves desire to be classed as depressed or exterior and in fact strongly object to it. . . .

'Again:

"The Education Department in 1915 provided three general dining halls and four separate rooms and the understanding has always been that the upper caste boys are to dine in the general dining halls and the depressed or backward class boys are to use the above four rooms. . . . For the last two years, there has been a very strong movement for admitting these remaining 'backward' caste boys into the general dining hall— there is an overwhelming majority in their favour, only a small minority of about five or six still being in the opposition."

'Professor Sen Gupta has subsequently informed me that the movement referred to in the last paragraph of his note resulted in August 1931 in the abolition of the remaining restriction and that—as a tentative measure—permission was given to the students who had formerly dined in the four rooms set apart to dine in the general dining hall. The Professor thinks it probable that the concession will continue.

'This last piece of information, I confess, surprised me. If the concession is allowed to continue, it will reflect great credit on the liberal spirit of Professor Sen Gupta's mess and may, in time, have a far-reaching effect on social custom in the Assam Valley. It does not, however, change my opinion that the Kaibarttas and Banias are definitely "exterior castes".

'On the whole I feel fairly confident that my classification of exterior castes in the Assam Valley is correct. . . .

'I only wish I felt as confident about the exterior castes in the Surma Valley.

'Conditions in that Valley are very different from those in the Assam Valley. Sylhet is linguistically and ethnologically connected with Bengal, and the inclusion of this large district in Assam was originally merely a measure of administrative convenience.

'Sylhet and Cachar (which is largely populated by people of Sylhetti origin) are therefore essentially Bengali in their culture. Hence there are many more functional castes than in the Assam Valley where, as I have already explained, caste is largely racial. Moreover, the presence of a large upper-caste zamindar class in Sylhet—the arbitrators of social usage—has not tended to encourage any relaxation in the treatment of the lower orders of society. . . . Take, for example, the case of a M.A. of the Sylhet Mali caste occupying a good Government post. Many responsible Hindu officers have informed me definitely that if such a person came alone to see them in their paternal homes a chair would not be offered to the guest. A *jol-chauki* (small wooden stool) *might* be offered. Even Muslims treat these low castes in the same way. A Muslim Sub-Divisional Officer tells me that if a Dhubi [8] friend of his occupying a good position in Government service were to come to his house to see him " I would not offer him a chair. I would simply say 'sit down' and the Dhubi would not take a chair."

'Surely if the upper-caste Hindus wished to help the lower castes the least they might do is to treat the educated men among the lower castes with the same courtesy as they would extend to an educated Muslim.

'The following opinion of a responsible Hindu Government officer is of interest: "Some low-caste men by their *submissive attitude* win the hearts of the upper-caste men and get partial admission into society. Others claim as of right and get refused. A lot depends on the man himself. If he claims too much, he gets badly snubbed. In places where orthodoxy is strong he will not, in any case, get fair treatment. In the towns treatment is more liberal than in the villages. In the villages orthodoxy still prevails. If a Patni is the tenant of a Zemindar, he will never get fair social treatment however highly educated he is. Orthodoxy is strongest amongst the Zemindars. But if the low-caste man is an executive officer such as a Sub-Deputy Collector or an Extra Assistant Commissioner, he would be given better treatment than a non-executive officer, e.g. than a Deputy Inspector of Schools." The above remarks refer, of course, only to private social intercourse. On all social and public occasions the educated Mali [9] or Patni is simply nowhere. He has (if he goes to the ceremony) to sit along with his other caste-men outside the house on the mat provided for their caste, while the higher castes sit inside the house.

[8] Washerman.
[9] The Sylhet ' Mali ' caste here referred to is the caste more accurately called ' Bhuinmali ', which is much lower in the social scale than the ' Mali ' gardener caste.

'Add the following facts:

(1) Members of castes like Mali, Patni, Muchi, etc., are not allowed to enter into the temples set up by the higher castes;

(2) The upper castes will not take water or food touched by them; and one begins to realize the dreadful sense of mingled inferiority and hatred which an educated member of one of these exterior castes must feel in most cases towards the higher castes.

'The exterior castes themselves are, however, guilty of similar treatment to each other, and an exterior caste which considers itself to be on a higher social level than another exterior caste adopts exactly the same attitude as the higher castes do towards the exterior castes. A case which recently happened in Sunam-ganj illustrates this point. The local ferryman there (a Patni by caste) was prosecuted for refusing to row a Muchi across the river. His defence was that, according to social custom, a Patni could not row for a Muchi and that it has always been the practice, if a Muchi wanted to cross the river, for the paddle to be given to him so that he could row himself across.

'After careful consideration and analysis of the evidence I have collected, I have come to the conclusion that the following are the main castes in the Surma Valley which should be classed as exterior. They are arranged in alphabetical order:

1. Dhupi or Dhobi.	6. Mahara.
2. Dugla or Dholi.	7. Mali (Bhuinmali).
3. Jhalo and Malo.	8. Namasudra.
4. Yogi (Jugi) (Nath).	9. Patni.
5. Kaibartta (Jalliya).	10. Sutradhar.

'There is general consensus of evidence that these castes are exterior throughout the Surma Valley, though the position of some of them seems to be much more hopeful in Cachar than it is in Sylhet. I have no doubt that this is due largely to the absence of a Zemindari class in Cachar which is a temporarily settled district. . . . I have been told by several officers that the Maharas are a *jal-chal* caste, and that people of this caste were made " clean " by some ancient Raja of Sylhet—the idea being that the Maharas used to carry the Raja's palanquin and, as the Raja wanted to smoke in it, he had to have as palanquin-bearers people who could attend to his smoking requirements. On the other hand, some officers completely deny this story and say that the Maharas are not a *jal-chal* caste . . . the Maharas are princi-pally to be found in South Sylhet. The Sub-Divisional Officer (a Muslim) reported as follows:

" I have made close and careful enquiries and there is a general consensus of opinion that the Mahars are not *jal-chal* and are a depressed class. The story that Raja Subid Narayan made them *jal-chal* for smoking requirements only, seems to be true. If the Maharas are at all *jal-chal*, they are *jal-chal* only in the sense that a man of higher caste can smoke a *huka* filled with water by a Mahara. There is not a single graduate among the Maharas in this sub-division and not even a single matriculate can be found. The Deputy Inspector of Schools reports that the only educated Maharas he has met in the whole sub-division are three persons working as Vernacular teachers in Primary and Middle English Schools. So the Maharas are depressed both socially and educationally. . . ."

'One gentleman from Karimganj—himself a Nath—has, indeed, no hesitation in including his community among the exterior castes. He writes as follows:

" So far as my knowledge goes, amongst the Hindus inhabiting this sub-division the Patnis, Jogis (Naths), Namasudras, Malis, Dhubis and Duglas are to be properly included in the list of depressed classes. The reasons of depression regarding each of these communities are almost the same, namely:

"(1) The members of these communities are not allowed by the so-called high-caste Hindus to enter the temple; even their shadow defiles the image in the temple.

"(2) The high-class Hindus never take any food and water touched or shadowed by these people.

"(3) Brahmins of caste Hindus [10] never agree to officiate as priests in ceremonies performed by these people, even if they request them.

"(4) Some of these communities are not allowed to have the same barber who works amongst the high-class Hindus to work for them.

" In conclusion I beg to say that these are but few amongst the many disadvantages from which these people suffer."

'Previous census reports show that for the last forty years the Naths have been endeavouring to raise their social position by giving up widow remarriage and refusing food prepared by other castes. In spite, however, of these efforts the Nath community of the Surma Valley is still very much looked down upon and I must, I consider, class them as an " exterior caste ".

'This classification may seem peculiar inasmuch as I have not classed the Naths (Katonis) of the Assam Valley as exterior. How far the Assam Naths are connected with the Sylhet Naths is a matter into which I intend to inquire further, but I doubt whether there is any very close connexion. In any case, a sufficient explanation of this difference in treatment would appear to be that Hinduism in Sylhet is not so tolerant as it is in the Assam Valley. Even in the Murarichand College caste restrictions seem to be much more closely observed than in the Cotton College. I have received a note on the system of messing

----

[10] i.e. Brahmans who officiate as priests for caste Hindus.

in that college, and it appears that even the Sahas [Shahas] are not allowed to take their meals in the general dining hall reserved for the upper-caste students. In fact, the *jal-chal* line is strictly observed there—at least nominally—and the students who do not belong to the upper castes have their meals served to them "either in their own room or in those set apart in the main block or in two out-houses provided for the purpose".'

BALUCHISTAN.

Of the Chuhras the Census Superintendent (1931) of Baluchistan writes:

'The Chuhras censused in Baluchistan have returned themselves as belonging to the religious groups named below:

Caste or Tribe	Religion
Chuhra	Hindu Balmiki
Chuhra	Hindu Lal Begi
Chuhra	Musalman Lal Begi
Chuhra	Musalman Balashai
Chuhra	Sikh Mazhabi
Chuhra	Chuhra

'Although these persons without exception are not allowed to drink from wells belonging to real Hindus, Muslims or Sikhs, and are not permitted to enter their places of worship, I include them in the figures for the various religions to which they claim to belong, giving separately the numbers (males and females) of these untouchables in a footnote in each case.'

MADRAS.

The following extracts are taken from the Census Report (1931) for Madras, where the Census Superintendent gives as the total number of depressed classes 7,300,000 in round figures, or $15\frac{1}{2}$ per cent of the population of that province. He goes on:

'For reasons already given this figure cannot be taken as an absolute tale of those to whom the peculiar disabilities summed up in the broad term "depressed" attach. There are many Christian converts on whom disabilities press no whit lighter than in the untouchable communities they owned before. These are not included, for personal and local and sectarian variations enter too largely for census allocation to be possible. There are other bodies the difficulties of whose life are hardly less than those of any Adi-Dravida, but to whom the technical stigma of untouchability does not apply. Such do not figure in the census list. The census total therefore can fairly be termed only an approximation. It is, however, a good approximation and, as an indication of the general dimensions of untouchability and through it of the depressed classes problem, is absolutely reliable.

Whether its approximation is above or below would depend on the point from which approached. If this is viewed primarily as the existence of heavy social disabilities, the figure 7,300,000 is a minimum, if it considers strict personal polluting power it is a maximum. The general dimensions of seven millions are beyond contest.

'The 7,300,000 figure and the discussions above refer of course only to persons enumerated within the province on census night. . . . A third of the emigrants belong to the depressed classes and consequently, were the natural population to be considered, eight millions would have to be taken as the round figure for them instead of seven. . . .

'. . . It cannot be said that the social disabilities under which these communities labour are in sight of extinction despite the growth of tolerance and the inevitable effect of the development of communications and of urban life. Distinguished individual effort . . . is by no means rare, but it remains individual. Communities cannot yet be said even to have altered appreciably in outlook. I came across in a Telugu delta district a subordinate officer of the Labour Department occupying the dak bungalow, an unusual thing for such officers, who ordinarily put up with some casteman in the village. His castemen however shied off him, because of his employment, which brought him into constant association with the depressed classes. This man was of no notably exalted caste, but a Telaga. It is probable that resentment at special consideration shown to the depressed classes in land assignment and other directions is reflected also in such an attitude, the resentment that the rising of the underdog never fails to arouse in those who have kept him down, a feature not peculiar to India. It remains however an indication of the true position in the rural areas where the depressed classes are most represented. . . .

'A peculiar refinement of the untouchability theory was distance pollution. This set out certain castes as polluting not merely on contact but by mere approach. The Nayadis were the backmarkers in this handicapping system and were practically denied ordinary use of public ways. When the system was in full force Nayadi progress must have borne a strong resemblance to that of a malefactor for whom a warrant is out and whose one object is to avoid close contact with his fellow men. A lifetime so spent can hardly produce elevation of thought or desire, and a community whose chief aspiration is to avoid notice cannot contribute much to national life. This remarkable development of the superiority theory was practically confined to the west coast and of late years has greatly weakened even there, probably more because of development of communications and increase of population than from any conscious realization that there is in such a system something hardly compatible with claims to culture and advancement. It is probably becoming evident that a person of such rare texture that a presence sixty feet away pollutes him had better park himself on a desert island or develop a less fragile purity. The train began the breakdown of this preposterous system; the bus may complete it.[11]

'Contact pollution on the other hand existed and exists all over the presidency.

'An instance of the modification and at the same time of the persistence of discrimination is afforded by the river and canal ferries of the Telugu delta districts. According to petitions quoted in a Government Order of 1919 a member of the depressed classes might have to wait for hours before being taken over as he and a Brahman would never be taken together and the Brahman always had priority. In the bigger boats plying on the two rivers and larger canals there is now no such preference; any person waiting is admitted on board. Depressed classes, however, have to keep to a different end of the boat from Brahmans. In the cross-river ferries the disappearance is not so complete and an influential Brahman would be taken over in preference to a crowd of depressed classes of prior arrival. In other cases either the Brahman or the depressed class person would hold back to avoid travelling with the other. The extent to which prejudice and preference have scope varies from village to village and with the importance of the Brahman or enlightenment of the depressed. It has been noticed that Christians of depressed class origin make no bones about getting into the boat whether a Brahman is waiting or not. The ferryman occasionally too has prejudices.

'On the small canal ferries Brahman precedence is still the general rule, but where the traffic is considerable and the balakats big, as at Nidadavole before the bridge was built, conditions resembled those on the river boats.

'The same petition complained that in certain municipalities depressed classes were denied the use of water taps reserved for higher castes, despite circumstances of proximity and convenience. Such restriction if it ever existed as an official practice no longer does.

'Despite their lowly status, these communities play a large and important part in the life of the presidency. It is they who furnish the backbone of agricultural labour in the chief rice-growing districts. In one form or another they have been the

[11] A recent observer, Mr Eric Miller, reports that distance pollution is now seen only in ritual situations, and he mentions the case of a particular Nayar who insisted that a man of an exterior caste should remain at a distance when bringing him a formal offering on a ritual occasion, but had no hesitation in approaching a man of the same caste who had cut his hand and needed assistance in attending to the wound. This was in 1948-9.

victims of an agrestic serfdom wherever they have been. This generally took (and still takes) the form of compulsory advances from their employers which could never be repaid in full and thus tied the borrower to the soil. This was most noticeable in Tanjore, but a parallel system of advances produced the same effect in South Kanara. It must be laid to the credit of Ceylon and other estates that they have done more to raise the self-respect of the South Indian depressed classes worker than any other single circumstance. It is possible for the same reason that emigration is opposed in certain quarters. The Madras Government appointed an officer as Commissioner of Labour and among his particular functions is the attending to the needs of depressed classes. The decade has seen much expenditure on provision of wells for them, of schools, and a most important feature, the buying of house sites for them mainly in the delta areas. A notable example of a breakaway from caste traditions is in the Nambudri who was schoolmaster in a depressed classes school in Malabar. The Nayadi colony of Olavakkot formed to house members of possibly the most contemned community in Malabar has been able to develop its activities more than it anticipated. Recently, however, some difficulties have arisen through a boycott by other castes of a school which received some Nayadi pupils.'

APPENDIX B

HINDUISM IN ITS RELATION TO PRIMITIVE RELIGIONS IN INDIA [1]

THOUGH derived no doubt from multiple sources, the Hindu religion may fairly be said to have taken its final form as the result of the impact of the social ascendancy of the Indo-European invaders of the second millennium B.C. on pre-existing religious institutions.[2] The first occupants of India were probably Negritos, and elements of their belief, perhaps including the reverence for the pipal tree and possibly a primitive phallic fertility cult, both of which are found in the Andaman Islands, may have been perpetuated by the proto-Australoids, who were the next comers and possibly contributed the totemic theory, or at least the basis thereof. Later elements were probably of Mediterranean and Iranian origin, and may have contributed a phallic and a megalithic culture and the life-essence theory, but the relative positions and identities of the Dravidian-speaking, Mediterranean, Armenoid, Eurasiatic, proto-Australoid, Kolarian and Mon-Khmer or Austro-Asiatic peoples are difficult to determine and there is little material from which to draw a conclusion; some would identify the proto-Australoid and the Kolarian-speaking racial elements. If the latter elements be distinct from the proto-Australoid, it would be convenient to suppose that the Kolarians came after them with a life-essence theory and the Mediterraneans still later to develop it into one of reincarnation, while bringing in the worship of the Great Mother, but it is conceivable that the Mediterraneans brought both the theory and its development and the Kolarian came later as a barbarian invader, though no doubt already in possession of the soul-matter philosophy. At any rate, the hill tribes of Assam, Burma, and Indo-China appear to contain an element of Caucasian stock which penetrated to the south-east of Asia before the southern migration of Mongolians of the Pareoean branch, and the soul-matter theory must have arisen very early in the history of the human race. Both Kolarian and Mediterranean must have been followed by religious elements from Asia Minor, brought via Mesopotamia by traders and settlers from the west, which no doubt superseded a fertility and soul-matter cult by one of personified deities, sacrificial propitiation and a formalized worship, again with phallic elements and such

[1] This appendix is little but a reprint of the greater part of § 176 in ch. XI of my *Report on the Census of India*, 1931. Such changes as there are are due to minor excisions, to a few alterations in wording or in punctuation, and to the addition of references.　　　　　　　[2] *Vide supra*, ch. I.

institutions as that of the *devadasi*,[3] together with astronomical lore and cults of the heavenly bodies and priestly institutions which formed the basis of modern Hinduism; the final form of which was no doubt determined by the successful conflict of this proto-Hinduism on the religious side with the imported religion of Iranian and 'Aryan' invaders, to whom, however, it had to concede much socially, resulting in the socio-religious position of the priestly order so familiar in India.

The generally accepted view of the Hindu religion, or society, used to regard it as originating in Aryan invaders of about 1500 B.C. who came in with a higher civilization and a fairer skin to find the great peninsula inhabited by dark-skinned barbarians on whom they imposed the religion of the vedas. This view can no longer be maintained, and the doubts cast on it appear to be confirmed by discoveries including that of a figure of Shiva among the remains at Mohenjodaro, while Sir John Marshall has clearly shown that the pre-Aryan religion of the Indus Valley involved a cult of the bull, and of the snake—typical Mediterranean cults, to be found in Crete—and also of phallic symbols, including 'ring' and baetylic stones, which are probably all part of the soul-fertility cult which is associated throughout India with menhirs, dolmens, and a megalithic culture generally; indeed, Heine-Geldern connects the megalithic Mycenean theatre with India and so with the Far East and the Pacific Islands. It has been pointed out with some aptness that in modern Hinduism only those elements of vedic rites have survived which are essentially social, such as the marriage ceremonies; the argument being that though society was or aimed at being Aryan, its religion is older than that of the so-called Aryan invasion. The god of the Rigvedic Indo-Europeans is Indra, the thunder god, who fills in later developments an entirely minor role, apparently being absorbed into the Hindu pantheon, just as the minor gods of primitive tribes have been, retaining, however, his personal identity by virtue of a social prestige or privilege which other tribal gods have lost in the process of assimilation. The historical Hindu religion first appears not in the Punjab, which must be regarded as the area most completely occupied by the Indo-European invaders, but to the east of it in the Brahmarshidesha, where stable fusion between these Indo-European invaders and the previous inhabitants probably took place. When alien cultures and religions fuse to form a new culture or religion, it will not be found that this fusion takes place where the intrusive culture is strong enough to predominate. It will rather appear, away from the centre where the intrusion is strongest, in some area where the previous culture was strong enough to resist complete suppression and make its influence

3 *Vide supra,* pp. 162 sqq.

felt on the new one. Thus it is that the efflorescence of Greek culture took place not in Sparta, where was the purest blood of the northern invaders, but in Athens, where the grasshopper-wearing inhabitants regarded themselves as autochthones and where there was probably effective fusion between the fair-haired northerner and the dark-haired Pelasgian. Similarly, there is some reason to believe that Rome grew from a fusion between the ancient Etruscans and later invaders, whether the latter came from the east or from the north. In the same way it is suggested that Hindu religion and society finally took form and flourished as a result of the impact of the invading Indo-European on the indigenous religion that he found in India. It is quite clear that the previous inhabitants of India lived in cities and had a high civilization, probably of western Asiatic origin, and it is significant that Hinduism is remarkable for the similarity of many of its tenets and practices to those of Asia Minor and Mesopotamia. The indigenous religion of any country inevitably starts with an advantage over that of an invading people, since it is the priest of the country who knows how to approach the gods of the soil and propitiate them, and for that reason there is always a tendency for a local religion to establish its ascendancy over an intrusive one. This appears to have been the case in India, where the important position of Shiva, Vishnu, and Kali, as compared to the unimportant one which Indra now holds, signalizes the triumph of the older gods. The religious history of pre-vedic India was probably similar and parallel to that of the eastern Mediterranean and of Asia Minor. Professor Tucci points out [4] that though the moon does not appear to have been an independent divinity, ancient lunar cults have been assimilated by Devi in the forms of Durga, Kali and Tripurasundari. The cult of snakes, and the worship of a mother goddess, were probably brought in by earlier invaders of Mediterranean or of Armenoid race, speaking no doubt a Dravidian language, whose religion must also be associated with fertility cults, phallic symbolism, the *devadasi* cult, and probably human sacrifice. Recent discoveries in Crete have revealed a remarkable snake cult associated with the symbol of the double axe. With Mesopotamia, too, we must perhaps associate a moon god and sun goddess, whose sex was changed with a change from matrilineal to patrilineal descent perhaps under the influence of the Rigvedic invaders. It is worth pointing out that the deification and worship of kings, very typical of the Hindu attitude to kingship, is stated by Langdon [5] to be characteristic of Sumerian religion in contrast to Semitic. It would also appear not characteristic of the religion of the Rigveda, but on

[4] In a note on ' Traces of Lunar Cult in India ' in *Rivista degli Studi Orientali*, vol. XII (1930), fasc. iv, quoted in *The Indian Antiquary* for January 1932, p. 17.   [5] *J.R.A.S.*, 1931, p. 367.

the contrary to be connected with the beliefs in the external soul and in life-essence discussed below, inasmuch as the king contains or represents the life principle of the community he rules. Like the cult of the snake, the transmigration of souls too appears to be a doctrine in no way typical of northern religions, in which the dead live on underground, and Fustel de Coulanges has pointed out [6] that it is not a feature of any northern religion though it has survived and been incorporated in them from the more ancient religions of Greece and Italy. Ancestor worship again is very strong in India, and this, too, would appear foreign to northern European religion, and indeed it is almost impossible that nomads should be ancestor worshippers, and the Aryan invasion, so-called, was probably an invasion of steppe-dwelling tribes, pastoral in habit and still nomadic. Cremation they may have brought in, and if so, they gave it a social cachet which is still leading to its gradual adoption by tribes which have previously practised burial or exposure, but it seems much more likely that the Rigvedic Aryans buried their dead and adopted cremation from the inhabitants whom they conquered. The eighth book of the Rigveda contains the following words addressed to the dead: ' I place this barrier (of stones) for the living . . . that no other may go beyond it. May they live a hundred numerous autumns, keeping death at a distance by this hill. . . . Enter the mother earth. . . . Earth, let his breath rise upward (easily); oppress him not. . . . Even as a mother covers her son with the end of her cloth, so do ye, earth, cover him . . . may these homes . . . for all time be his asylum. I heap up earth above thee,' etc.[7] This passage seems very clearly to indicate burial in a tumulus, and the word translated ' barrier ' is stated in a note to be *paridhi*, which may mean part of a circle of stones.[8] It is true that the tenth hymn of the Rigveda clearly refers to cremation, but the author above quoted regards it, rightly no doubt, as the later passage, and suggests that ritual exigencies involved the dislocation of the verses and their fusion for ceremonial purposes in the Yajurveda and the Sutras, the reference to inhumation being then interpreted as indicating the burial of the ashes. It appears, however, quite clear that the hymn quoted above can only refer to the inhumation of the body, and that this practice as well as that of cremation was in use at the time of the Rigveda, while cremation is not mentioned until the tenth hymn, admittedly a much later composition than the earlier ones; cremation also seems definitely to have been the practice in the Indus valley of the Mohenjodaro period, and therefore

[6] *La Cité Antique,* pp. 7 sq.

[7] Rajendralala Mitra, *Indo-Aryans,* II. p. 123.

[8] Mr H. J. E. Peake thought that it refers originally to a wooden fence, which may have been translated into stone later (*personal communication*).

the more likely one of the two to have been adopted as an alternative by the Rigvedic Aryans at their period of fusion with the pre-existing population. The Aryan sanctity of fire seems likely to have been incompatible with cremation, and it will be remembered that Herodotus [9] taxes Cambyses with impiety for having had the body of Amasis burned, 'for the Persians regard fire as a god and therefore to burn the dead is on no account allowed . . . for they say that it is not right to offer to a god the corpse of a man'. It may be noticed that Wilson [10] remarks of the Rajputs of Kachh and Kathiawar that they encouraged their concubines to commit *sătī* in preference to their wives, and he actually gives as the reason that *sati* was a custom of low castes and therefore derogatory to Rajputs; and it may be noted also that Rajputs in Gujarat who forbid widow remarriage are called *Vankā*, 'crooked', and those who allow it *Pādhrā*, 'straight'.[11]

With Asia Minor or Mesopotamia again we must associate astronomy and the worship of the heavenly bodies, which form an important part of Hindu culture, and in particular the cult of the moon god. Sun worship appears to be less important in the Rigveda than at a later date, when the Bhavishya Purana is largely devoted to a cult of the sun. It is, however, possible that it was the influence of Rigvedic invaders which changed the sex of the sun in India from female to male and gave rise to the sun-descended nobility as distinct from the moon-descended. In Rigveda X Soma the moon is represented as male and as marrying Sūryā the daughter of the Sun. The name of the latter suggests that the Sun himself, Sūryā, was originally the female that married the Moon, and that there has been a change of sex associated in so many parts of the world with variations of the Phaëthon legend. Similarly, again, the existing holy places of the Hindus are outside Brahmavartta where one might have expected to find them, if it were really the fact that the religion actually arose in that area, while to find them elsewhere is consistent with a view that they are places regarded with devotion by the religions which preceded the invasion. This view is sometimes emphasized by the existence of Hindu shrines where priests and custodians are not Brahmans but some pseudo-Brahman or Sudra caste, e.g. the Malis who are the officiating priests of some Orissa temples and probably the Panda Brahmans of the same region.[12] It is doubtless significant that sacrifice of cattle was 'detested by the public' though enjoined by the earlier vedas, the inference from which is that the reverence paid to cattle predates the Rigvedic invasion, and Buddhism and

[9] III, 16.
[10] *Infanticide in Western India*, p. 74.
[11] Campbell, *Bombay Gazetteer*, IX, i, p. 183 n.
[12] Cf. also Wise, op. cit., p. 270.

Jainism, the latter of which contains extremely ancient ceremonial survivals, may represent a reaction towards the pre-vedic religion to which the majority of the inhabitants of northern India were attached and which was modified but not destroyed by contact with the invaders. The first prohibition of cow-killing seems to be found in the comparatively late Atharvaveda and to be applied specially, if not exclusively, to Brahmans, while elsewhere we learn that the cow, although a fit offering for Mitra and Varuna, should not be sacrificed because such sacrifice is opposed to public feeling, a clear indication of the contrast between the religions of the socially superior Aryan invaders and the cattle-cherishing inhabitants who formed the bulk of the population. 'Let not the Rajanya desire to eat the inedible cow of a Brahman' (*Atharvaveda*, v.18.1). In southern India 'the cow is as much revered in those areas of the presidency with the lightest tincture of Brahmanism as in those more affected', which 'may be taken to indicate that reverence for the cow in India is older than the vedic religion'.[13] In any case the sanctity of the cow is foreign to the Rigveda and appears far more suggestive of the religions of Asia Minor, Egypt, and Crete than of the Indo-European invaders who came from the steppes of the north-west to conquer northern India in the strength of their horses and of their iron. Indra, moreover, appears as the author of sacrifice, and in the Yajurveda it seems still to be Indra and Varuna who are the principal recipients of sacrificed cattle. Nor is it possible to accept Sir John Marshall's anti-thesis between the worship of the bull and the worship of the cow. Both are surely different aspects of the same reverence for cattle which characterizes the pre-equine civilizations of the Mediterranean basin, and in India are pre-'Aryan' in origin. The vedas after all enjoined *gaumedha*, and the Black Yajur-veda lays down an elaborate list of deities to whom bulls, oxen and cows can be appropriately sacrificed. Vishnu, Shiva, and Kali, the great gods of Hinduism, are not Rigvedic deities at all. Sakti is probably a cult derived from the Great Mother goddess of Asia Minor, and the cult of Shiva is inevitably associated with it, the two being bound up with the phallic religion of southern Asia and of the eastern Mediterranean. It is probably significant that the word *lingam* is definitely of non-Aryan origin, as Przyluski has demonstrated, while the word *puja* is also believed to be a non-Sanskritic loan word. With the worship of Shiva, too, is to be associated the snake cult of which there are so many survivals in southern India and which appears to have been at an early date in definite opposition to Brah-manistic Hinduism, the conflict between the two being indi-cated, for instance, by Krishna's exploits against serpents, by the destruction of serpents at the burning of the forests of

---

13 Yeatts, *Report on the Census of Madras*, 1931, p. 320.

Khandava and the slaughter of serpents in the Mahabharata. Vishnu, apparently a post-Rigvedic god, is perhaps the fruit of the reaction of what we may call proto-Hinduism to the Rigvedic invaders, as also the present ascendancy of male over female conceptions of the deity, and Przyluski ascribes a Dravidian origin to the name 'Vishnu'.[14] At the same time Vishnu would seem to have some associations with religious beliefs which must be regarded as represented chiefly in beliefs yet surviving among primitive tribes. Indra apparently is himself declared in the Mahabharata to be guilty of brahmanicide in killing Vrtra and Namuci who were Danavas, though the Rigveda praises him for the same deed. Pargiter adduces considerable evidence to show that the true Brahman families were of pre-Rigvedic origin, and that the Aryan kings of Madhyadesha were their own priests and in the earliest times had no Brahmans. Strabo remarks that it is recorded that 'The Indians worshipped Zeus Ombrios, the river Ganges, and the indigenous gods',[15] and as Zeus Ombrios is clearly Indra, the thunder god, the suggestion that the other gods worshipped are of indigenous origin is probably very near to the truth, and the traditional view that the Hindu religion is a growth entirely subsequent to the Rigveda, or rather to the Rigvedic invasions, is no longer tenable. Rai Bahadur Ramaprasad Chanda, in a paper on the 'Non-vedic Elements in Brahmanism',[16] has made a number of points which indicate the continued existence of the pre-Rigvedic religions alongside of or in opposition to the orthodox Hinduism of the Brahmarshidesha. Quoting Kumārila and Medhātithi he points out that the Smartas include non-vedic elements; that thus of the four orders named in the Dharmasutra of Gautama (Student, Householder, Ascetic and Hermit) only that of householder (*grihastha*) is prescribed in the vedas; that the Upanishads were not originally recognized as part of the vedic canon at all and had their origin outside vedic Hinduism; that the Yatis destroyed by Indra are probably the forerunners of the Yatis of the Upanishads and the Smritis and that the latter order were organized on a pre-vedic model; that the Pancharatra and Pasupata systems were condemned by Kumārila as non-vedic and that the Vaishnavite and Saivite sects are derived respectively from those two systems; that contact with Pasupatas, Saivas, Jainas, etc., involved purification; that by the time of the Mahabharata, however, Pancharatra and Pasupata are placed on a footing of recognized and orthodox religious authority. His general conclusion is that the cults of Vishnu, Shiva, and Sakti 'originated among a people of different ethnic origins from the midlandic Aryans'. The point to be

[14] *Archiv Orientálni*, IV, p. 2 (August 1932).
[15] '*tous egchorious daimonas*', bk. xv, p. 718.
[16] MS. (unpublished?) in the author's possession.

emphasized here is not so much Chanda's precise conclusions as the evidence he adduces of the survival of pre-vedic religion alongside and inside the later forms of Hinduism, and of their gradual absorption and acceptance as a recognized part of it, which has perhaps since developed into the position of their forming the most important part of it.

If the view be accepted that the Hindu religion has its origin in pre-vedic times and that in its later form it is the result of the reaction by the religion of the country to the intrusive beliefs of the northern invaders, many features of Hinduism will become at once more comprehensible, while the very striking difference between the religion of the Rigveda and that of the Dharmashastras will seem natural. It will, however, be still necessary to look westward for the source of Hindu religion; though its spread in India was possibly in the nature of a peaceful infiltration, along the trade routes from Asia Minor, of beliefs and practices which associated themselves with those already followed by the indigenous inhabitants. This would explain Hinduism's amalgamation with and absorption of local cults and its excessive multiformity, and is, moreover, in entire accordance with the manner in which it still spreads at the present day, absorbing tribal religions by virtue of its social prestige, by identification of local gods with its own, by the experimental resort to Hindu priests, and by the social promotion of pagan chiefs who are provided with suitable mythological pedigrees. Into the early Hindu beliefs spread in this manner the religion of the Rigveda has been imposed and absorbed. Features survive curiously in out-of-the-way parts beyond the pale of Hinduism itself. Thus the horse sacrifice has become a fertility rite among the non-Hindu Garos of the Assam hills and appears likewise in the wilds of Sumatra, though it has failed to establish itself in orthodox Hinduism. Similarly, though the sacrifice of cattle is anathema to the true Hindu, the Taittiriya Brahmana recommended a whole series of animal slaughterings, including both bulls and cows, to be performed at the *Panchasaradiya Sava* and at the *Asvamedha*, a series extremely suggestive of the scales laid down for successive feasts for the acquirement of social merit at such ceremonies as the *Terhengi* of the Angami Nagas, while the Grihya Sutra enjoins the *Sulagava*—'spitted cow'—ceremony (corresponding roughly to the Angami *Sekrengi*, as the *Panchasaradiya* does to the *Terhengi*) at which the beast was killed, as today by Sema Nagas, with a pointed stake, and its death was accompanied by the erection of a wooden post with a round top mortised on to it and by the distribution of the animal's flesh.[17]

Viewed in this light it is not difficult to understand the claim

[17] *Vide* Mitra, op. cit., I, pp. 369 sqq. and Hutton, *The Sema Nagas*, p. 229.

of certain politicians that the term Hinduism should cover all religions having their origin in India, even though we hold that the original impulse came from the Mediterranean or Asia Minor, since Jainism, Buddhism, and Sikhism are all offshoots of the same root. The claim is less logical when applied to tribal religions which have not yet reached the stage of accepting Brahmans as priests or of attaching any sanctity to the cow or of worshipping in Hindu temples in their own villages. An occasional visit to Hindu temples away from home is not quite a safe test, since many such shrines undoubtedly occupy sites dedicated originally to more ancient indigenous deities and subsequently Hinduized, and in any case it is typical of primitive religions to propitiate the gods of any locality they may visit. Admittedly, however, the line is hard to draw between Hinduism and tribal religions. The inclusion of the latter within the Hindu fold is easy, and wherever hill or forest tribes live in permanent daily contact with Hindus their religion rapidly assimilates itself to that of their neighbours though the old method of thinking is unchanged. Thus it is that religious or quasi-religious beliefs and practices among Hindus appear very frequently to be based on the principles of magic, *mana* or other ideas common in primitive religion. The very word *brahma* itself seems to have possibly connoted originally supernatural power or influence of the nature of *mana*—a view apparently supported by the Atharvaveda—and these beliefs and practices survive and operate with all their primitive qualities alongside the loftiest heights of asceticism and philosophy. If it appears that the latter aspect of the Hindu religion is lost sight of in these pages, it is because their purpose is rather to articulate the fragments of the more primitive and material philosophy that preceded it, than to emphasize what is already of long-standing and undisputed recognition.

We may therefore expect to find very ancient and primitive beliefs continuing under the guise of Hinduism, or even constituting its major content. The sanctity of the fig-tree, for instance, is possibly to be associated with the beliefs of the Negrito inhabitants who appear to have formed the earliest population of India. It is probably on account of its milk-like sap that the *ficus* is associated with fertility cults in Africa, Italy, and New Guinea as well as in Assam and in southern India, and it is generally also connected with the spirits of the dead. This cult appears to be shared by the Andamanese who are an approximately pure Negrito race and perhaps the only race still surviving in the world comparatively unmixed in blood. At any rate they and their beliefs have probably been isolated for some five thousand years at least. Similarly, though the probability is that this element of Hinduism is due to some pre-Aryan immigrant cult from the direction of Asia Minor, the possibility that some tribal and totemic taboo has acted as a contributory factor in the religious sanctity attaching to cattle cannot be entirely over-looked. Thus the flesh of cattle is tabooed by certain clans among primitive tribes of Assam and Indonesia who do not appear to have come even remotely under the influence of Hinduism, while on the other hand the cow is regarded as com-pletely tabooed by the Shins of Chilas, who are described by Leitner as a Hindu tribe with nowadays a veneer of Islam, the highest caste in Dardistan, and really Brahmans themselves, though expelled from India or from Kashmir by Brahmans. Not only do they taboo the flesh of the cow but also its milk, and they only touch a calf at the end of a prong.[18]

Pargiter's view of the original conception of *brahma* as akin to that of *mana* has already been mentioned, and the view seems naturally to associate itself with the views on soul-matter, or life itself, as a transferable and material substance, which are so familiar in Indonesia and further India, but which are actually common enough in India itself. It is on this theory of the indestructibility and transferability of life-matter that the underlying principle of head-hunting is based in Assam; in other parts of the same cultural area it has been manifest in human sacrifice or in cannibalism, the latter perhaps being its most primitive manifestation and the former its most developed. That the principle is still strong in India may be inferred from a number of recent instances, several of which are given later. In the form of head-hunting this theory involves that which regards the head as the particular seat of the soul, and this belief is apparent in India proper in the sanctity which attaches to the head or to the hair, as also in many cases where the (soul-impregnated?) hair does duty for the individual. Thus, in the case of the Naga who dies far from home, a portion of his hair is brought back by his companions to be attached to the head of the wooden effigy, which is then the subject of the usual funeral ceremonies, and one may compare the way in which the head-hunter so often substitutes the hair of his dead or even of his living, and unwitting, victim for the head he cannot carry off.[19] The Ujli Minas when unsuccessful in dacoity will only shave at home and after propitiating their goddess. Probably they fear that they may be suffering from a loss of life-essence as Samson did when his hair was cut. Conversely, a Korku woman of the Central Provinces tries to obtain as a cure for barrenness a hair from the mother of a large family which she buries under her bathing stone.[20] The same theory may per-haps be the origin of the familiar ' caste mark ' placed in front of the forehead just between the eyebrows. The Angami Naga

---

[18] Leitner, *Dardistan in* 1866, 1886 *and* 1893, Appendices VI, p. 1 and VIII, p. 15 ; cf. Biddulph, *Tribes of the Hindoo Koosh*, p. 113.
[19] Cf. also *supra*, pp. 163-4.   [20] Russell, op. cit., III, p. 563.

tribe regard this particular place as the special seat of the soul, conceived of as a diminutive human shape, which it is necessary to guard from the infectious influence of strangers by means of disinfectants. This is done by attaching to that particular spot on the forehead a small fragment of the leaf of the worm-wood—an effective disinfectant of spiritual influences, like other aromatic plants. It seems likely that it is in a practice of this sort and as a protection against danger to the soul that the use of the so-called caste mark may have first originated.[21]

Fertility cults have already been mentioned. These, like head-hunting and human sacrifice, are intimately associated with agriculture, and the line is hard to draw at the point at which a purely magical fertility rite begins to develop into ceremonial of a genuinely religious nature. At any rate a point is easily reached by the former which is correlated to the latter, and the tribal cult ceases to be purely tribal and is identified with some definitely religious festival so that the magical, cere-monial and devotional aspects become merged. Magical ferti-lity rites, originally regarded as necessary to ensure the processes of nature, are thus conserved and crystallized and continue to be accepted as a natural feature in the ceremony when the reason of their being there is forgotten. So, too, features of such rites which in the beginning are natural and inevitable, since they are regarded as essentially necessary to make the rite effective, and for this reason are performed without any sense of impropriety or obscenity, become, when they cease to be essential to the ceremony, effectively indecent, but are not recog-nized as such as long as the traditional form of the ceremony continues to be unquestioned. In this form ceremonies and practices survive long after the conditions of society in which they originated have changed. Thus rites essentially priapic survived at Isernia near Naples at any rate into the nineteenth century actually under aegis of the Church,[22] and it is only on contact with and under criticism from some external source that familiar and therefore unquestioned practices are seen in a new and critical light. That this process is now taking place in Hindu society is sufficiently obvious. The Cochin Government prohibited the singing of obscene songs, etc., at the *Holi* festival, and advanced Hindu opinion would probably welcome a similar prohibition in many other parts of India, where already the festival seems to be generally celebrated with less excess than used to be the case. The Government of Mysore abolished the institution of *devadasis*, and here again an influential element in Hindu society was loud in its approval.

[21] See Hutton, *The Angami Nagas*, p. 179, and cf. the Mexican custom of sticking a small black disc of cloth called *chiqueadores* on to the forehead as a cure for headache (*Antiquity*, March 1936, p. 97).

[22] Dulaure, *Des Divinités Génératrices*, pp. 257 sqq.

It is perhaps symptomatic of the tendency to reform, and towards even more drastic change in Hinduism, that it should prove possible, as apparently it has in Bombay, to constitute an ' Anti-Priestcraft Association ', the professed purpose of which is ' to combat all religious and social beliefs and customs and institutions which cannot stand the test of reason ', and members of which are reported to entertain a frankly bolshevist attitude towards all religions and to advocate the destruction of all temples, churches and mosques. On the other hand, little effective has been accomplished in the way of removing untouchability in its real sense. It is often said that the conditions of modern life have broken down the idea that contact with certain castes involves pollution and this is true just to that extent to which the use of conveniences such as trams, buses and trains necessitates a relaxation of the rule that certain castes pollute by touch and still more that they can pollute by mere proximity. Further, there is a tendency, obviously consequent on the necessity of the relaxation referred to above, to relax the rule of pollution by touch in the case of members of untouchable castes who do not pursue untouchable avocations. This does not necessarily involve any real abandonment of the attitude of caste Hindus to what the Census Superintendent of Assam [1931] conveniently described as the ' Exterior Castes '. The water they touch is still undrinkable, food they touch becomes impure, and they are not admitted to places of worship or to restaurants, nor will the ordinary barbers serve them. Indeed, the most that seems to have been yet accomplished is the occasional staging of inter-caste meals, gestures which appear so far to have had little practical effect on the general attitude of the caste to the outcaste Hindu, though it is only fair to add that in Assam and Bengal, at any rate, students and schoolboys have shown a manifestly more tolerant attitude than their elders. Moreover, it must not be forgotten that the attempts of the depressed classes to obtain the right of entry to temples are perhaps sometimes as much inspired by social motives as by religious ones, and produce an antagonistic reaction which might be absent if religion alone were involved.

The tribal religions, as has been indicated already, represent, as it were, surplus material not yet built into the temple of Hinduism. How similar this surplus is to the material already used will appear in many ways and may be noticed, to start with, in the cults of the dead. The Hindu rites of the *shradh* provide for the creation of a new body to house the soul of the deceased and, though theoretically renewed every year to maintain it, they are usually as a matter of fact gradually abandoned with the lapse of time. In the tribal religions this cult of the dead is seen in a precisely parallel form, but at a very much more matter-of-fact and materialistic stage of the development of the idea. Thus in Mysore the Hasala caste redeem the soul with a pig from the magician who has caused the death and domicile it in a pot where it is supplied with food and water.[23] The Nicobarese and some Naga tribes fashion wooden figures on which the skull of the deceased is placed in order that the soul may leave it and enter the wooden figure.[24] It is for a time kept supplied with all worldly necessities. A similar practice must formerly have obtained among the Garo of Assam, but it has disappeared, and in the wooden figures now used the pegs that held the skull in place have become unrecognizable, surviving apparently as a sort of a pair of ornamental horns,[25] though an obsolete grave figure in the Indian Museum in Calcutta has a pair of horns much more nearly approximating to the trans-frontier Konyak Naga type. Farther west and south the Sawara of the Ganjam Agency tracts use a similar but more conventionalized wooden figure to accommodate the soul of their cremated dead during the interval between death and cremation and the time for the erection of a stone or stones for the souls of the dead during the year past, which is done annually about the time of the transplantation of the crop.[26] Still farther west the Kunbi of the Central Provinces [27] make an image of their dead in brass, which is kept until the superfluity of such images necessitates their deposit in the water of some sacred river. In the north the statues of the dead made by the head-hunting Kafirs of the western Himalayas had probably a similar purpose, while in western India may be seen the chattries of deceased Hindu Maratha rulers in which the recumbent bull and a lingam face the waxen images of the dead prince and his wife, which latter are piously supplied with food and other requisites and are entertained with music and have their clothes changed regularly once a week. In the very south of India the Mala-Arayan of Travancore make a metal effigy of their dead, which is kept in a miniature stone cist covered with a capstone (like the tattooed skull of a Konyak Naga in the north-east) and erected on high ground. The image is brought out annually and feasted and worshipped with tulsi leaves on its head.[28]

[23] Iyer, *Mysore Tribes and Castes,* III, p. 306.
[24] Bonington, ' Ossuary Practices in the Nicobars ', in *Man,* XXXII, 133 (May 1932) ; Hutton, ' Two Tours East of the Naga Hills ', in *M.A.S.B.,* XI, no. 1 (1929).
[25] Playfair, *The Garos,* p. 113.
[26] Hutton, *Census of India,* 1931, I, pt. III B, p. 4. Dr Elwin writes in 1950 that he can find no trace among the Sawara of the use of such a conventional wooden figure, but I saw one myself in March 1931, and it was explained to me as set down here.
[27] Russell, op. cit., IV, p. 39.
[28] Mateer, *Native Life in Travancore,* p. 75 ; L. A. K. Iyer, *Travancore Castes and Tribes,* I, pp. 179-90.

Allusion [29] has already been made to the theory of soul-matter as a fertilizer of the crops and a producer of life generally, a theory which appears to pervade magico-religious thought and practice throughout Indonesia and south-west Asia and survives in strength in farther India. The collective disposal of the village's dead at the time of sowing is clearly associated in some Naga tribes with their aspect as crop fertilizers, while the Oraons of Chota Nagpur again, if the paddy has sprouted, inter their dead temporarily to cremate them the following year before it sprouts. The connexion between the souls of the dead and the fertilization of the ground is reflected again in their very frequent association with water. It is hardly necessary to call to mind the value set by Hindus upon the immersion of their dead in the Ganges, but there are a number of parallel beliefs in more or less primitive tribes which do not seem to owe their existence to Hindu influence but rather to share their origin with the ingredients of that religious system. Thus the Meithei practice of disposing of the frontal bone of the deceased in the Ganges appears, at first sight, to be the result of their Hinduization, and no doubt their choice of the Ganges is such a result, but their neighbours the Kacharis, when yet un-Hinduized, used to consign their frontal bones to the Kopili river after the harvest, while the Rengma Naga make a pool for water at the grave of any notable man that the rain, and rice, may be plentiful; and at least one other Naga tribe pours water on a grave to cause rain, while the Palaung of eastern Burma fetch a bier pole from a grave and put it in a stream for the same purpose. The Santal again have the practice, at any rate under certain circumstances, of consigning a piece of bone from the head and another from the breast of the dead to the waters of the Damodar river.[30] The Panwar mourner,[31] besides throwing into the Narbada the bones of the dead, throws in with them some of his own hair also, thus perhaps vicariously accompanying the soul. The Kunbi practice of consigning to the Ganges the brass images of their ancestors has already been mentioned, and the Bishnoi Brahmans of Sind were described by Tod as burying their dead at their thresholds and raising over them small altars on which they place an image of Shiva (*sc.* a lingam?) and a jar of water.[32] Though nothing is said of any fertilizing effect, these various practices would seem not unconnected. It is even possible that there may be some similar association with the dead or their avenging spirits in the ordeal by water described in a communication from Warren Hastings [33] as practised by Hindus in the Ganges, the accused man submerging himself and

[29] See above on p. 232 and, for an instance of such a specific theory, p. 250, below. [30] Dalton, *Ethnology of Bengal*, p. 218. [31] Russell, op. cit., IV, p. 348. [32] *Rajasthan*, VIII, ii (vol. III, p. 1297). [33] ' On the Trial by Ordeal among the Hindus ', by Ali Ibrahim Khan in *Asiatick Researches*, I, p. 390.

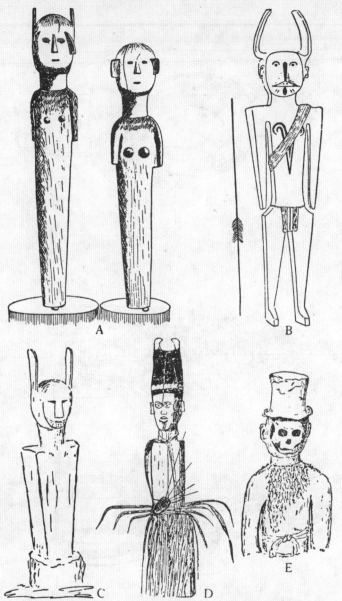

A. Obsolete type of Garo Grave Figure (Kima) from specimens now in the Indian Museum, Calcutta.

B. Statue of dead man with skull receptacle on head. Ukha Village, Konyak Naga.

C. Soul-figure of a woman at Chongvi, with horns for keeping her skull in place (Konyak Naga tribe).

D. So-called 'Devil-Scarer' in the Nicobars, with horns projecting from his top hat.

E. Statue of Nicobarese with skull of deceased as head. The wooden body serves as a cupboard for his bones (Teressa Is., 1930).

Kafir memorial effigies, A & B male, C female, set up one year after death.
Sketched by the late General R. G. Woodthorpe at Apsai, Bashtol R. Kafiristan, 29th September, 1885.

holding to the foot of a Brahman, a form of ritual parallels to
which are practised by a number of primitive tribes from western
India to Vizagapatam and from the Central Provinces via Assam
and Burma to Indo-China. Even in the Rigveda itself there
seems to be some notion of the departure of the souls of the
dead to the waters or into vegetation, in spite of the more definite and prevailing idea of a house of the dead, and in the later
vedic rite of *garbhadhana* to promote conception the husband
infused grass in water and then poured the water down his wife's
nostril, which looks as though it were intended that soul-matter
from the grass should enter the woman to cause her to conceive.

The idea of soul-matter as a fertilizing agent is probably also
responsible for distinctive treatment of the bodies of those who
die by 'bad' deaths and are therefore probably either unfertile
or unsuitable or likely to lead to the reproduction of bad results.
It is thus that we find everywhere special treatment accorded to
the bodies of women who die in child-birth, while other forms
of death are treated differently, i.e. as bad or otherwise, by different tribes. In the case of persons killed by wild beasts the
idea is perhaps that the soul-stuff of the dead is absorbed by
the wild animal, and this is illustrated by the widespread belief
that the soul of the dead rides on the tiger, as told, for instance,
by the Annamites of Cambodia and the Baigas of Central India.
The idea that the soul of a person killed enters the killer is
found elsewhere, e.g. in Australia.

The same doctrine of soul-matter is probably the principle
which underlies head-hunting, human sacrifice, and cannibalism.
The first of these has been recognized in India only in Kafiristan
and in Assam, though it is reported by Colonel Cole of the
Bhils [34] that they were at one time accustomed to bring back
the heads of their enemies and hang them up in trees; and the
Kondhs circulated a head, hair and fingers as a signal for a
rising in 1882, and of four heads taken in that rising one at any
rate was 'affixed as a trophy' to a tamarind tree near Billat
village; [35] again, a Brahui clan explain their name of Sarparra
as meaning 'decapitator',[36] and have been identified with
Strabo's 'Saraparae, that is Decapitators', who lived near the
Guranii and the Medes, and were 'savage intractable mountainy
men' who 'slash round the legs and cut off the heads of
strangers'.[37] The theory, however, on which it is based, that

[34] *Report on the Census of the Rajputana Agency*, 1931, p. 125.
[35] Thurston, *Castes and Tribes*, III, pp. 411 sq.
[36] Bray, *Report on the Census of Baluchistan*, 1911, p. 186 ; R. Hughes-
Buller in Risley, *Ethnographic Appendices*, p. 68.
[37] Strabo, XI, 531. The generally preferred reading, *periskuthistas* for
periskelistas, is translated ' scalp in the Scythian manner ', but this is hardly
compatible with decapitation ; either would seem to be *hapax legomenon*,
and the former reading is much more likely the emendation of a scholiast
who knew his Herodotus, but was as unacquainted with what is a common

the soul-matter is specially located in the head, may be detected
elsewhere. Thus the Andamanese attach special importance to
the jaw [38] and to the skull in mourning, and at any rate one
case is recorded of their carrying off the cranium of a victim
killed in warfare.[39] The Newars of Nepal apparently [40] show
traces of the separate treatment of the head in disposing of
their dead, a feature frequently associated with head-hunting
in Assam, Indonesia, and Oceania, Melanesia in particular, and
undoubtedly based on the same idea. Head-hunting as a necessary preliminary to marriage, as it is in most if not all genuine
head-hunting tribes, is to be explained by the idea that unless a
man has taken heads he has no surplus soul-matter about him
to beget offspring.[41] Probably the same notion is to be seen in
the Chang Naga practice of naming a child after a village raided
by his father. Thus the chief of Yongemdi was named Long-
khong and his brother Ongli after the Ao villages Lungkhung
and Ungr which were successfully raided by their father with
considerable slaughter about the time that they came respectively
into this world. The same notion is clearly present in the cases
that come to light from time to time in India of murder as a
remedy for barrenness in women. Thus in October 1929 the
High Court of the Punjab had to deal with a case in which a
girl, desperately anxious to bear her husband a son, killed a
child, cut off its hands and feet and bathed herself standing upon
them. It cannot be doubted but that the idea was that the life
of the dead child should become the life of a fresh child in her
womb. Again early in 1930 a case occurred in Gujarat of the
murder by means of sulphuric acid of a 12 months old boy by a
girl of 20 who had no child, and it was part of the prosecution
case that it was a comparatively common practice on the part
of barren women to attempt to quicken themselves by burning
marks on children in the street, a practice no doubt ultimately

feature of head-hunting practice as with the unusual word coined by
Strabo to describe it ; Casaubon indeed explains the name of the tribe as
a facetious metaphor from Persian trousers (*sarabara* = ' jodhpurs ') ' dimin-
ishing at the knee '. A Naga head-hunter who does not actually remove
and suspend from the village head-tree the foot and leg of his victim will
frequently slash the legs in order to entitle him to wear the embroidered
gaiters of a warrior who has taken his enemy's legs, while some tribes on
the north bank of the Brahmaputra are reported to cut off the hands and
feet of their enemies (though they do not decapitate), probably to hamper
possible attempts of the ghost to pursue and harm them.

[38] Special importance often attaches to the lower jaw among head-hunters
in both Asia and Africa, and sometimes to the tongue, which is regarded as
the seat of life.

[39] Portman, *Relations with the Andamanese*, i, p. 182.

[40] Northey and Morris, *The Gurkhas*, p. 183.

[41] Conversely I have known a gardener in the Simla Hills refrain from
setting grafts himself since to do so would prejudice his chance of begetting
children, clearly on account of the loss of life-matter ; instead he called
in an old man past the breeding age to do it for him.

derived from one which involved the taking of the child's life, and comparable with that referred to below of branding children offered to the Syrian goddess.[42] And if head-hunting is rare in India, human sacrifice, on the other hand, has been widespread and has clearly been ultimately based on the same conception of the necessity or at any rate the desirability of releasing soul-matter to fertilize the earth. No doubt it was later interpreted as the placation or propitiation of an earth deity, but this must be regarded as a sophisticated justification of a practice the true meaning of which had become obscure or been forgotten. The Kondhs [43] are described as having performed their *meriah* sacrifices to the earth mother, but the details of the ceremony and the practice of distributing fragments of the sacrificial meat in their fields and granaries show a very patent connexion with the disposal of enemy flesh by head-hunting Nagas and the underlying idea is undoubtedly the same. In one form of the sacrifice the victim was squeezed to death in a cleft in a green tree, and in another the tears caused by his sufferings brought rain in proportion to their profusion. Similarly, the Wa of Burma definitely associate their head-hunting with the sowing of the crop,[44] while the successful Kafir head-hunter was greeted, on his return from the foray with his trophy, by a shower of grain.[45] In Kulu the transplanting of the rice is accompanied by the sacrifice of a rough dough image of a man to the house god.[46] So again the Dasehra festival, now associated by all Hindus with the killing of Ravana by Rama, coincides throughout most of India with the sowing of the winter crops, in particular with that of millet, a more ancient staple in south Asia than rice, as well as with that of wheat. It is this festival that is associated in western India with the worship of weapons of war (and it is still regarded there as a proper day on which to go forth and loot), while it is then that human sacrifices used to be performed in eastern India; and it is still on this festival that the *gupta puja*, the hidden rite, to ensure the prosperity of the person, house or family, would be resorted to if ever. The association of human sacrifice with the prosperity of the individual and with the success of the State in war seems clear enough, and its association with crops may be inferred with equal safety. It was probably some such association of soul-substance with fertility, and perhaps with some notion

[42] p. 254, *infra.*
[43] Macpherson, *Memorials of Service in India*, pp. 113 sqq.; Thurston, *Castes and Tribes*, III, 369 sqq., and see Reclus, *Primitive Folk*, pp. 304-35.
[44] Scott and Hardiman, *Gazetteer of Upper Burma and the Shan States*, I, pp. 500 sq.   [45] Robertson, *Kāfirs of the Hindu-Kush*, p. 123.
[46] Crooke, *Religion and Folklore*, p. 253, and cf. Pant, *Social Economy of the Himalayans*, p. 111, where he says that the women transplanting rice offer ' a red powder . . . to heaven ' and apply it to their foreheads. Ochre has definitely some ceremonial association with fertility, probably being associated with blood and semen.

16

of a higher fertility value attaching to Europeans, that led Oraons to remove portions of the body of a recently buried European not so very long ago. The evidence at the trial made it clear that special value attached to European bones for magical purposes.[47] The location of the soul in the head and the confusion of the soul with the shadow are illustrated in the Himalayan cure for fever in which the patient stands in the sun and a bone filled with grain is buried in the spot where the head of the shadow falls.[48] The idea of soul-matter as a fertilizer again is probably at the bottom of human sacrifice as a cure for illness, as in the case of a Santal of Dhanbad who in 1931 garlanded and then beheaded his infant son in order to effect a cure of his own maladies.

True cannibalism is only traditional in India but vestiges of ceremonial cannibalism survive in many places or have done until recently. Thus Portman records [49] the practice of Andamanese homicides, who drank of the blood and ate of the raw fat of the victim and of the flesh of his breast, the latter apparently cooked. In the north-west the Kafirs used to eat a piece of the heart and drink some of the blood of the enemies they killed.[50] In the north-east the Lushei of Assam used to taste the liver and lick from the spear-head the blood of the first victim slain in war.[51] The nearly related Thado eats his first meal after taking life with hands deliberately imbrued with his enemy's blood and still uncleansed therefrom, a custom practised as lately as 1919, and the same custom obtains in a decayed form among the independent Semas of the Assam frontier, where a returning head-taker must eat at least a morsel of food before entering his village; the insistence is on the meal now, but it is eaten with still ensanguined fingers, as he may not cleanse himself until after he has taken this meal. The intention in all these cases is certainly to transfer to the slayer the soul-matter or life-matter of the slain, just as the soul-matter of so many kings has been transferred to their successors by their murder. Similar in principle is the practice of anointing at his succession the intrusive Rajput ruler with the blood of the indigenous Bhil who regards the right to give it as a precious privilege, even though the giver is believed always to die within the year, his soul-matter exhausted no doubt in providing for the fertility and prosperity of the State (compare Forsyth, *Highlands of Central India*, p. 145). It was no doubt a similar idea to that of the Kafir and the Thado which inspired the action of Nana Pharari, a notorious dacoit of Nasik in Bombay Presidency, who stabbed a personal enemy in July 1930, pulled out his knife from

[47] See *Indian Antiquary*, December 1929.
[48] Crooke, *Religion and Folklore*, p. 222.
[49] *Relations with the Andamanese*, I, pp. 31, 115.
[50] Leitner, op. cit., pp. 14, 53, 61.
[51] Lewin, *Wild Races of South-Eastern India*, p. 269.

the victim and applied its gory blade to his forehead and to his tongue. The action of applying the blood to the forehead offers a very close parallel to that of the Angami Naga who never drinks liquor without-applying on the tips of his fingers a drop to his forehead for the benefit of the material soul resident within. The drinking of human blood and the tasting of human flesh are common in Indonesia and Oceania, and it is likely that it has at one time been more prevalent in India than it is now. It was reported of the Wa of Burma by Sir George Scott [52] that probably human flesh was eaten on special occasions, possibly at the harvest festival. The Wa are also credited by the Shans with eating their dead relatives [53] like the Batak of Sumatra, and this, a practice probably arising rather from a belief in reincarnation than directly from that in life-, or soul-matter, has also been reported of some tribes in India. Thus Gardiner reports it of a tribe in the Himalayas, who 'eat the heart and liver of their own dead'. The Kafirs too, he says, occasionally eat the ashes of these organs, mixed with herbs, 'as a sign of affection'.[54] Herodotus mentions the Callatians as an Indian tribe known by Darius to practise this,[55] and he attributes [56] the same custom to the Padaei, for whom an identification has been suggested with the Birhor of Chota Nagpur whom Dalton states to have admitted its former practice by their tribe.[57] The same custom has been likewise attributed to the Lobas of north-east Assam [58] (called Mishu Ting Ba by the Tibetans) in particular, to the hill tribes of Chhattisgarh and of the Amarkantak tableland,[59] as to the hill tribes of Assam in general, and to some of the transfrontier Kachins of north-west Burma, though in these cases there is no well-authenticated evidence. A possible survival of the same practice is to be found in the Kharia custom in the Central Provinces of catching, and eating, communally, a fish on the third day after a person's death,[60] the fish being a common vehicle of the soul as is noted elsewhere in this chapter. All this points to some pre-existence of this practice and to a clear cultural link between the more primitive tribes of India and those of the Indian archipelago.

[52] Scott and Hardiman, op. cit., I, p. 497.
[53] Scott and Hardiman, op. cit., I, p. 498. The same authority says that the Shans eat human flesh at certain tattooing ceremonies (ibid., p. 327).
[54] Edgeworth, 'Abstract of a Journal kept by Mr Gardiner during his Travels in Central Asia', in *J.A.S.B.*, no. 3 of 1853, p. 302.
[55] III, 38.   [56] III, 99.
[57] *Ethnology of Bengal*, pp. 158, 220 sq.
[58] Duff-Sutherland-Dunbar, *Abors and Galongs*, p. 5.
[59] Rowney, *Wild Tribes of India*, p. 7 ; Wilson, *Indian Caste*, I, p. 328.
[60] Russell, op. cit., III, p. 450 ; Roy, *The Kharias*, I, p. 295 sq.; Crooke, *Religion and Folklore*, p. 228 sq. (and cf. p. 244). Dr Verrier Elwin tells me that this custom is not confined to the Kharia tribe, but known and practised all over the Central Provinces.

Perhaps the crudest form in which the doctrine of soul-substance appears is the vulgar but widely credited superstition [61]. which attributes to the European the practice of catching fat black boys and hanging them by the heels over a slow fire to distil from a puncture in the skull the seven drops of vital essence which impart to sahibs in general their energy in field sports and their activity of mind and body. Curiously enough this life-essence, this *momiyai*, seems to have started as bitumen simply,[62] or some similar mineral substance, and to have been used as a quite legitimate medicine, then to have become a spurious substitute in the form of resin, the supposed virtues of which were later attributed by confusion to the embalmed bodies from which this resin was most readily obtained. From the dead body a fourth transfer has taken place and superstition now imputes the virtue of the medicine to its distillation from the living body in the form of its life-essence. This belief caused several harmless strangers to be beaten in Saharanpur not long ago on the suspicion that they were manufacturers of this elixir. Enthoven [63] mentions that this belief gave some trouble during the outbreak of plague in 1896 in Bombay, and is clearly still active. Possibly it has some bearing on the reluctance felt in India to remain in a hospital. Here again it is by Hindus, or persons classified as such, that this superstition is generally held, and the Kabuli trader who brings *momiyai* for sale from Afghanistan is probably under no delusion as to its composition or virtue. The theory is also to be seen in the Aghoripanth philosophy [64] and in occasional cases of cannibalism that come to light in the criminal courts. Thus in September 1931 two men, one apparently a Rarhi Brahman ascetic and the other a Mahabrahman, were accused in Bankura of having dug up the newly buried corpse of a child, of having taken it to their *asram*, and of having there cooked and eaten part of it; the Rarhi Brahman admitted having eaten a little of the heart ' as he believed it was a part of his religion to do so '. It is perhaps partly due to the influence of the primitive belief in this life-giving soul-matter that so much importance is attached in India to the reproduction of the species to pass it on reduplicated to the next generation, so that among the more primitive tribes the penalty of failure to marry is extinction at the hands of a demon who bars the pathway of the dead, while among a number of Hindu castes, as also among the Toda of southern India,[65]

[61] Crooke, *Religion and Folklore*, pp. 111 sq.; Gordon, ' Momiyāi ', in *Man*, XXIX, 160, XXXIII, 163, XXXIV, 83.

[62] Russell, op. cit., I, p. 409 ; Dawson, *The Bridle of Pegasus*, ch. VIII ; Nazaroff, ' The White Lady ', in *Blackwood's Magazine*, August 1931, pp. 217 sq.; Huntingford, ' Momiyai ', in *Man*, XXXIV, 22 ; Gordon, loc. cit.

[63] In his introduction to Crooke's *Religion and Folklore of Northern India* (1926), p. 2.   [64] Russell, *Tribes and Castes of the C.P.*, II, p. 15.

[65] Rivers, *The Todas*, p. 392 ; Thurston, *Ethnographic Notes*, p. 105.

the corpse of a person dying unmarried is married before cremation as a necessary qualification for future happiness.[66] The
doctrine of soul-substance as a fertilizer is naturally not less
applicable to animals than to human beings, and it is therefore
not surprising to find the Mala of southern India and Ahir at
the Gaidaur festival causing their cattle—the young in particular—to trample a pig to death, after which, according to the
ancient custom, the corpse of the pig is eaten by the Ahir who
thus share in the transfer of the porcine life-substance to their
cattle. In the case of the Korava, who have a similar practice,
an instance of the substitution of a human being for the more
usual pig is actually on record,[67] the unfortunate victim having
been buried to his neck before the cattle were driven over him.

Involved again in the belief in soul-matter probably are the
practices of erecting megalithic monuments and wooden images
of the dead. The two practices are not completely separable,
as both appear primarily to be intended to afford a temporary
dwelling for the soul pending its operation as a fertilizer of the
crop. The megalithic monument appears very often as merely
a permanent substitute for the impermanent wooden statue
which can be given greater resemblance to the human body.
Thus the wooden statues of the dead put up by the Angami
Nagas of Assam are in some villages destroyed after the harvest
and the others have a small stone erected behind them to do
duty when they have perished. In other villages again a man's
youngest son, on succeeding as he does to his father's dwelling-
house, must put up a monolith for his deceased parents, an act
corresponding to that of some other villages in which the monoliths are erected during their lifetime by specially prosperous
persons to enhance the prosperity of the community as a whole.[68]
The significance of the latter monolith is quite definitely phallic,
and ancient specimens still exist elsewhere in Assam [69] whose
form puts this beyond dispute, both as solid menhir and as
hollow monolith which contained the ashes of the dead; and
there is no doubt but the association is here again with the soul-
matter as a fertility agent, and an echo of the doctrine is perhaps
to be found in the Vijayanagara legend of the head of the hero
Ramanatha which, when returned to Kummata, became united
with the lingam of Shiva. .It may be noted that Kampila, the
defender of Kummata, appeared, or at least his troops did, under

[66] Thurston, ibid., pp. 106 sq.; *Omens and Superstitions*, p. 51 ; *Castes and
Tribes*, I, pp. 250 sq., V, p. 197, VI, pp. 22, 111 ; Iyer, *Cochin Tribes and
Castes*, II, p. 198 (quoting the report of the Malabar Marriage Commission,
which his own inquiries did not confirm); Wilson, *Indian Caste*, II, pp. 75,
77. [67] Thurston, *Castes and Tribes*, III, pp. 463 sq.
[68] Hutton, *Angami Nagas*, pp. 136, 233 ; *Monoliths at Dimapur*, pp. 58,
67 ; *Erection of Monoliths*, pp. 242 sq.; *Use of Stone*, p. 82.
[69] Mills and Hutton, *Monoliths of North Cachar* ; Hutton, *Monoliths at
Dimapur* ; *Monoliths at Jamuguri* ; *Significance of Head-hunting*.

the guise of head-hunter,[70] while dolmens have actually been used as Saivite temples; in the Naga Hills the cult of head-hunting is, like that of the dead, associated with menhirs and dolmens and other symbols of fertility like the milky *ficus* or *euphorbia* trees.[71] The remains of this megalithic culture in India are widespread though in most places completely decadent, and they generally show sporadically very similar traits. Thus the disposal of the dead of the community during the sowing season has already been mentioned, and in farther India it is, or used to be, associated with a certain amount of mummification of the dead to make them keep, some tribes, e.g. the Ao Naga, smoke-drying the body, others, e.g. the Khasi, embalming it in honey. The use of a soul-figure is merely a different method of obtaining the same end, and by the Konyak Naga of Assam a wooden figure is provided to house the soul until the head can be separated and disposed of in a phallic stone cist.[72] Soul-figures, probably of similar purpose in the first instance, are made in earth by the Handi Jogi of Mysore.[73] The Nicobarese, like some Naga, place the skull of the dead on a wooden body, and at the census of 1931 such a figure was to be seen on the island of Teressa, the skull doing duty as a head incongruously surmounted by an old top hat, the treasured headgear of the dead man.[74] It is impossible not to see the same idea underlying the waxen figures of deceased Hindu princes already referred to, accompanied as they are by a stone lingam. It seems therefore not unlikely that the carved stones erected to the memory of Rajput dead of both sexes have a similar origin, and table stones may occasionally be seen in Rajputana erected to mark the site of a *sati*, recalling the fact that the dolmen is used as a memorial of the dead by the Munda of Chota Nagpur, while by some Assam tribes the upright mono-lith and recumbent dolmen are used to correspond respectively to the male and to the female sexes. A reference to vol. ix of the *Bombay Gazetteer* definitely confirms the supposition that the Rajput memorial stone has the same origin as the Naga or Khasi menhir. Unhewn stones (*khatra*) or carved stones are raised, we learn, by most classes of Hindus in Gujarat for deceased persons, sometimes for all, but more particularly for those that have died a violent death [75] or been remarkable for

[70] *Journal of the Mythic Society*, January 1930.
[71] Hutton, *Two Tours East of the Naga Hills*, pp. 6, 30, 39, 41, 42 ; Mills, *Lhota Nagas*, pp. 28, 108, 129.
[72] Hutton, ' The Disposal of the Dead at Wakching ', in *Man*, xxvii, 44.
[73] L. K. A. Iyer, *Mysore Tribes and Castes*, iii, p. 500.
[74] Bonington, loc. cit.
[75] The Census Superintendent of Madras may be conveniently quoted here on similar practices in South India:
' *Pudams* or shrines exist to which no priests or temples are attached and the prevailing worship is in fact a kind of goblin propitiation, the goblins being usually the spirits of persons who died a violent death.

their holiness. These stones are sometimes placed in a shrine, sometimes under a pipal tree. Until the shrine is set up the spirit of the deceased is dangerous. We may perhaps infer that the reason why such stones are set up, particularly for persons whose spirits are likely to be dangerous, is in order to appease them by providing an abiding place for them and so conforming to an ancient custom otherwise liable to be forgone. The carved stones take the ordinary form of a Rajputana or Kathiawar memorial stone or may be replaced by 'a bust of black marble, brick or wood', but it is significant that they are worshipped by the newly married, or by a bridegroom on the way to fetch the bride, recalling the ceremony performed by childless Konyak Nagas on their phallic stone skull cists, and the practice of barren women to strip themselves at dawn and embrace naked the stone slab carved with the image of Hanuman.[76] At certain temples in southern India barren women are or were seated astride a particular stone to get offspring, success depending upon the experience of an orgasm while in this position. In the Punjab hills again (in Chamba, for instance), monoliths, or wooden substitutes, are put up for the dead, with feasting on a great scale, and for the sake of acquiring merit. A rough effigy of the deceased is usually carved on the stone, and the wooden substitute sometimes has a hole and a spout for water, when it is set up in the stream beside which it would otherwise be placed. Sometimes a circular stone is placed on the top of the monolith (recalling the former Khasi practice), and in the case of ruling families (e.g. of Mandi and Suket, where the practice is confined to royalty) the wife and concubines of the deceased are also represented on the stones, as they are by Assam hill tribes. The Mala-Arayan of Travancore make a metal

Animal sacrifice and frequent admixture of human blood are commonplaces in their ceremonies. One such shrine in Tinnevelly district is to the spirit of a European killed in the Travancore wars and the offerings made are of articles considered peculiarly acceptable to one of his race: bread, fowls, cheroots and brandy. The spirit of Muhammad even is said to inform one granite pillar in Tinnevelly where daily " puja " is done by Hindu votaries. Vows are made to it by Hindus who flock to seek cure of disease, rain, and other boons. Ganja and cheroots are the form the offerings take, these being considered peculiarly attractive to Muhammadans. . . . In effect the real religion of the presidency, in the south, at any rate, is directed rather towards shrines and saints than towards deities.' (Yeatts, op. cit., p. 320.)

[76] One may compare with these practices that of embracing a certain pillar in the church of the Virgin at Orcival in Auvergne or sitting in the chair of St Fiacre in the church of the village of that name, the stone seat of which, like the pillar at Orcival, had the power of rendering barren women fertile. It was necessary, however, that there should be no garment between the stone and the sitter's body. Similarly in the chapel of St Antoine de Paule at Saragossa there was a tombstone on which barren women lay in order to become fruitful. (Dulaure, *Des Divinités Génératrices*, p. 251.)

effigy of the dead and put it into a miniature cist of stone verticals and a capstone which is erected on high ground and worshipped annually. Even the method of transporting megaliths seems to have left traces in western India. The Naga of Assam, like the people of Nias in the Indian archipelago, transport megaliths on wooden sledges made from the forked trunks of trees which are dragged by very large numbers of men pulling on cane or creeper ropes. In the case of the Naga, at any rate, an essential implication of the ceremony is the infection of the village with the prosperity of the celebrant, and when the ceremony is performed with wooden instead of stone emblems these emblems are formally dragged all round the village with this express purpose.[77] Very suggestive of a degenerate form of this ceremony is the village festival (*ghasbavji*) in Rajputana at which the 'god', consisting of a large waterworn boulder, is dragged round the village on a sled made out of a forked tree trunk. Probably of similar origin also is the general veneration paid to stones throughout India, particularly of course to those of queer or unusual shape. Crooke gives a very large number of examples [78] which it is unnecessary to recapitulate, but it may be recorded here that a suit was argued in the Calcutta High Court on 25 April 1929 about a stone about 5 ft. square, apparently of black slate or marble from Jaipur (Jeypore), which changed hands for Rs. 10,000 (£750) as being ' very efficacious in the matter of getting a son'. The suit arose because the stone failed to function, and it was stated in evidence that numbers of even quite well-educated Hindus believed in the efficacy of stones of this kind when used with the correct rites, and that so much as a lakh might be paid for such a stone. It was also mentioned that sitting on a stone is an essential feature in many Jain rites.

It may here be urged that the reverence and superstition paid to stones in general, is not, as Crooke suggests, a vague superstition which develops into the use of memorial stones, but on the contrary is the degenerated remnant of the life-essence fertility cult. The use of a stone or mere pebble as a *pretyasila*, 'stone of the disembodied spirit', by Hindus in western India seems a definite instance of this process of decay. The stone is picked up by the chief mourner at the place where the corpse was put down and is anointed with oil (recalling the baetyls of Naga fertility cults [79]), a crow is induced to eat corn scattered about it and the pebble is then thrown into running water or kept among the household deities. Similarly, the Komati caste of Mysore invokes the soul of the deceased to enter a pebble temporarily, while the ashes of the deceased

[77] Hutton, ' Carved Monoliths at Dimapur and an Angami Naga Ceremony ' ; ' Meaning and Method of the Erection of Monolithis by the Angami Nagas ', in *J.R.A.I.*, LII.   [78] *Religion and Folklore,* ch. xii.
[79] Hutton, *The Sema Nagas,* p. 254.

are cast into a sacred river or some other water.[80] It seems therefore much more likely that a veneration of stones on account of the indwelling soul has been transferred to peculiar stones in general on account of similar possibilities, than that a vague reverence of stones should exist without reason and be elaborated into a coherent creed which really turns on a belief in the power of soul-matter to promote the fertility of nature. An extension of the same idea would seem to appear in the practice of requiring spirit or soul-matter of the dead to impart permanence or, to use our own metaphor, 'life', to buildings. This practice is referred to as that of foundation 'sacrifices', but the idea of sacrifice, if present at all, is clearly later than the practice itself, which is essentially of the same origin in India, where at least a belief in the necessity survives, and in Oceania, where in Fiji and in the Marquesas, for instance, human sacrifices were required to invest a building or a canoe with the necessary *mana*. This belief is still so prevalent in India as to be the cause of a good deal of disturbance from time to time. In 1922 the Deputy Commissioner of Dibrugarh had to issue a notice reassuring people against *mur katas* (= 'head-cutters') coming to kill or behead male children for some unknown purpose, and to threaten with prosecution anyone assisting to spread the rumour. In May 1923 a riot took place on Cinnamara tea estate on account of a scare about the kidnapping of children for the foundation of a new bridge. In June 1924 a rumour in Calcutta that the Port Commissioners were seeking for children to bury in the foundation of the new Kidderpore dockyard led to Punjabi taxi-drivers being killed in the belief that they were agents decoying children for this purpose, and in the same month strangers in Patna were maltreated in connexion with a similar scare about a bridge in Bihar. In 1926 in North Lakhimpur there was a rumour that *arkas* (i.e. head-takers?) were trying to obtain children's heads for the construction of a railway bridge. In the same year the district engineer constructing a recent bridge on the Sibsagar Road-Khowang Railway had trouble from a kidnapping scare, which was so much intensified when a retaining wall burst that schoolboys asked leave in order to stay at home for fear of being kidnapped on their way to school. Several petitions were filed in the S.D.O.'s office, also against suspected kidnappers, while villagers insisted on visiting and counting tea-garden coolies during the night in order to assure themselves that they were not concealing victims in their lines, and a number of assaults took place, one serious. In July of the same year there was a scare in Cachar that a human sacrifice was required for the oil-borings to promote the flow of oil in the Burmah Oil Company's wells. A strange coolie was

[80] L. K. A. Iyer, *Mysore Tribes and Castes*, III, pp. 571 sq.

roughly handled on the 12th of that month in Cachar and a stranger from Sylhet was beaten and confined on the same suspicion on the 10th. In January 1929 a rumour in Bombay that children were being kidnapped for the construction of a bridge in Baroda led to an attack on Pathans and on a Greek engineer, to the death of a Hindu carpenter, and ultimately during two days' time to the killing of seventeen Pathans, while two other Muslims and three Hindus were killed in the consequent affrays, very many other persons being injured.⁻ In the subsequent riots 149 people were killed and the damage to property came to at least 5 lakhs of rupees (£37,500). In May 1929, in Bihar again this time, a man was beaten to death in the belief that he was seeking to kidnap a child as a 'foundation sacrifice' for a bridge at Jamshedpur, while the floods in the Surma valley of the same year led to a scare that children were being kidnapped for the reconstruction of certain embankments in the Manipur State. In certain tribes of the Naga Hills in Assam a live chicken is still placed in the hole dug for the main house post and the post stepped on to it, while it is asserted that certain transfrontier tribes use a human being thus, as formerly in Fiji, 'to hold up the post'. The same idea is to be seen in a practice attributed by Mr S. N. Roy [81] to Bengali boat-builders who have had to dispute their dues with a customer; a few drops of the shipwright's blood are plugged into a cavity in the planking, when the boat acquires a malevolent vitality, drowns its crew and continues an independent existence as an aquatic phantom. A sword used in sacrifice acquires a similar vitality from the blood of the victims it decapitates, and, like boats, it is furnished with eyes painted in vermilion.

It has already been indicated that the soul is often conceived of in the tribal religions of India as having the form of a manikin and being located in the head, and though this conception is apparently at conflict with the theory of soul-matter or a material life-substance, it is held concurrently with it without any consciousness of inconsistency. There is nothing remarkable in this, but the question arises whether these two conceptions are of different origin or may have come into being from the same source, and it is here submitted that the conception of the soul as a manikin is merely the effect, on a rather vague conception as to the nature of life, of that tendency towards anthropomorphism which is inevitable when man is to conceive of a material with some of his own attributes and no known shape, a tendency which is apparent in the conception of the deity in the great majority of religions. The Karen of Burma [82] have a doctrine of a material substance which is the cause of life, or rather which is actually life itself, a sort of ectoplasm of life, which

[81] *Man in India*, IX, no. 4, p. 272.
[82] Marshall, *Karen People of Burma*, p. 222.

leaves the dying body to enter the herbs of the field or the seeds of the earth, and which then passes through grass into cattle and through grain, or indirectly through the meat of grazing animals, into man and passes through the seminal fluid to generate fresh life, almost as if it consisted of carbohydrates.[83] This doctrine may perhaps be regarded as having arisen very early in the history of mankind as a natural result of speculation as to the cause of the change that takes place at death and as to the nature of that which has left the body. Speculation of some kind would be inevitable, if only as a result of the natural curiosity required by any animal, human or otherwise, to adapt itself to environment in the struggle to survive. Abstract ideas come late in the development of a language and presumably therefore late in the development of thought, and hence the necessity, before any philosophic idea of life can be framed, of regarding it as a material substance and of thinking of that substance as taking some form. The idea then of a manikin living behind the forehead whose movements are registered on an infant's fontanelle is a not unnatural symptom of the development, or degeneration, of the life-substance theory and may perhaps be traced in that doctrine of the Vedanta school of Hindu philosophy which regards the soul as encased in a series of sheaths, the interior of which accompany the soul on its migration while the exterior constitute the material body; and the location of the soul in the head is illustrated by the Hindu belief that it escapes through the 'crevice of Brahma', through which ascetics can project their soul (and so die) at will, while for less holy persons it is necessary to fracture the skull with a conch shell to let out the soul. The *sālăgrămă* held to the aperture perhaps served the same purpose as the *pretyasila* mentioned above. One is also reminded of the story in the Aitareya Brahmana [84] of how the gods killed a man for their sacrifice, but the part in him fit for an offering went out, leaving him deformed, and entered a horse, and so on through an ox (which turned to a gayal when the fit part left it), a sheep and a goat and entered the earth, where the gods surrounded it so that no escape was possible, when it turned into rice. Father Schmidt considers that in India 'the materialistic Sankhyan philosophy most certainly arose from matrilineal animism', and he suggests that the spiritual philosophies of classical Greece may have had at least in part a similar source. Having got as far as materializing our life principle, its conception as similar in feature to the human body is inescapable, and the way is clear

[83] It seems certain that the strange provision in the Brahmanical code which makes the Telis an untouchable caste (but not the Tilis, who only sell and do not press oil) is due to their practice of destroying the seed in the pursuit of their occupation without provision for its transfer to another living organism, a suggestion confirmed, I think, by Manu, IV, 85.
[84] *Vide* Rajendralala Mitra, *Indo-Aryans*, II, p. 76.

for the doctrine of reincarnation. The doctrine reached is logically irreconcilable with the theory with which we started, but experience shows that the two can be held simultaneously, at any rate by primitive man, without any consciousness of inconsistency. There are probably, however, steps by the way which contribute to this belief—the idea of the soul coming back as an insect is one, and one to which the conception of the soul as able to leave the body and flit about at night, derived in part no doubt if not entirely from the phenomena of dreams, has contributed. As instances the Lhota Naga of Assam, the Kunbi of Bombay, and the Kami and Bhuiya of Bengal may all be quoted as watching for an insect after a person's death, or the Ahir and Gond who go to a river and bring back an insect or a fish as containing the soul and sometimes, in the case of the Gond at least, eat it to ensure its rebirth.[85] Another contributory observation to the insect notion is perhaps the mysterious way in which large numbers of insects appear from nowhere in particular, as if caused by superfluity as it were of life-substance, an idea which would have been comprehensible enough to the ancient world, which regarded, for instance, insect life as spontaneously engendered in dung dropped under a waxing moon, etc.,[86] or which regarded the Nile floods as pouring soul into the sods so as to fashion live creatures from the very soil,[87] bringing us back again to that fertility cult which associates soul with water. Similarly, Diodorus Siculus says, 'moisture generates creatures from heat, as from a seminal principle', and a little farther on, 'they say that about Thebes in Egypt, after the overflowing of the river Nile, the earth thereby being covered with mud and slime, many places putrify through the heat of the sun, and thence are bred multitudes of mice. It is certain, therefore, that out of the earth . . . animals are generated'.[88] These ideas of life in dung and water seem to have been combined in the practice which so disgusted the Abbe Dubois at the temple of Nanjanagud in Mysore some 150 years ago. Barren women and their husbands were described by him as drinking out of the temple sewer from hands soiled by setting aside a portion of the ordure to be examined a few days later whether insects or vermin were engendered in it, which was regarded as 'a favourable prognostic for the women'.[89] Whatever be its origin, however, a vague belief in reincarnation is common to most of the tribal religions in India and is generally associated more or less with some degree of ancestor worship,

---

[85] Crooke, *Religion and Folklore*, p. 381 ; Roy, *Hill Bhuiyas*, p. 202 ; Risley, *Tribes and Castes*, I, p. 395 ; Russell, op. cit., II, p. 28, III, p. 94.

[86] *Vide* Pliny, *Nat. Hist.*, bk. xviii, ch. xxxii, editor's note.

[87] [*Nilus*] . . . *glaebis etiam infundat animas, ex ipsaque humo vitalia effingat*—Pomponius Mela, I, 52.

[88] *History*, I, i.   [89] *People of India*, pp. 396 sq. (pt. III, ch. iii).

a tendency to which is everywhere apparent. This reincarnation belief is to be seen very clearly in the ancient Brahmanic theory that after the birth of a son the sexual relationship of husband and wife should end, since the son is the father's self and the father's wife has become his mother also. It is stated of the Kochhar subcaste of the Khatri, a trading caste of the Punjab, that funeral rites are performed for a father in the fifth month of his wife's first pregnancy, which points to the same idea.[90] The Bishnoi of Hissar bury an infant at the threshold that its soul may re-enter the mother and be born again.[91] Among the Bhuiya every child is regarded as a reincarnation of some deceased relative,[92] while the Mikir, it may be noticed, believe in reincarnation except for the souls of those who have been killed by tigers. Among the Lushei the reincarnated soul sometimes appears as a hornet, sometimes as dew,[93] and in the latter form the belief is hardly distinguishable from the Karen theory of life-substance. So again it is a common practice with the tribes mentioned that while a dead grandfather's name or that of another ancestor must be given to a child, the name of a living ancestor shall not be given, as, if it were, either he or the new-born child would die. The practice was perhaps similar in ancient Indian society, as in old lists of kings it is common to find a grandson named after the grandfather. This practice seems, however, to have changed, as the name of any ancestor living or dead is reported now to be avoided by Hindus.

The association of reincarnation with the soul-fertility cult is perhaps confirmed to some extent by Malcolm's record[94] of the practice of jumping off certain high rocks in central India in order to be reborn in a royal house. Forsyth also records[95] the account of an eyewitness, Captain Douglas, Political Assistant in Nimar, of a scene at Omkar, a shrine of Shiva on Mandhatta island in the Narbada, at which a young man leaped off a rock 90 ft. high to his death in 1822, and mentions a later case of an old woman who hesitated and was pushed over. In the case of this rock apparently if the jumper survived he was killed by a 'priestess' with a dagger, but in the case of another of these rocks if a man survived the fall he was made Raja, and the association between the soul and the fertility of the land impinges on that between the fertility of the land and the king as the living receptacle or embodiment of the life-spirit, and one which must not be allowed to grow old. One is reminded, however, by this habit of jumping off a cliff to royal incarnation, of a number of similar practices associated in each case with the

[90] Frazer, *Golden Bough*, IV, p. 189, and cf. Crooke, *Northern India*, pp. 202 sq.   [91] Kaul, *Report on the Census of the Punjab*, 1911, I, p. 299.
[92] Roy, *Hill Bhuiyas*, p. 186.
[93] Shakespear, *Lushei Kuki Clans*, pp. 64 sq.
[94] *Memoir of Central India*, II, p. 210.
[95] *Highlands of Central India*, pp. 180 sqq.

fertility of the soil.[96] Thus rope-sliding (*beduart*) in the Himalayas would appear to be a definite survival of a similar form of voluntary or involuntary human sacrifice. The slider, an acrobat or dancer (*beda*) by caste, is worshipped as Mahadeo, bathed in milk, dressed in new clothes, and carried round the village fields before the ceremony, which is resorted to when harvests have been bad.[97] That this is a survival of human sacrifice is clearly indicated by the fact that both the rope used and the hair of the slider are distributed as fertility charms, while the slider himself becomes infertile, for his fields go barren and the seed he sows fails to burgeon. He is, in fact, spiritually dead[98] and his life-matter has been distributed to his neighbours. We are recalled to the Kondh *meriah* whose parent was consoled by his neighbours in words which Macpherson has recorded: 'Your child has died that all the world may live.'[99] It is worth remarking that the hereditary caste of rope-sliders is the Nat caste, and that the women of that caste are associated in many parts of India with dancing and prostitution. Both are probably closely connected with fertility rites, and it may be that the professions of tight-rope walker, acrobat, dancer, and prostitute take their origin in services performed primarily for the benefit of the crops. It is said that in former days the slider who fell off the rope was cut to pieces at the bottom, and the rite as a whole suggests a chastened form of human sacrifice in which it was essential that the victim should fall from a great height. It recalls insistently the ceremony described as practised at the temple of the Syrian Goddess where from a very lofty porch between two gigantic phalli the animal or sometimes apparently human victims were hurled to the ground, and where worshippers let their children down in a sack after branding them[1] as devoted to the deity. In the north-east corner of India the Angami Naga still hurls from the roof of a house his sacrificial victim, a puppy dog invested with the symbolic attributes of a man, while a calf released below is literally torn to pieces by the crowd. Meanwhile ashes representing clouds and cotton seeds representing hail are thrown by the priest from the roof, clearly showing that not only is a distribution of the victims' life-essence involved but a fall of fertilizing water is probably intended to be magically ensured by a fall of the victim

---

[96] Tod (*Annals*, XI, ch. iv) says 'love of offspring' is the motive, but he does not explain, and one is almost inclined to suspect him of a subtle pun.
[97] Rose, *Tribes and Castes*, I, pp. 345 sqq.
[98] Like the Maithil Brahman mentioned by Wilson (*Indian Caste*, II, p. 194) who was outcasted by his family because he recovered after his funeral ceremonies had actually been performed in expectation of his decease (cf. *supra*, pp. 109-10), and like the Bhil referred to above (p. 242) who died within a year of the use of his blood for anointing his lord as king.
[99] Macpherson, op. cit., p. 115.
[1] See *Purchas his Pilgrimage*, bk. I, ch. 15.

from above.[2] The practice of 'hook-swinging', i.e. suspending a devotee on hooks inserted through the flesh under the muscles of the back and rotating him at the end of a horizontal pole mounted high on a vertical bearing, a practice at one time widely used in Bengal and in most of southern India, was undoubtedly another manifestation of the same fertility cult.[3]

One phenomenon of primitive religion which cannot be ignored when writing of India is totemism, traces of which are shown by primitive tribes in all parts of India and by not a few castes that have reached or retained a high social position. From the Bhils in the west to the Wa of eastern Burma; from the Kanets of the Simla hills to members of Telugu castes of southern India, clear traces of totemism are found to survive, and it is needless here to go into details already sufficiently well known and recorded. It may be enough to recall 'the long-tailed Ranas of Saurashtra', Jethwa Rajputs who claim descent from Hanuman, and the ruler of the Malabar coast whose death involves abstention from fishing lest the soul-inhabited fish be captured, to show that totemistic ideas are not entirely confined to primitive tribes and to castes low in the social scale. What is called totemism is no doubt remarkable for the extreme variety of its manifestations, ranging from the sacramental consumption of the totem or its use for magical augmentation of the food supply, to the merest peg for exogamy to hang upon, and it is in the latter form that it is commonest in India, where it has generally decayed into a mere totemistic clan name. There are, however, traces of taboos and beliefs essential to it at an earlier stage. Some tribes having what appear to be totemistic clan names no longer regard them as such. Thus the Thevoma clan of the Angami Nagas and the Awomi of the Sema would appear in both cases to bear names translatable as 'Pigmen', but no such meaning is ascribed by the Angamis, who explain the name as a human patronymic, while the corresponding Sema clan gives an adventitious explanation of an ancestor who was bitten by a pig; on the other hand, the Ao Naga neighbours of these tribes have a dog clan which still claims canine characteristics, e.g. speed of foot and doglike features;[4] moreover, they taboo the dog as food or rather used to taboo it until recently they found it desirable to break the taboo in order to benefit by the medicinal virtues of dog-flesh. Another Ao clan again, the

---

[2] Hutton, *Monoliths at Dimapur*, p. 69.

[3] A full account with references to the older reports will be found in an article by Prebendary J. H. Powell in *Folk-Lore*, vol. xxv, pp. 147 sqq.

[4] In the Nicobars, where descent is claimed from a dog and a woman, the dress of man is said to be intended to simulate a doggy appearance, consisting of a fillet round the head with two ends sticking up from the knot on the forehead to resemble dog's ears, while the private parts are concealed in a blue bag with a long red point to it, and the waist-band is arranged to fall down behind in a tail.

Wozakumr, i.e. Hornbill people, claim descent from a woman who conceived as a result of a feather dropping in her lap from a hornbill flying overhead, and it is taboo for them to kill a hornbill or even to see a dead one. It may likewise be noted that the Hindu Chasa of Orissa regard the injuring of their clan totem as punished by leprosy, an affliction which the Brahman regards as the punishment for killing a cow.

Into totemism the belief in life-matter seems hardly to enter, perhaps, but the idea of the external soul, which seems to be a development of the life-matter belief, does appear as connected with totemism in India much as it is in parts of Africa. As a possible source of the connexion between totemism and the external soul the phenomena of birth may be suggested. The afterbirth is well known to be intimately associated with the idea of the external soul and is regarded in some cases as actually containing it. Thus among the Baganda it is buried under a plantain tree, and a woman may conceive if pollinated, as it were, by the dropping on her of a plantain flower.[5] In the case of the chief, however, the placenta is carefully preserved and brought to him to handle and return to safe keeping on State occasions. Here we are reminded of the placenta standard on the palette of Narmer.[6] No doubt as the abode of the king's vital essence the proximity of such a standard in time of danger would be useful, and if the standard be the abode of the external soul we have the explanation both of the association of totems with standards and the apparent paradox of taking into danger a very highly prized emblem the capture of which is regarded by the enemy as of great significance.[7] One may recall the Fairy Banner of the McLeods, which not only brings victory but causes a cow to drop her calf or a pregnant woman to give birth on the sight of it. It may be inferred that its quickening property is due to its being the seat of external soul-matter.[8] If the placenta be thus regarded as the location of the external soul, a possible origin of totemic belief at once

[5] Frazer, *Totemism and Exogamy*, II, p. 507.
[6] Seligman and Murray, ' Note on an Early Egyptian Standard ', in *Man*, XI, 97.
[7] The earliest Roman standards are said to have consisted of a bundle of hay on a pole. Can it have been held that such a bundle of hay would be, like a growth of mistletoe, a convenient hiding place for external soul-matter, just as the Kayan leaves the leafy tops of trees unpruned in order to afford a refuge for the spirits of vegetation when clearing the fields? It might be that the same idea was present in the bandaged pole which on an Egyptian temple represented the god, the hieroglyphic for which resembles a flag though it is described as a hatchet and stated to be in effect a bandaged pole with a loose flap projecting.
[8] Strasser (*The Mongolian Horde*, p. 104) relates that the Tashai Lama of Urga in Mongolia ' pressed his standards to the slit throats of his victims, saturating them in their spurting life blood '. One is tempted to see in this an attempt to imbue the standards with soul-matter which would no doubt contribute towards their victorious progress.

suggests itself in the possibility of the placenta being devoured by some scavenging animal or bird, or being associated with the tree on which it is placed for security or with some plant which springs up on the spot where it is buried. It is necessary, of course, to postulate a subsequent transfer of the totem from the individual to the exogamous clan descended from him or her, but such an origin would perhaps account for a purely social form of totemism in which there was no sacramental element and no magical food production. It would also account for a soul-transmigration form of totemism.

It is worth while in this connexion to draw attention to the case of the plantain tree as deriving Baganda soul-matter from a placenta at its root in Africa and as being used as the equivalent of a human being in Assam and Oceania.[9] Thus a 'plantain tree' is in many parts of the Naga Hills an euphemism for a slave for decapitation. The same equation appears in Micronesia, Fiji, Polynesia, Madagascar and nearer home among the Palaungs of Burma, with whom the tree is also an emblem of fertility, while it is frequently a plantain tree which is used in India in the mock marriages sometimes performed for elder children to enable their juniors to be married before them. A close parallel to the Baganda theory of conception from a plantain flower is to be found in India in the Muslim belief that a woman may conceive if the flowers of a rose tree or jasmine which is growing from the tomb of a dead saint should fall upon her. One may also call attention to the existence in the case of the Ho tribe of a clan whose peculiar totem is the hole of a mouse or rat, a totem immediately explicable on the placenta theory when one is informed that the clan is descended from a person whose placenta at his birth was buried in a rat hole.[10] The same placenta theory perhaps also appears in the Kora story reported by Risley [11] from Bengal to account for the fruit of a certain tree being taboo to the tribe, since their ancestor once accidentally ate a human placenta which had been exposed in a tree of that particular variety. The existence of clans with a placenta totem has also been reported from the Agariya and Gond tribes [12] of the Central Provinces.

Another origin of totems has been suggested as likely to be found in food restrictions. We should be inclined rather to put it the other way round and regard it as perhaps to be found in peculiarities of diet. The discovery and search for forms of vegetable food must have held a very important place in early

---

[9] Cf. also J. G. S. Turner, *Census of Nigeria*, 1931, VI, p. 7: 'It is said that some of the Yoruba eat the placenta. . . . In the Cameroons it is usually buried under a plantain tree and the fruit is henceforth taken by the native doctor and later by the child.'

[10] Majumdar, *Tribe in Transition*, p. 206.

[11] *Tribes and Castes*, I, p. 507.

[12] V. Elwin, *The Agaria*, p. 76 sq.; Hivale, *The Pardhans*, p. 40.

domestic economy. Under any conditions in which food was scarce and its collection uncertain and laborious, as is probably frequently if not normally the case in a pre-agricultural stage of existence, there must have been a tendency to conceal as long as possible the source of some hitherto unknown supply of food lest that supply be exhausted by other gatherers. Experiment in strange vegetables is dangerous, particularly in the tropics. It is therefore suggested that to the discovery and communication to the kindred and concealment from other clans of new forms of vegetable food must be ascribed the importance of certain wild vegetables in clan ceremonial among the Naga tribes of Assam. The test of whether a clan in one tribe is to be identified or not with a clan in another tribe speaking a totally different language often depends on the vegetable used in certain ceremonies. If the identical plant is used, the clans would be regarded as related, and clansmen of one tribe going on a trading expedition into the territory of another will feel secure in a house of a related clan, whereas otherwise they would lie down, if at all, in fear of their slumbers being sublimated by the sharp *dao* of decapitation. It is true that the wild vegetables used in these clan ceremonies are not always regular articles of food, but it is the writer's impression that they are always edible. Here surely is another possible source of ideas leading to the adoption of a vegetable totem by a given clan.

It is not argued that all totems are accounted for directly by any of the ideas suggested above. Pig's tripe, for instance, will not quite fit, though we might perhaps suppose a fragment to have got left in a pot in which an after-birth was hung up; buffalo dung is harder still, unless dung be regarded (*vide supra*, pp. 252 sq.) as a source of spontaneous life. It is, however, likely from every point of view that totemism in general has received accretions from a number of sources, and that while it may have originally started with, say, Frazer's theory of conception in ignorance of the fact of paternity, it has been encouraged and perpetuated by the ideas of life-matter, a separable soul, transmigration and probably other connected ideas, and that a number of these have contributed to totemism as still found in India.

Magic, when limited to purely imitative or sympathetic magic, is rather nearer the domain of science than of religion. There is nothing religious at all about the effort of an Ao Naga to influence the rice by planting a root or two in earth put in the hollow top of a bamboo, and so raised above the rest of the field which is thus induced to grow high; in the rather inconsiderate Kuki plan of putting a bug into the bundle of the departing guest in order that the rest of the vermin may leave the house likewise; or in the custom of giving a Prabhu bride a grindstone to hold which she gives to her husband saying 'take the baby'.

When, however, the efficacy of such magic depends not on the practice but on the practitioner, we may suspect that the idea of soul-matter is present and that it is, often at any rate, the superfluity of this material that enables the magician to make his magic successful. Here again one may perhaps see the reaction of the simple belief that like produces like to an independent belief in the existence of soul-matter. However that may be, a belief in magic both white and black pervades all the more ignorant classes in India and is frequently responsible for serious crime; nor is it always eliminated by culture and education, as witness the comparatively educated persons frequently victimized by rogues who profess to be able to double currency notes miraculously. Thus, to give a single instance, in May 1931, a well-to-do merchant of Indore imprudently handed over Rs. 2,800 to one Pandit Sri Krishna who claimed to have a marvellous process of doubling notes. Ignorant villagers are much more easily imposed on, as in the case of a village near Multan in the Punjab which about the same time parted with Rs. 15,000 in cash and ornaments to a Muslim fakir who first called down a few rupees from heaven to inspire confidence in his piety and miraculous powers, and then professed to be able to turn silver ornaments into gold or one rupee into three. A belief in magic again, for it can hardly be described as anything else, even if it involve the theory of the impregnation of matter with soul-essence, appears in the practice, reported on good authority in Rangoon, of a director of an international trading corporation who, when ill, had sewn into the seat of his pyjama trousers by his Catholic wife a pious fragment of the holy St Theresa's petticoat. What the effect on a male Naga would be of wearing a piece of any woman's petticoat, however holy, we hesitate to set down in print, but presumably Herr Direktor experienced benefit.

Often a belief in witchcraft leads to the murder of the reputed witch.[13] In 1928 in Bihar, for instance, nine cases of murder were ascribed to witchcraft, and in 1931 in the Yarpur mahalla of Patna a small Lohar girl was murdered in retaliation for the supposed enchantments of her mother, while an 'aboriginal' woman suspected of being a witch was killed near Ghatsila. In Faizabad, in 1927, a man was killed on the advice of a medicine man as being the cause of another's prolonged dysentery, and in Budaun a Chamar, who was suspected of having bewitched an idiot of good family, was pegged out and periodically belaboured while the bewitched one was watched for improvement in his condition. Ultimately, as there was none, the Chamar succumbed. In July 1920 a mob in the Nizam's

[13] See also Elwin, *Maria Murder and Suicide*, ch. v, and C. R. Hemeon, ' Short Notes of some Remarkable Crimes in the Central Provinces and Berar ' in *Man in India*, September 1943.

Dominions killed a woman who was believed to have brought cholera on the village, a belief arising from the hysterical statement of a possessed woman into whom had entered the spirit of the goddess who was being worshipped at the time by the village. In November 1930 in Gonda in the United Provinces a wizard was murdered by his own pupil in the belief that he, the wizard, had caused an evil spirit to destroy his pupil's wife and would cause it also to destroy him himself; and as the pupil was one of ten years' standing, this instance testifies to the wizard's belief in his own system.

On the other hand the witches themselves likewise commit murders for their own ends, and to that extent anyhow justify their persecution. A boy was sacrificed in Bhagalpur in 1928, for the purpose of exorcising evil spirits from a possessed woman, and on the eve of the Dasehra festival of 1930 two sorcerers of Sambalpur, described by the High Court as 'men of standing', sacrificed a boy for some nefarious purpose of their own. This case, however, may possibly have been one rather of a homicide of the kind alluded to above as occasioned by the belief in the need for soul-matter. The use of human sacrifice in order to exorcise spirits is probably unusual, as it is commoner to treat the body of the possessed by more direct methods. Indeed, a Hindu girl was beaten to death in Lahore in November 1929, in the attempt to cure her of possession, and this apparently at a shrine frequented by persons in order to experience possession by the deity. In view, however, of the extent of illiteracy and of the population concerned, the amount of violent crime actually due to a belief in witchcraft appears to be unexpectedly small, though naturally apt to increase with the appearance of calamities or epidemics, which are ascribable to the malevolence of witches. In Chota Nagpur there are professional witch doctors called *sokha* whose business it is to indicate the witch responsible for any calamity or epidemic that has occurred.

Personal magic, however, is not the only form in which magic appears. Tribal magic, in which the community combines, usually at some festival, in rites or dances intended to secure fertility or prosperity, is a normal feature of tribal religion. Such festivals or rites are usually associated with the agricultural year and may involve sexual licence which is probably intended to have a magical effect on the fertility of the crop and of the community itself, and no better instance of such a festival can be quoted than the *Holi*, which has survived as a Hindu festival throughout India.[14] It is tempting, if possibly fanciful, to

[14] Unless it be the marriage festival annually celebrated in June by the lord of a feudal manor in Normandy, who after participating in the bridal festivities of his serfs picked out the couples who appeared to him to be the most amorous, and caused them to consummate their marriages in the boughs of trees or in the waters of the local river. Dulaure speaks of this practice as one of tyrannical jesting, but the interpretation here assumed

trace the origin of the widespread belief in the magic effect of coition on the fertility of the soil, of animals and of people in general to a period in human history when the relation between cause and effect in the begetting of children was not yet fully comprehended, but when the two were already seen to have some association, so that what was really the cause of the conception of one particular child was regarded as merely the cause of parturition in general.[15] Such a stage in the process of deduction from observed facts, if its existence be credible, would account for the common practice of assisting the fertility of the crops by the act of sexual coition. A reference has already been made [16] to the probable connexion between fertility cults and the practice of sacred prostitution. An explanation may here be offered of the peculiar part played by strangers in this cult. In the sacred prostitution of both Babylon and Byblos it is clear that the dedicated woman gave herself to strangers; similarly, it was commerce with strangers which was so necessary to the fertility of the fields of Kamul and so contributive to the prosperity of the people of Caindu. Yule mentions [17] the custom as reported of the Hazaras and of other peoples, including even the Nayars. It seems not unlikely that the underlying motive is the acquisition from the stranger of additional life-matter not already inherent in the soil or its inhabitants. The soul-matter of any given place may be regarded as limited in extent and the transfer from one individual to another merely redistributes but does not increase, whereas the reception of soul-material from a stranger is additional to that already in circulation and will naturally therefore increase fertility. This hypothesis likewise offers a possible explanation of the custom mentioned by Gait [18] of the Todas, who are reported to call in a person from another village to deflower a girl about to attain puberty, who otherwise finds it difficult to marry, and perhaps also of the *talikettu* ceremony in south India generally. Approval of commerce with strangers, which is perhaps associated always with the fertility of the soil, is reported of the Uighúrs, Hazaras, Chukchis, Koryaks [19] and (by a tenth-century Arab traveller) of some Turks. Dancing likewise has probably a magical origin, and it certainly has a magical aspect as when it

is perhaps more likely. Fertility rites survived in Europe in spite of the Church: ' *les femmes prostituées . . . qui suivaient la Cour . . . étaient tenues, tant que le mois de mai durait, de faire le lit du roi des ribauds* ' (Dulaure, op. cit., pp. 275 sq., 280); and sometimes even under its auspices, as at Isernia.

[15] I have heard a Sema chief of great tribal authority and experience, Inato of Lumitsami, affirm that it was ridiculous to suppose that pregnancy would result from coition on one occasion only, which indicates that even now the relation between cause and effect in this particular is not completely grasped in that tribe.   [16] *Vide supra*, pp. 163 sqq.

[17] *Marco Polo*, I, p. 212 n.; II, p. 56 n.

[18] *Census of India*, 1911, I, p. 260.   [19] *Vide* Yule, *Marco Polo*, loc. cit.

involves leaping up in the air to encourage the growth of paddy, and Russell has acutely suggested that acrobatic displays have originated in the same idea. Similarly, animal dancing, such as that for instance of the Gonds and Bhatras of the Central Provinces, probably originates in an attempt to increase, or perhaps merely to assemble, by magic the wild animals on which the community partly depends for its food supply. Even the highly mimetic dancing of the Juang of Orissa [20] may have originated in that way. When, however, the spring hunting is considered, it is apparent that the soul-matter cult is again prominent. The *Aheria* of the Rajput in western India, the hunting festival of the Halvakki Vakkals in Kanara, the *Jur Sital* of Bihar, the spring hunt of the Chota Nagpur tribes, and of the Bhatras, Gonds and Gadabas of the Central Provinces and Orissa, the *Sekrengi* hunt of the Angami Nagas and the corresponding festivals of other Assam tribes are all designed to secure prosperity through the coming year, and inasmuch as all manner of living things are destroyed they are probably intended (the *Sekrengi* certainly is) to collect a supply of life-essence and are to be regarded in much the same light as the spring man-hunt of the Wa of Burma.

It would be impossible here to go into all the aspects of the tribal religion in India, but enough has perhaps been said to show that the beliefs held are not mere vague imaginings of superstitious and untaught minds, ‘amorphous’ as they were described in the Census report of 1911, but the debris of a real religious system, a definite philosophy, to the one-time wide-spread prevalence of which the manifold survivals in Hinduism testify, linking together geographically the Austro-Asiatic and Australoid cultures of the forest-clad hills where the isolated remains of the original religion still hold out in an unassimilated form. It is probably this philosophy of life-matter which accounts for the fact that in so many parts of the world, e.g. in India and southern and eastern Europe, Greece and Italy in particular, the real religion of the people is hagiolatry. It is less the orthodox gods of the religion who are worshipped than shrines and holy places, generally tombs particularly associated with some deceased saint or hero likely to have been rich in soul-stuff, the benefit of which may be obtained at the grave, originally no doubt in the form of material emanation. Be that as it may, showing traces in Europe on the one hand and stretching down into Australasia on the other, this creed must have been in its time a great religion, not so great perhaps in altruism, but great in extent and in constituting a very definite rung in that poor ladder up which our race still tries to climb in its effort to ascertain the unknowable, to scale the ramparts of infinity.

[20] *Vide* Dalton, *Ethnography of Bengal*, p. 156.

PART FIVE

BIBLIOGRAPHY

REFERENCE will be found in the text or notes to the following periodicals and works. Both the periodicals and books are sometimes referred to by the abbreviated letters or titles indicated, and in the case of the books the date of the first publication is given in this list wherever possible, while the edition used is also indicated where that is other than the original. Where the book has not been published in London the place of publication is given.

PERIODICALS

Antiquity	*Antiquity, a Quarterly Review of Archaeology.* Gloucester.
A.R.	*The Asiatic Review.*
B.S.O.A.S.	*Bulletin of the School of Oriental and African Studies,* University of London.
C.J.S.	*The Ceylon Journal of Science.* Colombo.
Folk-Lore	*Folk-Lore, a Quarterly Review of Myth, Tradition, Institution and Custom,* being the Transactions of the Folk-Lore Society.
I.A.	*The Indian Antiquary.* Bombay.
J.A.O.S.	*Journal of the American Oriental Society.* Newhaven, Conn.
J.A.S.B. (and	*J.R.A.S.B.*) *The Journal of the (Royal) Asiatic Society of Bengal.* Calcutta.
M.A.S.B.	*Memoirs* of the above Society. Calcutta.
J.R.A.I.	*The Journal of the Royal Anthropological Institute.*
J.R.A.S.	*The Journal of the Royal Asiatic Society.*
J.M.S.	*The Journal of the Mythic Society.* Bangalore.
Man	*Man, a Monthly Record of Anthropological Science,* published by the R.A.I.
Man in India	*Man in India, a Quarterly Record of Anthropological Science with Special Reference to India.* Ranchi.

AUTHORS

ABBOTT, J. *The Keys of Power, a Study of Indian Ritual and Belief.* 1932.

ACHAN, P. A. ' A Hebrew Inscription from Chennamangalam ', in *I.A.* for July 1930. Bombay, 1930.

AIYANGAR, M. S. *Tamil Studies.* Madras, 1914.

AIYAPPAN, A. *Anthropology of the Nayadis.* (Madras Govt. Museum Bulletins, N.S., vol. II, no. 4.) Madras, 1937.

ANSARI, G. ' Muslim Caste in India ' in *Wiener Völkerkundliche Mitteilungen,* 2 Jahrgang, Nr. 2, pp. 165-70. Vienna, 1954.

—— *Muslim Caste in Uttar Pradesh* (a study of culture contact). Lucknow, 1960.

BAILEY, F. G. *Caste and the Economic Frontier.* Manchester, 1957.

BAINES, A. ' Ethnography (Castes and Tribes). With a list of the more important works on Indian ethnography by Dr W. Siegling ', in *Grundriss der Indo-Arischen Philologie und Altertumskunde,* II Band, 5 Heft. Strassburg, 1912.

BANERJEE, A. R. See Sarkar, S. S.

BANERJI-SASTRI, A. ' Mother-Goddess Cult in Magadha ' in *The Searchlight* (Anniversary Number, 1929). Patna, 1930.

BARBOSA, DUARTE. *A Description of the Coasts of East Africa and Malabar in the Beginning of the Sixteenth Century.* (Hakluyt Society.) 1866.

BARTLETT, F. C. *Anthropology in Reconstruction,* 1943. (Huxley Memorial Lecture.)

BARTON, W. *India's North-West Frontier,* 1939.

BERNIER, F. *Voyages de François Bernier, Docteur en Médecine de la Faculté de Montpellier, Contenant la Description des Etats du Grand Mogol,* etc. Amsterdam, 1709.

BHATTACHARJEE, PAPIA. See Sarkar, S. S.

BHATTACHARYA, J. N. *Hindu Castes and Sects. An Exposition of the Origin of the Hindu Caste System and the Bearing of the Sects towards each other and towards other Religious Systems.* Calcutta, 1896.

BIDDULPH, J. *Tribes of the Hindoo Koosh.* Calcutta, 1880.

BLUNT, E. A. H. *Report on the Census of the United Provinces of Agra and Oudh,* 1911 (vol. XV, pt. i, of the *Census of India,* 1911). Allahabad, 1912 (cited as *Census of the U.P.*).

—— *The Caste System of Northern India,* 1931 (cited as *Caste System*).

BONINGTON, C. J. ' Ossuary Practices in the Nicobars ', in *Man,* XXXII, 133. May 1932.

BONNERJEA, B. ' Possible Origin of the Caste System in India ', in *I.A.,* March, April, May 1931. Bombay, 1931.

BOR, N. L. ' The Daflas and their Oaths ', in *J.A.S.B.,* II, i, 1936.

BOUGLE, C. *Essais sur le Régime des Castes (Travaux de l'Année Sociologique).* Paris, 1908.

BRADLEY-BIRT, F. B. *The Story of an Indian Upland.* 1905.

BRAY, D. *Report on the Census of Baluchistan,* 1911 (vol. IV of *The Census of India,* 1911). Calcutta, 1913.

BRIFFAULT, R. *The Mothers. A Study of the Origins of Sentiments and Institutions.* 1927.

BROUGH, J. *The Early Brahminical System of Gotra and Pravara. A Translation of the* ' Gotra-pravara-manjarī ' *of Purusottamapandita.* Cambridge, 1953.

BUCHANAN, F. *Journey through Mysore, Canara and Malabar,* 1807. (The edition used is that of 1870 published in Madras; as the original edition is in three volumes and that of 1870 in two only, chapter references are given as well as pages.)

—— *An Account of Assam with some notices concerning The Neighbouring Territories.* By Francis Hamilton, M.D., F.R.S. Edited by Dr S. K. Bhuyan. Gauhati, 1940.

BÜHLER, G. *The Sacred Laws of the Āryas as taught in the Schools of Āpastamba, Gautama, Vāsishtha and Baudhāyana* (vol. II in *The Sacred Books of the East,* edited by Max Müller). Oxford, 1879. (Cited as *Sacred Laws.*)

Bühler, G. *The Laws of Manu*, translated with extracts from seven commentaries. (Ibid. vol. xxv.) Oxford, 1886.

Burnell, A. C. See Yule.

Burton, R. F. *Sindh, and the Races that inhabit the Valley of the Indus; with Notices of the Topography and History of the Province.* 1851.

Campbell, J. M. *Gujarat Population: Hindus* (*Gazetteer of the Bombay Presidency*, vol. ix). Bombay, 1901.

Cappieri, M. ' Le Caste degli intoccabili in India ', in *Rivista di Antropologia*, vol. xxxv. Rome, 1947.

Carre, l'Abbe. *The Travels of the Abbé Carré in India and the Near East, 1672-1674.* Translated by Lady Fawcett and edited by Sir Charles Fawcett with the assistance of Sir Richard Burn. Hakluyt Society, 2nd Series, nos. xcv-xcvii. 1947-8.

Chakravartti, M. R. See Sarkar, S. S.

Chanda, R. *The Indo-Aryan Races. A Study of the Origin of Indo-Aryan People and Institutions.* Rajshahi, 1916.

—— *Non-Vedic Elements in Brahmanism.* Unpublished (?) MS. in author's possession.

Cole, B. L. *Rajputana Classes compiled under the orders of the Government of India* (Handbooks for the Indian Army, 1921). Simla, 1922.

—— *Report on the Census of the Rajputana Agency*, 1931 (vol. xxvii of the *Census of India*, 1931). Meerut, 1932.

Colebrooke, H. T. *Enumeration of Indian Classes*, in vol. v of *Asiatick Researches*, 1788. (The edition used is the 4th edition, London, 1807.)

Cornford, F. M. *Plato's Cosmology. The Timaeus of Plato translated with a running commentary.* 1937.

Crooke, W. *Religion and Folklore of Northern India.* Oxford, 1926. (Crooke's *An Introduction to the Popular Religion and Folk-lore of Northern India* was published in 1894 and was followed by a second edition called *Popular Religion and Folklore*, etc., the edition used here being the third.)

—— *Tribes and Castes of the North-West Provinces and Oudh.* Calcutta, 1896 (cited as *Tribes and Castes*).

—— *Things Indian. Being Discursive Notes on Various Subjects connected with India.* 1906.

—— *Natives of Northern India*, in ' The Native Races of the British Empire ' series. 1907 (cited as *Northern India*).

—— (Editor). *Tod's Annals and Antiquities of Rajasthan.* Oxford, 1920 (cited as Tod's *Annals*, etc.).

Dahlmann, J. *Das Altindische Volkstum und seine Bedeutung für die Gesellschaftskunde.* Köln, 1899.

Dalton, E. T. *Descriptive Ethnology of Bengal.* Calcutta, 1872.

Dames, M. L. *The Baloch Race* (Asiatic Society Monographs, vol. iv). 1904.

Dawson, W. R. *The Bridle of Pegasus. Studies in Magic, Mythology and Folklore.* 1930.

Day, F. *The Land of the Permauls, or Cochin, its Past and its Present.* Madras, 1863.

Desai, G. H. *A Glossary of Castes, Tribes and Races in the Baroda State.* Bombay, 1912.

DILL, S. *Roman Society in the Last Century of the Western Empire.* 1898. (The edition used is that of 1899.)

DIODORUS SICULUS. (The edition used is *The Historical Library of Diodorus the Sicilian*, translated by G. Booth, Esq., 1814.)

DOWSON, J. *A Classical Dictionary of Hindu Mythology and Religion, Geography, History and Literature.* (Trübner's Oriental Series, vol. VI, 1879.) (The edition used is the 4th edition of 1903.)

DRURY, R. *See* Oliver.

DUBE, S. C. *The Kamar.* Lucknow, 1951.

DUBOIS, J. A. *A Description of the People of India.* 1817. (The translation used is the Madras reprint of 1879, but chapter as well as paginal references are given.)

DULAURE, J. A. *Des Divinités Génératrices ou du Culte du Phallus chez les Anciens et les Modernes.* Paris, 1825. (The edition used is the reprint of 1885.)

DUMONT, L. *Hierarchy and Marriage Alliance in South Indian Kinship*, in Occasional Papers of the Royal Anthropological Institute, 1957.

DUNBAR, G. D.-S.- ' Abors and Galongs ', in *M.A.S.B.*, vol. v, extra no. Calcutta, 1916.

DUNCAN, J. ' Historical Remarks on the Coast of Malabar, with some Description of the Manners of its Inhabitants ', in vol. v of *Asiatick Researches*, Calcutta, 1788 and after. (The edition used is the 4th edition printed in 8vo in London, 1807.)

DUTT, N. K. *Origin and Growth of Caste in India*, i. Calcutta, 1931.

EDGEWORTH, M. P. ' Abstract of a Journal kept by Mr Gardiner during his travels in Central Asia—with a Note and Introduction ', in *J.A.S.B.*, no. 3 of 1853.

EHRENFELS, O. R. *Mother-right in India.* Hyderabad, Deccan, 1941.

ELLIS, R. H. *A Short Account of the Laccadive Islands and Minicoy.* Madras, 1924 (cited as *Laccadive Islands*).

ELLIS, W. *History of Madagascar.* 1838.

ELWIN, V. *The Baiga.* 1939.

—— *The Agaria.* Bombay, 1942.

—— *Maria Murder and Suicide.* Bombay, 1943.

—— *The Muria and their Ghotul.* Bombay, 1947.

ENTHOVEN, R. E. *The Tribes and Castes of Bombay.* Bombay, 1920-2 (cited as *Tribes and Castes*).

—— Review of Dutt's *Origin and Growth of Caste in India*, in *J.R.A.S.*, Jan. 1932.

EVANS, F. B. *See* Innes.

EVANS, I. H. N. ' Kempunan ', in *Man*, xx, 38, 1920.

FITZGERALD, S. V. Review of *Caste in India* in *B.S.O.A.S.*, vol. XII, pt. 1, p. 245. 1947.

FLEURE, H. J. *See* Peake.

FORBES, A. K. *Rás Mala; or Hindoo Annals of the Province of Goozerat, in Western India.* 1856.

FORBES, J. *Oriental Memoirs.* 1813. (The edition used is that of 1834.)

FORSYTH, J. *The Highlands of Central India. Notes on their Forests and Wild Tribes, Natural History, and Sports.* 1876. (The edition used is that of 1889.)

FRAZER, J. G. *Totemism and Exogamy. A Treatise on Certain Early Forms of Superstition and Society.* 1910.

—— *The Golden Bough* (3rd edition). 1911-15.

FUCHS, S. *The Gond and Bhumia of Eastern Mandla.* Bombay, 1960.

VON FÜRER-HAIMENDORF, CH. *The Raj Gonds of Adilabad.* 1948.

FURNIVALL, J. S. *Netherlands India, A Study of Plural Economy.* Cambridge, 1939.

FUSTEL DE COULANGES, N. D. *La Cité antique.* Paris, 1864. (The edition used is the 1929 edition in the *Librairie Hachette.*)

GAIT, E. A. *Report on the Census of Bengal, Bihar and Orissa, and Sikkim* (vol. VI of *Census of India,* 1901). Calcutta, 1903.

—— *Report on the Census of India,* 1911, vol. I, pt. i. Calcutta, 1913.

—— *See also* Risley.

GARDINER. *See* Edgeworth.

Genesis, Book of. Authorized Version.

GHOSH, A. *The Original Inhabitants of the United Provinces: a Study in Ethnology,* in vol. XI of Allahabad University Studies. 1935.

GHURYE, G. S. *Caste and Race in India.* 1932.

GILBERT, W. H., Jr. *Peoples of India* (Smithsonian Institution War Background Studies, no. 18). Washington, 1944.

GIUFFRIDA-RUGGERI, V. *First Outlines of a Systematic Anthropology of Asia.* Calcutta, 1921.

GORDON, D. H. 'Momiyāi', in *Man,* XXIX, 160 (Dec. 1929), XXXIII, 163 (Sept. 1933), XXXIV, 83 (April 1934).

GREEN, M. M. *Ibo Village Affairs.* 1947.

GUHA, B. S. 'An Outline of the Racial Ethnology of India ', in *An Outline of the Field Sciences of India.* Calcutta, 1937.

GURDON, P. R. T. *The Khasis.* 1907. (The edition used is that of 1914.)

HAMILTON, A. *New Account of the East Indies.* Edinburgh, 1727.

HAMILTON, F. = BUCHANAN, q.v.

HAMILTON, W. *The East India Gazetteer.* 1815.

HANDY, E. S. C. *Polynesian Religion* (Bernice P. Bishop Museum Bulletin no. 34). Honolulu, 1927.

HARDIMAN, J. P. *See* Scott.

HATCH, W. J. *The Land Pirates of India.* 1928.

HAUGHTON, G. C. *Dictionary, Bengali and Sanskrit.* 1833.

HEMEON, C. R. 'Short Notes of some Remarkable Crimes in the Central Provinces and Berar ', in *Man in India,* XXIII, no. 3. Ranchi, 1943.

HERODOTUS. *Historiai.* (The edition used is that edited by Blakesley, 1854.)

HILL, S. C. 'Origin of the Caste System in India ', in *I.A.,* March-October 1930. Bombay, 1930.

HIRA LAL. *See* Russell.

HIVALE, S. *The Pardhans of the Upper Narbada Valley.* Bombay, 1946.

HOBSON-JOBSON. *See* Yule.

268   BIBLIOGRAPHY

HOCART, A. M. 'India and the Pacific', in the *Ceylon Journal of Science*, Section G. Archaeology, Ethnology, etc., vol. I, pt. 2. Colombo, 1925.

—— *The Temple of the Tooth in Kandy.* 1930.

——' The Basis of Caste in India ', in *Acta Orientalia*, XIV. Leyden, 1936.

—— *Kings and Councillors.* Cairo, 1936.

—— ' The Estates of the Realm in Thakaundrove, Fiji ', in *B.S.O.A.S.*, vol. IX, pt. 2, 1937-9.

—— *Les Castes* (Annales du Musée Guimet). Paris, 1938.[1]

HODSON, T. C. ' The " Genna " : mong the Tribes of Assam ', in *J.R.A.I.*, vol. XXXVI, 1906.

—— *The Meitheis.* 1908.

—— *The Naga Tribes of Manipur.* 1911.

—— ' Meithei Literature ', in *Folk-Lore*, vol. XXIII, 1912.

HOLDICH, T. H. *India.* (The Regions of the World, edited by H. J. Mackinder.) 1904.

HOLLAND, T. H. ' The Coorgs and Yeruvas, an ethnological contrast ', in *J.A.S.B.*, vol. LXX, pt. iii, no. 2, 1901.

HOPKINS, E. W. *The Social and Military Position of the Ruling Caste in Ancient India as represented by the Sanskrit Epic; with an Appendix on the Status of Woman.* (From *J.A.O.S.*, vol. XIII). New Haven, Connecticut, 1889.

HUNTER, W. W. *Annals of Rural Bengal.* 1868. (The edition used is the 7th edition published in 1897.)

—— *Orissa, or The Vicissitudes of an Indian Province under Native and British Rule.* 1872.

HUNTINGFORD, G. W. B. Letter on ' Momiyai ' in *Man*, XXXIV, 22 (January), 1934.

HUTTON, J. *A Popular Account of the Thugs and Dacoits, the Hereditary Garotters and Gang-Robbers of India.* 1857.

HUTTON, J. H. *The Angami Nagas.* 1921.

—— *The Sema Nagas.* 1921.

—— ' Carved Monoliths at Dimapur and an Angami Naga Ceremony ', in *J.R.A.I.*, vol. LII, 1922.

—— ' Meaning and Method of the Erection of Monoliths by the Angami Nagas.' Ibid.

—— ' Carved Monoliths at Jamuguri in Assam ', in *J.R.A.I.*, vol. LIII, 1923.

—— ' The Use of Stone in the Naga Hills ', in *J.R.A.I.*, vol. LVI, 1926.

—— ' The Disposal of the Dead at Wakching ', in *Man*, XXVII, 44, 1927.

—— ' The Significance of Head-hunting in Assam ', *J.R.A.I.*, vol. LVIII, 1928.

—— ' Diaries of Two Tours in the Unadministered Area East of the Naga Hills ', in *M.A.S.B.*, vol. XI, no. 1. Calcutta, 1929.

—— *Report on the Census of India*, 1931 (vol. I of the *Census of India*, 1931). Delhi, 1933.

—— *A Primitive Philosophy of Life* (Frazer Lecture). Oxford, 1938.

—— See also Mills.

[1] The original English version has since been published (1950) as *Caste: a Comparative Study*. With a preface by Lord Raglan.

IBBETSON, D. *Panjab Castes, Being a reprint of the Chapter on ' The Races, Castes and Tribes of the People' in the Report on the Census of the Punjab published in 1883 by the late Sir Denzil Ibbetson, K.C.S.I.* Lahore, 1916.

INNES, C. A. *Gazetteer of the Malabar and Anjengo Districts.* Edited by F. B. Evans. Madras, 1908.

IYER, L. A. K. *The Travancore Tribes and Castes.* Trivandrum, 1937-41.

IYER, L. K. A. *Lectures on Ethnography.* Calcutta, 1925.

—— *The Cochin Tribes and Castes.* Madras, 1909-12.

—— *Anthropology of the Syrian Christians.* Ernakulam, 1926.

IYER, L. K. A. and NANJUNDAYYA, H. V. *The Mysore Tribes and Castes* Bangalore, 1928-35.

JACKSON, A. M. T. ' Note on the History of the Caste System ', in *J.A.S.B.*, vol. III, no. 7, for July. Calcutta, 1907.

JEVONS, F. B. (Editor). *Plutarch's Romane Questions. Translated* A.D. 1603 *by Philemon Holland* (Bibliothèque de Carabas, VII). 1892.

JOLLY, J. *The Institutes of Vishnu* (vol. VII in *The Sacred Books of the East*, edited by Max Müller). Oxford, 1880.

KAPADIA, K. M. *Hindu Kinship.* Bombay, 1947.

KARANDIKAR, S. V. *Hindu Exogamy.* Bombay, 1929.

KARVE, I. *Kinship Organization in India.* Poona, 1953.

—— *Changing India; Aspects of Caste Society.* Bombay, 1961.

—— *Hindu Society: An Interpretation.* Poona, 1961.

KAUL, H. *Report on the Census of the Punjab*, 1911 (vol. XIV of the *Census of India*, 1911). Lahore, 1912.

KEITH, A. B. Chap. IV, ' The Age of the Rigveda ', in *The Cambridge History of India*, vol. I ' Ancient India ', edited by E. J. Rapson. Cambridge, 1922.

KETKAR, S. V. *History of Caste in India.* Ithaca, N.Y., 1909.

—— *Essay on Hinduism, Its Formation and Future.* 1911.

KHAN, A. I. *On the Trial by Ordeal among the Hindus*, communicated by Warren Hastings to *Asiatick Researches*, vol. I. Calcutta, 1788. (The edition used is the 5th, London, 1806.)

KIRKPATRICK, W. ' Primitive Exogamy and the Caste System ', in *Proceedings, A.S.B.*, vol. VIII, no. 3. Calcutta, 1912.

KITTS, E. J. *A Compendium of the castes and tribes found in India.* . . . Bombay, 1885.

LACROIX, P. *Mœurs, Usages et Costumes au Moyen Age et à l'Epoque de la Renaissance.* Paris, 1871.

LANGDON, S. ' A Sumerian hymn to Ishtar (Innini) and the deified Ishme-Dagan ', in *J.R.A.S.*, 1931.

LEACH, E. R. (Editor). *Aspects of Caste in South India, Ceylon and North-West Pakistan.* Cambridge, 1960.

LEITNER, G. W. *Dardistan in 1866, 1886 and 1893 being* An Account of the History, Religions, Customs, Legends, Fables, and Songs of Gilgit, Chilás, Kandiá (Gabriál), Yasin, Chitrál, Hunza, Nagyr and other Parts of the Hindukush, as also a supplement to the second edition of The Hunza and Nagyr Handbook (printed by the Government of

India in 1889), and an epitome of Part III of the Author's *The Languages and Races of Dardistan.* Woking, N.D. (*c.* 1895).

LEWIN, T. H. *Wild Races of South-eastern India.* 1870.

LINTON, R. *The Tanala, A Hill Tribe of Madagascar* (Field Museum Publication 317). Chicago, 1933.

LITTLE, K. L. ' The Psychological Background of White-Coloured Contacts in Britain ', in *The Sociological Review*, vol. XXXV. 1944.

LOGAN, W. *Malabar.* Madras, 1887.

LOVE, H. D. *Vestiges of Old Madras, 1640-1800,* in Indian Records Series. 1913.

LOWIE, R. H. *The Origin of the State.* New York, 1927.

LUARD, C. E. *Ethnographical Survey of the Central India Agency.* Lucknow, 1909.

LUCIAN. *The Works of Lucian from the Greek,* by Thomas Francklin. 1781.

MCCRINDLE, J. W. *Ancient India as described by Megasthenes and Arrian.* 1877. (The edition used is the Calcutta reprint of 1926.)

MACDONELL, A. A. *India's Past.* Oxford, 1927.

MACGREGOR, G. L. See Mead.

MACPHERSON, W. (Editor). *Memorials of Service in India. From the correspondence of the late Major Samuel Charters Macpherson, C.B., Political Agent at Gwalior during the Mutiny, and formerly employed in the suppression of human sacrifices in Orissa.* 1865.

MAINE, H. S. *Ancient Law; its Connection with the Early History of Society and its Relation to Modern Ideas.* 1861. (The edition used is the eighth, 1880.)

MAJUMDAR, D. N. ' Pseudo-Rajputs ', in *Man in India*, vol. VI, no. 3. Ranchi, 1926.

—— *A Tribe in Transition, A Study in Culture Pattern.* Calcutta, 1937.

—— ' Some Aspects of the Cultural Life of the Khasas of the cis-Himalayan Region ', in *J.R.A.S.B., Letters*, vol. VI, no. I. Calcutta, 1940.

MALCOLM, J. *A Memoir of Central India, including Malwa, and Adjoining Provinces. With the History, and Copious Illustrations, of the Past and Present Conditions of that Country.* 1823.

MARETT, R. R. and PENNIMAN, T. K. (Editors). *Spencer's Last Journey, being the Journal of an Expedition to Tierra del Fuego by Sir Baldwin Spencer.* Oxford, 1931.

MARRIOTT, McK. (Editor). *Village India.* Chicago, 1955.

—— *Caste Ranking and Community Structure in Five Regions of India and Pakistan* (Deccan College Monograph Series, 23.) Poona, 1960.

MARSHALL, H. I. *The Karen People of Burma: A Study in Anthropology and Ethnology.* (Ohio State University Bulletin, XXVI.) Columbus, Ohio, U.S.A., 1922.

MARSHALL, J. *Mohenjo-daro and the Indus Civilization.* 1931.

MARTIŃ, M. *The History, Antiquities, Topography and Statistics of Eastern India.* (Three volumes.) 1838.

MATEER, S. ' The Land of Charity ': a descriptive account of Travancore and its People with especial reference to missionary labour.* 1871.

—— *Native Life in Travancore.* 1883.

MAYER, A. C. *Caste and Kinship in Central India.* 1960.

MEAD, P. J. and MACGREGOR, G. L. *Report on the Census of Bombay, 1911.* (Vol. VII of the *Census of India*, 1911.) Bombay, 1912.

MEEK, C. K. *A Sudanese Kingdom.* 1931.

MELA, P. *Pomponii Melae de Chorographia libri tres.* (The edition used is that edited by G. Parthey and published in Berlin, 1867.)

MENON, C. A. *Report on the Census of Cochin State*, 1911 (vol. XVIII of the *Census of India*, 1911). Ernakulam, 1912.

MILLS, J. P. *The Lhota Nagas.* 1922.

—— *The Ao Nagas.* 1926.

MILLS, J. P. and HUTTON, J. H. ' Ancient Monoliths of North Cachar ', in *J.A.S.B.*, vol. XXV, no. 1 (1929). Calcutta, 1930.

MINCHIN, C. F. *Las Béla* (vol. VIII, Baluchistan District Gazetteers). Allahabad, 1907.

MITRA, R. *Indo-Aryans: contributions towards the elucidation of their Ancient and Mediaeval History.* Calcutta, 1881.

MOLONY, J. C. *Report on the Census of Madras*, 1911 (vol. XII of the *Census of India*, 1911). Madras, 1912.

—— *A Book of South India.* 1926.

MORRIS, C. J. *See* Northey.

MURPHY, J. *Lamps of Anthropology.* Manchester, 1943.

MURRAY, M. A. *See* Seligman.

NANJUNDAYYA, H. V. *See* Iyer, L. K. A.

NAZAROFF, P. S. ' The White Lady ', in *Blackwood's Magazine*, August 1931.

NESFIELD, J. C. *Brief View of the Caste System of the North-West Provinces and Oudh.* Allahabad, 1885.

NEWELL, W. H. ' The Brahman and Caste Isogamy in North India ' in *J.R.A.I.* vol. LXXXV, pp. 101-10, 1955.

NORTHEY, W. B. and MORRIS, C. J. *The Gurkhas, their Manners, Customs and Country.* 1928.

OLDENBERG, H. ' Zur Geschichte des indischen Kastenwesens ', in *Zeitschrift der Deutschen Morgenländischen Gesellschaft*, vol. LI, pt. 2. Leipzig, 1897.

OLDHAM. C. E. A. W. Review of *Caste and Race in India* by G. S. Ghurye, in *Man*, XXXII, 316. 1932.

OLIVER, P. (Editor). *Madagascar; or Robert Drury's Journal, during Fifteen Years' Captivity on that Island, and a Further Description of Madagascar by the Abbé Alexis Rochon.* 1890.

O'MALLEY, L. S. S. *Indian Caste Customs.* 1932.

—— *Popular Hinduism.* 1935.

—— (Editor). *Modern India and the West.* 1941.

OPPERT, G. *On the Original Inhabitants of Bharatavarsa or India.* Westminster, 1893.

PANT, S. D. *The Social Economy of the Himalayans Based on a survey in the Kumaon Himalayas.* 1935.

PARGITER, F. E. *Ancient Indian Historical Tradition.* 1922.

PARRY, N. E. *The Lakhers.* 1932.

PATE, H. R. *Tinnevelly*. (Madras District Gazetteers.) Madras, 1917.

PEAKE, H. and FLEURE, H. J. *Merchant Venturers in Bronze.* 1931.

PEATE, I. C. *The Welsh House.* Liverpool, 1944.

PENNIMAN, T. K. *See* Marett.

PIOLET, J.-B. *Madagascar et les Hova.* Paris, 1895.

PITT-RIVERS, G. H. LANE-FOX. *The Clash of Culture and the Contact of Races.* 1927.

PLAYFAIR, A. *The Garos.* 1909.

PLINY. *C. Plinii Secundi Naturalis Historia.* (The edition used is that published by Hackius in Leyden and Rotterdam in 1669.)

PLUTARCH. *The Roman Questions.* (The edition used is the translation by H. J. Rose. Oxford, 1924.)

POLO, M. *The Book of Ser Marco Polo the Venetian concerning the Kingdoms and Marvels of the East,* translated and edited by Col. Sir Henry Yule, 1871. (The edition used is the third edition of 1921, revised by Henri Cordier.)

PORTMAN, M. V. *A History of our Relations with the Andamanese compiled from Histories and Travels, and from the Records of the Government of India.* Calcutta, 1899.

POWELL, J. H. ' "Hook-swinging" in India ', in *Folk-Lore*, vol. xxv. 1914.

PRZYLUSKI, J. ' Le nom de dieu Visnu et la légende de Kṛsna ', in *Archiv Orientálni*, IV, 2. Prague, 1932.

PTOLEMY. *KLAUDIOU PTOLEMAIOU ALEXANDREOS peri tēs GEO-GRAPHIAS biblia oktō.* (The edition used is that of P. Bertius published in Amsterdam in 1618.)

PURCHAS, S. *Purchas his Pilgrimage, or Relations of the World, etc.* (The edition used is the fourth, 1626.)

RAJKHOWA, B. *Short Accounts of Assam.* Dibrugarh, 1915.

RAKSHIT, H. K. *See* Sarkar.

RANGACHARI, K. *See* Thurston.

RAO, H. *Indian Caste System.* Bangalore, 1931.

RAPSON, E. J. (Editor). *The Cambridge History of India.* Vol. I, *Ancient India.* Cambridge, 1922.

RAY, GAUTAMSANKAR. *See* Sarkar, S. S.

RECLUS, E. *Primitive Folk. Studies in Comparative Ethnology* (in the Contemporary Science Series edited by Havelock Ellis and published by Walter Scott). N.D.

REVILLOUT, M.-E. *Cours de Droit égyptien.* (Ecole du Louvre.) Paris, 1884.

RICE, S. ' The Origin of Caste ', in *A.R.*, vol. xxv. 1929.

—— *Hindu Customs and their Origins.* 1937.

RICHTER, E. *Manual of Coorg.* Mangalore, 1870.

RISLEY, H. H. *Tribes and Castes of Bengal—Ethnographic Glossary.* Calcutta, 1891. (Cited as *Tribes and Castes.*)

—— *Tribes and Castes of Bengal—Anthropometric Data.* Calcutta, 1891. (Cited by title in full.)

—— *Report on the Census of India,* 1901. Vol. I. Ethnographic Appendices. Calcutta, 1903. (Cited as *Ethnographic Appendices.*)

RISLEY, H. H. *The People of India.* 1908. (The edition used here is that of 1915 edited by Crooke.)

RISLEY, H. H. and GAIT, E. A. *Report on the Census of India,* 1901, vol. I, pt. i. (Vol. I of the *Census of India,* 1901.) Calcutta, 1903.

RIVERS, W. H. R. *The Todas.* 1906.

—— ' The Origin of Hypergamy ', in the *Journal of the Bihar and Orissa Research Society,* March 1921. Patna, 1921.

ROBERTSON, G. S. *The Káfirs of the Hindu-Kush.* 1896.

ROCHON, A. *See* Oliver.

RODRIGUEZ, E. A. *The Hindoo Castes. The History of the Braminical Castes, containing a minute description of the origin, ceremonies, idolatry, manners, customs, etc. Of the Forty Two sects of Bramins of the British Indian Empire: deduced from authentic manuscripts after particular investigations and inquiries.* 1846.

ROSCOE, J. ' Immigrants and their Influence in the Lake Region of Central Africa ' in *The Frazer Lectures,* 1922-1932, by divers hands, edited by Warren R. Dawson. 1932.

ROSE, H. A. *A Glossary of the Tribes and Castes of the Punjab and North-West Frontier Province.* Lahore, 1911-19. (Cited as *Tribes and Castes.*)

—— ' Caste ', in the *Encyclopaedia Britannica,* 14th edition, vol. IV, 1929. (Cited as *Caste.*)

ROWE, G. S. *See* Williams.

ROWNEY, H. B. *The Wild Tribes of India.* 1882.

ROY, SACHIN. *Aspects of Padam-Minyong Culture.* Shillong, 1960.

ROY, S. C. *The Oraons of Chota Nagpur.* Ranchi, 1915.

—— *The Hill Bhuiyas of Orissa.* Ranchi, 1935.

—— *The Khārias.* Ranchi, 1937.

—— ' Caste, Ra and Religion in India ', in *Man in India,* vols. XIV, vol. 2 ; XVII, no. 4 ; XVIII, nos. 2 and 3. Ranchi, 1934, 1937, 1938.

ROY, S. N. ' Supposed Animation of Inanimate Objects ', in *Man in India,* vol. IX, no. 4. Ranchi, 1929.

RUSSELL, R. V. and LAL, H. *The Tribes and Castes of the Central Provinces of India.* 1916.

RYAN, BRUCE. *Caste in Modern Ceylon.* New Jersey, 1953.

SARKAR, B. K., assisted by H. K. RAKSHIT. *Folk Element in Hindu Culture: a contribution to socio-religious studies in Hindu folk-institutions.* 1917.

SARKAR, S. S.; RAY, GAUTAMSANKAR; CHAKRAVARTTI, M. R.; BANERJEE, A. R., & BHATTACHARJEE, PAPIA. *A Physical Survey of the Kadar of Kerala.* Memoir No. 6, 1959, of the Anthropological Survey of the Government of India. Calcutta, 1961.

SAYCE, A. H. ' The Aryan Problem—fifty years later ', in *Antiquity,* I, ii (June, 1927), p. 205n.

SCHOEBEL, C. *L'Histoire des Origines et du Développement des Castes de l'Inde.* (Extraits, nos. 8 et 18, du *Bulletin de la Société Académique Indo-Chinoise,* 2 série, t. II et III, Novembre 1882 et Janvier 1883.) Paris, 1884.

SCOTT, J. G. and HARDIMAN, J. P. *Gazetteer of Upper Burma and the Shan States,* Part I. Rangoon, 1900.

[SCOTT, J. G.] SHWAY YOE. *The Burman: His Life and Notions.* 1882.

18

SEDGWICK, L. J. *Report on the Census of Bombay Presidency* (vol. VIII of *Census of India*, 1921). Bombay, 1922.

SELIGMAN, C. G. and MURRAY, M. A. ' Note on an Early Egyptian Standard '; in *Man*, XI, 97. 1911.

SENART, E. *Les Castes dans l'Inde*. Paris, 1896.[1] (The edition used here is that of 1927.)

SHAKESPEAR, J. *Lushei Kuki Clans*. 1912.

SHAW, W. *Notes on the Thadou Kukis*. (*J.A.S.B.*, vol. XXIV, 1928, no. 1.) Calcutta, 1929.

SHERRING, M. A. *Hindu Tribes and Castes*. Calcutta, 1881.

SLATER, G. *The Dravidian Element in Indian Culture*. 1924.

SLEEMAN, J. L. *Thug, or A Million Murders*. N.D. (*c.* 1939, but compiled from General W. H. Sleeman's notes of 1839).

SLEEMAN, W. H. *Rambles and Recollections of an Indian Official*. 1844. (The edition used is that edited by V. A. Smith. Constable, 1893.)

SONNERAT, M. *Voyages aux Indes Orientales et à la Chine*. Paris, 1782.

SPENCER, B. *See* Marett.

SRINIVAS, M. N. *Religion and Society among the Coorgs of South India*. Oxford, 1952.

—— *Caste in Modern India and Other Essays*. Bombay, 1962.

STEELE, A. *Law and Custom of Hindoo Castes within the Dekhun Provinces subject to the Presidency of Bombay*. 1868. (This edition, published in London, is called a ' new edition '; an earlier one seems to have been published in Bombay in 1827.)

STEVENSON, H. N. C. ' Status Evaluation in the Hindu Caste System ', in *J.R.A.I.*, vol. LXXXIV, 1954.

STEVENSON, S. *The Rites of the Twice-Born* (in ' The Religious Quest of India ' Series). Oxford, 1920.

STRABO. *Geographika*. (The edition used is that published by Wolters, Amsterdam, 1707.)

STRASSER, R. *The Mongolian Horde*: translated from the German by ' R.T.G.' with an introduction by Sir M. Sadler. 1930.

THOOTHI, N. A. *The Vaishnavas of Gujarat/being a study in methods of investigation of social phenomena*. 1935.

THURSTON, E. *Ethnographic Notes in Southern India*. Madras, 1906.

—— (assisted by K. RANGACHARI). *Castes and Tribes of Southern India*. Madras, 1909.

—— *Omens and Superstitions of Southern India*. 1912.

TOD, JAMES. *Annals and Antiquities of Rajasthan*. 1829-32. (The edition used is that of 1920, Oxford, edited by Crooke.)

TURNER, A. C. *Report on the Census of the United Provinces of Agra and Oudh*, 1931. (Vol. XVIII of the *Census of India*, 1931.) Allahabad, 1933.

TURNER, J. G. S. *Medical Census, Southern Provinces*. (*Census of Nigeria*, 1931, vol. VI.) 1932.

WEBB, A. W. T. *These Ten Years*. (*Rajputana*, vol. XXIV, pt. 1 of the *Census of India*, 1941.) Bombay, 1941.

[1] Translated into English by Sir Denison Ross in 1930 as *Caste in India*.

WESTERMARCK, E. *The History of Human Marriage.* 1891. (The edition used is the 3rd edition, published in 1901.)

WILLIAMS, T. *Fiji and the Fijians.* 1858. (The edition used is that of 1870 bound in one volume with James Calvert's *Missionary Labours among the Cannibals,* and edited by G. S. Rowe.)

WILSON, J. *History of the suppression of infanticide in Western India under the Government of Bombay.* Bombay, 1855.

—— *Indian Caste.* 1877.

WISE, J. *Notes on the Races, Castes and Trades of Eastern Bengal.* 1883. (The volume, printed by Harrison & Sons, is described on the title-page as ' not published '.)

YEATTS, M. W. M. *Report on the Census of Madras,* 1931. (Vol. XIV of the *Census of India,* 1931.) Madras, 1932.

YULE, H. *See* Polo.

YULE, H. and BURNELL, A. C. *Hobson-Jobson.* 1886. (The edition used is that of 1903, edited by Crooke.)

ZINKIN, TAYA. *Caste Today.* 1962.

GLOSSARY

Ābor	Assam tribe now known as Adi (*abor* = ' uncivilized ' or ' untamed ').
Āgāriya	A primitive tribe of central India whose principal occupation is smelting and forging iron.
Agarwāla	An important mercantile caste of upper India with traditions of descent from a Naga (snake) ancestress. Many are Jains by religion (see Crooke, *Tribes and Castes*, I, pp. 13 sqq.).
Aghoripanthi	A mendicant sect whose philosophic tenets lead them to feed on human corpses and excrement.
Agnikula	Division of the Rājputs regarded as descended from Fire (*agni*), as distinct from those descended from the sun and moon, probably because descended from foreign tribes ' reborn ' as Rajputs after a symbolic purification by fire.
Ahār	A caste of graziers and herdsmen in Rohilkhand.
Ahīr	A caste primarily of graziers and cowherds, also of cultivators, widely distributed in northern and central India.
Āhom	Shan tribe from which Assam takes its name.
Ambalavāsi	A caste, or perhaps rather a group of castes, of temple servants, having many subdivisions, in Malabar (see Thurston, *Castes and Tribes*, I p. 30). The term *Ambalavāsi* is also reported to be used sometimes as a synonym of *Nambīssan*, the name for a particular caste, or subcaste, of Ambalavasi.
Ambattan	A Tamil barber caste.
Andē Koraga	See Koraga.
Angami	A Naga tribe of Assam.
anulōmǎ	See p. 55.
Ao	A Naga (q.v.) tribe of Assam.
Āpastamba	An ancient writer on ritual and law.
Āpa Tani	Assam hill tribe north of the Brahmaputra River.
Āratta	An ancient Punjab tribe with matrilineal inheritance.
Arorā	A trading caste of the Punjab and north-west India with some affinity to the Khatri, in regard to whom they stand in some sort of inferior relationship.
āsram	Religious order; hermitage; school or college.
Āsura	A divine being hostile to the Aryan gods; a pre-Aryan people with magical powers and a knowledge of the working of metals.
Asvamedha	Horse-sacrifice; one of the great vedic rites.
Atharvaveda	The fourth veda, characterized by a large number of spells and incantations.
Avesta	The collective sacred writings of the Zoroastrians.
Awān	A Muslim landed and cultivating caste or tribe, claiming Arab extraction, in the Punjab.
Āyar	See Idaiyan.
Ayyar (Aiyar)	An honorific title of Tamil Brāhmans.

Bābhan	(=Bhuīnhār) A landowning and cultivating caste of upper India, particularly of Bihar; they claim to be of Brahman extraction, but it is not unlikely that they are really of Rajput derivation. See Risley, *Tribes and Castes*, 1, s.v. Bābhan.
Badaga	A cultivating tribe (or caste) of the Nilgiri Hills; fire-walkers.
Bāgdi	A caste of fishermen, palanquin-bearers, and field labourers in central and western Bengal, and in Bihar.
Baidya	A caste of physicians in Bengal (=Vaid).
Baiga	A primitive tribe of central India.
Bāiti (Bāoti)	A small caste engaged in the manufacture of lime from shells, also in the making of mats, and of music. Known otherwise as Chunāri, Chuniyā (from the word for lime), or Dhōli (drum), or Dugla.
Balija	An important Telugu trading caste.
Bālti	A Himalayan tribe.
Balūchi (Baloch)	A tribe of Baluchistan (see pp. 40 sqq.).
Banajiga	A Kanarese trading caste corresponding to the Telugu ' Balija '.
Baniyā	A term applied to traders, moneylenders and shop-keepers, and often used for various trading castes, particularly those of Rajputana and western India.
Banjāra	A caste of carriers, traders, and cattle-herders more or less nomadic. Also known as ' Vanjāra ', ' Lambādi ', ' Labānā ' (see p. 21).
Barhai	A caste of carpenters in upper India.
Bārui	A caste of *pān* growers in Bengal.
basavi	A girl dedicated to a god after the custom of some Kanarese castes, who, when they have no male children, marry a daughter to the deity. She lives in her father's home and her children take his name and no stigma attaches to her or to them.
Bauri	A caste of field labourers in Bengal and Bihar.
Bēdar	A Kanarese fighting caste of southern India (=Bōya).
Bēkanwāla	Pork-butchers, a subcaste of Khatīk (< bacon).
Ben-i-Israel	A Jewish caste of Bombay (see p. 19).
Bēri Chetti	A caste of traders in south India (see Chetti).
Bhangi	Caste of sweepers and scavengers over all India except the south.
Bhar	A tribe of the United Provinces and Bihar, formerly of some political and social importance, now reduced to a caste of low status.
Bharbūnja	A caste of grain-parchers in upper India.
Bhāt	A caste in upper India of hereditary bards, genealo-gists, and heralds, probably of mixed Brahman and Rajput extraction, but claiming Brahman descent. They used to have the reputation of compelling the performance of any promise made to them, or of extorting money, merely by threatening to kill them-selves or some member of the family in case of non-compliance. They had also the reputation of abiding

18

by threats of this kind (cf. ' Chāran '). There are some Muslim Bhāts following a mixture of Muslim and Hindu practices.

Bhātia   A trading caste of western India.

Bhatra   A forest or hill tribe (or caste) in Orissa.

Bhīl   An important tribe of west central India noted as bowmen and bandits.

Bhīlāla   A tribe in western India of mixed Bhīl and Rājput extraction.

Bhoksa   A tribe in the Himalayan foothills of the United Provinces, and claiming Rajput extraction (see Crooke, *Tribes and Castes*, ii, pp. 35 sqq.).

Bhotiya   A Mongoloid tribe of the lower Himalayas claiming an origin from Bhutwal in Nepal and now transformed into a Hinduized caste (see Crooke, *Tribes and Castes*, ii, p. 61).

Bhuīnhār   See Bābhan.

Bhuinmāli   A cultivating, palanquin-bearing and menial caste of eastern Bengal, probably representing an aboriginal tribe: in Sylhet it now calls itself ' Māli '.

Bhuiya   A Kolarian tribe of Chota Nagpur and Bengal.

Bhumi   Belonging to the soil, from the Sanskrit *bhu* = ' earth ', and thus sometimes used in the names or titles of castes or tribes claiming to be the original cultivators of the soil or to be the lords thereof.

Bind   A caste of cultivators and field labourers in the United Provinces, probably of Kolarian tribal origin.

biradari   See p. 99.

Birhor   A quasi-nomadic Kolarian forest tribe of Chota Nagpur and Orissa.

Bishnoi   A caste of sectarian origin in Rajputana and adjoining areas. Though spoken of as Bishnoi Brahmans by Tod, they are, in fact, derived from various castes, particularly (according to Rose, *Tribes and Castes*, ii, s.v. Bishnoi) from Jats and Khatris.

Bōhra   A trading caste of western India now predominantly Muslim (see Enthoven, *Tribes and Castes*, i, p. 197, s.v. ' Bohora '; Russell, op. cit., ii, p. 345 ; Ibbetson, op. cit., p. 245).

Bondo Parja   A primitive Kolarian tribe of Orissa.

Brāhman   A *varna* comprising a large number of castes whose traditional occupation is that of priests and who stand as a rule at the apex of Hindu society (see pp. 64-7). They are divided roughly into two great classes said to be of five orders each, the Panch Dravida and the Panch Gaur, roughly south and north of the Vindhya Hills respectively, but there are other classes no longer recognized as belonging to either of these two groups and in some cases regarded as degraded.

brāhmanas   Religious works of the post-vedic period consisting in theological treatises explaining the vedas. They expound the sacrificial ceremonial in minute detail with speculations as to origin, etc. The *brāhmanas* probably belong to about the seventh century B.C.

Brahmarshidēsha	'The country of the holy sages', i.e. the upper region between the Jumna and Ganges rivers.
Brahmāvartta	'The holy land', i.e. the country about the river Saraswati, in the neighbourhood of Sirhind and Ambāla in the Punjab south-east of the Sutlej River.
Brāhui	A Muslim tribe of Baluchistan speaking a Dravidian language (see pp. 41, 151).
Brittiāl Baniyā	An exterior caste of Assam (see pp. 113, 213 sq.).
Brokpa	A Himalayan tribe of the Hindu Kush.
Būrusho	A Himalayan tribe of the Hindu Kush speaking a language so far not identified as belonging to any recorded linguistic family.
Chakkiliyan	A Tamil caste of leather-workers corresponding to Chamār in the north, and Mādiga in Telingana.
Chakli	See Chakkiliyan.
Chakmā	Tribe of Chittagong Hill Tracts in East Pakistan.
Chāliyan	A caste of cotton-weavers now found in Malabar.
Chamār	Skinners, tanners, and workers in leather; northern and central India generally.
Chamārgaur	A subcaste of Rājput with both Hindu and Muslim branches.
Chandāl	An exterior caste, traditionally the lowest in Hindu society and sprung from the union of a Brahman woman with a Sudra man; specifically a caste of cultivators, boatmen and fishermen in Bengal (=Namasudra).
Chang	A Naga tribe of Assam.
chāpāti	See p. 73.
Charāl	=Chanrāl or Chandāl, q.v.
Chāran	A caste in Gujarāt of hereditary bards, genealogists, and heralds claiming Rājput origin, and possibly of mixed Rājput and Brāhman extraction, with customs similar to those of Bhāt (q.v.), like whom they had the reputation that they would keep their word or die.
Chāsā	A cultivating caste of Orissa.
Chattarkhai	A caste in Orissa derived from persons who lost their caste in 1886 by eating in relief kitchens (chattra) during the famine (see Risley, Tribes and Castes, I, p. 196).
chattri	A platform, generally of stone, covered by a domed roof but with open sides—a sort of loggia.
Chaubē	=Chaturvedi, so named because they follow the fourth, Atharva, veda—a caste of Kānyakubja or Kanaujya Brāhman in upper India.
Chenchu	A Telugu-speaking forest tribe, mostly food-collecting and non-cultivating, of southern India.
Chero	A caste of cultivators of tribal origin and Kolarian affinities in the Mirzapur district of the United Provinces and in adjoining areas (see Crooke, Tribes and Castes, II, p. 241).
Cheruman	A caste of agrestic serfs in part of South Kanara and in southern Malabar corresponding to, or identical

	with, Pulayan (q.v.) in northern Malabar, Cochin, and Travancore.
Chetti	A caste of bankers, brokers, shopkeepers, money-lenders, etc., in southern India; corresponds to Baniya.
Chin	A group of hill tribes in Burma and Assam.
Chitpāvan	A caste of Brahman from the Konkan in western India distinguished for their administrative capacity and their fairness of complexion.
Chōdhra	A more or less nomadic hill tribe or caste of Bombay.
Chūhra	A caste (or tribe?) of scavengers in the Punjab and north-west India (see pp. 38-9, 219).

Dafla	An Assam tribe on the north bank of the Brahmaputra.
Daitya	A race of demons or titans that fought against the gods; representing, perhaps, the indigenous inhabitants of India who fought against the Aryan-speaking invaders.
dao	A bill or broad-bladed hacker with a single cutting edge.
Dard	Himalayan tribe of Dardistan.
darga	The shrine of a Muslim saint (properly = ' a royal court ').
Darzi	Tailor caste in India generally.
Dāsyu	A race of dark-coloured evil beings, enemies of gods and men; probably representing aboriginal inhabitants of India who fought against the Aryan-speaking invaders, and/or perhaps against more civilized inhabitants who preceded those invaders as immigrants.

Deōri (or Deori Chutiya) A tribe in Assam credited with magical powers.

Dēshasth	A caste of Maharashtra Brahman coming originally from the *dēsha*, i.e. the country above the Sahya Ghats in western India.
Dēvā	The race of gods, no doubt representing in effect the Aryan-speaking invaders of India who fought against the Daityas, q.v.
dēvadāsi	Girl dedicated to the service of a deity, and generally to temple prostitution.
Dēvānga	A caste of weavers in the Carnatic country.
Dēvēndrakula Vellālan	A fancy name for the Pallan (q.v.) caste, who, it is thereby claimed, were created by Devendra, the king of the gods, to labour for the Vellāla.
Dhangar	A shepherd caste of western India.
Dhānuk	A caste of field labourers in upper India.
dhărămsālā	Rest-house for wayfarers (lit. ' pious edifice ').
Dhārhi (or Dhādhi)	A caste of musicians or panegyrists.
dhărmă	Duty; conformity to the laws; justice; piety. See p. 124.
dharmasāstra	See *sāstra*.
Dhēd	An exterior caste of field labourers and private servants in western India.

Dhōbi	A widespread caste of washermen standing low in the social scale on account of their occupation (=Dhubi, Dhupi).
Dhōli	See Bāiti.
Dogrā	An inhabitant of the Dugar tract in the Himalayan state of Jammu.
Dōm	A widespread caste of scavengers, musicians, and sometimes weavers, traders, or even moneylenders; possibly representing an aboriginal tribe of some influence and power (=Dōmra, Dōmbu). See pp. 34-5.
Dōmbo	=Dōm.
Dugla	See Bāiti.
Dumāl	An agricultural caste of Orissa, claiming affinities to the Goala.
Ernādan	A Malabar hill and forest tribe of very low social status and apparently having unusually pronounced brachycephaly. See also footnote 27 on p. 80.
Feringhī	A Christian caste of Bengal claiming descent from Portuguese pirates (*Feringhi* < ' Frank ', i.e. ' European ').
Gadabā	A primitive Kolarian tribe of Orissa.
Gaddī	A caste of graziers in the Punjab, partly Muslim, partly Hindu (see Rose, *Tribes and Castes*, II, pp. 255 sq.)
Garhwāli	An inhabitant of Garhwāl in the Himalayas.
Gāro	A matrilineal hill tribe of Assam.
gaumedha	The sacrifice of cattle.
Gautama	The founder of the Nyāya school of philosophy and author of a *dharmasāstra* or law book.
Gayawāl (or Gayāli)	A subcaste of mendicant Brahman maintaining themselves on the offerings of pilgrims in the city of Gaya.
Ghānchī	A caste of oil-pressers and sellers in western India (corresponds to Teli).
Ghāsiyā	A caste of musicians, fishermen, and artificers in brass, of low status in upper central India.
ghee (or *ghi*)	Clarified butter.
Ghōshī	A pastoral caste, commonly but not always Muslim, acting as milkmen in the Punjab.
Goāla	A caste of cattle-breeders and milkmen in northern India generally.
Golapurāb	An agricultural caste, probably of Brahman extraction, in the district of Agra.
Golla	A Telugu caste of herdsmen, cattle-breeders, and milkmen in southern India.
Gōnd	A widespread tribe in central India.
Gōpa	A caste of herdsmen, cattle-breeders, and milkmen in Bengal (=Goāla, Ahīr, etc.).
gōtra	An exogamous group, descended from a common ancestor, inside the endogamous caste (see pp. 47 sqq. and index s.v. *gōtra*).

Gūjar	A grazier caste of the Punjab and north-west India generally; their origin is attributed to the White Huns or Ephthalites who came into India in the third century A.D. (see p. 38). Many are Muslims, e.g. in Kashmir.
Gujarāti	Inhabitant of Gujarāt, formerly a part of the Bombay Presidency, and the language of that area.
guru	Spiritual adviser.
Halālkhor	A subcaste of Bhangi, q.v.
Haldiya	A subcaste of Agarwala < haldi = ' turmeric ', the eating of which is taboo to them.
Hāliya Kaibartta	Kaibartta of the plough (=Chāsi Kaibartta or Mahishya).
Halvakki Vakkal	A cultivating caste of Kanara with quasi-totemistic clans.
Halwai	A caste of confectioners in northern India generally.
Handi Jōgi	A caste of mendicants, pig-breeders, quacks and snake-charmers in southern India.
Hārī	A scavenger caste of eastern India (=Haddi).
Hasāla	A caste (or tribe) of agrestic serfs and collectors of forest produce on the Kanara border of Mysore State.
Hazāra	A Himalayan tribe of the Hindu Kush.
Hīra	A subcaste of Chandāl (q.v.) Apparently makers of pots and of brass wire, vide F. Hamilton's Account of Assam, pp. 55, 60, and Martin, Eastern India, III, pp. 676, 679.
Ho	A Kolarian tribe of east central India.
Holeya	A Kanarese caste of field labourers and village servants, formerly agrestic serfs (corresponding to Paraiyan).
Holi	The Spring festival. See Crooke, Things Indian, s.v. Festivals and Hobson-Jobson s.v. Hooly.
Huligamma	A southern Indian goddess, with a temple in Dharwar District, who is worshipped by eunuchs or by male priests in the dress of women (see Fawcett, ' On Basivis ', Journ. Anthropol. Soc. of Bombay, II, p. 343).
huqqa	Tobacco-pipe in which the smoke is drawn through a water-container.
Hur	Quasi-religious follower (bandit) of the Pir Pagaro in Sind (see p. 40).
hypergamy	The system under which women from a group of lower status are married to men in a higher group.
hypogamy	The reverse of hypergamy.
Idaiyan	A Tamil caste of herdsmen, shepherds, cattle-breeders, and milkmen in southern India (=Āyar, Golla).
Idayar	See Idaiyan.
Ilavan	See Izhavan.
Iluvan	See Izhavan.
Iravan	See Izhavan.

Irula	A tribe of the Nilgiri Hills and related caste of the same name in the Madras plains.
Iruvan	See Izhavan.
Izhavan	(=Iravan, Ilavan, etc.) A toddy-drawing caste of the Malabar coast nearly related to the Tiyan, and believed to have come from Ceylon, or from Indonesia by way of Ceylon. They are matrilineal in Travancore and southern Cochin, but patrilineal in northern Cochin and southern Malabar.
Jaiswāl	A trading caste of Rajputāna.
Jāliya Kaibartta	Kaibartta (q.v.) of the net—a fishing caste of Bengal.
Jalua (Jaliya)	A term applied in Bengal to fishing castes in general, but in Noakhali district apparently to a specific caste with endogamous groups (see Risley, *Tribes and Castes*, I, p. 340).
Janappan	A Telugu caste which make gunny-bags of hemp fibre and act as hawkers and cattle-brokers.
Jāt	An agricultural caste of upper India (see pp. 36 sqq.).
jātakas	A collection of the birth stories of Buddhas that preceded Gautama.
Jhālo	Probably a synonym for Mālo (q.v.); in any case it refers to a caste of fishermen in Bengal.
Jolāhā	A caste of Muslim weavers widespread in upper India (see Crooke, *Tribes and Castes*, III, p. 69).
Juang	A primitive Kolarian tribe in the Orissa hills.
Jūgi	A caste of rearers of silkworms and weavers of silk in Assam.
Kabīrpanthi	A sectarian caste drawn largely from weavers; the followers of the reformer Kabīr, who flourished at the end of the fifteenth century; it has Muslim as well as Hindu practices.
Kābuli	A native of Kābul; an Afghan or Pathān.
Kachāri	An Assam tribe, now mainly Hinduized (see Kōchh).
Kāchhī	A caste of opium-growers and market-gardeners in upper India (=Saḥnai).
Kachin	A group of hill tribes in Burma and on its northern borders.
Kādar	A food-collecting (non-cultivating) forest tribe of southern India.
Kadva Kunbī	A subcaste of Kunbī practising periodic marriage (see p. 19).
Kāfir	A Himalayan tribe in the neighbourhood of Gilgit (see p. 43).
Kahār	A caste of fishermen, porters, and domestic servants in upper India. Kahārs also commonly act as well-sinkers and cultivators of water-nuts.
Kaibartta	Originally apparently a tribe, now a caste or castes of Bengal and adjoining areas, their occupation being fishing or cultivation (?=Kēwat, see pp. 52, 208).
Kaikōlan	A Tamil caste of weavers.

Kalitā	A cultivating caste of Assam (? = Kaltā of Orissa).
Kallan	A cultivating and predatory Tamil caste notable for their efficient agriculture, expert thieving, robbery, cattle-lifting, lengthened ear lobes, use of the Indian boomerang, and practice of a sort of bull-fighting (see Thurston, *Castes and Tribes*, III, pp. 53 sqq.).
Kaltā (or Koltā)	A cultivating caste of Orissa (? = Kalitā of Assam).
Kalwār	A caste of distillers and liquor-sellers in northern India (= Kalāl).
Kāmi	The blacksmith caste of Nepal; found also in adjoining areas.
Kamma	A numerous Telugu caste, so-called after an ear-jewel of the goddess Lakshmi, consisting of cultivators claiming Kshatriya origin; sometimes divided into five groups according to the manner in which they carry water, *viz.* on the head, on the hip, by the hand only, by two persons carrying between them, or on a pack-bullock. Besides *gotra* they have a number of exogamous septs, some with quasi-totemic names (*see* Thurston, *Castes and Tribes*, III, pp. 94 sqq.) *Cf. infra* s.v. ' Okkalīga '.
Kammālan	See Panchāla.
Kammavan	A Telugu caste of peasant owners and cultivators in Tinnevelly district; they practise a form of cross-cousin marriage in which a man must marry his father's sister's daughter, or his mother's sister's daughter, or his own sister's daughter.
Kanbī	See Kunbi.
Kanēt	A caste of peasants in the outer Himalayas formerly practising fraternal polyandry.
Kaniyan	A caste of astrologers on the Malabar coast (= Kanisan).
Kanjar	A gipsy caste of criminals and/or mat-makers in upper and central India.
Kansārā	See Kasēra.
Kāpu	A very numerous caste of south India primarily cultivators; in some districts they rank next to Brahmans and claim a Rajput origin. They use the title ' Reddi '.
Kārālar	= ' Rulers of Clouds '; applied to a tribe of cultivators and hunters in South Arcot district, to the Vellāla caste in Malabar, and to the Malayali of the Shevaroy hills in Salem district in southern India.
Karan	A writer caste of Orissa (corresponding to Kāyastha).
kărmă	See p. 125.
Karuppan	A South Indian god associated especially with the Kallar caste.
Kasērā	A caste of brass-founders and coppersmiths in northern India generally (= Kāsār).
Kātkarī	A more or less nomadic forest tribe of Bombay.
Kātoni	A caste of weavers in Assam (also known as Nāth).
Kāyastha (Kāyasth)	A writer caste of upper and of eastern India (ranks next to Brahman in Bengal).

Kēwat	A fishing and cultivating caste of upper India (corresponds to Kaibartta).
Khandait	A quasi-military cultivating and landowning caste of Orissa.
Khangār	A caste of watchmen in the Central Provinces.
Khariā	A Kolarian tribe of Chota Nagpur and central India.
Khārvā	A seafaring and salt-making caste of western India.
Kharwār	A cultivating caste of tribal origin and Kolarian affinities in Bihar, Chota Nagpur and adjoining areas.
Khas	A tribe (or caste) of Nepal.
Khāsi	A matrilineal tribe of Assam speaking a Mon-Khmēr language.
Khātī	A caste of cartwrights and carpenters in the Punjab.
Khatīk	A caste of labourers, butchers, and vegetable sellers, etc., in northern India.
Khatrī	A trading caste of the Punjab and north-west India.
Kho	A Himalayan tribe of the Gilgit area.
Khōja	The name of two Muslim trading castes of western India; the Khoja of the Punjab are Sunni and are largely derived from the Hindu caste Khatri; the Khoja of Sind, who are Shi'ah, are similarly largely derived from the Lohāna caste of Hindus of that province.
Kisān	A cultivating caste of upper India, probably allied to Kāchhī, Koiri, and Kurmi, q.v.
Kōchh	A tribe of Assam and northern Bengal; in latter area generally Hinduized as the caste of Rajbansi, but in Assam ' Kōchh ' is used as a caste label for several tribes when Hinduized, particularly Kachāris, Lālungs, and Mikirs.
Kodaga (or Koṟaga)	The warrior caste or tribe of Coorg.
Koiri (or Koeri)	A cultivating and market-gardening caste of upper India.
Kōl	A Kolarian tribe of central India and Orissa.
Kolarian	Possessing a language or culture associated with a group of peoples of which the principal entities are the Mundā, Kōl, and Santāl tribes.
Kōlī	A caste of cultivators and labourers in western India possibly of Kolarian affinities.
Koltä	= Kaltā, q.v.
Kōmati	A Telugu trading caste.
Kond (or Kondh)	A hill tribe of Orissa, noted for human sacrifice and infanticide, nearly allied to Gond (spelled commonly Khond, also Khaund, Kandh, etc.). See pp. 25-6.
Konkan	The coastal area of Maharashtra.
Konyak	A group of Naga tribes in Assam.
Korā	A caste of earthworkers of Kolarian extraction in Chota Nagpur and Bengal.
Koraga	An exterior caste of basket-makers and labourers in South Kanara district. The women wear petticoats of leaves. The Andē (' pot ') Koraga had to wear a small pot suspended to a string round the neck in which to spit so as to avoid polluting the roads.

Koraga	See Kodaga.
Korava	A nomad Tamil caste (or tribe) of fortune-tellers, quacks, and thieves operating particularly on railways.
Korku	A hill or forest tribe of central India.
Korwa	A hill or forest tribe of central India.
Kōta	A tribe, or low caste, of the Nilgiris; musicians and artisans.
Kōttai Vellāla	A small and exclusive subcaste of Vellāla (q.v.) living within a fort (kottai) in the Tinnevelly district of southern India.
Kshatriya	A varna; the ruling and warrior class of the vedas, now represented by Rajputs, and by other castes claiming Kshatriya origin (see pp. 64-7).
Kudumi	A caste of servants, firework-makers, and (formerly) soldiers in Travancore.
Kuki	A group of hill tribes in Assam and Burma.
Kulin	See pp. 53 sqq. of this volume.
Kumhār	The potter caste; all India except the south. The Kumhār have many endogamous subcastes.
Kunbi	A cultivating caste of western India (=Kurmi ; also =Kanbī).
Kurava	A Malabar caste of agrestic serfs.
Kuricchan	A caste (or tribe) in Malabar which subsists by hunting and by shifting cultivation.
Kurmi	A widely distributed cultivating caste of northern India (=Kunbi).
Kuruba	A caste of shepherds, weavers, and stone-masons in southern India, probably identical originally with Kurumba or Kuruman (see Thurston, Castes and Tribes, IV, pp. 155 sq.)
Kusavan	A Tamil caste of potters (corresponds to Kumhār).
Lālbegi (or Lāl-Begi)	A scavenging caste of upper India with customs partly Hindu, partly Muslim (see Crooke, Tribes and Castes, I, s.v. Bhangi).
Lambādi	See Banjāra.
Lapcha	A hill tribe of the Himalayas, Bengal.
Let	A subcaste of Bāgdi (q.v.) in the Murshidabad and Birbhum districts.
Lhota	A Naga tribe of Assam.
lingam	The symbol of the God Shiva: a stone of cylindrical or phallic shape.
Lingāyat	A numerous caste of sectarian origin derived from different strata, from Brahman downwards, in the west of India, and frequently in rivalry with the Okkalīga, q.v. (see Enthoven, Tribes and Castes, II, pp. 343 sqq. and also L.K.A. Iyer, Mysore Tribes and Castes, IV, pp. 81 sqq.)

Lodhā	A caste of cultivators and labourers in the United Provinces of Agra and Oudh, probably identical with Lodhi, a caste of landowners, probably of Rajput affinities in central India (see Russell, op. cit., IV, p. 112, and Rose, *Tribes and Castes*, III, p. 35).
Lōhāna	A trading caste in Sind.
Lōhār	A blacksmith caste, widespread in India north of the Godāvari River.
Loi	A tribe of Manipur State.
Lōk Sabha	The lower house of legislature.
Lori (or Lūri)	A nomad tribe of Baluchistan, tinkers and musicians, probably = Dōm. Lūri perhaps < Lūr, = Lūristan; or else Lūristan < Lūri.
Lushei	A Kuki-Chin tribe of Assam.
Mādiga	A Telugu caste of leather-workers, corresponding to Chamār and Chakkiliyan in northern India and the Tamilnad respectively.
Magh	A Buddhist tribe of Bengal; of Burmese, or rather Arakanese, affinities.
Mahābrāhman	A caste of Brahman, the function of which is to receive the funeral offerings of clothes, jewellery, etc., which belonged to the dead man, and by the wearing of which the soul of the dead is provided with necessities and luxuries in the next world.
Mahar	A clan of Huna extraction in Sind. Also a subcaste of Kahār (q.v., and p. 90).
Mahār	An exterior caste of field labourers and village servants in west and central India.
Maharā	Used in Sylhet probably for the caste of Kahār (q.v.).
Mahishya	A caste, according to one of the Sanskrit commentators on the Code of Manu, sprung from a Brahman father and a Kshatriya mother, or, according to others, of a Kshatriya father and a Vaishya mother, and ranking with Kayastha (see Wilson, *Indian Caste*, I, pp. 55, 65). Such a caste, however, is no longer known, at any rate by that name, and the name has been adopted by the Chāsi or Hāliya Kaibartta as a status-raising designation for themselves (see p. 113). See Gait, *Census of Bengal*, 1901, p. 380.
Māhli	A caste of labourers, porters, and basket-makers in central India, having affinities with the Santal, Ho, and Munda tribes (= Māhili).
mahwā	The flowering tree *Bassia latifolia* (Roxb.), wild, or *Bassia longifolia*, cultivated, from the blossom of which liquor is distilled.
Maithil Brāhman	A Brahman caste originally associated with the ancient kingdom of Mithila roughly corresponding to Bihar.
Majhwār	A forest tribe (or caste) apparently of mixed origin in upper central India.
makkathāyam	Descent in the male line, women being normally excluded from inheritance.
Māla	A Telugu caste of field labourers and village servants (corresponding to Pulayan).

Mala-Arayan	A hill tribe of Travancore who make miniature dolmens to house their dead, who are represented by a small brass image or a smooth stone.
Mala-Pantāram	Food-collecting (non-cultivating) forest tribe of Travancore.
Malavētan	A primitive tribe of southern India (= Vedan).
Malayālam	That branch of the Dravidian tongue spoken on the Malabar coast (Kerala) from Cannanore southwards to Cape Comorin.
Malayāli	A Tamil caste inhabiting the hills (*malai*) in Salem district; probably derived from the Vellāla caste (q.v.).
Malāyan	A patrilineal caste of Malabar which cures disease by expelling the demon responsible for it by dancing in masks and disguises (= Pānān; *malāyan* means ' hillman ').
Mālēr (Māl)	A hill tribe of Bihar and Bengal.
Māli	A caste of domestic and market gardeners in all India except the south.
Māli	(In Sylhet) = Bhuinmāli, q.v.
Mālo	A caste of boatmen and fishermen in Bengal.
māna	An Oceanic concept of mysterious impersonal power attaching to individuals, objects, places, or even words, and set in motion as a rule by ritual; the positive aspect of the supernatural as opposed to *taboo*, the negative aspect involving the avoidance of such power as dangerous.
Mannān	A Malabar caste of washermen, = Vannān but follows the *marumakkathāyam* system; not to be confused with the hill tribe of Travancore called Mannān.
mantra	A text of the vedas used as a magic formula.
Manu, Code of	A digest of existing laws and creeds probably of about the third century B.C. but based upon earlier works.
Marātha	A warlike community of western India (see pp. 19-20).
Maravan	A cultivating, marauding, cattle-lifting caste of the extreme south of India having obvious cultural affinities to the Kallan whose practice of bull-fighting they share as well as the use of boomerangs (see Thurston, *Castes and Tribes*, v, pp. 22 sqq.).
Mārāyan (or Mārān)	A caste of drummers, temple servants, and barbers serving Nayars and higher castes; their functions and status vary to north and south of the Malabar coast (see Thurston, *Castes and Tribes*, v, pp. 5 sqq.).
Māria	A subtribe of Gond in east central India.
marumakkathāyam	System of descent and inheritance in the female line, so that a man's heir is his sister or his sister's child.
Mārwāri	Strictly speaking an inhabitant of Mārwār in Rajputana, loosely used for Baniyā from that region.
Maurya	The name of the dynasty, and the empire associated with that dynasty, founded late in the fourth century B.C. by Chandragupta. It reached its zenith in the third century under the great Buddhist emperor Asoka, and broke up early in the second.

Mazhbi	A section of the Sikh community socially of inferior status as having been recruited from low or exterior Hindu castes.
Meithei	A tribe, the ruling people of the Manipur State (see p. 116).
Mēlakkāran	A name given to two castes of musicians in south India, the one Telugu, the other Tamil (see Thurston, *Castes and Tribes*, v. p. 59).
Mēmān	A Muslim section of the Lōhāna (q.v.) caste in Sind.
Mēo	A tribe in Rajputana and upper India following mixed Hindu and Islamic practices. When predominantly Muslim they are called Mewāti, but Meo when regarded as Hindu.
Mer, Merat	A tribe of Merwara in Rajputana. The Muslims call themselves ' Merat '; the Hindu ' Mer ' (also = Mair) generally use the title Rawat.
meriah	Person reserved, often hereditarily, for sacrifice, to promote the fertility of the soil, by the Kondhs of the Orissa hill tracts; loosely used also for the rite of such a sacrifice.
Mēwafarōsh	Fruiterer; a subcaste of Khatīk.
Mikir	A hill tribe of Assam.
Mīnā	A marauding tribe in Rajputana, probably of common origin with Meo (see Crooke, *Tribes and Castes*, s.v. Meo).
mirasdar	Proprietor.
Mīrāsī	A Muslim caste of genealogists and musicians in the Punjab.
Mishmi	An Assam tribe north of the Brahmaputra River.
Mōchi	See Muchī.
Momīn	(i) A caste of weavers (= Jolāhā) in northern India; (ii) = Mēmān.
Moplah (Māppila, Māpilla)	A fanatical Muslim tribe or caste of western India, traditionally of partly Arab extraction. They are matrilineal in north Malabar but patrilineal in the south of it. (See *Hobson-Jobson* s.v. Moplah.)
Morasu	A section of the Kāpu (q.v.) caste.
Mru	A Buddhist tribe in the Chittagong Hill Tracts of East Pakistan.
Muchī	A caste of workers in leather all over India except the south; commonly = Chamār (also Mōchi).
Mukkuvan	A Malabar caste of fishermen, litter-bearers, and boatmen.
Munda	A Kolarian hill tribe of Chota Nagpur. They put up megalithic monuments to their dead.
muni	' A holy sage, a pious and learned person, endowed with more or less of a divine nature, or having obtained it by rigid abstraction and mortification ' (Haughton, p. 2298). The title is applied to *rishis* and others.
Musāhār	A caste (or primitive tribe) of Kolarian affinities in Uttar Pradesh and Bihar.
salli	Muslim of inferior status socially on account of the low status of the Hindu caste of his extraction.

Nadiyāl	An exterior caste of boatmen and fishermen in Assam.
Naga	A group of hill tribes in Assam and Burma (see p. 183). *Naga lōg* = Naga (i.e. *nanga*—' naked '?) people.
Nāga	Literally = ' snake '; a pre-Aryan people in India, with whom the worship of snakes, particularly the cobra, is associated.
Nāgar Brāhman	A caste of Gujarati Brahman associated in origin with half a dozen towns in the north-east of Gujarat (< *nagar* = town).
Nai	A barber caste all over northern India (= Nhavi).
Namasūdra	A numerous exterior caste of cultivators and boatmen in Bengal, formerly known as Chandāl (q.v.). Risley (*Tribes and Castes*, I, p. 181) regards them as representing an aboriginal tribe and possibly allied to the Māler of the Rājmahal hills; their own traditions assign them an origin from Brahmans or other caste Hindus degraded for one reason or another.
Nambūdri	A caste of Brahman in Malabar in which it has been the practice for the eldest son to make a normal endogamous marriage while the younger sons contract with Nayar women unions governed by the matrilineal inheritance laws of the latter.
nāmghar	Communal house of meeting and worship in Assam.
Nānagōtri	A caste of Brahman in Garhwal (see p. 154).
Nat	A caste of singers, dancers, acrobats, and professional criminals (the feminine is *natni* or *noti*) who generally move about without a permanent territorial location (see F. Hamilton, op. cit., p. 55, Martin, op. cit., III, p. 676, and in particular Crooke, *Tribes and Castes*, IV, pp. 56 sqq.).
nat	A spirit or godling in Burma.
Nāth	= Jūgi or Kātoni (qq.v.).
Nāttukōttai	A subcaste of Chetti in Madura district who are moneylenders and traders, with distinctive customs of their own (see Thurston, *Castes and Tribes*, V, s.v. Nāttukōttai).
nattuvan	A name for teachers of dancing-girls whose performances they accompany as musicians. They may belong to any of several castes, Kaikōlan, Dēvānga, Occhan, for instance, among them.
Nāyādi	An exterior caste (or tribe) of the Malabar coast, hunters and beggars by profession, polluting to Brahmans at nearly 100 yards distance (see pp. 80-1).
Nāyar	An important aristocratic matrilineal caste of the Malabar coast whose traditional occupation is fighting in the case of the higher subcastes, but the caste as a whole includes oil-sellers, potters, herdsmen, barbers, washermen, and others by no means military.
Newār	A tribe of Nepal claiming to have been in occupation before the Gurkhas, and largely Buddhist in religion.
Nishada	An ancient caste derived traditionally from a Brahman and a Sudra woman; a dark-skinned people settled in the country before the Rigvedic invaders (see Wilson, *Indian Caste*, I, pp. 55, 116, 126n, 226, 241, 418).

Occhan	A caste of temple priests at village shrines in southern India.
Oddē	= Odh, q.v.
Odh	A migratory caste of earthworkers (= Orh, Vaddar, etc.) probably of Kolarian origin from Orissa.
Ojha	A caste or subcaste of medicine-men and magicians; there are Ojhas of Brahman as of other castes, and there is a subtribe of Gond of this name.
Okkalīga	A group of agricultural castes in Mysore and Kanara. Like the Kamma, they have a tradition of escape from persecution across a river which parted its waters for them as the Red Sea for the Israelites. Women practised mutilation of the hand at the ear-boring of children, like the Morasu section of the Kapu. *Cf. supra* p. 11 (*see* L. K. A. Iyer, *Mysore Tribes and Castes,* IV, pp. 225 sqq.).
Oraon	A hill tribe of Chota Nagpur using a Dravidian language.
Oswāl	A trading caste from Mewar in Rajputana. This caste is very largely Jain by religion, but Hindu and Jain Oswals recognize each other as caste-brethren.
paita	(Telugu) Outer end of sari draped over breasts and shoulder.
Paliyan	A primitive tribe of southern India subsisting mainly on hunting and food-collecting.
Pallan	An exterior Tamil caste of agricultural labourers.
Palli	An agricultural caste of southern India claiming Kshatriya origin (= Vanniyan). They are spoken of as painters by Carré (op. cit., II, p. 595), and in modern times have assumed the title Mudaliyar, used by the chief 'painters' of the Malabar (Tamil) caste in 1680 (*Madras Records,* quoted in a footnote to above by the Editors).
pān	< Sanskrit *parna* = 'leaf'; the plant *Piper betel* which is chewed with dried areca nut and lime as a masticatory. According to Sir Thomas Roe 'it bites in the mouth, accords rheums, cooles the head, strengthens the teeth '.
pān bari	An enclosed and shaded garden in which the creeper *Piper betel* is grown in rows on sticks.
Pānān	See Malāyan.
Panchāla	A group of five (*panch*) artisan castes—goldsmiths, braziers, carpenters, stonemasons, and blacksmiths—in southern India.
pănchāyăt	See above pp. 99 sq.
Pāndaian	Appertaining to Pāndya.
Pāndya	An ancient kingdom of southern India which had its capital at Madura.
Panikkan	A caste of barbers and weavers in the Madura and Tinnevelly districts of Madras.
Paniyan	A hill tribe of Malabar and the Nilgiris.
Pantāram	See Mala-Pantāram.

Panta Reddi	A subdivision of Kāpu (q.v.).
Panwār	One of the Agnikula (' fire-born ') Rājput clans (= Pramara, Ponwār).
Parahiya	A small hill tribe (or caste) in Mirzapur district of Uttar Pradesh.
Paraiyan	An exterior Tamil caste of field labourers and village servants whose caste name has given us the word ' pariah '.
Parasurāma	(i.e. ' Rāma with the axe '.) A Brahman hero of the epic *Mahābhārata* who cleared the earth of Kshatriyas twenty-one times and gave it to the Brahmans.
Parava	A caste of south Kanara which cures disease by exorcising devils by dancing, and which also makes baskets and umbrellas.
Parja	A tribe with a Kolarian language in Orissa; see also Bondo.
Parwār (or Parwāl)	A mercantile caste of Rajputana.
Pāsi	A caste of toddy-drawers in northern India who tap the *tari* palm for liquor.
Pathān	A Muslim tribe of the North-West Frontier. See p. 42.
Pātni	An exterior caste of fishermen and basket-makers in eastern Bengal and in Assam, probably nearly allied to Dōm.
Peravadar	A caste mentioned in early Tamil literature as living on the coast by fishing; probably = Paravan, a fishing, pearl-diving, and sea-going community on the extreme south-east coast of India.
Pīrali (or Pīr-Ali)	A subcaste of Brāhman in Bengal reputed to have become segregated from the Rārhi Brāhman caste as a consequence of smelling a Muslim meal.
Prabhu	The writer caste in the west of India; it claims a Kshatriya origin and can show much in support of its claim (see Enthoven, *Tribes and Castes*, III, p. 235).
prătilōmă	See p. 55.
prăjără	See p. 58.
pretyasilā	See p. 248.
pūjā	A Hindu religious ceremony; hence almost any kind of rite. See *Hobson-Jobson*, s.v. Pooja.
Pulayan	A caste of agrestic serfs in the north of Malabar district, in Cochin, and in Travancore, corresponding to the Tamil Paraiyan (q.v.).
Purāda Vannān	A caste of Tamil washermen who wash the clothes of exterior castes, and of whom the very sight is polluting.
purānas	Sacred books of the Hindus recording the pantheistic form of this religion which followed the vedic period; the earliest go back to at any rate the fourth century B.C. and the famous epics, the *Rāmāyana* and the *Mahābhārata*, were succeeded by *purānas* in the form of a dialogue between an inquirer and an exponent in verse. *Purāna* = ' ancient ', and different books have distinguishing names, e.g. *Padma-Purāna*,

the *purāna* which contains an account of the period when the world was a golden lotus (*padma*); *Agni-Puṛāna*, the one which was communicated by the deity of fire (*Agni*) to the vedic sage Vasishtha. The *Bhavishya Puṛāna*, nominally a book of prophecies, is actually more concerned with rites and ceremonies.

Rābhā	A tribe of Gāro and Kachāri affinities in Assam.
Rājanya	The aristocratic and ruling class of the Aryan invaders of India *circa* 1500 B.C. from which the Kshatriyas and Rājputs are derived.
Rājbansi	A caste formed from the Kōchh (q.v.) tribe, in northern Bengal and Assam.
Rājgar	A mason; a subcaste of Khatīk with the occupation of mason.
Rājput	An aristocratic caste, widespread in western, northern, and central India, whose traditional functions are fighting and ruling. They represent the ancient Kshatriya *varna*, and rank next to the Brāhmans socially (see pp. 33, 54-5, 66). See also s.v. Agnikula.
Rārhi	A Brāhman caste of Bengal.
rath	A wheeled car used in particular for carrying an idol in procession.
Rāthor	A clan of Rājputs, q.v.
Rāvulo	A caste of temple servants in Orissa.
Reddi	See Kāpu.
Rengma	A Naga tribe of Assam.
Rigveda	The original compilation of vedic hymns to nature deities. The Yajurvedas, Black and White, and the Sāmaveda were derived from it, and are chiefly concerned with sacrificial ceremonial.
rishi	An inspired poet or sage; in particular the inspired persons to whom the hymns of the vedas were revealed, and the ancestors of those Brahmanical *gōtra* in the *prăvără* of which they are named (see p. 59).
săbhā	An association, a council.
Sadgöp	A caste of cultivators in Bengal (=Chāsā).
Saka	A northern people—' Scythians '—who invaded India about the second century B.C.
Sākaldwipi	A caste of Brahmans in Bihar who are reported to be divided into a number of exogamous units known as *pur*, marriage being allowed within the *gōtra* but not within the *pur*.
Sākta	A worshipper of Sakti or the female energy of the wife of the deity, the deity generally being Shiva.
săkti	See p. 189.
Sakuntalā	The heroine of a play by Kālidāsa written in the fifth century A.D.
sālăgrămă	A pebble, found in certain rivers, having mystic virtues, and commonly containing the fossil known as an ammonite. See *Hobson-Jobson* s.v. Saligram. It is particularly associated with Vishnu.

19

Sāmaveda	See Rigveda.
Sānsiya	A vagrant criminal tribe of Rajputana and adjoining provinces, dependent for a livelihood on theft and robbery.
Santāl	A Kolarian tribe of Chota Nagpur, Bihar and Bengal.
sǎpindǎ	See page 60, n. 39.
Sārāk	A small caste of cultivators and weavers in eastern India; an archaic community originating from farther west and originally Jain, but now mostly Hinduized, though some are Buddhists (see Risley, *Tribes and Castes*, II, p. 236 ; Gait, *Census of Bengal*, p. 427).
Saraswat	A caste of Gaur Brahmans primarily in the Punjab and Sind which take their name from the river Saraswati, formerly a tributary of the Indus but now lost in the deserts north of Rajputana. They are reported to marry within the *gōtra* but to retain certain exogamous clans.
sāstra	A rule, or treatise. Any book recognized as having divine authority, but particularly the ancient books of Hindu law.
sāstri	Person learned in the religious law.
Satapatha Brāhmana	The Brāhmana of a Hundred Paths, the most important of the *brāhmanas*, q.v.
sati	Act of immolation of a living widow on her deceased husband's funeral pyre.
Satnāmi	(i) The name of a sect founded at the end of the seventeenth century by Jag-Jīwan Dās, a Rajput, and taking its name from its invocation of ' the God of Truth ', *Satyanāma*. (ii) A sect with similar tenets founded in the early nineteenth century by Rāē Dās and virtually confined to the Chamār caste.
satyagrāha	' Non-violent resistance.'
satyagrāhi	Person practising non-violent resistance.
Sawara	(Also spelled Savar, Sora, Saora, etc.) A Kolarian tribe of Orissa (= also Sahariya, central India).
Sema	A Naga tribe of Assam.
Sēniyan	A weaver caste of southern India (see Thurston, *Castes and Tribes*, VI, pp. 361 sq.).
Shāgirdpēshā	Caste of domestic servants in Orissa.
Shāhā	A caste of distillers, liquor-sellers, and shopkeepers in Bengal (= Sunri).
Shaiva	A Hindu sect worshipping Shiva as the greatest god.
Shānān	A Tamil toddy-drawing caste. Corresponds to Tīyan.
Shi'ah	*Vide infra* s.v. Sunni.
smārta	= Appertaining to the *smriti*, i.e. to ' what has been remembered ', that is, to traditional lore, thus including at its widest the epics (*Māhābhārata* and *Rāmāyana*), *purānas*, and *sutras*, but in particular the *dharmasāstras*, i.e. the law books or codes, particularly the Code of Manu, and the works of other sages who recorded the ' recollections ' of what they had received from a divine source. A Smārta Brahman is a student of the *smritis*, and the term is particularly applied to

the followers of Sankarāchārya, a Hindu philosopher of the ninth century A.D., prominent in the extirpation of Buddhism. Most Smārta Brahmans are Shaivas.

Sombatta	Rope-maker; a subcaste of Khatīk.
Sonār	Goldsmith caste, distributed all over India except in the south.
Soni	Goldsmith caste of western India—see Enthoven, *Tribes and Castes of Bombay*. Distinct from Sonār.
sradh	Obsequies and sacrifices performed for the manes of deceased ancestors.
Sūdra	The *varna* of indigenous castes not entitled to the initiation ceremony of rebirth (see pp. 64-7).
Sunni, Shi'ah	These are the two principal Muslim sects. The Sunni accept the authority of all the successors of Muhammad, whereas the Shi'ah regard the first three—Abu Bakr, Omar, and Osman—as interlopers, and Ali, the Prophet's son-in-law, as the first true Khalifa.
Sunri	A caste of liquor-sellers and distillers in Bengal (= Shāhā).
Sut	A cultivating caste of Assam; said to have a *pratiloma* descent from a Brahman mother and a low-caste father.
Sūta	An ancient caste of charioteers and bards, no longer existing; also *pratiloma* (see p. 151).
Sutār	A carpenter caste; found all over India except the south.
Sūtradhār	The carpenter caste of Bengal (< Sanskrit *sūtra* = a thread, because a thread is used to mark straight lines to work by).
sūtras	Religious books of Hinduism consisting of concise treatises which condense for practical purposes the earlier *brāhmanas*, which are theological treatises explaining the vedas. The *sūtras* were produced between about 500 B.C. and the beginning of the Christian era.
Tāgā	A land-holding caste of Rohilkhand, probably of Brahman extraction, and having Muslim as well as Hindu branches (see Crooke, *Tribes and Castes*, S.V. Taga).
tālikettu	The ceremony of the tying on of the *tāli*, or neck ornament emblematic of the married state, by the bridegroom, on to the bride, or nubile girl, in southern India. (In many castes the *tāli* must be tied before the girl reaches puberty, and often the *tāli*-tier is not the person who will ultimately be the girl's husband.)
tantras	The name given to a numerous class of religious and magical works, generally of later date than the *purānas*, and devoted in particular to the cult of the *śāktis* (see Sākta); *tantra* = ' rule ', ' ritual '.
Tawāïf	A caste of dancing girls and prostitutes both Hindu and Muslim; the men of the caste, who obtain wives from outside it, act as pimps and musicians (see Crooke, *Tribes and Castes*, IV, p. 364).

Telaga	A cultivating and military caste in Telingana.
Tēli	A caste of oil-seed crushers and oil merchants in upper and eastern India (see pp. 75, 89).
Telingāna	The Andhra Desha, or country inhabited by speakers of the Telugu tongue.
Thādo	A Kuki tribe in Assam.
thākurghar	Place of worship (Hindu).
Thantapulayan	A primitive tribe of southern India.
Thatherā	Caste of braziers in upper India.
Tīli	A caste of oil merchants in Bengal (= Tēli, but see p. 89).
Tirhut Brāhman	A synonym for Maithil Brāhman, q.v.
Tiyan	A toddy-drawing caste of the Malabar coast, matrilineal in the north of Malabar district, patrilineal in the south of it; corresponds to Shānān, and Izhavan, qq.v.
Toda	A matrilineal polyandrous tribe of the Nilgiri Hills; buffalo herdsmen and dairymen.
Tūri	A caste of cultivators, bamboo-workers, and basket-makers, originally derived from a forest tribe of Kolarian affinities in Chota Nagpur.
Ullādan	A forest tribe of hunters and food-collectors in Travancore.
Upănishads	Treatises forming the concluding portions of the veda, and called therefore the Vedānta, on which is based much of the later Indian philosophy.
Uppara	A Telugu caste of salt and saltpetre workers; also well and tank diggers and earth workers generally.
Uppāra	A Kanarese caste of salt workers corresponding to the Telugu Uppara.
Uppiliyan	A caste of salt workers in Malabar; corresponds to Uppara.
Urāli	A caste of agricultural labourers in Trichinopoly and Madura districts of southern India. There is a hill tribe of the same name in Travancore. According to Thurston (Castes and Tribes, VII, p. 242) urāli = ' ruler of a village '
Vaishnava	Hindu sect worshipping Vishnu instead of Shiva as the greatest god.
Vaishya	The third varna of the Indo-European invaders of the Rigvedic age; Vaishya, < vish = the people, represented the third estate of the invading community, i.e. farmers and perhaps traders, as distinct from the rulers and warriors (Kshatriya), and priests (Brāhmana) on the one hand, and the Sudra or servile indigenes on the other. The term is now generally used for the superior mercantile castes associated in particular with Rajputana and the rest of upper India (see pp. 65 sqq.).
Vania	= Baniyā, q.v.

Vāniyan	A Tamil caste of oil-pressers, corresponding to Teli in northern India.
Vannān	A Tamil caste of washermen, corresponding to Dhōbi (q.v.) in northern India.
Vanniyan	See Palli.
varna	See pp. 65 sqq.
Vedan	A Tamil labouring and hunting caste, formerly soldiers, corresponding to Bēdar.
vedas	Books of Divine Knowledge forming the earliest written records of Hinduism; see Rigveda and Atharvaveda.
Vēlan	Apparently an abbreviation of Vellāla and used as a title by several castes in southern India.
Vellāla	A Tamil caste of cultivators, very strong numerically.
Vēttuvan	A Tamil agricultural and hunting caste.
Wa	A primitive tribe of the Shan States in eastern Burma.
Yādava	Anciently a tribe of Rājputs. The term is now used collectively by cattle-grazing castes to cover a number of groups so employed; it has been chosen perhaps on account of some resemblance to the word Idaiyan and its use implies a claim to Rājput extraction.
Yajurveda	See Rigveda.
yăti	Holy men and wandering mendicants, some of whom were destroyed by Indra who gave them away to be devoured by wolves (*sālāvrīkas*) (see Chanda, *Memoirs of the Archaeological Survey of India*, no. 41, pp. 32, 33).
Yeruva	A primitive tribe or low caste of Coorg.

INDEX

N.B.—The numbers appearing in brackets after an author's name refer to different works by him in the order in which they appear under his name in the Bibliography, the reference to which precedes them. Where one work only has been used, the bibliographical reference is given in its paginal order.

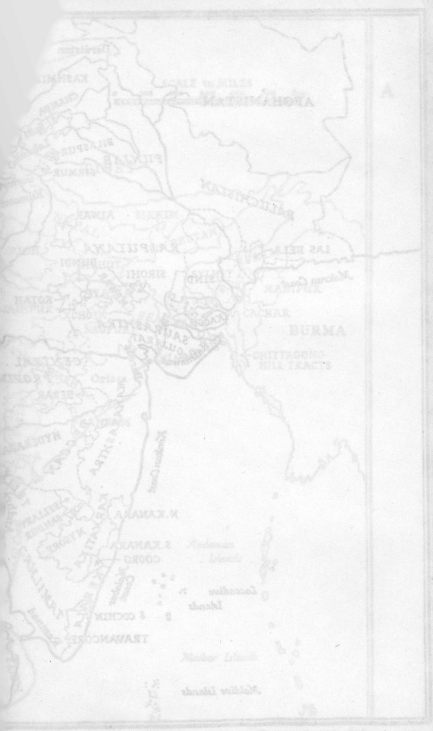